# ON MY MIND

# ON MY MIND

by
**Manfred R. Lehmann**

*Essays on Jewish history, literature, Dead Sea Scrolls, Zionism, Arabs,
Jewish communities, personalities, the Vatican
and the author's family cover the spectrum of Jewish existence*

**SHENGOLD PUBLISHERS, INC.**
NEW YORK

ISBN 0-88400-194-6
Library of Congress Catalog Card Number: 96-070932
Copyright © 1997 by M. R. Lehmann
All rights reserved

Published by Shengold Publishers, Inc.
18 West 45th Street
New York, NY 10036

Printed in the United States of America

# Table of Contents

*Introduction* . . . . . . . . . . . . . . . . . . . . . . . . . . . . . . . . . . . 9

*History* . . . . . . . . . . . . . . . . . . . . . . . . . . . . . . . . . . . . . . . *11*
    What the Maccabees Really Accomplished . . . . . . . . . . . . . . 11
    The Message of Jewish Coin Inscriptions . . . . . . . . . . . . . . 15
    Unbroken Jewish Presence in Israel: Christian Testimonies over the Ages  19
    Turning Toward Jerusalem . . . . . . . . . . . . . . . . . . . . . 25
    Chevron-Machpelah Campaign . . . . . . . . . . . . . . . . . . . 29
    Rabbi Akiva and Bar Kochba—Two National Heroes . . . . . . . . . 31
    How Shabatai Tzvi's Message Reached Norway in 1666 . . . . . . . 34
    An Historical Perspective Of Moshiach . . . . . . . . . . . . . . 38
    Remember When We Had No State? . . . . . . . . . . . . . . . . . 45
    100 Years Ago: The Dreyfus Case . . . . . . . . . . . . . . . . . 48
    The History of Jewish Banking . . . . . . . . . . . . . . . . . . 52
    Early Relations Between American Jews and Eretz Yisrael . . . . . 55
    The Rescue of the Previous Lubavitcher Rebbe . . . . . . . . . . 59
    How the U.S. Government Treated Enemy Terrorists in 1942 . . . . 63
    How Hitler Began—The Relevance for Today . . . . . . . . . . . . 66
    Brazil . . . . . . . . . . . . . . . . . . . . . . . . . . . . . . 68
    Marienbad, 1937 . . . . . . . . . . . . . . . . . . . . . . . . . 71
    Oral History: Personal Memories from Hitler's Germany . . . . . . 74

*Hebrew Literature* . . . . . . . . . . . . . . . . . . . . . . . . . . . . . . . *79*
    The Book of Ben Sira . . . . . . . . . . . . . . . . . . . . . . . 79
    A Book Lover Caresses His Sefarim . . . . . . . . . . . . . . . . 82
    Haggadah Thoughts . . . . . . . . . . . . . . . . . . . . . . . . 87
    The Publication of Three Outstanding Books . . . . . . . . . . . 92
    The Rambam as Revealed Through His Teshuvot (Responsa) . . . . . 96
    Encounter With The Rambam . . . . . . . . . . . . . . . . . . . . 102
    *"Libelli Fata Sua Habent"* Books Have Their Own Fate . . . . . . 106
    Assuring Perpetual Jewish Learning:
        The Halberstadt Archive of 1713–1847 . . . . . . . . . . . . 110

*The Vatican* . . . . . . . . . . . . . . . . . . . . . . . . . . . . . . . . . . . *115*
    The Story of the Hebrew Manuscripts in the Vatican Library . . . 115
    Unsung Jewish Martyrs—Victims of the Church . . . . . . . . . . . 118
    Sainthood for Pope Pius XII? . . . . . . . . . . . . . . . . . . 124
    Worst Anti-Semitic Outrage in 1,000 Years Perpetrated by the Church . 130
    A Confrontation With The Vatican . . . . . . . . . . . . . . . . 133
    Do We Not Deserve the Same Consideration as Galileo? . . . . . . 135
    "Rome Reborn"—A Thoroughly De-Judaized Vatican Exhibition . . . 140

*Dead Sea Scrolls* . . . . . . . . . . . . . . . . . . . . . *145*
   The Dead Sea Scrolls in the Jewish Tradition . . . . . . . . 145
   Last Gasp for Christological Dead Sea Scroll Interpretations . . . . . 149
   On The Dead Sea Scrolls— The Mysterious MMT Scroll . . . . . . . 153
   The 10 Greatest Archaeological Discoveries . . . . . . . . . . . 158

*Zionism* . . . . . . . . . . . . . . . . . . . . . . . . . . *163*
   Zionism Before Zionism . . . . . . . . . . . . . . . . . 163
   Who Are the Palestinians? The Giant Arab Propaganda Fraud . . . . 168
   Whose Land Is It Anyway? Who Has The Right to Give It Away? . . . 172
   Bosnia—Motherland Of "Palestinians" . . . . . . . . . . . . 176
   Ben-Gurion: Without Chasidim There Might Not Have Been
      a State of Israel . . . . . . . . . . . . . . . . . . . 178
   General Schwarzkopf Says: Don't Give Back The Golan Heights . . . . 182
   Entebbe Rescue Operation 20th Anniversary . . . . . . . . . . 184

*Arabs* . . . . . . . . . . . . . . . . . . . . . . . . . . . *189*
   Arafat's Secret Speech in Stockholm . . . . . . . . . . . . . 189
   Arafat's Ferocious Stockholm Speech Makes Major Impact
      on Public Opinion . . . . . . . . . . . . . . . . . . 193
   Islam in America . . . . . . . . . . . . . . . . . . . 196
   PLO Covenant Update: A Phony Abrogation in the Offing . . . . 201
   Africans Were Enslaved by Arabs—And Freed by Jews . . . . . . . 205
   The Slave Trade—An Arab Invention . . . . . . . . . . . . 207

*Personalities* . . . . . . . . . . . . . . . . . . . . . . . *211*
   Encounters With Lubavitch . . . . . . . . . . . . . . . 211
   Rabbi J. B. Soloveitchik at 90: His Father's and
      Grandfather's Testimony . . . . . . . . . . . . . . . 215
   Rembrandt—Painter of Jews . . . . . . . . . . . . . . . 219
   Winston Churchill—Hero, Villain or Pawn of Providence? . . . . . . 222
   William Foxwell Albright (1891–1971) A Righteous Gentile . . . . . 226
   Eugene V. Rostow—An Unsung Hero . . . . . . . . . . . . 229
   The Jew in Benjamin Disraeli, The Earl of Beaconsfeld . . . . . . . 231
   The Jew in Felix Mendelssohn (1809–1847) . . . . . . . . . . 236
   The Warburgs . . . . . . . . . . . . . . . . . . . . 241
   Heinrich (Chayim) Heine— the Great German Jewish Bard . . . . . 246
   Albert Einstein—Exponent of Outstanding Jewish Traits . . . . . . . 250
   Walther Rathenau (1867–1923): Jewish Foreign Minister
      and Tormented Jew . . . . . . . . . . . . . . . . . 256
   On Music Appreciation . . . . . . . . . . . . . . . . 258
   Mrs. Albright: You Can Be Proud of Your Centuries
      of Jewish Ancestors . . . . . . . . . . . . . . . . . 262

*Communities* . . . . . . . . . . . . . . . . . . . . . . . . . . . *265*
   Williamsburg, 1940 . . . . . . . . . . . . . . . . . . . . . 265
   Baltimore Half a Century Ago . . . . . . . . . . . . . . . 269
   Memories of Jewish Life In Boston 50 Years Ago . . . . . . . . 273
   Worms—One of Our "Mother Cities" . . . . . . . . . . . 278
   The Jews of Yemen . . . . . . . . . . . . . . . . . . . . 282
   The Jews of Gibraltar . . . . . . . . . . . . . . . . . . . 287
   Aleppo and Its Jews—A Proud History . . . . . . . . . . . . 292
   The Jewish Community in France . . . . . . . . . . . . . 296
   A Visit to the Synagogue of Piedmonte . . . . . . . . . . . . 300
   *Part II:* Travels in Piedmonte, the Northwestern Province of Italy . . . 303
   *Part III:* Travels in Piedmonte, the Northwestern Province of Italy . . . 305
   A "Shared" Jerusalem Equals a "Judenrein" Jerusalem . . . . . . . . 309

*Family* . . . . . . . . . . . . . . . . . . . . . . . . . . . . . *313*
   'D'Yukna Shel Abba': A Profile of My Father, *z"l* . . . . . . . . . 313
   Remembering My Son Jamie Lehmann *z"l* . . . . . . . . . . . . 317
   How One Jew Saved Yiddishkeit in His Country . . . . . . . . . 321
   My Wife . . . . . . . . . . . . . . . . . . . . . . . . . . 324
   Message to My Grandchildren . . . . . . . . . . . . . . . 331

Dedicated with abiding love
to my wife Anne.
**רבות בנות עשו חיל**
**ואת עלית על כלנה**

To my children and to my grandchildren.
**בבנינו ובבנותנו נלך**


In memory
of our beloved son
Jamie
**חיים מנחם ז״ל**

# Introduction:

In the present collection, I have made a selection from some 900 essays published over the last ten years. The vast panorama of Jewish experience makes it incumbent on an author to give prominence to as many areas of Jewish religion, history and experience as possible in order to inspire the reader to continue on his own with the pursuit of the many facts and phases of the 4000 years of our existence. It is a monumental task which I cannot claim to exhaust. Yet, as Pirkey Avot teaches us: While you are not expected to finalize your task, neither are you free to withdraw from it.

My essays on History include the 10 Greatest Archaeological Discoveries. The Machpelah in Hebron is one of our oldest ties, going back thousands of years. Sometimes the message of our history is enshrined in ancient Jewish coins, closely connected with the Chanukah story. The role of Rabbi Akiva and Bar Kochba is related in one essay. This touches on Messianism which was so important throughout our history to this day. The unbroken presence of Jews in Eretz Yisrael forms a central part of our attachment to the Land in answer to the question "Whose Land is it, Anyway?" "Zionism Before Zionism" gives an additional dimension to our ties with the Land.

The bridge between Biblical and Talmudic literature is now established through the all-important Dead Sea Scrolls and a few of my essays reflect the extensive work I have done in this field. In the course of our history we were attacked again and again from a variety of sources, but mainly by the Christian Church, as my essays show.

Throughout our long history, Jews have lived in fascinating communities. These have always intrigued me, and therefore many essays relate to a variety of locations and their unique features and activities. These accounts cover such widely-extended communities as Worms, Gibraltar, Aleppo, France, Piedmonte, Brazil, Yemen, Boston and Bosnia.

Our glorious history is made up of the lives of outstanding men, whose biographies have always inspired me. It was my late father who passed on to me the enthusiasm he felt for these great men. I have therefore included biographies of such men as Einstein, Heinrich Heine, Rembrandt, Churchill, Ben Gurion, Rathenau, the Warburgs, Albright, Eugene Rostow, Disraeli, Felix Mendelssohn and General Schwarzkopf. Outstanding among these essays is the description of Rav J. B. Soloveichick written in 1935 by his own father. Included also are the biographies of outstanding famous musicians.

Because of my life-long interest in Jewish scholarship, I have included essays on my love for Jewish books, thoughts on the Haggadah, and my abiding interest in the Rambam and his writings. I have also included memories of my encounters with Lubavitch.

My contacts with Africa resulted in such essays as my account of the Entebbe rescue and the history of black slavery by Africans and Arabs.

My political analyses of historic events are reflected in such essays as "Islam in America" and several reports on secret and threatening PLO speeches.

The writings which are the most meaningful to me are the recollections of my childhood home and the influence my father had on me, and the wonderful memories our family shared.

This book is dedicated to the memory of my dear son Jamie (1950–1982) who would have shared in my experiences and observations. If he had lived he would have made my life much more meaningful. Now I leave my impressions behind to remind my children and grandchildren of the heritage in which Jamie was such an important link. May these essays be a lasting memorial to him.

I hope that my readers will share in this enormously rich tradition which I trust will inspire the coming generations in my family.

I wish to express my abiding love, admiration and gratitude to my dear wife Anne who for almost half a century has shared my life and has been a partner in all the experiences which this book reflects.

# History

In no other religion or culture does history play a greater role than among Jews. In *The Book of Kuzari* by Yehuda Halevy, the faith of a Jew is sought throughout the course of our history. Our history proves the truth of the Jewish religion without the need for any philosophical sets of proof. G-d's providence controls the fate of the nation. In every period we can spot G-d's intentions for our survival—even if it sometimes takes centuries to realize the purpose of our historic fate. My articles trace Providence from earliest times including the message of Jewish coins struck in Jerusalem and the accomplishments of the Maccabees to preserve our heritage, to the tribulations in the Middle Ages and modern times. The awakening of our surge back to our land is traced in the manifestation of Shabatai Tzvi and modern Zionism.

## What the Maccabees Really Accomplished

When we teach our children about Chanukah, we usually tell them about the wickedness of Antiochus, the martyrdom of Mattityahu, the heroism of Judah Maccabee, and the miracle of the oil burning for eight days. But there is much, much more to the story.

Let us first contemplate the story's setting: The great ancient empires from the beginning of history—Egypt, Assyria, Babylonia and Persia—had already vanished. When Alexander the Great conquered what was then the known world, in approximately 330 B.C.E., all those ancient civilizations and their religions disappeared for all practical purposes. It took another two thousand years for man to again be able to read their ancient writings and inscriptions. Alexander's military victories caused Greek culture, philosophy, religion, art, sports, etc., to sweep over the world. But Rome with its might was already lurking in the wings right behind the Greeks, waiting for its turn to take over.

The Romans first had to destroy the last vestige of Oriental power, that of the Phoenicians, who, centered in Carthage, controlled the western Mediterranean and northern Africa. After the Punic Wars of 149–146 B.C.E., Rome was ready to turn its attention toward the east. From 60 B.C.E. on, the eminent Romans—Pompey, Caesar, Marc Anthony, Octavian (later Augustus)—appeared on the world's stage; the 200 years from 27 B.C.E. on, when Augustus became the first Roman Emperor, are known in history as "Pax Romana," the Roman Peace. The whole known world, from England to India, was under Roman rule.

Seen against this evolution and transfiguration of cultures, one little sliver of land stood out: Judea, the Jewish State, which withstood all the onslaughts of the times, and overcame and survived with its exalted traditions intact. It may seem that what happened to the Jews was only a "sideshow" of history, but it certainly was not. After Alexander's empire had been divided three ways, and Palestine fell into the sphere of the Macedonian General Seleucus I, the Jews experienced an onslaught against their religion, led by Antiochus IV (Ephiphanes), which led to history's first revolt based on religious values. And the "Pax Romana" certainly brought no peace to the Jews, for two Jewish revolts broke out during that period, again, to assert Judaism: the revolt against Vespasian in 66 C.E., and the revolt against Hadrian in 132 C.E.

The Seleucids, as well as the Roman rulers, saw in that little sliver of land a challenge that they could not stomach. They could not tolerate a people unwilling to give up their old mores and laws for the splendors and riches of the new world powers. Otherwise, it is incomprehensible why the Seleucids and the Romans would repeatedly mobilize their mightiest armies under their most successful generals to crush that miniscule, stubborn and proud nation of Jews. As proof of this, in the year 70 C.E., and for 50 years thereafter during the "Pax Romana," when Jerusalem had been captured, three Roman Emperors—Vespasian, Titus and Domitian—struck commemorative coins with the legend "Judea Capta." No other victory meant so much to them. They would, of course, turn in their graves, if they could see how in our times, on the triumphant Arch of Titus in Rome, one may always see written in chalk: "Am Yisrael Chai."

The only "Pax" Jews knew was the period from 161 B.C.E. till 37 B.C.E. This peaceful interlude, brought about by the Maccabeans, should perhaps be called "Pax Judaica." The only ancient civilization and religion that continued to exist and flourish, weathering all the storms and cruel vicissitudes of thousands of years of history, was that of the Jews, a testimony to the miracle of survival.

So the history and miracle of Chanukah must be viewed as evidence of our ability to swim against every hostile stream, throughout every chapter of our long history, emerging intact and stronger from the experience. Every crisis period also turned into a period of strengthening of Jewish learning and observance: Under the early Seleucids, the Anshei Knesset Hagedolah flourished; under the Maccabees, great Tannaim, such as Shimon ben Shetach, lived; under the Romans, Hillel and Shammai established their schools; and under the nose of Vespasian, the yeshiva of Yavneh and its scholars was founded, destined to outlive Roman rule, and flourish forever.

Luckily, we have important historical sources which relate the history of the fabulous family of Mattityahu and his sons. Among the books of the Apocrypha—Sefarim Chitzonim in Hebrew—there are the First and Second Books of the Maccabees, which, together with some references in the history books of Flavius Josephus, document almost every twist and turn of that era. I recommend that Jews read these works in time for Chanukah. They tell about the intrigues and "politics" instigated by Hellenized Jews against the authentic priesthood in the Temple, and how these squabbles, as often in Jewish history, brought about intervention from the non-Jewish powers: Antiochus sent his general Apollonius to occupy Jerusalem. He burned parts of the city, tore down its walls, took control of the Temple and stopped the traditional sacrifices.

At this point, many Jews fled Jerusalem. Mattityahu and his sons became the central force among these refugees. Religious oppression grew as observance of Torah and mitzvot was outlawed and pagan worship was introduced. These measures were recommended and encouraged by Hellenized Jews (today we would call them Reform Jews), who collaborated and complied with the Seleucid powers.

Meanwhile, the Hasmoneans, as Mattityahu and his family are called (probably because they originated in the town of Hashmon, which is mentioned in the Bible), were joined by the Chasidim (Asidaioi in Greek). These pious Jews became the role models for religious piety and strict observance of the mitzvot and dinim, but they were also staunch fighters for Judaism and the Jewish people. When 1000 of them were attacked by the Seleucid army on a Shabbat, they all perished because they would not violate the holiness of the day. After this disaster, defensive fighting on Shabbat was encouraged—which saved countless Jewish fighters throughout our history.

The Chasidim of those days are important for our story: We learn about them and their history through the Dead Sea Scrolls, because they existed for a long time after the Maccabees. The Talmud, hundreds of years later, still talks about the Chasidim harishonim and their unbelievable piety.

The militant Jewish rebels grew in number, as the Seleucid oppression and the treachery of the Hellenized Jews grew. We know many stories of their personal heroism and martyrdom. The many battles which had to be fought are also generally known. Judah Maccabee stood out as a great military leader, but he was also a good diplomat. Thus, he sent envoys to Rome, which at that time was not yet a "player" in the area, in order to enlist Roman support.

Finally, Jerusalem was recaptured and cleansed of the pagans, and the Temple was rededicated. The first sacrifices were brought again on Kislev 25, in the year 164 B.C.E., starting an eight-day commemoration, similar to the eight-day celebration at the inauguration of the Ohel Moed in the desert under Moshe Rabbeinu, or the eight days of King Solomon's dedication of his Temple.

But the fighting was far from over. In fact, tragically, Judah fell in one of the ongoing battles. Since he left no heir, the mantle of Maccabean leadership fell to his brother Shimon, who then became the founder of the 130-year Maccabean or Hasmonean dynasty.

Of Shimon's descendants, Alexander Yannai, or Alexander Janneus, and his wife, Queen Salome Alexandra (Shelom-Zion in Hebrew), were the most important. It was during their rule that the purity of our tradition in the hands of the Pharisees

(Perushim in Hebrew) was won, over the objections of the more severe Sadducees (Tzedukkim in Hebrew). This, too, is reflected in the Dead Sea Scrolls. Unfortunately, the disunity and infighting among their two sons, Aristobulus and Hyrcanus, led to the intervention of Roman General Pompey, who occupied Palestine in 63 B.C.E., never again to give the Jews back their full freedom and independence. It took 2000 years till we won those back in 1948, truly a fulfillment of such a long messianic hope.

The Books of the Maccabees contain many interesting pronouncements which have relevance to us today. Let us just quote what is said about Judah and his valiant men: "The man Judah and his brothers were greatly honored among all Israel and among the Gentiles, wherever their name was heard; and people joined them, praising them" (Maccabees I, 6:24; 7:6). That praise has been kept alive by Jews throughout time. Even famous composers and painters have dedicated outstanding works to the valiant Maccabees, such as the opera *Judas Maccabeus* by George Handel, the opera on the same theme by Russian composer Anton Rubinstein, and a magnificent painting by Rubens.

Therefore, when we kindle the menorah on each of the eight nights of Chanukah, we can relive in our minds the triumphs of the Maccabees and all of our heroes, giving us the fortitude to continue their struggle for the survival and strengthening of Judaism today.

# The Message of Jewish Coin Inscriptions

A sign of a people's civilization and cultural advance is its ability to produce a written script—to be able to convey from generation to generation information of important events and personalities, whose memory is considered precious enough to pass on to future generations.

Almost every nation has, throughout history, produced a script with which to eternalize its history. Interestingly, only one continent is absent from the chart of scripts: that of Africa. No black nation has ever produced a written script. (The Egyptians who produced the hieroglyphics were not a Negroid people.)

It is true that instead of script they have devised other means of passing on messages from generation to generation. For example, in Ghana, the former Gold Coast, the "talking drums" replace the task of writing. Professional drummers are trained in passing on entire epics and narratives by way of hours and hours of drumming. (I have attended such sessions and know that the African sense of hearing is much more developed than that of white nations. I heard hours of drumming with what sounded to me like the same beat and rhythm over and over. The Africans listening to the drumming, however, told me of the wonderful stories that the drumming conveyed.)

No wonder that the Mishnah in Avoth 5:9 proclaims "the script and the writing tool" as part of the original Creation of the World. Many types of materials have been used on which writing can be inscribed, engraved or chiseled. The most enduring material is metal, whether gold, silver, copper or bronze. And so, eventually coins were picked to be the carriers of important political, religious and social messages from generation to generation.

Mention of coins appears in the earliest books of the Torah, for example, in the purchase of the Machpelah by our patriarch Abraham.

### *The Persian and Hellenistic Periods*

During the period of about 300 B.C.E, coins were produced bearing the legend "YHD," or "YHDH," or "Judah." The Jewish land was considered a Persian or Greek province; its coins bore no particularly Jewish text or element.

### *Hasmonean Coins*

Jewish texts began to appear openly on coins after the Maccabeans had cleansed the land of pagan influences. Judah Maccabee's brother, John Hyrkanos I, declared himself High Priest and King in about 140 B.C.E., and used as an emblem the lily of Jerusalem. Evidently the coin was struck for use by Jews, mainly in Jerusalem.

The most prolific producer of coins among the Maccabees was King Alexander Jannaeus (in Hebrew Yonatan or Yannai), who ruled from 103 to 76 B.C.E. He fought many wars against the Syrians. As a Sadducee, he also fought a religious war against the Pharisees (Perushim), although his own brother-in-law, Shimon ben Shetach, was a leader of the Perushim.

When Yannai died, his widow, Queen Alexandra, who was a sister of Shimon ben Shetach, took over the rule. Yannai's coins were the first Jewish coins to bear an extended text. Using the ancient Hebrew script, the coins made reference to Yannai being Kohen Gadol and the head of a council called "*Chever ha'Yehudim* (Jewish Brotherhood)." The exact nature of this council is not clear; this might well be a reference to the Anshei Knesset Hagedolah, the men of the great synod which plays such an important role in the Talmud. Thus the brief text on these coins gives us information on the political, social and religious organization of the Jewish community in Eretz Yisrael at the time.

The tragedy that befell the Jewish State after the deaths of King Yannai and Queen Salome Alexandra is well known. The surviving brothers, John Hyrkanos and Judah Aristobulus, engaged in fratricide which eventually led to the invasion of Rome by Pompey and the eventual ending of Jewish independence. We find now on the coins that Hyrkanos (Yehochanan) was both High Priest and the "*Rosh ha'-Chever ha'Yehudim*"; the religious and political offices were combined.

## *Herodian Coins*

King Herod (40 B.C.E to 4 C.E.) was a mighty builder and ruler. Rome had a preference for him and supported him politically. Although a descendant of Edom, he qualified as a Jewish king by virtue of being married to Mariamne, a Maccabean princess. Because of family rivalry, Herod finally had Mariamne executed.

We know him mainly as a magnificent builder of the largest constructions in the entire Middle East. The fact that he undertook to rebuild the Temple shows how much he strove for the acceptance of the religious leadership of the Jews. He also rebuilt the second most sacred structure in the Holy Land—the Machpelah. He turned this structure in Hebron into a magnificent building, in exactly the same style of masonry as the Temple itself. Almost all of his coins bear Greek legends only. He is called "*Basileus* (King)," on these coins.

Of the remaining coins of the Herodian family, only those of Agrippa (37-44 C.E.) are of interest to us. Agrippa, who is mentioned often in the Talmud, had a checkered rule. As grandson of the last Hasmonian ruler, Mariamne, he was given much respect and honor by the rabbis. His coins bear only Greek legends. One of the most remarkable ones is the text: "A vow and treaty of friendship and alliance between the great King Agrippa and Augustus Caesar, the Senate and the people of Rome."

### Roman Procurators and Their Coins

Judea was ruled by Rome-appointed procurators for a long time, under the emperors Augustus, Tiberius, Claudius and Nero.

### Jewish Coins of the First Revolt

With the unbearable oppression of Jews under the Romans, the seed for the First Revolt (66-70 C.E.) was apparent. In the vast expanse of the Roman Empire, from England to India, only Judea, the tiny country, posed a real threat to Rome. Jewish independence was a thorn in the side of the old Roman establishment. Paganism was long undermined by doctrines of Judaism, and the foundation of Rome was seriously threatened. Any political victory of Judea over Rome could lead to the collapse of the entire Empire. Therefore, when the revolt broke out in 66 C.E., Rome brought its most powerful generals and armies to bear. The revolt had to be subdued at any cost.

Thus Jews immediately signified to the world their independence by striking beautiful coins with magnificent Jewish themes and texts. The centrality of Jerusalem and its sanctity was clearly demonstrated on the coins. The number of the year of the revolt was carefully engraved on the coins. To show that the shekel used by the men of the great revolt lay in the direct line of the biblical shekels, the legends stressed again and again the sanctity of the shekel, by calling it *"Shekel ha'Kodesh* (Holy Shekel)." As the revolt succeeded, the date of the revolt took a prominent place in inscriptions: "*Cherut Zion* (Freedom of Zion);" "*Geulat Zion* (Redemption of Zion)" from "Year 1" to "Year 5." These coins exist until this day. The coins of this period were also found at Massada, where the Jews took refuge until its fall in the year 73 C.E.

### Second Revolt, 132–135

Then years of suffering and renewed oppression followed. In 132 C.E., under Emperor Hadrian, the Jews took to arms again, under the heroic and mighty figure of Shimon Bar Kochba. It is not clear whether he, in keeping with the requirements of a legitimate, genuine Messiah, rebuilt the Temple. But many of his coins show the Temple and its implements, and Bar Kochba is called the "*Nessi Yisrael* (Prince of Israel)." Assisting him on his coins was Elazar, the High Priest, so that the revolt had a military-political as well as a priestly-religious leadership. No wonder that Rabbi Akiva declared his faith in Bar Kochba as the Messiah.

A multitude of coins has been found from this period. This evidence has been dramatically augmented by letters, contracts and other documents found in the caves near the Dead Sea.

### Sanctity of Ancient Hebrew Script

Throughout the 300 years that Jewish coins were struck, only the ancient, biblical script was used, never the *ktav Ashuri*, the script which was brought back from the Babylonian Exile from which our modern Hebrew script is derived. It is also interesting that in the Dead Sea Scrolls, which are mostly written in *ktav Ashuri*, the Divine Name is often written in the ancient script. This script was therefore considered more sacred than the later, "modern" script.

The tragic end of 1,135 years of Jewish independence in Jerusalem is documented by the cruel Roman coins issued to tell the world that "*Judea Capta*," (Judah is captured)." The small area of the Jewish State was so important to the political and religious life of humanity that emperor after emperor announced to the world through coins that the Jewish State was no more.

### *Jewish Survival*

We are privileged to live to see and proclaim to the world that the Jewish State is alive. When you visit the Titus Arch in Rome, raised to commemorate the defeat of the Jews, you will always find that someone has written in chalk these words: "*Am Yisrael Chai!*" Those words tell the whole story of the perilous victory of the Jewish people and the Jewish religion over its enemies. The chain of the story can be traced through the long trail of Jewish coins—contemporary evidence of Jewish heroism and resilience. We can only exclaim in awe and gratitude to Hashem: "*Am Yisrael Chai!*" Ancient Jewish coins are therefore a source of great inspiration and faith.

# Unbroken Jewish Presence in Israel: Christian Testimonies over the Ages

I have always wondered how non-Jews see us, and how our most intimate character traits and customs strike them, especially as practiced in Eretz Yisrael. For this reason I have collected a large number of books written over the past 300-400 years, containing travel reports by Christians—Englishmen, Frenchmen, Swedes and Americans—who visited the Holy Land and observed the Jewish population there. Needless to say, such books are an inestimable source of historic information. We read of the number of Jews there, usually higher than we would otherwise estimate; the presence of the Arab population, which was practically non-existent outside of a few cities; religious observance, which was extremely intense and therefore misunderstood by Christians; the extremely harsh political oppression by the Turkish rulers; and the very severe economic conditions.

For this column I have selected excerpts from ten of my books. The earliest, from a trip begun in 1610, almost 400 years ago, describes the conditions shortly after the Kabalists had arrived from Spain and the Ottoman Empire. Travelers reported that Spanish was the spoken language before the influx of the Ashkenazic immigrants. "Spanish in Hebrew letters" refers to Ladino, probably the popular work *Me'am Loez*, a commentary on the Bible.

The Swede, Mikael Eneman, visited Smyrna before he came to Jerusalem, and had learnt a lot from the followers of Shabatai Tzvi about Kabala. Swedish travelers, influenced by the botanist Carl Linné, were more interested in plants and flowers than in people. The British and Americans who came later were often missionaries, and were on the lookout for opportunities to proselytize among the poor and sick Jews who had come from Russia after the days of the Baal Hatanya and the Vilna Gaon. The exceptional treatment afforded Sir Moses Montefiore shows the suffering, by contrast, which Jews experienced under the Moslems for centuries.

It is interesting how consistent the reaction of Christian visitors was to Jewish worship which, with its spontaneity and intimacy with G-d, makes the stiff, formal and impersonal Church services, by contrast, seem arid and stale. It is obvious that the Christians are overcome by this contrast, and being unable to admit the superiority of the Jewish religious experience, pretended that the Jewish format of synagogue worship was "savage," "ridiculous," "barbaric," "outrageous" and "vehement," etc.

Here we have probably the earliest eye-witness accounts of the appearance of the Ashkenazic immigrants, either Chasidim or Mitnagdim, wearing "broad brimmed hats," and "twisting, jerking, wriggling and swinging back and forth like the pendulum of a clock" in prayer. We all recognize the fervor of the *davening* of our devout Jews, an everyday occurrence in our lives, of which we can be justly proud.

These books offer clear testimony to the strong Jewish claim to the land of Israel, where throughout the centuries Jews lived and died, and where a pulsating Jewish religious life always existed, carried forward by the certainty that a Messianic age would dawn when Jews would have their land and their beloved eternal capital of Jerusalem back again. It is therefore highly significant that in 1783 the Arabs still admitted that the name "El Kuds" for Jerusalem does not at all indicate any "Moslem" sanctity, but strictly refers to the old Jewish Temple, the *Beit Hamikdash* that stood there and gave the city its sanctity. (El Kuds is an abbreviation of the fuller Arabic term for the Jewish Temple, "al-Bayit al-Mukadash.")

All of the translations which follow are my own:

## *"A Relation of a Journey Begun in A.D. 1610," Sandys, London, 1615*

In Jerusalem, besides Moors, Greeks and other Christians, there are also some Jews. They inherit no part of the land, but in their own country do live as aliens, a people scattered throughout the whole world and hated by those amongst whom they live, yet suffered, subject to all wrongs and contumlies, which they support with an invincible patience. Many of them have been abused, some of them beaten, yet never saw I a Jew with angry countenance.

Throughout the Turks' dominion they are allowed their synagogues. Their synagogues have in their midst a scaffold, wherein stands he that reads from their law and sings their liturgy. They read in savage tones, and sing in tunes that have no affinity with music, joining voices at the several closes. But their fantastical gestures exceed all barbarism, continually weaving with their bodies, and often jumping upright, as in the manner of dancers, by them esteemed an action of zeal, and figure of spiritual elevation. They pray silently with ridiculous and continual nodding of their heads, not to be seen and not laughed at.

During the time of service their heads are veiled in linen, fringed with knots, in number answerable to the number of their laws, which they carry in procession. They have it stuck in the jambs of their doors and covered with glass, written by their *chacham* and signed with the name of G-d, which they kiss next their hearts in their going forth and in their returns.

Many of their books are in the Spanish tongue and Hebrew characters. Their only studies are Divinity and physics. Their occupation is brokerage and usury, yet take they no interest of one another nor lend but upon pawns, which once forfeited are unredeemable.

They live through the Turks' dominions, and when they die, and the flesh is consumed in the grave, they dig up the bones of those that are of their families, whereof whole shipfuls not seldom do arrive in Jaffa, to be conveyed and again interred at Jerusalem.

## "Relation Fidèle du Voyage de la Terre Sainte,"
## Franciscan Traveler, Paris, 1699 (translated from the French)

The Jews are divided into two sects, one whose followers observe purely the law of Moses, and another which considers the first as heretics. Both parties hate Jews who, coming from Europe, have had contact with Christians. However, they all get along with one another in business, for they all have correspondents in all parts of the world.

In their religion they have three main holidays which are celebrated with great solemnity: One is the Passover, when each family pulls out a lamb according to the law of Moses. There is another holiday for which they assemble in the Galilee, the small town of Safed where they believe the Messiah will arrive. The feast of Tabernacles is also celebrated with great solemnity.

On October 15, 1699, I was at Scide in Syria, where there is a great number of Jews. I entered one of their Spanish-speaking synagogues and observed that its walls were beautifully decorated with branches of trees. I was received with great courtesy, as was the Spanish priest who accompanied me. The venerable elders of the community got up from their seats and offered their seats to us. There was a platform elevated some ten feet, where a cantor and eight small boys cried like possessed by demons, their bodies shaking and moving back and forth as the pendulum of a clock.

Although the Jews are dispersed throughout the world, they consider Jerusalem their native city. That is why a large number of them come there to die and to be buried in the soil of their ancestors.

## "Resa i Orienten," M. Eneman, Stockholm, 1711
## (translated from old Swedish)

The Jews believe in what they call *gilgul*. Their bodies will somehow arrive in the Holy Land through dales and mountains, rocks and rivers, till they arrive in Jerusalem to be present when the Messiah (who Christians believe will never come) arrives. Those who go through the sufferings of this gilgul, instead of enjoying tranquility and good days in other countries, believe that they will be rewarded by being treated like princes and noblemen in the realm of the Messiah.

Those who come to the Holy Land want to see the *Shechina* with their own eyes, which they believe still dwells at *Kotel Hamaaravi*, the last part of the Temple, where they pray incessantly. When I asked an old Jew there why the Messiah is tarrying for so long, he smiled and quoted to me a verse from the Song of Songs, indicating that he is about to come: "Lo, he stands behind our wall (kotel) and looks through the window" (Songs 2:9).

The Jews venerate several old sacred sites, such as the Tombs of Kings, Absholom's and Zacharia's Tombs, those of Hagai and Malachi on Mt. Olives, and also the Prophet Elijah's tomb. They also go day and night to a site in Bethlehem, to pray there. In Jerusalem they have two synagogues, one called the German Jews' synagogue, the other, the Frankish or Italian synagogue, also used by Spanish refugees.

They send out emissaries throughout the world to collect alms for the Jews in Hebron, Safed and Bethulia, near Tiberias. The Jews are not engaged in any commerce, but maintain a few soap-making shops.

### *"Voyages and Travels in the Levant,"*
### *Fredrick Hasselquist, Sweden, 1749*

Tiberias is a little town, half of it is inhabited by Arabs, who are the masters, and the other half by Jews, who pay taxes to the former. The Christians have no liberty here. We saw Bethulia or Saphet, whither the Jews go out of devotion to spend their vacant time.

### *"Stora Swenska Herrars Rese-Beskrivning," 1783*
### *(translated from old Swedish)*

In Jerusalem, where the Holy Sepulchre Church is located, there is in front of it a marble-covered square, on which no Jew is allowed to step. The city is rather well populated, partly by Moslems, partly by Christians, partly by Jews who come here in their advanced age to die and be buried in the valley of Joshafat.

Jerusalem is called in Arabic *"Beit al-Mokdesh,"* for the Holy House of the Temple that stood there.

### *"The Land and the Book," W.M. Thompson, New York, 1834*

My cicerone took me to a large synagogue in Jerusalem which was crowded with worshippers. There was something inexpressibly sad in the features, deportment and costume of these children of Abraham, as they grope about the ruins of their once joyous city.

The Jews come to Jerusalem to die, which accounts for the ever-increasing multitude of their graves, which are gradually covering the side of [the Mount of] Olives. A community gathering for that specific purpose will not be particularly gay, nor very careful about appearances.

The behavior of the worshippers was very peculiar and somewhat ridiculous. The men, with broad-brimmed hats, or whatever other headdress they possessed, were reading or muttering prayers, and while doing so twisted, jerked and wriggled about incessantly, and at times with great vehemence, so that "all their bones should praise the L-rd," as one of them explained to me. When they began what was understood to be singing, it was the most outrageous concert of harsh nasal sounds I ever heard. It was Hebrew, too, but if David thus "praises the L-rd," I should never have thought of calling him the "sweet singer of Israel."

As to Safed, its prosperity is entirely owing to the constant influx of foreign

Jews, drawn hither by the sanctity of the place. The population is about 5000, more than half of them Jews.

### *"Narrative," Church of Scotland, 1839*

The Turkish Governor of Jerusalem allowed Sir Moses Montefiore and his attendants to enter the tomb of David upon Mount Zion, and to pray over it, a privilege not granted to a Jew for many centuries. The Jews recited a long form of prayer and read many Psalms, such as the 15th, 72nd and 76th chapters, over the tomb of the sweet singer of Israel. It was a solemn and affecting scene.

The British Consul, Mr. Young, gave the following statistics of the Jews in the Holy Land:

| | | | |
|---|---|---|---|
| Jerusalem | 6000 | Kaipha | 200 |
| Nablus | 200 | Sidon | 300 |
| Tiberias | 800 | Tyre | 150 |
| Safed | 2000 | Jaffa | 60 |
| Acco | 200 | Villages of Galilee | 580 |

On the whole, Mr. Young reckoned that there are in round numbers about 10,000 Jews in the whole of Palestine. There is without doubt a constant influx of Jews into this country.

### *"The City and Environs of Jerusalem," W.H. Barlett, London, 1842*

Christians and Jews live side by side within her walls, in nearly equal numbers, of from four to five thousand each. The Jews occupy the rugged slope of Mt. Zion, over against the Temple. One can divide them into classes: those who are natives, descendants of Jews banished from Europe by Charles V, and who are in more comfortable circumstances; and a crowd of Polish and German exiles, wholly without resources, except contributions gathered for them in Europe and Turkey. They are described as more fervent in their devotion to the Holy City than their native brethren, they pass much of their time in the synagogue and their rabbis are possessed of a larger share of the peculiar learning of their sect than those born on the spot.

### *"Palestina," W. F. Palmblad, 1842 (translated from Swedish)*

Jerusalem has nine soap-making shops, nine sesame oil presses, one large tannery, but otherwise no factories, no export except for antiquities, and no commerce. However, during Easter, the pilgrims stream here and traders from Damascus come here to sell their ware. The city which in the days of Alexander counted some 120,000 inhabitants, up to one million during the Passover, in our own days has some 12,000 inhabitants, of which 4500 are Moslems, 3000 Jews, 130 Armenian, 460 Greek Orthodox, 260 Catholic and the rest are Christians of various denominations.

***"Those Holy Fields," Samuel Manning, London, 1846***

We come to the Wailing Place of the Jews. It is closer to the Jewish quarter, the foulest, most squalid and wretched part of the city. The masonry here is the finest, and in the best preservation, of any part of the enclosure. Many of the stones are twenty-five feet in length and apparently have remained undisturbed since the time of the first builders. Here the Jews assemble every Friday to mourn over the fallen state.

These travel accounts, even if colored by Christian bias, are testimony to the devout Jews who, under very difficult political and economic conditions, overcame every hardship and sacrifice just to live and die on the ancestral soil of the Land of Israel. Through the deep impression these Jews made on these chance observers, they left behind a lasting heritage to stand their descendants in good stead centuries later. They were links in the unbroken chain of permanent Jewish presence on our holy soil, which none of our enemies can deny. The eternal love of Jews for Jerusalem is beautifully expressed by the Franciscan priest 300 years ago: "Although the Jews are dispersed throughout the world, they consider Jerusalem their native city."

# Turning Toward Jerusalem

Jerusalem is the eternal Jewish capital. There can be no doubt about that. And it is an undoubted fact that all Jews—even the most leftist "liberals" and most alienated Reform Jews among us—agree that Jerusalem must remain the eternal, undivided capital of Israel. Therefore, the continuity of Jerusalem as the Jewish capital can never be placed on the agenda of any political dialogue with our adversaries. We must never allow the slightest doubt about our loyalty to Israel on this point to creep into any discussion of Israel's future.

It is, however, timely that we, between ourselves, fortify our position by studying the historic and documentary background to our claim to Jerusalem, and at the same time educate ourselves as to claims made by Moslems and Christians to Jerusalem, so that a comparison between the claims can be made.

Let us remember that Jerusalem is mentioned about 800 times in the Hebrew Bible. Just look into any available Concordance of the Bible and you will find the exact listings of all references to Jerusalem in the Tanach. The city is mentioned about a thousand times, throughout most of the books of the Tanach.

Next, ask yourself, "How many times is Jerusalem mentioned in the Koran, the Holy Book of the Moslems?" You may be amazed at the answer, because the answer is—zero times! Nowhere in the Koran is Jerusalem mentioned!

The most Moslem apologists can come up with is a single reference in the Koran to "el-Aqsa," translated as "the furthest Mosque." Moslems apply this to the famous Aqsa Mosque in Jerusalem. However, the flaw in this argument is that at the time of Mohammed, Jerusalem was a Christian Byzantine city, part of the Byzantine Empire. What is today the Aqsa Mosque as then a Byzantine Christian church (Church of St. Mary)! Anyone familiar with the architecture of the Aqsa Mosque will immediately recognize that characteristic, typical Byzantine church structure of the building which is hardly changed from its Christian days. Therefore, Mohammed could not have thought of this church in Jerusalem, but must have thought of a mosque in some other location.

But did Mohammed show any affinity to Jerusalem, regardless of the fact that he did not mention the city in the Koran? Let us look at the history of Islam. Mohammed, in the beginning of his career as the founder of a new religion, failed to capture Medinah, a city he aimed for. He enlisted thereupon the help of a Jewish army which captured Medinah for him. Mohammed then thought that the Jews would also be candidates for conversion to Islam. Knowing the central position of Jerusalem in Judaism and that Jews turn to Jerusalem in their daily prayers, Mohammed adopted—temporarily—this practice to make the transition to Islam easier for Jews. He declared the *Qibla*, the direction in prayer, to be Jerusalem.

When, however, after two years, he noticed that Jews would not convert to Islam and that his efforts to win them over had failed, he suspended the practice. On February 12th in the year 624, he issued a prohibition against facing Jerusalem, and proclaimed that from then on the *Qibla* was Mecca. Ever since then Moslems have been turning to Mecca in their prayers.

I once had an interesting personal experience on this point. In February 1978, as part of an American Jewish delegation, I found myself in Cairo for meetings with President Anwar Sadat and other important Moslem personalities. One of them was the aged Sheikh al-Azhar, the head of the world's leading Moslem University, the Al Azhar University. This was at the time when the talks between Menachem Begin and Sadat were far from conclusion. The Sheikh expressed to us his own idea for a solution of the problem. He told us that in his opinion, if the Jews would give up Jerusalem and the rest of "Palestine," he would be in favor of—giving them back their banks and shops in Cairo! We were, of course, all stunned and shocked by this utterly intransigent and hostile attitude. Seeing that no reasonable dialogue was possible with the Sheikh, I decided to challenge him, as a scholar and historian, on the question of Jerusalem. I asked him, through his interpreter, how he could claim that Jerusalem was holy to Mohammed if he himself had forbidden his followers in 624 even to face the city in prayer. The Sheikh was visibly taken aback by the question. He had probably not counted on anyone in the audience being knowledgeable about this problematic point in Moslem theology. After some moments and after some quick whispered exchanges with the interpreter, the Sheikh said, 'Yes, but still, Jerusalem was close to the Prophet's heart." Frankly, it did not sound very convincing.

Actually, if we look further into the history of Islam, we find evidence that the name "El Kuds (the Holy One)," the Arab name today for Jerusalem, was unknown in the early generations of Islam. After Mohammed's death, the rulers of the Moslem world were called Caliphs. The second such Caliph was Omar, who was a mighty warrior and who captured Egypt, Syria and Iraq. In 638 he captured Jerusalem from the Byzantine Christians. It is highly significant that in the treaty signed by both sides after the capture of Jerusalem, Omar referred to the city as "Aelia," which was the pagan name given by Emperor Hadrian in 135 C.E. after the defeat of the Bar Kochba revolt. (The full pagan name was Aelia Capitolina.) This shows, of course, that Jerusalem held no special sanctity to Omar and that the name El-Kuds was unknown to him. Incidentally, the same treaty also contained a provision that all Jews had to be expelled from Jerusalem after its surrender to the Moslem forces. I have often wondered if anyone who heard Sadat's Knesset speech in November 1977, when he ended with the words, "Let us invoke the spirit of Omar," understood that these words could have had a sinister and grave meaning as to what he thought should happen concerning the Jews of Jerusalem.

Where does the name "El Kuds" come from? Does this name mean that Jerusalem has a special Moslem sanctity based on Islam? Here is the amazing answer to this question, found in the newly-published *Encyclopedia of Islam*: "Al Kuds = so-called from 'al-Bayit al-Muqqadas', 'the Holy House,' that is, the Temple of Solomon. Its holiness for the Moslems derives, in the first place, from its association with the Old Testament Prophets who are also Prophets in Islam." In other words, "El Kuds" is an abbreviation of "Beth Hamikdash," in Hebrew, and its sanctity is based on the Jewish Temple there and the presence there of all the Jewish personalities of the Hebrew Bible! It is a tragedy that the Jewish ties of Moslems to Jerusalem as the Jewish capital have either been forgotten or deliberately suppressed.

It is not the only factor which has been suppressed, but which could prove helpful in changing Moslem hostility to Jews, to a peaceful acceptance and friendship for each other. There is no doubt that Mohammed had high regard for the Jewish people. In a few places in the Koran, he says in the name of Allah, "O children of Israel! Remember my favor which I bestowed upon you and that I exalted you above all the people" (Koran 2:48 and 123). But, furthermore, the Koran clearly promises and foretells the return of the Jewish people to their land: "We said to the children of Israel: 'Dwell ye in the land, and when the time of the promise of the latter days comes, We shall bring you together again out of the various peoples" (Koran 17:105). Nothing more "Zionist" could be imagined, and it represents the words of Mohammed himself! I hope that this passage from the Koran could be spread among the Moslem world again.

We shall now turn to the Christian claim to Jerusalem, or at least their insistence that the city *not* be a Jewish city, by pressing for its internationalization. It is clear that all Christian ties and associations with Jerusalem are wholly Jewish in character. Their affinity to Jerusalem is derived from the fact that the city was the Jewish capital with the Jewish Temple standing there, during the time when the events of their Gospels are said to have taken place. The persons and events in these accounts were all Jewish, with the Romans present as an alien power. Nothing is "Christian" about these associations. Only centuries later, in their on-going efforts to delegitimize and eradicate Judaism, did they think of a scheme to deprive the Jews of the ancient homeland and capital, by usurping these names for themselves. The Church called itself "Verus Israel (the true Israel)," and Jerusalem was delegated to a place in heaven, not on earth. The current Pope is said—by people who know his thinking—to share this view, which is the main reason for his refusal to recognize the newly reborn State of Israel, his calling for the creation of a Palestinian State, and for the internationalization of Jerusalem. Such artificial contortions have of course been gainsaid by history itself, since Jews never throughout history left the soil of the Holy Land, and in every waking moment have turned their hearts to Jerusalem for the last two thousand years. Only during one short period, in the 11th century, when Christians ruled over Jerusalem as Crusaders, was the city made "Judenrein." Immediately after the capture of Jerusalem in 1099, the Christians killed its entire Jewish population. However, soon thereafter, Jews settled there again. Large groups of Jewish immigrants came from France and Spain. Yehuda ha-

Levy, the great 11th century Spanish bard and philosopher, and French Tosafists were among them. Another famous immigrant was Reb. Moses ben Nahman (Nahmanides), who migrated to Jerusalem after his successful disputation with the renegade Jew Pablo Christiano in Barcelona in 1263. Reb. Moses' synagogue is still in daily use today.

In sum, all claims to Jerusalem are based on the Jewish history and character of the city. If there had not been a Jewish Jerusalem, there would have been neither a Christian or Moslem interest in the city. Even today, these two religions seem to perk up about Jerusalem only in a negative way—to take it away from the Jews, its oldest inhabitants. It is interesting that the Saudi Arabian royal family, which claims to be the "Protectors" of the holy Moslem shrines in Jerusalem, never once visited Jerusalem during its nineteen years of occupation by Jordan. King Feisal, who was the Saudi king during that period, never took the trouble to visit the city.

Much Jewish blood was spilled because of Jerusalem. The valiant fight of the Maccabees 2,200 years ago, which ended in the freeing and purifying of Jerusalem, is a reminder for us during the Chanukah season of the central role which Jerusalem has played for thousands of years. All our dreams, hopes and prayers center on Jerusalem.

Only we have an uninterrupted chain of historic, political and religious ties with the City. Only Jews say, year after year, "Next year in Jerusalem."

Let us hope that the eternal, undivided capital of the Jewish State will enjoy peace and tranquility for all years to come. Our strengthened knowledge of the city's history will redouble our pride and loyalty to Jerusalem.

# Chevron-Machpelah Campaign

I was recently invited to attend the founding meeting of Jews and Christians concerned with the future of Chevron, the second most holy city in Judaism. It was decided to launch a world-wide campaign to raise, through gifts of $10 or more from a million people, enough money to pay for the restoration of the city, which through neglect by its Arab inhabitants in the past, has fallen into disrepair.

Also, the rapidly deteriorating security situation makes it incumbent on Israel to increase Chevron's Jewish population and tighten military and police protection there. Too many victims of PLO-sponsored terrorism, especially after the signing of the Peres-Arafat "peace" agreement, have paid with their lives in Chevron at the hands of Arabs being groomed for "police" service during the "autonomy" period.

Project Machpelah has the active endorsement of such Christian leaders as Richard Helman of CIPAC, Grant Livingstone of Shalom Israel Ministries, Ed McAteer of the Roundtable Organization and Edwood McQuade of Christian Friends of Israel. At the coming National Conference of Christian Broadcasters in Washington, Project Machpelah will have a booth, which will be manned by Jewish activist Mrs. Ruth Matar, and Grant Livingstone.

Mrs. Matar will address the Conference, which caters to the 65 million American Bible-believing Christians, who are opposed to surrendering to the Arabs land divinely promised to the Jews. This Project deserves our warm support.

Since 1967 when Chevron returned to Jewish hands, many have attempted to explore the lower sections of the city's Cave of Machpelah (the Double Cave) where our Patriarchs are buried. The farthest that archaeologists—including Moshe Dayan—had explored was the area below the main floor, the "cellar."

Now a report has appeared with the extraordinary news that archaeologists have reached the very "basement" of the Machpelah below the "cellar."

And, indeed, it holds two caves! Explorers have discovered, as well, ancient bones and implements dating to the Patriarchal age. This find confirms the definition of the name "Machpelah," meaning "the double one." The Talmud in Eruvin (53a) quotes two opinions. According to Rav, "Machpelah" means two levels, one behind the other. According to Shmuel, it means two floors, one above the other. As the chart shows, both are right: there are two levels, one above the other, but also at the lowest level, one next to the other.

The Cave of Machpelah is prominently mentioned in the Torah. Abraham's purchase of the burial site for his wife Sarah and the legal procedure by binding contract through which he purchased it, have been scientifically examined and found fully consistent with Hittite contract law for real estate at the time. My findings in this regard were published in the Bulletin of the American Oriental Society many years ago and were endorsed by the late Professor William Foxwell Albright, this century's greatest Orientalist.

Throughout the Talmud and later rabbinical writings, the Machpelah is prominently mentioned as a holy site conducive to praying. Unfortunately throughout the 700 years that the Machpelah was under Moslem possession, Jews and Christians were barred from entering the ancient structure holding the graves of the Patriarchs. Non-Arabs were only allowed to reach the seventh step on a staircase leading to the building.

The Arabs now aim to return to this outrageous discrimination.

No wonder that the Machpelah has held our attention and devotion throughout history. As an unusual example of that devotion I can cite a tomb inscription, which I copied some years ago at the old Jewish cemetery on the Island of Barbados in the Caribbean. A pious lady named Rachel Chanah Louzada died on October 28, 1741, and in the Hebrew text on her tombstone these words are included: "May her soul travel to the Cave of Machpelah." It is remarkable to think that the Machpelah was venerated in such a far-off and isolated place as colonial Barbados!

Now the PLO is clamoring for possession of Chevron, and the Beilin-Peres crowd apparently has no qualms about giving into this demand. But the entire Jewish world should rise in protest and demand that the Israeli government retain our second holiest site!

# Rabbi Akiva and Bar Kochba—Two National Heroes

In many communities, children celebrate Lag B'Omer by going out to the forests with bows and arrows. Do they play Cowboys and Indians? No, they reenact the heroic fights of Bar Kochba's fighters against the Roman oppressors. Many of these fighters were the disciples of the famous Rabbi Akiva, and when many of them died during those tragic days, the mourning of *Sefira* was instituted. On Lag B'Omer the deaths stopped, at least for a while. Who was this Bar Kochba, who left behind such a deep impression on the Jewish people?

The Jews revolted twice against the mighty Roman Empire. The first revolution took place in 68 C.E., and it ended in the destruction of the Temple on the 9th of Av, in 70 C.E. However, the Jews stayed in the land, and when Emperor Hadrian, in 132 C.E., imposed oppressive measures against the Jewish religion, a mighty fighter named Ben Kosiba rallied the Jewish people to revolt again, the so-called "Second Revolt." Unlike the first revolt, the second revolt was 100% successful, at least initially. To the utter consternation of the Roman rulers, who controlled the entire known world from India to England, the tiny Jewish people, for the first time in Roman history, was able to expel the occupation army from every inch of its soil!

At this point, Rabbi Akiva and his contemporary *chachamim* pronounced Ben Kosiba the long-awaited Moshiach, and bestowed upon him a royal title of "*melech*" and "*nassi*."

What do we know about this electrifying event in our history? Till now we knew very little. Roman historians understandably keep quiet about this latter-day David, who vanquished mighty Goliath-Rome. Christians hated him outright, for reasons which will soon become apparent.

At first all we knew about this great leader came from some cryptic references to him in the Talmud, Tractate Sanhedrin, and in Seder Olam. We also knew about him from the huge quantity of coins which he struck. In my own numismatic collection I have a large number of his copper and silver coins. Some are overstruck Roman coins, captured during the fighting. On some of them you can still see the Latin inscription underlying the proud Hebrew text (in ancient Hebrew script) proclaiming the "*ge'ulat Yisrael*," or "*cherut Yerushalayim*." Some large silver coins show the front of the *Beit Hamikdash*, with the Yochin u'Boaz pillars and the *Shulchan*. There are scholars who take this to mean that Ben Kosiba, or Bar Kochba as he was later called, actually started to rebuild the Temple! Some coins show the trumpets, the lyre and other instruments used by the Levites in the Temple.

Some years ago the famous archaeologist Yigal Yadin made some sensational finds when he excavated the caves along the Dead Sea. Among his discoveries were a large number of letters and contracts written by Jews in Bar Kochba's camp, and some written by Bar Kochba himself!

These writings throw an entirely new light on this heroic figure in our history: He was a first-class administrator, who declared the land to be the property of the State, to be distributed to farmers on a share-cropping basis. He gave vivid instructions to his people, calling on them to follow the mitzvot in every detail: to take *maaser*, to keep the Shabbat and the other commandments.

One very moving letter Bar Kochba wrote to his commander in Ein Gedi, noting that he was sending him donkeys laden with *lulavim* and *etrogim*, and instructing the commander to return the donkeys with *hadasim* and *aravot*, so that in both camps they would have the "four species" needed for the holiday of Sukot—and that in the heat of ferocious battles against the Romans!

Another letter throws extremely important light on the history of the cleavage between the Jews and the early Christians. These early Christians considered themselves to be good Jews, but since they believed that their Messiah had already come, they could not accept Bar Kochba as the Moshiach, and therefore did not join the national uprising headed by him. In one letter, therefore, we find that Bar Kochba gives harsh instructions to arrest and shackle any Galilean (Christian) who acts treasonably! In fact, the Bar Kochba revolt marked the clear parting of the ways between the Jews and the early Christians. No wonder that the latter had no love for Bar Kochba, who to us, however, is the epitome of a Jewish hero.

After the initial triumph of the rebels, Emperor Hadrian was desperate. He could not tolerate that such a small band of renegades had ousted his proud army. He searched his entire Empire to find his most gifted general, and finally he recalled General Severus from England, where he gained recognition by fighting off the fierce English barbarians, north of the so-called "Hadrian's Wall," which till this day cuts across the English countryside.

Emperor Hadrian ordered Severus to mobilize a special army against Bar Kochba. When the skilled general arrived in the holy land, he decided to conduct a "guerilla-style" campaign: slowly whittling away at Jewish strongholds, and not engaging them in open battle. Finally, the Romans captured Bar Kochba's largest base, the city of Betar, on the 9th of Av in 135 C.E. The massacre that ensued, which no doubt also involved Rabbi Akiva's disciples, really defies description, although our sages graphically recorded what they could in the Talmud and Midrash. According to their testimony, Bar Kochba died in the besieged city.

The Roman Senate did not think very highly of the performance of Hadrian's troops, and did not salute them with the customary congratulatory salutation upon their return to Rome. This was an indirect tribute to the heroism of the Jews.

How has Jewish history treated Bar Kochba? First, by changing his native name, Ben Kosiba, to Bar Kochba, the messianic nature of his character has been confirmed forever, for that designation is based on the prophetic saying of Bilaam (Numbers 24:17), "*darach kochav mi'Yaakov*, A star will shoot forth from

Jacob"—which the commentators agree is a messianic reference. Secondly, although it is not generally known, we commemorate Bar Kochba and his valiant fighters at every meal we eat, for the fourth blessing of the "Grace after Meals" was added as thanks to G-d for the burial of Bar Kochba's fallen, who for some time had been forbidden to be buried by the Romans.

But beyond this, Bar Kochba has entered *halacha* forever: The Rambam legislates (Hilchot Melochim 11:2) that Bar Kochba personifies the exact characteristics of the legitimate Moshiach—he has to be true to the Torah, must teach the Written and Oral Law and strengthen their observance, and although he does not have to perform any miracles, he must accomplish the political freeing of Jews from oppression. Therefore, when Bar Kochba failed, the Moshiach title was removed from him.

At the end of this law, the Rambam writes an unusual addition: "the Torah's statutes and rules are eternal and forever. They may not be added to or subtracted from." I see in these words a hint regarding other religions, like Christianity, which attribute the Messiahship to a man who passed none of the tests set down in the halacha! The one they glorify was not an expert in Torah—in fact, he caused his followers to abandon the Torah—and he made no dent in the political oppression exercised by Rome. As the Rambam stresses, instead of bringing peace and tranquility to his people, as the Moshiach should, he brought them nothing but suffering and death.

Despite the tragic ending of the Bar Kochba revolt, we celebrate Lag B'Omer joyously. Maybe this is in part because of the appearance of Bar Kochba—and through him Rabbi Akiva's lasting definition of the qualifications for the authentic Moshiach—which instills in us the clear hope that the authentic Moshiach will come soon, and bring our ultimate deliverance from all persecution and suffering. Can there be greater grounds for joyous celebration?

# How Shabatai Tzvi's Message Reached Norway in 1666

In my articles, I have from time to time written about the electrifying effect which the presumed Messianic appearance of Shabatai Tzvi had on European Jews everywhere. The year 1666 was a crucial year in that historic episode. It was then that his "revelation" as the Messiah took place. The effect was two-fold: On one hand, Jews in many countries far and wide liquidated their possessions and embarked on the voyage to Turkey to see with their own eyes the Messiah about whom they had just heard. They also heard of his assistant, a man who was called Nathan the Prophet of Gaza. On the other hand, a vigorous campaign was launched by rabbis and community leaders who suspected that Shabatai Tzvi was a fraud. It was, of course, the latter group which was proved correct when Shabatai Tzvi, to everyone's consternation, submitted to the pressure of Sultan Mohammed IV, and "took on the turban," or, in other words, converted to Islam.

The Christian world, naturally unnerved by the appearance of a Jewish Messiah (since they had preached that a Messiah had already appeared sixteen hundred years earlier), did everything it could to ridicule and mock the Jews who were still waiting for the coming of a Messiah. Many publications on this theme appeared in Christian lands. I could illustrate this with a booklet, printed in Germany, entitled "The Story of the Great Deceiver, or the False King of the Jews, Shabatai Tzvi of Smyrna."

I have now found rather unexpected and amazing evidence that the news of Shabatai Tzvi travelled even further and faster than usually assumed. I have come across an unusual letter, written in a mixture of Hebrew and Yiddish, by a Jewish woman, Schoenchen Sossmann, in Copenhagen, to her husband Jacob Sossmann in Oslo, in 1666. The letter is now in the royal archives of the Norwegian Government. Her husband had run afoul of the law in Norway and was held by the police. His wife kept him informed of news and current events. At the end of the letter she wrote: "Now I wish to inform you of news about the *melech hamoshiach* [King Messiah] and about Nathan the Prophet from Gaza, who together with ten *chachomim* are arriving in Constantinople. There the *geulah* [redemption] will become *mefursam* [publicized]."

Because the letter is written almost contemporaneously with the event in far-off Turkey, it is amazing how quickly the news reached the far north of Europe, where very few Jews lived at the time (Jews were not officially permitted entry into Norway for another two hundred years). We must be grateful to that lady who left for posterity such valuable testimony of the burning expectation of the Moshiach at that tragic time in Jewish history, after the Chmielnitzky pogroms in the Ukraine had just caused the loss of a substantial part of the Jewish people. Some have estimated that only one hundred thousand Jews survived those massacres. Therefore, the news of a Moshiach was the sorely needed event to inject new hope and *bitochen* in the Jewish people's eternal survival and ultimate redemption.

Since we have mentioned Norway in connection with this amazing letter, it is worthwhile reflecting on the fate of Jews in that far northern country.

Norway was for much of her history, either a Danish or Swedish province or colony. In the seventeenth century, Norway was part of Denmark. Later she became Swedish, in a union which lasted till 1905. That is why the Nobel Peace Prize is given out each year in Oslo, and not in Stockholm, as the rest of the Nobel Prizes are. Alfred Nobel knew Norway as a Swedish province and wanted her to share in the honors he sponsored.

The Church had a stronger hold on the Norwegian people than she had on the Danish people. As a consequence, hostility to Jews and Judaism lasted longer in Norway than in any other Scandinavian country, as in many other countries where the Church held sway. Christians were afraid that people would be attracted to Judaism, which was clearly recognized as the true religion of Biblical days.

The fear of mass conversions to Judaism prompted the clergy to insist on strict separation of Christians from Jews and Jewish practices. In Norway, as early as 1436, the arch-Bishop issued an edict in Latin in which it was forbidden to celebrate the "Sabbath in the Jewish manner." After the Lutheran reformation, things became even tougher: An edict issued in 1569 declared it a capital crime, punishable by death, for any non-Lutheran to stay in Norway for more than three days.

Although in later centuries Jewish bankers and financiers made important contributions to the economy of Denmark, and therefore also of Norway, the land was closed to Jewish immigration until the middle of the nineteenth century. The Norwegian law of 1814—at a time when Jews had already been admitted into Denmark and Sweden for a long time—said: "Jews are excluded from entry into the country."

Things changed when a highly respected young poet and playwright, Henrik Wergeland, championed the entry of the Jews. Another Norwegian poet, Andreas Munch, likewise fought for the liberalization of the immigration law in favor of the Jews. In one of his poems he pleaded for freedom for the Jews, because, as he wrote: "He is your brother, and you are his." He severely criticized his countrymen in a poem with the following lines (my translation):

> *And you, my Norway, freedom's sons*
> *You land of the future, so young, so beautiful*
> *You are proud of being free and light*
> *But you close your ports when*
> *The Jews seek safe haven*
> *You rebuff a people*
> *Is that being freedom's spokesman?*

Wergeland, too, wrote several poems in support of Jewish immigration. Despite vehement objections from the Church, the Norwegian parliament finally passed a law on June 13, 1851, allowing Jews to enter the country.

The Norwegian Jewish community always remained small. Just before the Holocaust they numbered about 1100, with most of them living in the capital, Oslo, while some had a small congregation in the most northern location of any Jewish community in the world, in Trondjem, near the Polar Circle. The Oslo community had engaged a charismatic German rabbi, Julius Isak Samuel, whom I was privileged to know when he used to visit our home in Stockholm before the War. My late father and he were good friends, and therefore it was a deeply felt tragedy in our family when the news came that Rabbi Samuel and most of his congregants had been murdered by the Germans after they were deported in 1942. Of the 740 Jews deported only 24 survived.

On the other hand, the community of Trondjem, perhaps because its location was far removed from the German headquarters, managed to smuggle a few Jews over the border to Sweden. Records found after the War show that the Germans wrote furious letters to Berlin, lamenting the fact that 400 Norwegian Jews had managed to escape into Sweden, and tried to intimidate the Swedish Government to surrender them to the Germans. Sweden refused.

The rabbi of Trondjem, a very great *talmid chacham* and true giant among the Jewish leadership in our times, was Rabbi A.I. Jacobson. He was a very colorful person, born in Tiberias, who came to Norway before the War, and managed to flee to Sweden—where my late father helped engage him for the "Jeshurun Synagogue" which my father saved from destruction during the Kristallnacht and physically transported to Stockholm. There Rabbi Jacobson was a pillar of strength for the Danish and other Jews who, during and after the War, saved themselves by fleeing to Sweden. He lived to rededicate his Trondjem synagogue in 1947, and he was active in our family *shule* till he died in the 50's.

The name "Quisling" has become synonymous with one who is a traitor to his own people. Vidkun Quisling was a small-time Norwegian "red neck" who caught the fancy of the Nazi barbarians in Berlin. They raised him to the top position, with full powers over every Norwegian's life and death. His pathological hatred for Jews resulted in one of the most complete eradications of a Jewish community anywhere during the Holocaust. After the War he tried to plead that he was a Norwegian patriot. He was executed as the most hated man in his own land. His name then became a synonym for "traitor," a latter-day version of Benedict Arnold in American history, only much more ferocious and lethal. His name comes to mind when, in our own ranks, Jews pose as friends of the PLO and other enemies of Israel.

May we never encounter another Quisling in our history, either from the Christian world or from among our own ranks!

This year many Jewish travelers will want to visit Scandinavia. In Denmark, the fiftieth anniversary of the heroic rescue of Danish Jews from Nazi deportations will be celebrated. In Stockholm, Sweden, the newly redecorated Jeshurun Synagogue is a worthwhile tourist attraction because it represents a live, continuous testimony to German-Jewish places of worship. Norway has recently celebrated an anniversary of its synagogue in Oslo.

Several touring companies specialize in Jewish tours of Scandinavia; one of the better known is Friends of Scandinavia Tours, at 405 East 63rd Street, New York, N.Y. 10021.

# An Historical Perspective Of Moshiach

The belief in an ultimate redeemer is as old as Judaism itself, a faith beautifully enunciated by our Prophets, up to the very last one, Malachi. This faith, coupled with the power of prophecy, is so unique and so characteristically Jewish, that the nations of the world have tried since time immemorial to wrest it away from us and make it their own. Christianity claims that their founder was the last prophet and redeemer. The Moslems claim that Mohammed was the last prophet and redeemer. Many other lesser-known sects have tried as well, all without success. For we know better. The process of redemption, or Messianism, is a long process, spanning the millennia, and only Jews have the true promise and the vantage point of thousands of years of history.

From time to time, over the years, expectations of the redeemer have grown and intensified. One such time is now. You can hardly open a paper without reading about the rumors and claims of a Moshiach coming or not coming. The debate and discussion is on, worldwide. Quite a phenomenon, after so many thousands of years, when the idea of redemption was first brought to the world by Judaism! In fact, this in itself is almost miraculous. It certainly coincides with what the Rambam legislated in his great Code about the Messianic times. There we read:

*"The world is already filled with talk of the Moshiach, and of the Torah and of the mitzvot, and these things have even spread to the far off islands and among uncircumcised peoples; they all discuss and debate these issues"* (Chapter 11 of the Laws of Kingship).

Mind you, this section, along with other passages on Messianism, was cut out from the Rambam by the ferocious censorship of the Church, due to its highly compromising nature for Christianity. Luckily, however, there was no censorship in the Moslem world, and the uncensored Rambam can therefore be found in editions printed in the Moslem Ottoman Empire. The above quotation is taken from the 1509 Constantinople edition in my possession.

While every Jew expects the Moshiach momentarily, every day, there have been situations in our history when such expectations reached the boiling point. One such episode revolved around David Reubeni, who appeared in Europe with all the pomp of an Oriental potentate in 1524. He claimed to come from the Arabian peninsula, where the ten lost tribes were still reported to exist, and that he came from the tribe of Reuben. He, of course, electrified the oppressed Jews of Europe, especially as his appearance came shortly after the tragedy of the expulsion from Spain in 1492. Christians, too, were smitten by his appeal. He appeared before Pope Clement VII and promised him a Jewish army which could capture Jerusalem, if only the Pope would support the enterprise. The Pope was sufficiently impressed to give

Reubeni a letter of introduction to King Manoel II of Portugal.

Once in Portugal, the appearance of this pseudo-Messiah made a profound impression on the Marranos, Jews forced into conversion. One of these "new Christians" was a 25-year-old man named Diego Pires, a secretary to the King. Unafraid of the Inquisition, he was so enthused by Reubeni's appearance that he converted to Judaism and took on the name Shlomo Molcho. He had himself circumcised and fled to Turkey in order to study Judaism undisturbed by the Church, and visited Venice, Salonika and Safed to study Torah with the greatest of his generation, including Rabbi Joseph Karo.

In 1531 he rejoined his master, David Reubeni, who by now had appeared before the German ruler, King Charles V, the victor of Rome. Shlomo Molcho, delirious in his Messianic zeal, produced a white flag, embroidered with verses from the *Tanach*, and wore a white cloak. But their luck ran out. The German Emperor was afraid of Reubeni's militant plans, coupled with his messianic vision of the reestablishment of a Jewish State around Jerusalem. Charles V dispatched Shlomo Molcho to the Inquisition in Ancona, Italy, where he was condemned to die at the stake because he refused to reconvert to Christianity. According to eyewitnesses he died in the flames, crying out *Shema Yisrael*—a true martyr, at 32 years old.

There is, however, a long and almost supernatural history attached to Molcho's cloak and flag, guarded by generation after generation as the relics of a martyr. They eventually reached Prague, where they were kept in the famous Altneuschul, and later were housed in the nearby Jewish Museum.

I remember seeing them as a young boy in 1937, after just having read the book *David Reubeni* by Max Brod. I must confess that I was deeply moved by the sight. Miraculously, the Nazis did not touch them during the years of their occupation of Prague. I saw them again after the War, in 1947 and in 1962, each time equally moved. These relics have now made their way to the destination Shlomo Molcho had in mind for them—Jerusalem—where they are about to be displayed.

The origins and end of David Reubeni are shrouded in deep mystery, but this episode brought the awareness of Jews everywhere nearer to a Messianic expectation. Although the Moshiach did not materialize in the year 1540, calculated by some to be the year in which the Messiah would arrive, the Jews continued to wait for him.

I have previously written in this column about Shabatai Tzvi (*Algemeiner Journal*, January 17, 1992). His appearance as a declared Moshiach around 1666 again electrified Jews all over Europe, and, although he proved a false Messiah, his appearance, as damaging as it was, certainly brought the redemption nearer: The scattered, impotent and isolated Jewish communities of Europe were forged together for the first time in one international enterprise—with the goal of leaving the *galut* and migrating back to the Land of Israel!

Although Emperor Napoleon Bonaparte was not a Jew, he had tremendous interest in Jews, Judaism, and—something which is not generally known—the re-establishment of the Jewish homeland!

First, Napoleon was the liberator of Jews wherever his armies went. After the peace treaty was signed at Charasco in northern Italy in 1797, he opened up all the ghettoes of the Italian Jews in the Piedmonte area and was practically worshipped by them as their saviour.

When he landed in Palestine in 1799, he made Jerusalem his headquarters, and issued a remarkable declaration to the Jews of the world:

*General Headquarters, Jerusalem*
*1st Floreal in the year 7 of the French Republic*
*[April 20, 1799]*

*Bonaparte, Commander-in-Chief of the Armies of the French Republic in Africa and Asia, to the Rightful Heirs of Palestine:*

*Israelites, unique nation, whom, in thousands of years, lust of conquest and tyranny were able to deprive of the ancestral lands only, but not of name and national existence!*

*Attentive and impartial observers of the destinies of nations, even though not endowed with the gifts of seers like Isaiah and Joel, have also felt, long since, what these, with beautiful and uplifting faith, foretold when they saw the approaching destruction of their kingdom and fatherland; that the ransomed of the L-rd shall return, and come with singing unto Zion, and the enjoyment of henceforth undisturbed possession of their heritage will send an everlasting joy upon their heads (Isaiah 35:10).*

*Arise then, with gladness, ye exiled! A war unexampled in the annals of history, waged in self-defense by a nation whose hereditary lands were regarded by her enemies as plunder to be divided, arbitrarily and at their convenience, by a stroke of the pen of Cabinets, avenges her own shame and the shame of the remotest nations, long forgotten under the yoke of slavery, and, too, the almost two-thousand-year-old ignominy put upon you; and while time and circumstances would seem to be least favorable to a restatement of your claims or even to their expression, and indeed to be compelling their complete abandonment, she [France] offers to you at this very time, and contrary to all expectations, Israel's patrimony!*

*The undefiled army with which Providence has sent me hither, led by justice and accompanied by victory, has made Jerusalem my headquarters, and will, within a few days, transfer them to Damascus, a proximity which is no longer terrifying to David's city.*

*Rightful Heirs of Palestine!*

*The great nation which does not trade in men and countries as did those who sold your ancestors unto all peoples (Joel 4:6) hereby calls on you not indeed to conquer your patrimony, nay, only to take over that which has been conquered, and, with that nation's warranty and support, to maintain it against all comers.*

*Arise! Show that the once overwhelming might of your oppressors has not repressed the courage of the descendants of those heroes whose brotherly alliance did honor to Sparta and Rome (Macc. 12:15), but that all the two thousand years of slavish treatment have not succeeded in stifling it.*

*Hasten! Now is the moment which may not return for thousands of years, to claim the restoration of your rights among the population of the universe which had been shamefully withheld from you for thousands of years, your political existence as a nation among the nations, and the unlimited natural right to worship G-d in accordance with your faith, publicly and in likelihood forever (Joel 4:20).*

Napoleon clearly saw himself as the redeemer of the Jewish people. No wonder that Jews in places as far away as Russia saw in him the forerunner of the Moshiach.

In Paris he called together a *sanhedrin* of Jews from many European countries in an effort to bring about cultural and political emancipation. In 1807, the participants in the sanhedrin issued a prayer for Napoleon's victory of which I have a copy.

When Napoleon's armies penetrated deep into Russia, many, although not all Jews, most notably Rabbi Schneur Zalman of Liadi, author of the *Shulchan Aruch Harav* and the *Tanya*, prayed for his victory, which, in 1812 the year immortalized by Tchaikovsky's "1812 Overture" turned into defeat before the bitter Russian winter (which also vanquished Hitler's armies in 1941).

By 1815, the dreams of Napoleon and his Jewish admirers were in ruins. Napoleon ended his days on the island of St. Helena, and the Jews were herded back into the ghettos of northern Italy. But it took only a few more decades before their emancipation came about officially. Napoleon's plans were thus fulfilled.

The effect of Napoleon on the Messianic process of the Jews was enormous and of decisive proportions in my opinion: Napoleon's visit to the Middle East, Egypt and Palestine, brought back vast treasures of ancient Oriental art. Egyptian obelisks were now being seen in Paris, Rome and London. The museums—especially the Louvre and the British Museum—were filled with Egyptian, Babylonian and Assyrian relics from antiquity. The study of Holy Land archaeology commenced as teams of scholars descended on Palestine without interruption.

Attention to the Orient was also seen in music and fashions. Operas on Oriental themes, by Mozart and others, abounded. All this anticipated the next great Messianic expectation:

Some Kabbalists had calculated that 1840 would be the year that Moshiach would come. As I wrote in a past article ("Zionism before Zionism," *Algemeiner*, March 15, 1991), this expectation led to the great *aliyot* (migrations) to the Land of Israel by the Chasidim, starting around 1775, and by the disciples of the Vilna Gaon around 1809.

This expectation was also widely spoken of in Christian lands—in England, Russia, and elsewhere. These Christians started their own migrations to Palestine, as attested to by the various Church properties they still own in Israel today. All this had political consequences: When the High Church of England, or Anglican Church, sent their first Bishop to Jerusalem in 1840—the renegade Jew, Shlomo Michoel Alexander—in the misguided hope that the Jews would be ready victims for proselytization by missionaries, it also opened the eyes of the British Government, which then made plans to wrest the Middle East from the Turks.

Don Isaac Abarbanel, no doubt the most aristocratic and scholarly personality in our history, used his deep erudition in statecraft and politics, gained at the courts of Spain and Portugal, in his voluminous commentaries on all books of the Tanach. In his commentary on the Book of Daniel, with its Messianic prophecies, Abarbanel enumerates 10 political events which must precede the coming of the Moshiach and which had not happened in his own days (he died in 1508). Among them he foresaw that the armies of the Christians and of the Moslems would have to engage in battles before the gates of Jerusalem. Since Abarbanel's death this has in fact happened: first, when Napoleon captured Jerusalem in 1799, and then again, when General Allenby captured Jerusalem from the Moslem Turks in 1917.

In either case, the Messianic expectation of 1840 was not in vain:

The year 1840 was a turning point in the history of the Jewish Land. A new government had just taken over in Turkey which was more benign than the previous rulers. Also, Sir Moses Montefiore started his series of visits which not only brought financial support for the *yishuv*, but also brought about some semblance of peace between the warring factions of the Sephardic and Ashkenazic communities. Without these developments, there could never have been a Zionist colonization of Eretz Yisrael when the first *Biluim* came, more than 100 years after the first Chasidic aliyah.

It is not generally known that the Koran holds out a most reassuring promise for the return of the Jewish people to their ancestral Land. In Sura XVII, Verse 104, Mohammed has this to say to the Jews:

*"We said to the Children of Israel: Dwell ye in the Land, and when the time of the promise of the latter days comes, we shall bring you together again out of the various peoples."*

Here, too, a faith is expressed in a Messianic period in which the Children of Israel will be brought back out of the various peoples where they now dwell, to return to the Land that was originally given unto them.

We can only blame ourselves for not making this fantastic profession of "Zionist" faith by Mohammed better known in our dealings with Moslem Arabs. We should remind them that Mohammed was extremely close to the Jews in the beginning of his campaigns, and could in fact only capture Mecca and Medina with Jewish help. For a while he hoped his Jewish friends would join Islam, even allowing, for a short time, prayers to be said facing Jerusalem, in the Jewish fashion, although Jerusalem, then a Christian city, held no sanctity for Mohammed himself. When he realized there was no hope that the Jews would join Islam, he stopped the practice and ordered all prayers to be said in the direction ("*qibla*") of Mecca, as it has remained ever since.

Mohammed later turned quite hostile to Jews and Christians alike, but it may be argued that this change was only because his fledgling religion felt threatened by the older religions of Judaism and Christianity. Mohammed feared his new religion might be gobbled up by the senior religions in the area, and therefore had to issue stern warnings against fraternizing with Christians and Jews.

The situation today is, of course, radically different: Islam is firmly established in a large part of the world and is in no way in danger of seeing its followers converted to either the Christian or Jewish religions. With this realization, Moslems should be convinced that in today's situation, Mohammed would have reverted to his original friendship with Jews. Certainly, he would have wanted the promise of the Jews' return to their promised Land, as stated in the Koran, fulfilled.

Much blood may have been spilled in vain over so many years because of lack of communication.

Another Moslem, who, in the modern era, understood that times have changed and the hand of brotherly neighborliness should be held out to the Jewish returnees to their Land, was King Feisal, the initial ruler over Syria after World War I. His famous letter to Judge Felix Frankfurter, written during the peace negotiations in Versailles, in 1919, reads as follows:

*Dear Dr. Frankfurter,*
*We Arabs look with the deepest sympathy on the Zionist Movement. We will wish the Jews a most hearty welcome home. I hope the Arabs may soon be in a position to make the Jews some return for their kindness. There is room in Syria for us both. Indeed, I think that neither can be a real success without the other.*

*Yours sincerely,*
*Feisal*

This letter is without doubt at least partly inspired by the Koran passage promising Jews the return to their Land. Why doesn't Israel's Government bring such information to the attention of President Assad of Syria and to the State Department? It would certainly facilitate the peace negotiations.

On the Jewish side, the Talmud abounds with symptoms heralding the Messianic era. I plan to elaborate on them on another occasion. They are mainly found in Tractate Sotah 49b, Tractate Sanhedrin 96b, and onward. One passage is of special significance for our discussion:

The Talmud says that the Moshiach is one of three things which come to us *"be'hessech ha'daat."* This term is usually translated as "when we pay no attention." The Lubavitcher Rebbe, just two years ago, told me in an animated discussion regarding the coming of the Moshiach, that one of his teachers told him a different translation: The term *"hessech ha'daat"* is related to the word *"masiach,"* which means to converse, to speak. Therefore, the Talmud teaches that Moshiach will come when the maximum number of people speak about him and discuss him. And that is certainly what we see before our own eyes in these days, largely through the Rebbe's own actions. And this fulfills the Rambam's words.

Our sweep of history has shown a tremendous tendency by Providence, throughout recent centuries, to direct and guide the Jewish masses in the direction of Eretz Yisrael. With all the apparent failures of Messianic expectations in the past, they have nevertheless served positive aims: They have not only prepared our minds for a Messianic period, but have also paved the political ground for such a development and have produced the recreation of a Jewish State. In this connection it is important to note the statement of the Rashbam on last week's portion: "After you have settled in Eretz Yisrael, G-d's kingdom will become known in all the realms" (Exodus 15:18). Thus, the Messianic ties depend on the Jews coming to live in Eretz Yisrael.

We must continue to watch with patience, goodwill and faith the further developments. We can learn our lessons from such verses as: "And the man was full of wonder about her, quietly watching to know whether G-d would lead his way to success or not" (Genesis 24:21), or "For the man will not rest until he has fulfilled his resolve" (Ruth 3:18).

# Remember When We Had No State?

Many of the deep disappointments that so many of us have with the new generation of Israeli leaders no doubt are derived from the fact the new generation has no way of knowing how the world looked before we had a state. As a result, the youngsters take a Jewish State for granted—they see nothing unnatural or supernatural in the existence of a Jewish State after 2,000 grueling years of the Diaspora. They are not conscious of the responsibility of our generation to protect and nurture the G-d-given, miraculous gift of a Jewish State. They think nothing of it to gamble away the Jewish State in all kinds of reckless schemes that may very well lead to the utter destruction of the state and our return to the indescribably tragic sufferings of the Diaspora.

Some time ago, I obtained an archive of columns written by the famous British leader and writer, Harry Aron Goodman, *z"l*, written from the 1930s until his death in 1961. These columns give us a true picture of the worries, crises and problems that harassed the Jews of Europe at a time when Hitler engulfed the entire continent, and the evil winds of the Holocaust were approaching. There was no protection for the Jews anywhere—no haven of refuge in those areas where the Hitlerian Angel of Death set out to utterly wipe out the Jewish people. Anyone who appreciates these facts, even the most alienated and indifferent Jews, should wake up to the need to protect and defend the State of Israel and not allow it to be destroyed again.

I quote herewith from a few Goodman essays, chronologically, to trace the tortured road of European Jews until the creation of the Jewish State:

"Sack the Mufti," 1937: The Mufti al-Haj Amin el Husseini—founder of the murderous Bosnian SS, whose kinsmen, Feisal el Husseini and Yasser Arafat el-Husseini, today continue the Mufti's bloody work—had instigated many of the bloody pogroms and riots in Palestine: "It is clear that there will be no peace in Palestine as long as this misguided person is allowed to direct Arab affairs. It is clear that the Mufti must go. There is no room in Palestine for this fratricidal strife. The inhabitants of Palestine must send forth the cry: 'Sack the Mufti!'"

Nothing has changed today: the Jewish government tolerates the descendants of the Mufti, Hitler's friend, and take little or no action to curb terrorism.

"Palestine in the Melting Pot," 1938: In this year Goodman wrote about the solutions for the tension in Palestine: "The British Government states that it is clear that the surest foundation for peace and progress in Palestine would be an understanding between the Arabs and the Jews. . . . Prior to any Arab-Jewish negotiations there must be held a Jewish roundtable conference at which all constructive pro-Palestine Jewish forces are represented. Then and then alone, can we hope for that unanimity of opinion which may yet lead to peace in the Land of Peace." (Today, 57 years later, unity still escapes the Jewish people.)

Goodman expressed premonitions of disaster approaching European Jews. "The sadism in Germany, the economic persecutions of Poland and Romania, the turmoil in Eretz Yisrael with a Jewish State looking ahead. What will 1938 bring?"

"Jerusalem—the Eternal City," 1939: Goodman quoted a statement by Chief Rabbi J. H. Hertz: "Like the Jew, this Holy City of Israel, the spiritual capital of humanity's magnet of the love and reverence of mankind, is deathless. Many conquerors have attacked Jerusalem and yet, like the Jew himself, marvelous to relate, it ever rises from its ashes to renewed life and glory." These sentiments sound hollow today, as the leftist government is making preparations for dismantling Jewish sovereignty over our eternal capital. The thousands of years of suffering—the torrents of blood shed for our capital—are ignored by the leftists now in charge, who are not concerned at the thought that their policies may lose us our most precious gift on earth.

"The Viennese Inferno," 1939: After Hitler's invasion of Austria and Czechoslovakia, a Jewish community of 200,000 souls has been reduced to pariahs. If proof is needed of the impotence of Jewry in political matters, the fate of Austria is a clear example." Goodman pointed to the core of the Jewish problem: Without a State of its own, the Jewish people are impotent and at the mercy of the anti-Semitic Christian world.

"Sabbath Violations and the Holy Land," 1939: Goodman became aware of the need to build up a strong religious community in the Holy Land. He lamented the desecration of the Sabbath by workers on land owned by the Jewish National Fund:

"Is it not enough that holy places and sacred scrolls have been desecrated and burned in Germany and elsewhere? Must desecrations be endured also in the Jewish homeland? Shall Sabbath violations in the Holy Land be condoned by labeling them "building the homeland?" Shall unity in Israel, of such vital importance to Jewry today, be thus flouted and broken up?"

The newly-born state was already being deprived of its Jewish character in 1949 by leftists, starting a long trail of the steadily declining Jewish character of the Jewish land, a development whose culmination we are watching today with horror.

"The Fate of Palestine," 1939: The British government called for a conference to settle the question of Palestine. Goodman recalled the tragic Munich conference, just a few months before, when the Czech Prime Minister was forced by the "peace loving" Chamberlain to sign away the independence and freedom of his country. "'The 400,000 Jewish souls in Palestine cry out to heaven for justice. Stand fast, we say to the Jewish leaders. The whole Jewish people looks to you in these days. We have suffered enough. Our backs are literally against the wall. The G-d of our fathers who led us from Egypt in Sinai—He neither slumbers nor sleeps. Stand fast!"

"San Francisco," 1945: On April 25 of that year an international conference gathered to decide on the founding of the United Nations. Goodman wrote: "Jews will have no seat at the conference. But the Jewish problem must loom large at its deliberations. Restoration of human rights, repatriation and migration, protection of human rights, abrogations of racial legislation, indemnification, statelessness, punishment of war crimes, all these are matter of vital concerns of the Jews, quite apart from the future of Palestine. Five million Jewish dead demand unity. San Francisco may revitalize a tombstone for our dead. We who have survived must decide." These words reflect the frustrations of a stateless people.

Goodman's assessment of the political and religious problems facing the Jewish survivors was prophetic. His concern for the future and his intercession on behalf of the Jewish people in the halls of governments and political forums made him the proverbial *shtadlan*—cut from the glorious cloth of centuries of Jewish intercessors.

I was privileged to observe Harry Goodman, always impeccably dressed, wearing his ever-present top hat and using his perfect English diction. Whether representing the view of Orthodox Jewry before the British Government, or participating in the deliberations of the great Torah leaders at the 1937 Knesset Gedoloh of the Agudah in Marienbad, he made an indelible impression. But apart from his official functions in private, he was a warm, outspoken human being, who was an outstanding father to his children. His home in Northwest London, which I visited on some occasions, was characterized by his lively, sometimes boisterous, expression of interest in an enormous variety of concerns.

We are fortunate that Harry Goodman left behind voluminous columns that mirror the tragic, but also glorious, chapters of the Jewish history of crucial decades. They give us a vivid picture of the helplessness and impotence that condemned so many millions of Jewish victims to their destruction. A people without a land, without diplomatic representation, without the slightest military power, suffered horrible disadvantage in dealing with the world's powers.

Today, looking back on 48 years of the fulfillment of our desperate aspirations, during which we have been in possession of a Jewish State, we take for granted that there is a Jewish State, with access to all the blessings for which generations of Jews have yearned. If we forget the supernatural blessings that we are enjoying, we are apt to lessen our idealism, patriotism and self-assertion. The great political and cultural disasters of the last three years and the prospect of the increased weakening of Israel's strategic capability, not to speak of the weakening of Jewish values, can all be blamed on our forgetting how the world of the Jews looked without a Jewish State.

Harry Goodman's voice can still be heard 35 years after he passed away—a timely reminder of the lessons that our history must teach us.

# 100 Years Ago: The Dreyfus Case

One hundred years ago, on October 15, 1894, a 35-year-old Jewish captain in the French artillery, Alfred Dreyfus, was called into the French War Ministry. He was asked to give a specimen of his handwriting. Moments later, he was placed under arrest for high treason. The authorities claimed that his handwriting matched the handwritten documents found in the ash can of the German Embassy in Paris. The charge was that Dreyfus had handed highly sensitive information—referred to as "the *bordereau*" throughout the case—on newly-developed French heavy guns to France's enemy, Imperial Germany.

This charge unleashed the case of the century. It involved anti-Semitism, the conflict between democracy and conservatism, the power of the French army over civilian rule, the influence of the Church and other issues that were explosive enough to keep the world vitally concerned for decades; the case is in fact not over yet, 100 years later.

It took five years for Captain Dreyfus to become a free man again and it took 12 years for him to be exonerated of the false, wrongful charge of treason. In those years Dreyfus had turned into a broken old man, whose sufferings made a him a true hero in his day.

We know of course that the trial—in which the words "Jew," "Jewish traitor," and "Judas" were freely hurled at the innocent Dreyfus—inspired one man, who heard these anti-Semitic outrages in court. This man was Theodor Herzl, a young Austrian-Hungarian journalist, who covered the trial for his newspaper, *Die Neue Freie Presse*, of Vienna. An assimilated Jew who had thought he had long escaped the "fate" of being Jewish, Herzl was shaken when he realized how deeply anti-Semitism was rooted in the Christian world and that assimilation was a total failure. It made him think of ways to protect the Jewish people, and he came to the conclusion that Jews needed a country of their own through a return to Zion, our ancient homeland.

He wrote profusely on the subject, including his outstanding book *Altneuland (The Ancient-New Land)*, which outlined Zionism. Therefore, the Dreyfus trial was providential in the way that we often find in Jewish history: a small, seemingly insignificant event, leads to momentous, historic developments for the Jewish people. Without the Dreyfus Affair there may not have been a Jewish State.

Dreyfus was a member of an old French Jewish family going back to Mulhouse (Müllhausen) in Alsace—that part of France, which had been wrested from her by Germany in the 1870-71 war of Bismarck, but which for centuries before had a German-speaking population.

Alsace was returned to France in the First World War but was taken away again by Hitler, only to be returned after France was liberated in 1944. Thus, living in a border area, the Jews of Alsace and neighboring Lorraine escaped the expulsion decrees against French Jews in the 14th century. Jewish life flourished there for centuries. Outstanding rabbis served there, including the Sha'agat Aryeh of the 18th century.

Capt. Dreyfus was a product of the emancipation, which had begun under the enlightened and democratic rule of Napoleon, that great liberator of Jews in France, Germany and Italy. That did not protect Dreyfus from the vicious anti-Semitism that his trial unleashed, egged on, of course by the Church. The public followed the line, "I have made up my mind; don't confuse me with the facts." The mass demonstrations by the anti-Semites against Dreyfus even before any evidence was presented showed how vulnerable a Jew still was in supposedly enlightened France.

Details of Dreyfus' family and its role in the history of the Jews of France can be found in the book, *Dreyfus, a Family Affair*, by American author Michael Burns. The legal ramifications of the trials—there was more than one trial throughout the years—can best be studied in the classic work on the case, *L'Affaire*, an 800-page tome by French author, Jean-Denis Bredin.

Dreyfus was sent to Devil's Island in French Guyana off the South American Coast. In inhuman conditions, including unbearable heat, he suffered greatly. His wife, who was the real heroine in the case, and his relatives worked incessantly for his release and exoneration.

The French people quickly divided into two camps—the pro-Dreyfus and the anti-Dreyfus. Even after the real perpetrator of the treason was discovered, the scoundrel Ferdinand Esterhazy, the anti-Semites did not want to admit that Dreyfus was innocent. It was Esterhazy who was the German spy and who had compromised French military capability.

And even the forger of documents in the case, an official by the name of Hubert Joseph Henry, was celebrated by the anti-Dreyfus camp as a martyr for France after he committed suicide in jail. The anti-Semites even planned to raise a monument to him. A collection for such a monument was sponsored by 350 Catholic clergymen.

The enemies of Dreyfus represented the old, conservative military establishment. They could not admit to the corruption and dishonesty in their ranks, which the Dreyfus trial uncovered. Therefore they hung onto their charges no matter how discredited they were. It took the courageous journalist and writer, Emile Zola, to rally most of France in support of Dreyfus with his famous manifesto, "J'Accuse." This manifesto was published in *L'Aurore*, the newspaper of the fiery liberal, Georges Clemenceau, who later led France to victory as its prime minister during World War I.

He condemned the conservative military establishment for using Dreyfus as its scapegoat for combating democracy and freedom. He showed that there were two Frances: one which was heir to the old royalist past of France; the other, the heir of the glorious French Revolution in 1789. It was thanks to Zola that Dreyfus was finally exonerated.

The two Frances are still visible today. I have met Frenchmen who until this day believe that Dreyfus was a German spy. That was, incidentally, also the belief of many outstanding artists and painters of the impressionist school, whom we treasure today for their art. In fact many of them, including Renoir, Monet and Cezanne, were hardened, vicious anti-Semites.

But what was the real object of the espionage accusation? As in other such sensational cases, the real core accusation is forgotten.

Has anybody ever asked what the Watergate burglars were looking for in the Democratic Party headquarters in the Watergate complex in Washington? All the attention was on the obstruction of justice, cover-ups, etc. But how is it that the real purpose of that infamous break-in was never investigated?

Books published later give a slight hint at the truth: the Watergate burglars looked for compromising documents relating to the Bay of Pigs invasion of Cuba during the Kennedy administration. Nixon wanted to prove that the disaster of that invasion was the doing of Democrats. Another explanation offered by these books is that Nixon wanted to remove documents embarrassing to the Republicans that the Democrats could use in that fall's presidential election.

But until this day nobody has bothered to find out the precise reason for the break-in! And yet this scandal caused the first-ever resignation of an American President.

What were the secret documents that the Dreyfus case was about? This has only come to light in a flood of books that have appeared in Europe, especially in connection with the centenary of the case.

France had developed a secret weapon: a formidable piece of artillery with an enormous range. The French army wished to keep news about it from the Germans and, in fact, wished to give the Germans the impression that France was impotent against superior German cannons.

The secret French weapon was called "Cannon No. 75." When the anti-Semites found themselves thwarted in their attempts to pin the writing of treasonable documents about this gun on Dreyfus, they came up with another canard. Dreyfus still had family in Alsace, the province west of the Rhine river, which Germany had occupied. Dreyfus visited his relatives there from time to time. The anti-Semites claimed that he went to that part of Germany in order to meet with German military personnel and to hand over secret information. That charge, too, proved baseless.

Dreyfus wrote down his personal reflections on his tragic fate in his book, *Cinque Anneés De Ma Vie (Five Years of My Life)*, published by him in 1901. It is characteristic of the French anti-Semites that once the Nazi regime of Marchal Pétain in Vichy was in power, they persecuted any descendants of Dreyfus, many of whom were sent to death camps.

Alfred Dreyfus had mercifully died in 1935 before the Holocaust, but his widow, Lucie, had to flee her beloved native land. Pétain stood for the discredited military establishment of old, which briefly had a vicious revival through him. He took out his revenge on the Jews, who—to the chagrin of the anti-Semites—had been proven innocent French patriots.

Actually, it must be remembered that the Dreyfus case came up only 70 years after Napoleon's death. Napoleon, too, suffered the animosity of the old guard from the French aristocratic world of the military and of the Church. Napoleon stood for emancipation of the Jews, enlightenment and democracy. The conservatives held it against him that he had instituted a Sanhedrin in Paris to give the rabbis of France a platform from which to address the needs of their newly won freedom.

The fruits of emancipation were promptly wrested from the Jews again, as soon as Napoleon fell. His emancipation of the Jews in northwestern Italy, for example, was not only canceled, but the walls of the ghetto were again raised around the Jewish communities there. Capt. Dreyfus, who was a product of Napoleon's emancipation and a graduate of the supreme French academic institution—the prestigious Ecole Polytechnique—was a thorn in the eyes of the Catholic Church and of the reactionary military.

Fortunately for the honor of French Jews, all Jews there stood firmly for Dreyfus' innocence. By contrast, today in the Dreyfus case of this century—the Pollard case—Reform and assimilationists among us unfortunately have refused to take up Pollard's cause. It says a lot about the destructive influence of Reform Judaism.

Let us, therefore, learn a lesson from the Dreyfus case: history will honor his memory and also the memory of all who defended him, but will dishonor those who fought against him or who failed to speak up for him. Jewish history will have the same to say in the Pollard case. The Dreyfus centenary is, therefore, a timely milestone in our history for reflection and re-dedication to the Jewish destiny.

Dr. Lehmann with Lord Rothschild of London,
at the opening of the Rothschild exhibition in Frankfurt.

# The History of Jewish Banking

Jewish bankers have been prominent throughout our history. It is fascinating to study their origin and development, because they played an important role in Jewish history as a whole. There is no doubt that they constituted a highly disproportionate segment of the banking world.

In my opinion, there must have been something basic in Judaism that formed the basis for this excellence. I would say that the Torah, before any other code or law, set down strict rules for commercial honesty and public-mindedness, so that a Jewish banker was always more trusted than other bankers. The biblical laws commanding honest and reliable weights and measurements, regulating interest-taking, and governing the handling of pawns, all set the basis for honest money lending. In the Talmud, laws controlling honest commerce and money lending abound. It is therefore not surprising that the basic Hebrew word for moneylender, "*shulchani* (money changer)"—found in the Mishnah—ultimately took the meaning "banker."

Similarly, the predominance of Jews in the medical profession—45 percent of all Nobel Prize winners in medicine have been Jews!—can, in my opinion, be traced to the unprecedented care for human health expressed in the Torah and in subsequent Jewish laws. No other nation ever cared so much for the physical well-being of each and every one of its members. Such attitudes and inclinations are carried over for hundreds of generations—either through education and personal example of elders, or by way of genes.

In the Tenach we find several transactions involving payment of money, such as Abraham's purchase of the Machpelah and Jeremiah's purchase of land in his native city. But there must also have been a thriving money lending business, since as soon as the Jews were exiled to Babylonia we surprisingly encounter at least two full-fledged Jewish banks operating there—the banking houses of Murashu and Egibi. Many cuneiform tablets evidencing their moneylending transactions and bearing Jewish names have been preserved. The "banking" skill of these Jews must have been preceded by generations of experience and tradition.

No wonder then that Jews were sought out by their rulers in the early days of exile in Europe. The Roman armies marching north in Europe, along the Rhine river, encouraged Jewish money lenders and traders to accompany them. They were the founders of the earliest Ashkenazic communities, such as Mainz, Speyer, Worms and Trier.

Before them, Jews in partnership with the Phoenicians had founded trading settlements along the Western Mediterranean. The outlook of Jewish businessmen and moneylenders, from the beginning, was international. The Diaspora itself offered the advantage of families having members in all corners of the world—Jews who could always trust each other. The worldwide trust remained the hallmark of Jewish bankers throughout the ages.

While Jews carried on money transactions in most countries of the Diaspora, their long-range success was most remarkable in Germany. In the documents found in the Cairo Geniza, covering the 11th to 13th centuries, we find adequate testimony of Jews carrying on commerce from one end of the then known world to the other—from Spain to India. But these communities, after flourishing for the some centuries, died out. German Jewry, however, existed for over 1,000 years.

In the Middle Ages, Jews were often restricted by law to money lending and tax collecting. Even a great man such as Rabbeinu Tam was a "banker" in the medieval sense—even operating his "bank" during Chol Hamoed.

German Jews came to their full bloom in the years shortly after the 30-year war, when the Germany of the monolithic "Holy Roman Empire" fell into several small duchies and municipalities, each with financial worries and needs for financing. The local dukes and princes would reach into the ghettos of Germany to select skilled Jews with proven ability to manipulate money. Some of these rulers had insatiable appetites for money—to be used on their lavish courts, their military campaigns and repayment of old debts. This need created the position of the Court Jew, occupied by an exceptionally fine class of Jews who excelled in finance but also in their concern for their suffering and oppressed brethren. Some of the finest Court Jews were Oppenheim, Wertheimer of Vienna and Behrend Lehmann of Halberstadt in the 17th century. Without them, German Judaism would have died out.

They also laid the foundation for the great banking families of the 18th century. As an example, Behrend Lehmann, who had achieved the position of virtual Minister of Finance to the King of Saxonia, established far-flung branches of his business with sons and nephews manning offices in various European cities. Lehmann's example was copied by the Rothschilds a few decades after his death. By distributing five sons—to Vienna, Paris, London, Naples and Frankfurt—the founder of the dynasty, Mayer Anshel Rothschild, established one of the most powerful financial empires the Jews ever possessed. But the Rothschilds were not alone in achieving banking greatness.

Here is a partial list of Jewish bankers and the dates when their banks were founded: 1750 N.M. Bamberger, Berlin; 1764 Gebrueder Veit, Berlin; 1795 Joseph Mendelsohn, Berlin; 1798 M.M. Warburg, Hamburg; 1803 S. Bleichroder, Berlin; 1811 Leopold Seligman, Cologne; 1815 A.S. Goldshmidt, Coblenz.

As Germany was unified into one empire in 1871, the need for large scale loans grew. Kaiser Wilhelm and Count Bismark founded their administration almost entirely on the financial help rendered by their Jewish banker, Bleichroeder.

In 1856, when the Russian Czar needed a large loan, Jewish bankers helped him out without regard to the oppression which their Jewish brethren suffered under him. Only one Jewish banker, Jacob I. Schiff—whose descendants founded the American private bank Kuhn, Loeb & Co.—refused to lend his money to a Russian czar!

English Jews, before their expulsion in 1290, had been outstanding bankers, who helped their sovereigns. Such Jews as Aaron of Lincoln and Aaron of York have gone into history as exemplary bankers. But all this did not help; after some terrible pogroms, all English Jews were expelled. It was only 400 years later, under Oliver Cromwell, that Jews were readmitted to England, after the famous Dutch-Portuguese philosopher Menasse ben Israel had lobbied in London. Since the early arrivals were of Portuguese ancestry, with outstanding commercial and banking traditions, it did not take long before important Jewish banking firms were established in London, after moving there from Amsterdam, such as the de Costa, de Medinas, Lopez and Salvador families. Many became stockbrokers. Later famous stockbrokers were the Montefiores, David Ricardo and Benjamin Gompertz from Amsterdam. When Ashkenazic Jews emigrated to England, some of them laid the foundations to well-known British banks. David Salomons, whose ancestors had come to England in 1689, became London's first Jewish mayor and was a founder of the Westminster Bank, today one of England's leading banks. Another early Jewish banking house was that of Mocatta and Goldsmid founded in 1782 and still flourishing today as bullion brokers.

The banking house of Samuel Montegue and Co. was established in 1863 and is still an important factor in London's City. Other banks, which are not clearly identified as of Jewish origin, are the Hambro Bank, of Danish-Jewish origin, and the Wagg banking firms, today known as J. Henry Schroder, Wagg and Co. go back to the famous Samuel family which produced Herbert Samuel, the first High Commissioner in the British Mandate of Palestine after World War I.

Dominating the field of English Jewish bankers are the Rothschilds. When Nathan M. Rothschild came from Frankfurt to England, he started a dynasty which until this day is outstanding in financial and Jewish life. His brother-in-law, Sir Moses Montefiore, although the legendary benefactor of Jews everywhere and a founder of modern Israel, never failed to attend board meetings of his companies, especially the Alliance Insurance Company which he and his brothers-in-law had founded in 1824 and which still today is a powerful insurance company.

Jewish bankers played a prominent role in the United States, France, Belgium, Holland, Vienna, Italy, Scandinavia, Russia, Egypt, Turkey, South Africa and, finally, today, in Israel. Many of them were interlocked through marriage and common family origins. They gave their Jewish communities much prestige and support.

The Holocaust gave, sadly, a fatal blow to Jewish banks in the lands under Hitler. Individual bankers were heroic in their fight to help their fellow Jews; the case of Max Warburg of Hamburg especially comes to mind. Most of the Jewish banks ravaged by Hitler have been rebuilt and are again flourishing. We must remember the Jewish banks of the past with reverence and respect. When Jewish communities were powerless, without political or military forces to defend them, many a staunch Jewish banker stood up for them and saved entire communities. If we take a look at the thousands of years of Jewish banking business, we realize with pride that their success can be laid at the feet of Mt. Sinai where their ancestors stood and learnt the laws of honesty and reliability in business.

# Early Relations Between American Jews and Eretz Yisrael

If you are looking for an accurate picture of Jewish life in Colonial America, before the American Revolution in 1776, you may be surprised to find that most Jews did not live in what is today considered the United States of America, in those days called the North American British Colonies. Most of them lived in the Caribbean area: Jamaica, Barbados, Curaçao, and Suriname had more Jews than lived in all of North America. Most of them were of Portuguese-Spanish origin, many former Marranos.

In North America, the main Jewish communities in the mid-1700's were in Newport, Rhode Island; New York; Philadelphia; Savanna, Georgia and Charleston, South Carolina. (Other Jewish communities developed only late into the 18th–19th centuries.) In many cases, the financial support came from the Caribbean communities, especially when synagogues had to be built.

We know how close the ties are today between Jews in the Americas and those living in Eretz Yisrael. How did those ties begin? A few important documents which I have recently acquired give us important clues.

As the American Jews developed financial wealth, the reputation of their charity reached the poor Jews of the Holy Land, who were languishing under the yoke of their Moslem masters. These few thousand Jews, partly of Sephardic, partly of Ashkenazic origins, were victims of unceasing attacks by the Arabs. Local governors were constantly holding Jews for unreasonably large amounts of ransom money, whereby the communities became totally impoverished. Added to this were occasional earthquakes, especially in the Safed area, as well as epidemics. "Intifada"-like uprisings were also the order of the day, not directed ultimately against Jews, but against the despotic Ottoman rulers who oppressed their citizens with inhumane harshness. But Jews, unfortunately, were their prime victims.

Little wonder that community leaders in Eretz Yisrael turned their attention to organizing visits to the Americas by qualified emissaries. We have many colorful accounts of the arrival of these unlikely emissaries, dressed in their Oriental garb, in the stern landscape of the American colonies. Some of these accounts come from non-Jewish observers. One prominent such observer was the famous Rev. Ezra Stiles, a Christian clergyman and later president of Yale University. His highly entertaining reports on his encounters with rabbis from the Holy Land are of greatest historic importance.

The first rabbi to come to Newport was the famous Talmudist and Kabbalist Hacham Hayim Isaac Carigal, who was sent by the Hebron community. After visiting Jamaica, Philadelphia and New York, he came to Newport in 1773 and immediately forged a close friendship with Stiles. He taught Stiles Hebrew, a language which Stiles later made an obligatory subject for all Yale students. Stiles wrote vivid and colorful accounts of Rabbi Carigal's sermons. He also described in greatest detail Carigal's splendid Oriental dress. Carigal also formed a close friendship with the leading Jewish merchant in Newport, Aaron Lopez, who, as a pseudo-Christian, had lived in Portugal, whence he came directly to Newport to cast off his Christian lifestyle and returned openly and enthusiastically to the Jewish religion of his forefathers.

Such quack black "historians" as the infamous Leonard Jeffries of CCNY have tried to pin the slave trade on Jewish merchants, especially Aaron Lopez. Jeffries would be surprised to see an original Bill of Lading in my possession issued by Aaron Lopez—covering a shipment not of slaves, but of kosher meat! As any reputable historian knows, the real slave traders were black Africans in West Africa, who sold their own kinsmen into slavery, and Arabs in East Africa, who rounded up Africans with the help of ferocious killer dogs and dragged them in chains to ships waiting along the coast.

After a few months in Newport, Carigal sailed to Suriname in 1773. Suriname was a unique community: Jews had established a semi-autonomous state in the jungle, complete with a Jewish army and a Court House. Great Talmudic scholars lived there and established an early yeshiva. Carigal must have felt that his presence was not needed in a community with such highly qualified rabbis and Hachamim, so he left for Barbados after just a few months.

The Jewish community of Barbados, called Nidchey Yisrael, enthusiastically appointed Carigal their rabbi in 1774. He ended his long and colorful life in that enchanting island where Jews had gained freedom in 1629, long before attaining freedom in practically any country in the world. When I visited Barbados some years ago, I came across the tombstone inscription over Carigal's grave, written in Hebrew and Portuguese. A short English text says: "Here lyeth the remains of the Learned and Revered Rabbi Raphael Hayim Isaac Carigal, Worthy Pastor of the Synagogue Nidchey Yisrael who departed this life on the 19th May 1777 aged 48 years." (The name Raphael had been given to him when he had suffered a serious sickness.)

I recently acquired the only handwritten letter by Hacham Carigal in existence outside of the collection placed in Yale University Library by Ezra Stiles. The letter, written in Barbados in 1774 in Spanish, is addressed to his friend Aaron Lopez. It ends with a startling sentence: "How is the *baño* (pronounced 'banyo')?" I immediately identified this word as synonymous with "mikvah." My identification was confirmed by my eminent friend, Professor Herman Salomon, a leading expert in Sephardic Jewish history. This shows that Carigal utilized his visits, primarily intended to raise money for the poor in Hebron, also to establish and fortify local Jewish institutions, including a mikvah in Newport. We know of mikva'ot in the Sephardic communities of Philadelphia and New York in the 1750's. But my document is the first reference to a mikvah in Newport—a historic "first."

Rev. Ezra Stiles, whose interest in all matters Jewish had been kindled by

Hacham Carigal, keenly awaited the arrival of the next emissary from Hebron. And in 1775 such a visitor did come: Rabbi Samuel Cohen. Who was he? I have a copy of the letter of introduction signed by the most famous rabbis of Hebron of the time, written in Portuguese in 1772. The letter introduces one Rabbi Shmuel Cohen to the Jews of the Americas to raise money for the impoverished Jews of Hebron, described as the site of the tombs of our Patriarchs Abraham, Isaac and Jacob, and details the sufferings and hardships experienced under Moslem rulers. The letter, attesting to Rabbi Cohen's high qualifications, is signed by the famous Rabbi Josef Hayim David Azulai ("Hida") and Rabbi Eliyahu ibn Archa. Rabbi Cohen, just as Carigal before him, made a profound impression on Rev. Stiles, who has been called "an early Zionist" because of his enchantment with the Holy Land and his vision of the Jews' return to their ancestral land as prophesied in the Bible.

I have just acquired a most interesting, in fact mystifying, document. Written in Italian, in Hebron, around 1770, it introduces the "Hida" himself to the Jews of "Italy, Romagna [area around Rome], France, Holland, England and America." We know many fascinating details of the Hida's extensive travels throughout Europe. He not only used his trips to raise money for his brethren in Hebron, but he also visited all leading libraries and took bibliographical notes of all the rare Hebrew books and manuscripts he saw there. His letter of introduction is signed by over 32 great rabbis; I own manuscript writings of many of them. But there is no evidence that the "Hida" actually set foot on American soil. Yet the intention was there, and it shows that the bonds between American Jews and Eretz Yisrael were already strong 250 years ago.

We see here a fantastic and immensely inspiring panorama of Providence at work in our history: The links established between the centers of learning and piety in Eretz Yisrael and the newly founded communities in the Americas led not only to the performance of the mitzvah of giving tzedaka, but also brought great scholars to our shores, who brought learning and Jewish institutions with them. These strengthened the practice of our religion in the most remote corners of the world, besides forging links of loyalty and compassion between Eretz Yisrael and the Diaspora. Thus what started in 1492 with the discovery of America through Columbus, himself of Jewish descent, developed by and by into a firm and strong haven for suffering Jews in all generations and for the survival of our religion. The thousands of miles of separation were no obstacle in these links of brotherhood across the seas.

All this became evident to me one day when I read the inscription on a tombstone in Barbados on the grave of a Jewish woman who had died almost 250 years ago: "May her soul travel to the Cave of Machpelah." To think that Jews in far off Barbados were dreaming of the Cave of Machpelah, in Hebron! But the history of the emissaries explained this mystery to me: the great rabbis from Hebron who dwelt in the Caribbean communities had brought with them a love for the Holy Land which the local Jews, otherwise, would never have heard about.

I recently bought a unique and historic document: the only surviving copy of a printed appeal to "our worthy Brethren of the United States of America," sent in

April 1835. It shows that a society had been formed in New York in 1832, called "Chevrat Trumat ha-Kodesh," for the purpose of collecting money for the Jews of Eretz Yisrael. It was headed by two leading German Jews, I.B. Kursheedt and G.A. Furst. Israel Baer Kursheedt (1766–1852) was married to the daughter of Gershom Mendes Seixas, a famous American-born Sephardic patriot during the War of Independence. After living in Richmond, Va., he moved to New York in 1824 and founded an Ashkenazic Orthodox synagogue, Cong. Bnai Jeshurun.

The idea of having a central organization for collecting donations for the poor in Eretz Yisrael had been conceived by the brothers H. and Meyer Lehren, great German Jewish Talmudists who had moved to Amsterdam. Joined by two Dutch Jews, Abraham A. Prins and S. B. Rubens, they formed what has gone down in history as the "Pekidim and Amarkelim of the Holy Land residing in Amsterdam." For decades they remained the only circuit for collecting and sending money to the poor, pious Jews of Jerusalem, Safed, Hebron and Tiberias. Their appeal to the North American Jews contains heartrending accounts of the suffering in the Holy Land: "An earthquake occurred in Jerusalem which destroyed a large number of houses. . . . Insurgents committed great depredations, having inhumanly murdered two of our people, plundered ten of the districts of the Portuguese Congregation. . . . The most dreadful calamities befell the Jews of Safed, nearly the whole [Arab] population having revolted against the government, plundering the Jews of nearly all their belongings and sparing neither sex nor age from the most abandoned indulgence of their savage propensities, destroying in their career the synagogues and holy books, and even barbarously murdering many of our people. . . ." Sadly, their account rings familiar to our ears when we hear similar accounts—of course in less flowery language—of Arab excesses and massacres perpetrated till this day. The often repeated Arab fable of "harmonious and peaceful co-existence of Jews and Arabs in Moslem countries" is proven a tragic falsehood. . . .

The compassionate and far-sighted Jews in Europe and America who put the alms collection on an organized basis played a historic role: they made it possible for the harassed Jewish communities of Eretz Yisrael, bolstered by the influx of Chassidic and Misnagdish Jews arriving from the beginning of the 19th century, to survive and expand. These staunch and pious Jews laid the foundation of the ever-growing Yishuv which, 100 years later, made it possible for Zionist settlers to find a livelihood and employment. Through my document we have evidence how American Jews made a meaningful contribution to these historic efforts, which inaugurated the Messianic period in our history.

In sum, the love for Eretz Yisrael among the Jews of America is as old as these communities themselves. You can say that this love is, to us, as American as "apple pie," an inheritance that has been handed over from generation to generation. It is our responsibility to nurture and strengthen it in our own days. For this we should be aware of and grateful to the great rabbis and scholars of old who braved the hazards and sacrifices of long journeys to bring the love for Eretz Yisrael to these shores.

# The Rescue of the Previous Lubavitcher Rebbe

We know the Biblical verse "*Podeh Hashem nefesh avadav...* (G-d redeems the soul of His servants...)" (Psalms 34:23). In no case is this verse more fully and miraculously fulfilled than in the rescue of the previous Lubavitcher Rebbe, Rabbi Yosef Yitzchak Schneerson, in 1939–1940, according to secret German War records, only recently made known.

Let us go back to September 1939: On September 1, Germany invaded—with all the fury of her overpowering military might—her neighbor, Poland. I remember well the indescribable terror in all our hearts on that day, even in neutral Sweden, where I was born. We all feared the worst: On the first day of that War, I took it on myself, as a youngster, to go out and buy gas masks for my entire family, as a gas war was more feared than any other type of war. (It turned out that gas was the one weapon neither warring side used throughout World War II. It was only used against the Jews in Auschwitz and other extermination camps.)

The Jews of Poland were soon the victims of Hitler's "*Endlösung* (Final Solution)." For the next three weeks Hitler's Blitzkrieg swept over Poland. Then the Russian army—under the treacherous Hitler–Stalin pact of the previous August—invaded Poland from the East. The Jews within this giant pincer were trapped. The chances for escape out of the jaws of death were minimal. We all know the tragic end of this, the saddest chapter in our long history.

In the midst of this furious destruction plan for the Jewish people, one person—unbeknownst to himself—was selected for an unbelievable drama of rescue, in which the most unlikely forces came together in a confluence of joint interests. The person selected for this miraculous rescue operation was the previous Lubavitcher Rebbe, Josef Yitshak Schneerson.

The Rebbe had already been rescued once before under miraculous circumstances—when in 1927, having been condemned to death by the Bolsheviks—his life was saved at the last minute by the intervention of President Calvin Coolidge. The Rebbe came to the United States in 1929 and visited President Herbert Hoover. He then settled in Riga as a Latvian citizen. In 1932 he established the Chabad Center in Otwotsk, a suburb of Warsaw. On the outbreak of the War, the Rebbe tried to save his extensive library of sacred books and manuscripts of the Lubavitcher Rebbeim, already packed in 140 cases. But the attempt failed.

Next, an enormous intervention effort was organized by the Rebbe's chasidim in America for his rescue from under the Nazi yoke. Among those who participated in this effort was Postmaster James A. Farley, President Roosevelt's leading politician in the Democratic Party; Sen. Robert F. Wagner (of German descent), father of the New York's mayor in the 1960s; and Supreme Court Justice Louis D.

Brandeis, who had retired from the Court by that time. Cordel Hull, the secretary of state, whose wife was Jewish, declined to officially intervene on the Rebbe's behalf on the grounds that the United States could not officially assist a citizen of another country.

Then Roosevelt's close Jewish advisor, Benjamin V. Cohen—who normally did nothing for Jewish causes—approached Robert T. Pell, deputy chief for Europe in the State Department, who approached Myron C. Taylor, Roosevelt's representative at the failed Evian Conference for the saving of Jewish refugees. While all these efforts, on the surface, did nothing to help the Rebbe get out of Nazi occupied Poland, they did bring his case to the attention of a high German official, Helmuth Wohlthat, who, while a senior member of the German government, was opposed to Hitler and cultivated relations with men later identified with the opposition within Germany.

He had studied at Columbia University and knew American political and commercial life well. A distant relative of Hitler's Central Bank chief, Hjalmar Schacht, Wohlthat had a meteoric career in Germany's Ministry of Commerce and became the confidant of Hermann Göring, Hitler's No. 2 man.

It was Göring's idea to let Wohlthat maintain contacts with such American officials as George F. Rublee and Robert T. Pell, both of the State Department. Wohlthat's job was to interest the Roosevelt administration in a peace agreement to be brokered between Hitler and Neville Chamberlain's England. After the end of the Polish campaign, there was a lull in the War theater, the so-called "Sitzkreig," with neither side engaged in any significant military activity. Hitler hoped that England would welcome a peaceful compromise during this lull in the fighting. He knew that England was feverishly arming herself after years of inertia and disarmament. This was also a time when the United States was seen as extremely weak, with no defense forces worth worrying about.

But the Germans had to first find a way to demonstrate their sincerity to the West. They decided to show their genuineness by performing an act of benevolence to the Jews of America—acceding to a request involving a concern in which large masses of American Jews were interested. Benjamin Cohen, Roosevelt's close Jewish adviser, came up with the suggestion to let the release of the Lubavitcher Rebbe be the test of German benevolence. Wohlthat was informed of this suggestion and he promptly mobilized his colleagues in the highest German circles to bring about the release of the Rebbe. This had to be done quickly and secretly because, as Wohlthat knew, his own boss, Foreign Minister Joachim von Ribbentrop, would object to saving a Jew.

To make the operation fully successful for the desired peace settlement, Wohlthat also contacted a number of wealthy American industrialists who had an interest in doing business with Nazi Germany. Among them were William Rhodes Davis, an oil millionaire, and James D. Mooney, president of General Motors, which had branches in Germany.

The Germans were convinced that the Rebbe had so many influential friends that his release could bring about a change in Roosevelt's policy in favor of a negotiated peace. The newly appointed American Ambassador in Berlin, Alexander C. Kirk, became the link between Washington and Berlin to realize the release of the Lubavitcher Rebbe.

But where was the Rebbe? Finding the Rebbe presented a more difficult problem than the intricate, secret negotiations that led to the decision to release him. The Germans turned to the intelligence and espionage system of Germany, which was known for its cunning. Headed by Adm. Canaris, the intelligence establishment was actually in opposition to the Nazis and operated quite apart from the dreaded Gestapo of the Nazi butchers.

Helmuth Wohlthat picked a German major of Jewish descent, Maj. Ernst Bloch, a war hero of the First World War, to organize the operation of locating the Rebbe and bringing him to safety in a neutral country. Maj. Bloch picked Maj. Johannes Horatzek, a Polish-speaking German intelligence officer, for the job. This happened on October 19, 1939, when Washington was informed that the rescue of the Lubavitcher Rebbe had been set into motion.

All this happened without the knowledge of the Rebbe himself, who meanwhile did everything to remain in hiding. Already in September of that year the Rebbe had been miraculously saved from certain death when the Warsaw building in which he lived was hit by a German bomb and demolished. The Rebbe had just left the building moments before the bomb struck. The trauma of this incident caused him severe shock and a nervous disorder.

The Rebbe moved into the house of Rabbi Hirsch Gourary where his whereabouts were kept secret. Therefore, when the uniformed Maj. Horatzek and his German associates came to the Gourary house, everyone there feared the worst and denied the Rebbe's presence. It took a while before it became known through the American ambassador in Warsaw that the Rebbe had nothing to fear from these German officers, but on the contrary, they had come for his deliverance.

Wohlthat reported to Washington on November 25 that the Rebbe had recovered sufficiently from the aftereffects of the bombing attack, and that he would undertake the planned trip to Riga. The costs of the travel were covered by the Rebbe's chasidim in the States.

The routing of the trip also posed a problem, because it was rightfully feared that any Christians—whether Germans or Latvians—who saw the bearded rabbi would attack him due to their ferocious hatred of any and every Jew at that time. The routing was discussed, on behalf of Robert T. Pell of the State Department, by attorney Max Rhoade. Finally on December 22, the American diplomat in Berlin could report to Washington that the Rebbe and his closest aides had left Warsaw and were on their way, escorted by Maj. Bloch, to Berlin.

After spending the night in the Jewish Center of Berlin, the travelers continued to Riga. One of those who traveled with him described the German soldiers whom they saw on the way as "acting like wild animal at the sight of Jews with beards." The 140 cases of books and 11 cases of silver and household articles of the Rebbe never made it. They were entrusted to the well-known freight forwarders Schenker & Co. for transmittal via Italy to the United States, but their transport was stopped by the Germans. Efforts to get the Rebbe's possessions released continued until September 23, 1941, but were in vain.

The Rebbe arrived from Riga in Stockholm in March. That is when I had the privilege to help him get to the railroad station and onto the train that took him to Gothenburg, Sweden, where the Swedish ocean liner, *Drottingholm*, took him to New York.

I will never forget the image of the Rebbe and his unbelievably dark, penetrating eyes, as he looked out of the train compartment window. He looked at those of us who had escorted him to the train, but he actually looked far, far beyond us. Now that I know the miraculous sequence of events that brought him out of the German hell to safety in Sweden and his way to America, I can—50 years later—begin to understand what heavy burdens rested on his mind, as he thought back to the tragedy of the Jews he had left behind and his worry about the future of the Jews in the new land of America.

As to the *Drottingholm*, the flagship of the Swedish-American line, I remember a saying during those months among Scandinavian Jews: Every nation has its line—the Germans have their Siegfried Line, the French have their Maginot Line, the Finns have their Mannerheim Line—and the Jews have the Swedish-American Line! Considering that the seas were infested with submarines at the time, every sailing of the *Drottingholm* was fraught with grave dangers. But it was providential—as so much in the rescue story of the Rebbe—that there was a Swedish-American Line whose neutrality was respected by both sides in the War.

It is of course public knowledge how enthusiastically the masses of chasidim greeted the Rebbe when the *Drottingholm* docked at the 57th Street pier in Manhattan on March 19, 1940. But probably few knew how miraculous and providential the entire rescue operation had been. It was a result of international interests converging at that precise moment, of high officials in enemy camps seeing a benefit to help each other, and the Rebbe being picked for the rescue operation. Of course, equally miraculous was the actual transport of the Rebbe through dangerous areas inside the Nazi hell and his ultimately safe voyage to the United States.

As I wrote recently, can we imagine how the world would look today if that rescue operation had not succeeded? We have reason to be thankful not only for the rescue itself, but also for the recent revelation of secret documents of all these details, which, providentially, were at work! As the *pasuk* (verse) says, "God redeems the soul of His servants."

# How the U.S. Government Treated Enemy Terrorists in 1942

Enemies of Israel from time to time criticize Israel's handling of terrorists it captures. Entire leftist organizations exist only to jump into action when Israeli-captured terrorists are interrogated, sentenced to prison and, sometimes, deported. Not one of these terrorists has been executed, no matter how murderous his activities have been. Extreme care has been taken to protect their civil rights. Because of Israeli leniency, such enemies of Israel as Feisal Husseini have been released from jail and now pose a grave threat to Israel's existence.

It is therefore timely to examine America's record when it comes to terrorists who have fallen into American hands. This happened in the midst of World War II. Hitler had declared war on the United States in December 1941. His huge war machine was poised to fight us on every front. Fortunately, German airplanes did not yet have the range to reach the United States. But their submarines reached the East Coast and sank many cargo ships off American ports. These submarines were a serious threat to our lifeline: our commerce with South America and Europe. It was at this time that German submarines were close to destroying Great Britain, by way of destroying huge quantities of vital cargo trying to reach the British Isles. But nobody expected another kind of assault on the United States from the sea.

In the June of 1942, a German submarine landed eight German terrorists, who had volunteered for the job of creating maximum damage to the United States and the war effort. They had been trained in Germany for months to familiarize them with American customs and mores. They had to read American newspapers and magazines. At the same time, they were trained in industrial sabotage. Their main aim was to destroy strategic bridges, railways and factories. A major target was to be the aluminum plants that supplied the American aircraft industry.

Six of the terrorists landed on Long Island, near Amagansett, while two landed in Florida. Together they carried nearly $200,000 and enough fuses and explosives to keep them busy for two years.

The public had never expected that enemy terrorists could reach their shores. Fortunately the terrorists were quickly apprehended by a lone Coast Guard on Long Island. The significance of this incident was the court case that followed and the law that was applied to the German spies.

President Franklin D. Roosevelt, as commander in chief, took the incident extremely seriously. On July 1 the president constituted a military commission consisting of seven top generals to try the Nazis. In a declaration the president stated: "All persons who are objects, citizens or residents of any nation at war with the United

States, who during time of war enter or attempt to enter the United States or any territory or possession thereof, through coastal or boundary defenses, and are charged with committing or attempting or preparing to commit sabotage, espionage, hostile or warlike acts, shall be subject to the law of war and to the jurisdiction of military tribunals, and such persons shall not be privileged to seek remedy or maintain any proceeding in the courts of the United States."

In short, saboteurs or terrorists had no right to civil trials. This point was challenged by the court-appointed defense attorneys of the Nazis. The case went all the way to the Supreme Court, which upheld the president's declarations and thus denied the terrorists the right to a civil trial. Here are excerpts from the government's arguments:

> Those whom the enemy sends to destroy our industries and lives and the very existence of the nation can hardly be in a position to claim constitutional rights, privileges or immunities from the nation that they seek to destroy. One privilege they seek is the freedom to ask our courts to help them now that they are caught.
>
> Traditionally all states in time of war have denied belligerent enemies access to their courts. That is one of the earliest and most rudimentary forms of political and economic warfare. It is an integral part of modern total warfare. *And today the nation that does not wage total warfare, usually meets total defeat* [my emphasis].
>
> Rights and privileges accorded to our residents—including those who disagree with us—should not be granted to belligerent enemies who, in time of war, enter this country in order to destroy it by acts of war.
>
> These petitioners, as enemies who crossed our borders after the declaration of war, *have no legal right to ask this court by habeas corpus or otherwise, to inquire into the lawfulness of their detention* [my emphasis].

In a desperate move to free themselves, the Nazi terrorists put up this unbelievable defense (from *The New York Times* of July 29, 1942): "While they were sent here by the German High Command to sabotage war industries, they actually made the submarine trip to escape from the German Reich and never intended to carry out their orders."

The death penalty, in a unanimous verdict, was imposed on six of the terrorists while two were given prison terms because they had cooperated with the United States. President Roosevelt approved the sentences, and on August 7 the six were executed in the electric chair.

Israel is facing a much graver danger from Arab terrorists than the United States faced from a group of six inept saboteurs who never managed to damage a single installation or hurt any human beings. Yet Israel is exercising immense restraint and tolerance. It has not executed a single terrorist.

The main points demonstrated by the Roosevelt verdict are that 1) terrorists must be tried before a military, not civilian court; 2) the court does not have to give the reason for the terrorists' arrest; 3) the death penalty is obligatory, except under mitigating circumstances.

Israel should be highly praised by "human rights" advocates, not faulted!

U.S. authorities are holding Islamic terrorists for such terror acts as the bombing of the World Trade Center. According to journalist Steve Emerson's reports, the fundamentalists consider themselves at war with the United States. There are also other cases of possible Islamic terrorism, such as the Oklahoma bombing; its connection with an Islamic group in the Philippines has never been brought to the open.

Have our authorities forgotten the law as applied by President Roosevelt in 1942? Instead of applying those lessons, months and years are spent wrangling with defense attorneys of the terrorists, even risking, as in the Meir Kahane murder case, that the terrorists go free because of technicalities.

In the light of the horrendous terror attack on TWA Flight 800 and the bomb attack in Saudi Arabia, the time has come to announce to the world Roosevelt's message as a warning to would-be Moslem terrorists.

# How Hitler Began—The Relevance for Today

Hitler was appointed Reichskanzler on January 30, 1933. Although everybody had read his *Mein Kampf*, in which he pronounced his plans to destroy the Jewish people, nobody believed he was serious about it. "He will mellow down," most Jews said. In the first few weeks his only anti-Semitic measures were to forbid *shechita* in most German states, but then his anti-Jewish machine slowly started to move, and we know the tragic end. How did it begin?

The German Jewish novelist, Lion Feuchtwanger, a descendant of an old Orthodox family in Munich, published a novel in 1934, called *The Oppermanns*, which shook up the world. In it he describes the horrible fate of a young member of the family.

The young Oppermann attended a German school, and was the only Jewish student in his class. They had just gotten a new history teacher, who one day asked Oppermann to stand before the class and relate what he had studied in Roman history.

The unsuspecting Oppermann proceeded to describe the battles of the barbarians and their attacks on Rome. He mentioned Armin the Teuton—when suddenly the teacher jumped up and screamed at the young Jewish student: "You are insulting our German honor! Don't you know that you are speaking about Herman the German, our great early German hero, and you call him Armin the Teuton?"

Of course, the name "Herman the German" did not appear in any history book, and Oppermann was perplexed. But the teacher did not stop screaming about how this Jew had insulted German honor, and that he would see to it that he would apologize before the entire school. He stormed out and ran to the school's principal, who was not yet a Nazi, but who allowed himself to be browbeaten by the furious Nazi teacher. In the end, Oppermann was hauled before an assembly of the entire school and ordered to apologize for having insulted German honor. The experience, as related in the book, was so traumatic that the young Jewish student committed suicide.

Let us now move on some 50 years, and observe a scene at the University of Pennsylvania—whose president, Sheldon Hackney, has just been nominated by President Clinton to become the head of the powerful National Endowment of the Humanities. This is the same Hackney who allowed black students to shred an entire issue of the school newspaper because they did not agree with one of its editorials, and in another incident, almost crucified a young Jewish student, Eden Jacobowitz, for having hurled the word "*behemoth*" (water buffalo) at some rowdy and noisy black women students who were disturbing his studies. A less-known incident at the University involved one of its most popular professors, Murray Dolfman, a lecturer in legal studies:

One day, teaching a class of black and white students, Prof. Dolfman came to the subject of the 13th Amendment which outlaws the practice of slavery. He asked his class if anyone knew the content of the 13th Amendment, but they all answered in the negative. He then said something to this effect: "It is curious that I, as a Jew, whose ancestors were slaves, celebrate the memory of my people's slavery and our freedom from slavery each year at Passover time, while you, whose ancestors were also slaves, do not know or celebrate the 13th Amendment which set your forefathers free!"

Pandemonium broke loose. Dolfman had called the black students "ex-slaves!" Such a racist statement could not be tolerated! Protests were raised by the Black Student League, a petition was signed by 109 black faculty members and administrators, and one demonstration after another was organized. The president of the University was pressed to conduct an investigation and to insist on a public apology by Dolfman.

Hackney gave in. He issued a statement that he regarded the incident as serious, and that an apology was in order. However, the black students were no longer satisfied, they now demanded that Dolfman—who had taught at the University for 21 years—should be dismissed. The incident was evidently deliberately intensified and fabricated as part of a premeditated power struggle at the University to show Hackney's subservience to the radicals, and to humiliate a Jew in the process. In the end Dolfman was suspended for one term, and then offered reinstatement on condition that he undergo "sensitivity and racial-awareness sessions."

Shades of Hitler? We know what followed the totally unfair and biased attacks on Jewish students in early Nazi days. Will the same happen here? Is the public aware of the potential danger that follows from pandering to racist bias and prejudice? Are the Crown Heights pogroms enough of a reminder? Were President Clinton and his wife aware of Hackney's docile, spineless conduct and his totally warped idea of freedom of speech before they appointed him to a position where he will dole out $150 million to support research, films and exhibitions in the humanities?

The anti-climax to this painful incident came a few days ago when the first African-American woman senator, Carol Moseley-Braun, caused a great stir in the Senate that led to the defeat of a motion to renew a patent on a Confederate emblem, by proudly invoking her slavery ancestry: If it is OK for a black senator to show pride in her slave ancestry, why is a Jewish professor ostracized for making an innocent reference to it, especially when he simultaneously mentions his own slave background, without a trace of prejudice or racial "hang up?"

After the Senate action I promptly wrote to Senator Moseley-Braun, bringing Prof. Dolfman's case to her attention, and asking her to intervene on his behalf so that his mention of black slavery should not be cause for apology or punishment. By defending his right to free speech on the subject of slavery she would help eradicate the double standards which are being used as a basis for inappropriate racist attacks.

Senator Moseley-Braun may never answer me, but at least it is our duty to speak up!

# Brazil

To most, the name "Brazil" brings home notions of the colorful Carnival, of samba rhythms, of beautiful Rio de Janeiro. But few realize how important Brazil was in the history of American Jewry. It is fair to say that without Brazil there would be no Jews, as we know them, in America today. How did this come about?

To answer this historic question we must go back a few hundred years to Portugal, the mother country of Brazil. During the 15th century—the century of navigational discoveries—Spain and Portugal were engaged in international competition for garnering colonies in all overseas continents. The Portuguese were the great navigators in Africa and the Far East. To this day, we hear echoes of these colonies in countries where Portuguese is still spoken, including Angola and Mozambique in Africa; and Goa, Timor and Macao in Asia.

Spain, on the other hand, captured most of the Americas: Florida in North America; and most countries in Central and South America, except Brazil, which by decision of one of the popes went to Portugal. Brazil had been discovered by Cabral and Ferdenando de Noronha—both Jews or Marranos—but remained undeveloped for a long time.

In 1492, the royal couple Ferdinand and Isabelle of Spain gave in to the cruel head of the Inquisition, Torquemada—himself perhaps of Jewish origin—and decreed the expulsion of the Jews from their land. The last-minute plea by Don Isaac Abarbanel, the minister of finance of Spain, and other leading Jews who offered the king and queen a huge amount of money if the decree were lifted, was brusquely brushed aside by Torquemada, who had an iron grip on the royal couple. He insisted on two choices: baptism or expulsion. We know the tragedies that followed.

The vast majority of Spanish Jews chose expulsion over baptism. Many of them migrated to nearby Portugal. But in 1497 a catastrophe hit them there. A newly crowned king, again under the diabolical influence of the Church, gave the Jews two new choices. This time they had to choose between baptism and death! That is why so many of them had to adopt Christianity as a sham, while continuing the practice of Judaism secretly. They were called "New Christians" or Marranos. They were the ones singled out by the Inquisition for barbaric tortures and *auto da fé* burnings.

However, a little known fact is that there was one way out of this cruel choice: any Jew who would go to Brazil and help colonize the newly won colony would be exempt for 100 years from the "Santo Oficio"—"Holy Office," the technical name given the Inquisition (some holiness!). And so a steady stream of New Christians immigrated to Brazil in the first years of the 1500s. They helped colonize the cities of Bahia, Recife and Rio de Janeiro and lived a free, undisturbed life. They must have been frightened to death when suddenly, 100 years later, the murder gangs of the Santo Oficio showed up in Brazil to carry out their cruel work.

The first recorded arrival of the Santo Oficio was in 1598 in Rio de Janeiro, followed by "visit" after "visit." The last burning of a Jew took place in 1769, when the famous Brazilian playwright, Antonio José da Silva, was burned to death for "Judaizing."

What is interesting for the history of Judaism is the study of the methods by which the agents of the Inquisition would discover who was a Jew. They would come into a community and would post on the door of the leading church a list of practices that informers were to report on their fellow citizens.

Some of these were:
> 1. anyone wearing a washed shirt (*camisa lavada*) on Saturday
> 2. anyone found fasting on March 10 or September 10 (These would be echoes of Taanit Esther and Yom Kippur. Taanit Esther was especially precious to Marranos, because Queen Esther, too, had to hide her Jewishness in the palace of King Ahashverosh. They, therefore, identified with her.)
> 3. anyone pouring out water from the house where someone had died. (This is an extremely interesting leftover of a very old Jewish practice, which only rarely is found in medieval *halachah*—where it is explained that the *Malach haMavet* (Angel of Death) washes his spade in the water, which therefore is infected. This practice is found as early as the Dead Sea Scrolls—over 2,000 years ago!)

In 1624 the situation was totally changed. The Dutch won a war against the Portuguese and turned northeastern Brazil into "Nova Holanda" (New Holland). The capital was the city of Recife in the province of Pernambuco. The suffering secret Jews could now live freely. They founded a congregation called "Tzur Yisrael" (the Rock of Israel, because the name Recife—similar to the Hebrew "*ritzpah*"—meant "rock.") They prospered and organized their congregation along the lines of the Portuguese community in Amsterdam.

When it came to choosing a rabbi they had two eminently qualified candidates: Menasse ben Israel, the great philosopher, rabbi, book printer and merchant; and Rabbi Yitzchak Ahoab da Fonseca. Brazil was an important outpost for an international Dutch trading firm. Menasse ben Israel had his sights set on doing some business with the company if he became rabbi of Recife. The Jews, however, selected da Fonseca, who later played a great role in Jewish life in Amsterdam.

Disaster struck in 1654, when the Portuguese made a comeback and defeated the Dutch, who had to evacuate their Nova Holanda. But what to do with their Jews? The Dutch Governor Mauritzio de Nassau managed to insert a clause in the Dutch version of the surrender document—which was omitted from the Portuguese version—allowing the Jews 90 days to leave the country without molestation by the Inquisition.

The Jews, after so much suffering for hundreds of years, had to pick up the staff of the wanderer again. This time their wandering took part of them to neighboring Surinam—a blessed choice as later history would prove—while the bulk sailed, along with their rabbis, either to Amsterdam or north to the Caribbean Islands and—when one of the ships lost its course in a storm—to New Amsterdam (later called New York). The Caribbean Islands benefiting most from these migrations were Barbados, Curaçao, St. Nevis, Martinique and a few lesser islands.

The Jews who sailed to Amsterdam took with them the *pinqasim*—communal archives—and some rare mahogany wood, which Rabbi da Fonseca installed in the Holy Ark of the magnificent Etz Hayim synagogue in Amsterdam, until today one of the most sought-out Jewish tourist attractions in Europe.

The migration of ex-Brazilian Jews thus populated the early Americas and set the stage for all Jewish immigration to the colonies. At first the Portuguese-Brazilian congregations of the Caribbean Islands were economically and spiritually much more important than the North American colonies. In Surinam alone, there were outstanding rabbis and Talmudic authorities over 100 years before any rabbinical personalities worth mentioning arose in North America. And it was money from the affluent and pious Jews of Surinam that financed the building of the famous synagogue in Newport, Rhode Island, and the Spanish-Portuguese congregation, Sheerith Israel, in New York.

What a marvel Jewish history is, and how unfathomable are G-d's manifestations in our history: The expulsion of the Jews from Spain and Portugal helped establish and enlarge the Jewish communities in North Africa and the Middle East, including Eretz Yisrael. At the same time, the same Sefardic families who emigrated from the South to North America helped establish the important Jewish communities in North America. Both these centers of Jewish population and scholarship were essential in assuring the survival of Judaism and the Jewish people—ultimately leading to the re-establishment of the Jewish State in Eretz Yisrael.

Brazil thus played a pivotal role in the history of the Jewish people, especially in the Americas. But what is even more important is that Brazil today has a very active Jewish life, with Jewish day schools and yeshivot in various places, and that Ashkenazim as well as Sefardim work together for the good of Jewish continuity and survival. The early colonizers would never have imagined that their dream would come true! But that is the imponderable secret of Jewish history.

# Marienbad, 1937

A few weeks ago, in the midst of the Israeli election campaign, a long-forgotten dateline was brought back to mind: Marienbad, 1937. During the campaign, the Sadegora Rebbe, Rav Abraham Jacob Friedman, issued his momentous appeal to Torah-true Jews to vote for Benjamin Netanyahu. In that document the rebbe said: "The Council of Torah Sages has already many times clarified its stand against giving up Jewish land, starting with the Knessia Gedolo in Marienbad of 1937."

Not too many people remember what took place in Marienbad in that summer, what led to it, and what the aftermath of it was. Not yet 15 years old, I was there, coming from my native Sweden with my family.

Marienbad is a small, world-renowned health spa, where the great rebbes of Eastern Europe used to go for their health during the summer. Although part of the Czechoslovak Republic founded by the famous democrat Dr. Thomas Masaryk, it was the heartland of the most ferocious Nazis and anti-Semites, namely, the Sudeten Germans. Although these Germans oozed with pretended hospitality and feigned friendliness to Jewish tourists during the summer, when the summer was over, they donned their Nazi uniforms and behaved in the same ferocious manner as the Nazis in the German "homeland." No wonder that the official Marienbader "Kurhaus," the main health and tourist installation, was graciously made available free of charge by the local Sudeten authorities to the 700 Jewish delegates and 2,000 guests, who came that summer to attend the third Knessia Gedola of the World Aguda to discuss the problems that weighed on Jews: problems in the Land of Israel; suffering from the onslaught of Arab terrorist murderers; and the problems looming on the horizon from Hitler and his gangs.

The Congress was officially opened on August 17 by "Moreinu" Jacob Rosenheim, the world president of Agudat Israel. This great German Jew, steeped in Jewish as well as in university learning, was the recognized guide and leader accepted by many of the great chasidic and Lithuanian sages. Perhaps in order not to frighten and alarm the delegates, Dr. Rosenheim alluded only slightly to the mortal danger that was approaching the Jewish people in Europe. The revolutionary, historic changes in the Aguda were reflected in Dr. Rosenheim's speech which called for the acceptance of Eretz Yisrael as the central force in the historical destiny of the Jewish people. This differed from the Aguda's stance in previous decades.

This was the summer when the so-called Peel Report was issued by the British government, which called for the partition of the Jewish land, leaving a pitifully small area in Jewish hands. The British government invited delegations from the

Jews and the Arabs to discuss the Partition Plan. The Arabs totally rejected the plan and so did staunch Zionist and religious groups.

Looking back it was, of course, providential that the Arabs in 1937—just as they would in 1948—rejected any kind of partition plan. Thereby Divine Providence gave Israel a chance to greatly expand on the Jewish land in the wars that ultimately erupted with the Arabs. Among the Jews, two camps developed: the so-called "Ja Sager," those who said "Yes" to partition; and "Nein Sager," those who rejected any kind of partition. Among the former were the general Zionists, under Weizmann and Ben Gurion; while the Aguda, the Revisionists of Vladimir Jabotinsky, and the extreme leftists of "Hashomer Hatzair"—a peculiar combination—were strongly opposed.

The debate that rocked the Jewish world seems to us now so futile and tragically unproductive, because nobody then knew that they were at the threshold of our history's greatest tragedy and slaughter of Jews. Also, with the advent of World War II just two years later, the British scrapped the Partition Plan and returned to a policy of suppression of Jewish nationalism. I remember how after the Knessia the delegates scrambled to climb into the Czech railroad car, which they thought would carry them back home—but their ultimate destination was Auschwitz. In hindsight, there are not enough tears to bemoan the tragedy and suffering that was facing the Jews who had gathered in Marienbad with so much *yirat shamayim* (fear of Heaven) and *bitachon* (trust) in the Ultimate Redemption of the Jewish people. But we are hardly permitted to search for an explanation.

The opening session was most impressive of all. I was not yet 15 years old but was allowed to enter the Plenary Session—with all the famous rebbes, rabbis and community leaders, sitting on the dais headed by the Gerer Rebbe, the Alexanderer Rebbe, the Sochaczover Rebbe and others. Also in the leadership was the outstanding personality of Rav Aron Lewin, of the Rzeszover dynasty, and member of the Polish Parliament. From Germany had come Rav Josef Carlebach, who would become a martyr just a few years later; and Rabbi Wolf Jacobson of Hamburg and Copenhagen. Never again would such an array of great Jewish leaders sit together. It was an unforgettable sight.

"The Jewish people must never be separated from the Jewish Land," Rav Lewin said. He also called on the assembly to eulogize the fallen victims of Arab terror. He, as well as most other speakers, reminded the delegates that the Land of Israel must be based on the Torah of Israel. Interestingly, Neville Laski, the president of the Board of Deputies of British Jews, and a secular Jew, sent a message to Harry Goodman, the British Aguda leader, in which he said: "A Jewish state has little hope for success if it is not based on a constitution founded on Torah and Jewish values."

A most deeply-felt impression was left with me of a youth session on Shabbat Ki Teitzei. A group of youngsters was addressed in the Shabbat afternoon session, both by Rav Elchonon Wasserman, the great rosh yeshiva of Baranovitch, and by Rav Josef Carlebach. I cannot forget Rav Carlebach's words, based on the Haftora of Parshat Ki Teitzei: "The prophet tells us to expand our tents, but to secure very deeply our pegs." He interpreted this to mean that the Aguda should expand and include as many Jews as possible but never dilute or water down its strong program. Such wise advice is valuable to us all.

The adherence of the Aguda to the totality of the G-d-given borders of the Land of Israel came forcefully to expression in the Resolution on the Land, which, to deafening applause, was read on behalf of Moetzet Gedole Hatorah: "The borders of our Holy Land were fixed by the Almighty, Creator of the Universe, and fixed for all time in the Holy Torah. Consequently it is impossible that the Jewish people, in any way or form whatsoever, would relinquish any part of the Land. Any such relinquishing is null and void."

At the same time, the congress called for Arab-Jewish reconciliation. A very significant speech was delivered by Dr. Maximilian Landau, who depicted the desperate economic and social conditions in Europe and the ever-growing crisis in trying to solve the problems of emigration and social welfare. This was all said before it became apparent that the Jews of Europe were destined for total eradication. Landau called for finding countries that were willing to take in Jewish refugees and pleaded for the opening of Eretz Yisrael to increased immigration. The Congo and Angola were mentioned as possible destinations for Jewish immigrants—a sign of the growing desperation.

A Women's Congress of the Aguda was taking place at the same time. Speakers called for increased education for Jewish women, for letting women take an increased role in Jewish affairs, and for strengthening the Beth Jacob schools.

The seriousness of the delegates in accomplishing concrete and effective help projects for the Jewish masses, while at the same time emphasizing Jewish Torah values in family life and education, was exemplary. Thus, even though many of the delegates perished before their mission could be accomplished, the Knessia Gedolo left behind an indelible legacy of self-sacrifice for the good of the Jewish *klal* (whole). The readiness of the delegates to apply *mesirat nefesh* (self-sacrifice) for Torah and the Land of Israel remains an inspiration which in our own recent history has proved itself. As we watch in wonderment the enormous increase in the power and influence of the religious Jews in Israel, we must realize that the seeds for such success were laid in Marienbad in 1937, exactly as the Sadegora Rebbe has just declared.

After attending the Aguda Congress, my parents gave me permission to proceed to Zurich to attend the 20th Zionist Congress. I give my parents enormous credit for permitting this venture—a 14-year-old boy crossing Nazi Germany by himself! I will report on this historical and memorable visit at another occasion. But it is hardly difficult to fathom that to a young boy the experience of two such historic congresses within a few weeks laid the foundation for life-long dedication to the betterment of the Jewish people.

# Oral History: Personal Memories from Hitler's Germany

This time of year I remember vividly my crossing Nazi Germany in the midst of World War II. This happened in May 1940. On May 12 I embarked alone as a 17-year-old traveler from my native Sweden on my trip to the United States, which took me right across Germany. The trip had been planned to take place during the so-called "Phony War," the period during World War II when no fighting took place between Germany and France.

True, the Russians, Hitler's allies at the time, had invaded Finland in November 1939 and were heroically held at bay until the Finns had to give up in March 1940. The Germans had invaded Norway and Denmark on April 8, 1940. But otherwise, things were quiet.

Then, suddenly, the Blitzkrieg broke out on Friday, May 10. The Germans invaded Holland, Belgium and France with sweeping armored attacks and Stuka bombers. Here I was holding tickets to start my trip to the United States. Would I go ahead despite the War, or not?

But first let me recall events going back to 1933. Our family had moved to Hamburg in Northern Germany in 1928 for the sake of my and my brothers' Jewish education. Sweden, with its assimilated Reform Judaism, offered no Jewish schooling, and we had been tutored by private teachers until early school age. Then we moved to Hamburg because of its well-known, magnificent *Talmud Torah Realschule*, organized by Rabbi Dr. Josef Carlebach, the brilliant educator—later martyred—who had formulated the school's religious and secular curriculum along the lines of "*Torah im Derech Eretz* (Torah with Secular Knowledge)" of Dr. Ezriel Hildesheimer of Berlin.

Hamburg was the most successful Jewish community in Germany because of its total integration of Portuguese, German and Lithuanian Jews, who had arrived there at different times in past centuries. Our family quickly became part of the pulsating, dynamic Jewish life of Hamburg. But then the skies darkened.

Throughout 1932, the political setup of Germany came to a boiling point. The Nazi hordes were terrorizing Germany with their Brown Shirt thugs, who incessantly carried out acts of violence against the democratic and leftist parties. The aged president, Field Marshal Paul von Hindenburg, was unable to stabilize the situation. He appointed one chancellor after another—von Schleicher, Bruening, von Papen—all of whom failed to quell the unrest.

The millions of German unemployed willingly listened to the Nazi rabble-rousers and demagogues, starting with Hitler himself.

Then I remember how one day, January 30, my late father told us, ashen-faced, that Hitler had been appointed chancellor in place of von Papen. The Jews were understandably shaken, knowing Hitler's ferocious anti-Semitism, which had propelled him into German leadership. Germany's defeat in World War I and all the ills of the depression, including the inflation of the 1920s and unemployment, were blamed on the Jews.

Yet, I remember clearly some Hamburg Jews telling us, "*Soll er nur kommen* (Let him just come). He will fall like all the others have fallen." Or worse, some said, "*Es wird alles nicht so heiss gegessen wie es gekocht wird* (Nothing is eaten as hot as it is cooked)." In other words, once in power, Hitler would not be as bad as he sounded in his political campaigns. These were famous last words, tragically, but they are indicative of the wishful thinking that is a natural human reaction to impending disaster.

A few weeks passed, and my father would report on anti-Semitic acts that he had experienced during trips to various German cities. One day he came home to report that *shechita* (kosher animal slaughter) had been banned in certain parts of Germany. He correctly predicted that this ominous sign would be followed by much worse attacks on Jews. Unfortunately, he was proved right.

Shabbat, April 1, 1933, was the crucial day: The Nazis had declared a "Boycott Saturday" to take revenge on the Jews for allegedly "fabricating *greulpropaganda* (malicious lies)," especially in America, against the Hitler regime. Brown Shirts were posted in front of all Jewish shops. They smashed windows or daubed them with signs, such as "*Jude*" or "*Kauft nicht bei Juden* (Don't buy from Jews)." (Today we see similarities to these racist boycotts in the Black boycotts in Brooklyn against Korean shops.)

It was Shabbat and Orthodox Jews did not open their shops, so they did not witness the boycott. But every Jew was terrified, especially since the Brown Shirts were also, as usual, marching through town screaming for the killing of all Jews! ("*Juda verrecke!*") For the first time that I can remember as a child, my family did not go to shul that Shabbat. We sat at home, huddled together, waiting for reports from our Christian maid, whom my father had sent into town to watch the happenings.

When her report came to us, my father gathered the family and told us that in his opinion Hitler was on his way to fulfill his anti-Jewish program spelled out in his book, *Mein Kampf* and that there was no future for Jews anymore in Germany. He had decided that we should forthwith leave Germany and return to Sweden. However, being democratically oriented, he polled each of us on whether we agreed with his decision.

One brother was eager to leave; another, who loved the academic atmosphere at the *Talmud Torah Realschule*, objected. In my own case, being 10-years-old, I confess that I did not worry about the political consequences. I simply asked, "Would we travel by sleeper?" since I just loved sleeper cars. When my question was answered in the affirmative, I joined the majority.

Our trip started the very next day. We first stopped at Copenhagen where we first witnessed the manifestation of Jewish loyalty and brotherhood among Orthodox Jews during the war. At the railroad station a committee of members of the Orthodox Machzikey Hadass community of Denmark met the train and asked any traveling Jew what help and support they could give him. From Denmark we continued to Sweden.

Years passed. From Sweden we watched the situation grow worse and worse for German Jews. Many refugees escaped to Sweden and were helped by our own small Orthodox congregation. In fact, my father rescued an entire synagogue congregation that had escaped destruction from the Kristallnacht of November 1938 and brought it to Stockholm. This feat was described by me in my column some years ago, when the 50th anniversary of the re-establishment in Sweden of this German shul was celebrated.

Two of my brothers had traveled to the yeshiva in Mir, Poland, in 1936 and 1938, respectively, but had returned to Sweden in time to escape the beginning of the war. But when the war broke out in 1939, close to 100 American yeshiva students were hurriedly evacuated from the various Lithuanian yeshivot and arrived in Sweden on their way home to the United States. My friends and I helped them on their arrival and also arranged their *yom tov* services during Rosh Hashana and Yom Kippur 1939, whereafter they continued their trips home.

I myself had crossed Nazi Germany in 1937 on my way to Marienbad and Zurich. In Marienbad, I witnessed the Knessia Gedolah, the Agudah World Congress, and in Zurich I served as an usher at the 20th Zionist Congress. Traveling through Nazi Germany was still an uneventful affair, but after the war broke out, things changed.

My teacher, Rav Shlomo Wolbe, whom my father had brought to Sweden to teach my brothers and me, urged me day after day to go to the United States to attend yeshiva there, since the yeshivot in the East, tragically, did not exist anymore. Much to the credit of my parents, they agreed to send their young son alone across the ocean to gain an advanced Jewish education in America. One of my brothers had already arrived in New York the year before, which made my own decision easier.

And so on that turbulent Sunday, May 12, I embarked on my long trip. My parents accompanied me until the southernmost tip of Sweden, Traelleborg, where I entered a train ferry to sail over to Germany. I will never forget the moment of separation from my parents. My father bore up bravely, but my mother broke into heavy crying: When would we meet again? (With G-d's help, Sweden miraculously escaped German invasion. It was the only European country to be saved. And five years later, at the end of 1945, we were reunited in New York!)

My first stop was Berlin. With a Swedish passport, properly authorized with a German swastika stamp, I had a visa to travel through the very same Germany where other Jews were rounded up and deported to concentration camps. (That is typical of the German mentality: You push one button and they smile at you; you push another button and they gas you. . . .)

However, I was not allowed to travel during the night and therefore had to stay in a hotel in Berlin. By arrangement with Rav Wolbe, his mother—a widow still living in Berlin—came to visit me in my hotel room. Immediately, before saying a word, she searched behind curtains and in closets for any possible Gestapo agent waiting to pounce on her.

I had brought food with me for her. She was a stately, handsome woman of noble family lineage. She spoke like an aristocrat, and I could well see how my teacher had had an exemplary upbringing with such a mother. Sadly, my encounter with her was the last contact anybody had with her from outside Germany. Soon she was deported and killed.

My trip continued to Munich. There a most dramatic scene met me, which I will always associate with the Holocaust: As I walked through the busy Munich railroad station, swarming with soldiers moving to the front in France, I heard a hissing sound. There in a corner, hidden behind a pole, stood a group of Jews signaling to me that they could help me find a hiding place from the Gestapo.

They constituted an emergency rescue committee, running an underground system that delivered Jews away from their homes to temporary hiding places where they thought—mistakenly, as it turned out—that Jews would be safe. When I assured them that I did not need any help, they were incredulous: Hows could a Jew feel safe in Germany? I had to explain that I was a Swedish citizen and had a German visa to cross the country.

I always wonder what the fate was of this courageous group of Jews, who in the midst of the flaming Holocaust worried about their fellow Jews and put their own lives at tremendous risk to carry out rescue work. This encounter inspired me, on arrival in New York, to do my bit—through the *Vaad Hatzalah*—to rescue as many Jews as possible from destruction in Nazi Europe.

At every stopover in Nazi Germany, I read the flaming newspaper headlines of the great victories the Nazis had won. Although the Nazi propaganda exaggerated these victories, we know of course that, sadly, these reports were true. French, Belgian and Dutch towns fell one after the other, following the brutal pounding of the dreaded Stuka bombers and the onslaught by the superior Nazi army.

I heaved a sigh of relief when our train crossed into Italy at Bozen (Belsano). Soon I was in Milan, Italy, where I had an uncle and two cousins. A year before, in 1938, when I visited them on a trip from my boarding school in French Switzerland, they had still admired Mussolini and were members of his Fascist party, assuring me that Mussolini would never persecute Italian Jews. This time, in May 1940, they told quite a different story: Their Fascist membership had been canceled, and anti-Jewish laws were in effect. One of my cousins later died at the hands of the Nazis.

Arriving in Genoa, just in time for the last sailing of an American ocean liner, the *Washington*, I recognized the miracle of my safe crossing of the Nazi hell.

On the day my ship landed in New York, May 28, 1940, the Belgians surrendered to the Germans and the war on the Western Front was practically over—

with tragic consequences to follow. But from then on, I watched the war through the eyes of America, putting my faith in Franklin Roosevelt, and of course, in Winston Churchill.

Contact with my parents, although often long-delayed by postal censors, fortunately continued throughout the war. But I was not at ease until I saw them again in 1945, when Hitler had been crushed, and we all looked forward to the establishment of a Jewish Land.

Many of the people who today are so glib about what happens in Israel are those who never knew what it meant for Jews to have no land of their own, no government that would protect them, nor a safe haven to go to in case of persecution.

That is why it is an inescapable duty for those who have memories to relate them to the generations who still have much to learn from the past. Reliving the past, through the process of oral history, is important and constructive for the survival of the Jewish people and the Jewish Land.

# Hebrew Literature

I have made here a brief selection of bodies of our literature which are not always well known, as the Book of Ben Sira. I have also recounted how Jewish learning was saved when threatened with extinction, such as in the days of the great Court Jew, Behrend Lehmann. I also describe the joys of being a book lover and contributions to the survival of our glorious literature.

## The Book of Ben Sira

The Tenach (Hebrew Bible) is known to us as a finite collection of 39 books: 5 Torah (the Five Books of Moses); 21 Neviim (Prophets); and 13 Ketuvim (Writings). This collection has a technical term in the English language: the Canon. Yet the Talmud reports that as late as the days of the Tannaim, the exact number of books to be included in the Canon was still "fluid." There are accounts of discussions as to whether this or that book should be excluded from the Canon, as for example, the Song of Songs, Kohelet, the Book of Ezekiel, which, of course, were finally included. But there was a large body of books that was left out or that was never considered for inclusion—the so-called Sefarim Chitzonim, or in English, the Apocrypha—for example, the Book of the Maccabees, the Book of Tobit and the Book of Judith.

One book in the Apocrypha occupied a very special position mainly because even though it was not included in the Tenach, it remained a border case—it was sometimes considered as part of the Ketuvim even though, as a whole, it was excluded and by some even banned. I am referring to the Book of Ben Sira or, in English, the Book of Ecclesiasticus. Despite its uncertain status, the Talmud swarms with quotations from the Book of Ben Sira; so it is obvious that it occupied a very special position among Jews for many centuries.

Another amazing feature of the history of this book is that until recently we did not even have a complete Hebrew text of it. It was only known in its Greek or Syriac translations, besides the individual single passages that were quoted in the Talmud and the Midrashim. Then a sensation occurred 100 years ago. Some old ladies browsing through the walls in the market in Cairo came across some pages of Hebrew text, which turned out to be parts of the Ben Sira—in Hebrew! They had come from the famous Genizah, which had just been discovered in Cairo. It did not take long before most of the rest of the book was also found in the Genizah and was soon published by a number of scholars in Europe.

This amazing find was a 12th century text—penned 1,400 years after its composition. The question, though, still remained: Was this Hebrew text the re-translation from the Greek or Syriac translations or was it the original Hebrew text?

Then, 50 years ago, an even greater sensation occurred when the Dead Sea Scrolls were discovered—biblical and non-biblical texts from the time before the destruction of the Second Temple. No text from Ben Sira was among them, but it was my contention, as early as 1951, that without doubt Ben Sira texts, in the original Hebrew, would be found among the Dead Sea Scrolls. I published my first papers on the subject over 40 years ago, and I traced very close similarities between passages from both bodies of Jewish documents.

My conviction was soon confirmed by another sensational find—this one at Massada—where a large portion of Ben Sira, in Hebrew, was found. Since Massada fell in 73 CE, it was evident that this text was not a medieval text as was the one from the Genizah manuscripts, but very close to the date of the author's life. Again I published a paper, showing how the Massada text coincided with quotations in the Talmud and with the Cairo Genizah text. The words are practically identical, despite the interval of centuries between the times of the scribes.

The Book of Ben Sira had fallen into oblivion among Jews for many centuries. Even Rashi and the Tosefites at times could only guess what a certain passage in Ben Sira must have been like. But before their time, R. Saadia Gaon (9th century) did know the book and knew the correct full name of its author: Shimon ben Yeshua ben Elazar ben Sira. As to his time, the best clue is found in the book itself: In his description of the Yom Kippur service in the Temple, he refers to Shimon ben Yochanan the High Priest. In fact, his description of the High Priest has remained part and parcel of our own Yom Kippur liturgy until this day, as included in the description of the Avodah of the Musaf service. Most of our text in the Yom Kippur Machzor is lifted directly out of the Book of Ben Sira, unbeknownst to most of us!

Based on the identification of this High Priest in Ben Sira, scholars place the composition of the book at around the year 250 B.C.E.—preceding the earliest Dead Sea Scrolls by over 100 years. The book therefore makes up an important "link" between the last book of the Tenach and the rabbinical literature. Although in past years, the span between these two bodies of our literature was "terra incognita," we now are blessed with an enormously rich number of writings by our forefathers covering every century from the ending of the Tenach until the ending of the Talmud.

Here is a partial list of the passages in the rabbinical literature where Ben Sira is quoted: Bereshit Rabba 73:12 (Veyetse); Vayikra Rabba 33:1 (Behar); Bavli Yebamoth 63b and Sanhedrin 1000b; Tanhuma 8 (Vayishlach); Bavli Shabbat 11a; Avoth IV:4; Bavli Betsa 32b; Bavli Baba Metsia 112a; Tanchuma 10 (Miketz); Shemot Rabbah 7:21 (Beshalach); Yerushalmi Taanit III:6; Bavli Eruvin 54a; Bavli Chagiga 13a; Yerushalmi Chagiga II:1; Bereshit Rabba 8:9.

It is the latter three quotations, which have been followed for centuries by many of our sages, that are perhaps the best known teachings of Ben Sira. The following passage from Ben Sira, quoted in Bavli Chagiga 13a, is also quoted by Ramban in his introduction to the commentary on the Torah.

> Do not investigate things which are above you;
> Do not inquire into what is hidden from you.
> Only study what has been passed to you in inheritance;
> You have no share in the mysteries.

In view of the vast number of quotations from Ben Sira in our rabbinical literature, it is mystifying why at the same time our rabbis warned us against the book. Yerushalmi Sanhedrin X:1 lists among those who do not have a share in the World to Come, anyone who reads the Book of Ben Sira. In Bavli Sanhedrin 100b, Rav Yosef says it is forbidden to read (*l'mikri*) the Book of Ben Sira. Yet surprisingly, the same Rav Yosef also says the opposite: "The valuable words in Ben Sira you are permitted to expound (*darshinon*)."

To solve this contradiction I suggest that there is a basic difference between *mikra* and *drasha*. The former can only refer to books that have the sanctity of the Tenach itself (*mikra*). Since the Ben Sira was excluded from the Tenach, it was not permitted to "read" it in the manner that you read any of the biblical books. On the other hand, it was permitted to expound and interpret the same book (*midrash*), which in itself did not elevate the book to biblical sanctity, but merely to a book of wisdom.

Since my first identification of close links between these two bodies of Jewish writings, many more Ben Sira texts have been found and identified. In particular, the so-called Psalm Scroll from Cave 11 contains many passages that—although not bearing the name of Ben Sira—were identified by me as having been lifted straight out from Ben Sira. I published these findings in 1979 in Hebrew and in 1983 in English. I have since lectured at Hebrew University and Bar Ilan University on these important links. They bear out the rich and reliable traditions among Jews in handing over from generation to generation the wisdom of our forefathers and the rich inheritance of our religion. I am confident that future students will find many more links that bind us faithfully to the very words and writings of our ancestors, which will add to the glory that is Judaism.

# A Book Lover Caresses His Sefarim

My collection of the earliest printed Hebrew books has a special mission and message for us: The books represent the earliest printings of Hebrew books, mainly printed during a period when the Church, through pope after pope, tried to eradicate Judaism by destroying our literature. They knew that without Jewish education Judaism could not exist. In order to throttle its continuation, the supply of sacred books had to be abolished. This was done by *papal bulae* calling for the total confiscation of Hebrew books and consigning them to flames. Starting in 1243 in Paris, generation after generation of popes have attempted this diabolical scheme of cultural genocide.

It is therefore a near miracle that regardless of these restrictions and prohibitions, Jews risked everything to replenish the ravaged and pilloried treasures. Whenever a load of a few thousand Hebrew manuscripts was consigned to the flames by the ferocious Church, diligent, pious Jewish scribes rushed to replace them—often at great personal risk. The editions printed during these horrible papal reigns are therefore especially precious to me, since they demonstrate better than any other human manifestation the rebellion and resilience of the Jewish spirit in resisting any attempt to destroy us. Such destruction throughout history has often take physical form: *autos-da-fé* during the Inquisition; massacres during the Crusades; forced conversions; impossible living conditions in cramped Ghettos; or in our times, through gassings and cremations. Yet our physical and spiritual survival, our comeback in even greater strength than before, is the greatest testimony to our abiding faith and to the supernatural assistance by the Almighty, who guides our history.

A large part of my library represents printings made during the so-called Renaissance period. It is this period that produced the most hateful, ferocious anti-Semites among the popes, who knew no limit to their obsession with destroying Hebrew books. Among them, Pope Clement VIII (1592–1605) and Paul IV (1555–1559) were probably history's greatest haters of Jews, and their edicts directed against Hebrew books are therefore the most extreme. Yet it is during their reign in the end of the 16th century that many of the Hebrew books in this catalogue were printed—a real miracle and great testimony to Jewish self-sacrifice for our heritage and religion. These heroes of our culture deserve the homage that my library bestows, for they brought about the victory of Judaism over Christianity. My library shows how the Church failed in its diabolical efforts to snuff out Judaism. It is paradoxical that the Vatican today spreads the fable that the Renaissance popes, including Clement VIII, were "lovers of Hebrew books" and therefore collected them for the Vatican Library. Anyone reading the *bull* with its detailed instruction for the total eradication of Hebrew books, whether in the possession of Jews or non-Jews, and the severe punishments for anyone maintaining such books, knows that his *bull* makes a mockery of the Vatican claim.

From among 42 *incunabula* in our family library printed before 1500, *Sefer Ha-Iqarim* (Soncino 1485) is unique in that the ink of the censor has faded away sufficiently to show what it was he tried to shield from our impressionable eyes. The most interesting censored section is a description of the mid-summer and mid-winter (Christmas) holidays, which Josef Albo ascribes to ancient pagan rites that the Christians adopted. As a Scandinavian born in Sweden, I can testify to this conclusion. Mid-summer is celebrated throughout Scandinavia with dances and songs to the sun, while Christmas still bears the pagan name "Jul" (Yule in English).

*Kol Bo* (Italy 1490) contains a section taken from the Tashbatz of R. Meir mi-Rothenburg. The book contains many other works and follows the pattern of some manuscripts of the time, which combine various works in one volume. In this it reminds me of one of my most cherished manuscripts, dated 1313, containing not only a *machzor*, which constitutes half of the manuscript, but also a large variety of works ranging from R. Nachshon Gaon to the contemporaries of R. Meir of Rothenburg. Thus, it contains the Tashbatz with several hundred paragraphs that I published in a study for Mekitze Nirdamim.

I was of course thrilled to discover parts of the Tashbatz inside the *Kol Bo*, too, but I soon found that it was a reduced version with only some 60 paragraphs.

I am particularly proud of the *incunabula* of works of Maimonides in my library, since our Foundation is deeply involved in research on hundreds of manuscript fragments of his *Mishneh Torah*, mainly from Yemen but also from Spain. This work has been going on for several years and consists of comparing these many fragments from the Middle Ages with our known printed editions and listing all the variants. My son, Jamie, *z"l*, was deeply interested in the works of Maimonides and as an undergraduate student had already published a study on Love of G-d and Fear of G-d in Maimonides' writings. We placed a plaque dedicated to Jamie on the tombstone of David ha-Naggid, the grandson of Maimonides, in Tiberias. (I recovered this tombstone in Cairo, which had been stolen from Tiberias in 1932.)

When it comes to the prints of 231 books after 1500 and before 1600, I find it extremely rewarding to study some of the colophons and other notations reflecting on the lives and feelings of the printers' proofreaders or patrons as well as the owners.

The *Arba Turim* (Augsburg, 1541) bears a notation that it belonged at one time to the "chaste and beautiful widow, Leah, the daughter of Moshe."

The book, *Meturgeman* (Isny, 1541), relates in the colophon how the printer felt the urgency to complete the printing of the book, since he felt he was getting older and older, with his eyesight diminishing. Hence, he feared that he would soon be unable to continue his work. He wished to end his days in his native Venice together with his aging wife: "I will not move my feet from her any more. May she close my eyes, and I will close her eyes. Only death will divide us from one another."

In the colophon to the book *Shaarey Dura* (Basel 1599) the printer expresses his hope that anyone seeing the printed book "will put forth gold from their pockets... not only for the price of the book but even double the value in price."

The *Machzor Rome* (Bologna, 1546) contains a prayer by the printers to their public in moving words: "Unto you, members of the congregation of holy men, holy seed, we raise our voices saying, 'Please buy our holy work at its full value, although its value is priceless. No homeowner, whether rich or poor, can afford to stay without this *machzor* and its commentaries because only through it can you learn true fear of G-d and the meaning of our holy men. It will be a merit in this world and the next.' "

The many words printed by Daniel Bomberg in my library are of course of special interest to students of these famous printings. Although a Christian, he lists his name in the Jewish fashion, as "Daniel ben Corniel Bomberg of Antwerp, who now lives in Venice, the great city. . . and because of my love for the city, I have appointed wise and precious, artistic men for the printing in a perfect and complete manner." He dates his work by the year, according to the rule of the different Doges; for example, "Year 16 of the Doge Leonardo Loreano the year 278, the 27th Kislev" (1517).

We can never be thankful enough to Daniel Bomberg. He invested and risked his money in printing a mass of Hebrew books at a time when Jews were not willing to do so (although this might have been the case because the Jews were afraid of the papal prohibition and confiscations). Could it be that Bomberg "fronted" for the Jews? Next, we owe thanks to him for standardizing the pagination of all tractates of the Babylonian Talmud, forever. Unfortunately, there was no Bomberg to do the same for the Palestinian Talmud, which therefore has remained without a standard set of pages.

The lament of printers is sometimes heard about the poor quality of the texts from which they had to copy. Thus, the proofreader for Bomberg in one instance—SC 50—complains that although the text offered him was supposed to be flawless, he found 27 mistakes, while in the Tosefta there "was no house in which there was no dead."

Another proofreader, Recanto (Bomberg, Venice 1523), was more philosophical, "Since the purpose of man's creation is to reach perfection, which results from the passage from the potential to the actual, in the intellectual conception, I therefore determined to proofread this work printed by Daniel Bomberg."

Some colophons demonstrate that sometimes very few copies of a work existed and that a particular work—even the most important works in our literature—risked being completely lost if it had not been printed at that time. For example, *Sifre* (Bomberg, Venice 1546) tell us: "The books *Sifra* and *Sifrey* were extremely rare and their memory was about to be extinguished, if it had not been for the prince of medical doctors, R. Yaakov Manten, the Spaniard who decided to publish from oblivion for the benefit of the public the books that were hidden in his treasure."

Three volumes of Maimonide's *Mishneh Torah*, printed in Venice, are particularly important because of the running marginal notes, handwritten by the great scholars in Hebron in the 18th century. I have attempted to publish these glosses by themselves. Interestingly, these were the scholars whose names also appear on letters of introduction for emissaries traveling from Hebron to Europe and the Caribbean. I own such letters of introduction printed in Italian and Portuguese, respectively, introducing R. Hayim David Azulay on his trips abroad for the benefit of the old Hebron community. In one of these volumes, a temporary bill of divorce was written by hand and given by Benjamin ben Yaakov to his wife, Luna, to go into effect if her husband did not return from overseas in 12 months. This document reflects the hazards that the pious emissaries of Hebron undertook on their voyages for their fellow Jews.

The danger of plunder of books is also shown in some cases. Thus, in *Klaley Hatalmud* (Mantua 1593) the printer laments the loss of most of his library, "I bring this book to print, which remained to me as a remnant from many other books and other property that the Ishmaelites [Arabs] in Egypt consumed in their inequities, criminality and trickery."

Printers also publicized the "copyright" protection that rabbis would give them: "The rabbis and leaders of Constantinople issued a strict rule that this book not be reprinted for 10 consecutive years. If a Christian should print it, no Jew would be permitted to buy it."

Some prints were dedicated to the king; for example, a book printed in Cracow is dedicated to King Siegmund Augustus, along with blessing for his royal reign. Other books were printed under King Siegmund III and under King Philip.

Prints from Riva de Trento are particularly dear to me because I cannot forget the breathless beauty of this little Italian town on the deep blue Lago di Garda. In 1928, when I was not even 6 years old, our family spent Pesach in Merano and took a car trip to Riva—at that time a rare way to travel. I never forgot the cry of exhilaration that was let out at the sight of that beautiful lake. In Riva I remember the miniature mandolin made of amber that my father bought for my mother there. Only many, many years later did I learn that the cardinal in Riva had sponsored a Hebrew printing press. In fact, it was here that a work by Josef Caro was printed in his own lifetime.

An unnamed later owner wrote these heart-rending words in the margin on page 67: "Woe and woe unto me. Woe unto my soul. I never thought that my home would be destroyed, and the wicked Neolog [the Hungarian term for reform] men would enter and defile my entire family. May G-d have mercy on me speedily."

Early Salonica prints are interesting in that the censor was especially ferocious in purging out not only possible Jewish references to Christianity but also Moslem reference to Ottoman rulers. Thus in *Yalkut Shimoni* (Salonika 1523) the censor painted over the name of the Sultan, whose name included Abdullah!

If you love your books, you can never get bored with them. Not only is the content a permanent stimulation to study, but knowledge of such details as their date, printing place, names of typesetters and proofreaders, and the personal notes of printers and owners, are an inexhaustible source of discoveries and information. No wonder that, as a book owner, you develop almost personal affinity and love for your *sefarim*. You often feel like caressing them, as a beloved possession. At that point you know that you are a real book lover.

# Haggadah Thoughts

I would like to share with my readers some thoughts which come to mind in preparation for the *seder*, based on sections of the *Haggadah*.

### *"Ma'aseh B'Rabbi Eliezer"* It Happened that Rabbi Eliezer...

I once heard that the Rov, Rabbi J. B. Soloveitchik, said that when he sits down to learn, he sees Rashi before him on his right, Rabbeinu Tam on his left, and the Rambam in front of him. In their presence the learning must be on the highest level.

The Haggadah, in the same way, endeavors to put us into a similar mood. By invoking the exalted personalities of five great rabbis and relating their way of celebrating the seder, we are one with them in spirit. Our seder must reach a high level of understanding and experience if we are in the literal company of the greatest of our teachers! No better introduction to the Haggadah could have been composed.

### *"Vayoreiu Otanu Hamitzrim"* The Egyptians Pictured Us as Bad...

Is the correct translation of this phrase "And the Egyptians treated us badly"? No, the correct meaning is that "the Egyptians *pictured us as bad*." In other words, they maligned us.

This is borne out by the fact that the Haggadah's proof for this statement is taken from Pharaoh's first appeal for the enslavement of the Jews: "*Hava nitchakma lo*," "Come, let us deal wisely with them." This plan could only be put into effect by launching a hate-propaganda campaign against the Jews, based on an alleged danger which the Jews represented.

Hitler, too, could not have gotten his people to participate in the physical destruction of six million Jews had he not, through such thugs as Goebbels and Streicher, previously pictured the Jews as dangerous vermin.

### *"V'Nosaf Gam Hu Al Sonenu"* And They Will Also Join Our Enemies...

One of the oldest and most sinister arguments of anti-Semites has been the accusation that Jews are disloyal and are a potential danger to the state's security.

Pharaoh, by using the word "*gam*," "also," implied that such a thing had happened before. Indeed, Egypt had seen the invasion of Semitic shepherd kings, the so-called Hyksos, who, once inside Egypt, took over the kingship and ruled Egypt for a long period of time. Only at the beginning of the 18th dynasty, around 1500 B.C.E., did the Egyptians rid themselves of the foreigners. The Jews came to Egypt about this time, so it made political sense for Pharaoh to invoke that relatively fresh memory of other Semites who had rebelled. Of course, no plan was further from the minds of the Jewish slaves than to make themselves rulers over Egypt; their only aim was to return to their own land, which had been promised them by G-d.

However, if we look at our history we find the same incident repeated again and again. For example, in the preamble to the Purim story, found in Chapter 4 of the Book of Ezra, we find that the Samaritans wrote a petition to Achashveirosh in which they pointed out that if the Jewish State were rebuilt, the king would lose almost half of his kingdom and the equivalent in tax receipts. The Jewish State, they said, had often rebelled against foreign rulers, whether Assyrian or Babylonian. This malicious lie convinced Achashveirosh to stop the rebuilding of Jerusalem and the Temple. It took much doing, and the efforts of Mordechai and Esther, to achieve the lifting of that prohibition and the resumption of the rebuilding of the Jewish State. The lie of our enemies became apparent in good time.

In more recent history, no better example can be found than the period of Napoleon. In my recent article on the history of Messianism, I quoted the extraordinary appeal by Napoleon for the reestablishment of a Jewish State in 1799. About this I received a letter from Mazal Linenberg, a highly respected historian and the sister of former President Yitzchak Navon:

"The period of Napoleon's campaign in the Holy Land was a very troubled and dangerous time for the Jews. The Moslems suspected them of being spies and traitors and of planning to join Napoleon. There was a rumor circulating that ten to twelve thousand Jews had joined his army. The danger and threat from the Turks and the Arab population were more imminent than the salvation offered by Napoleon.

"For a whole year, beginning from June 1798, the Jews were oppressed and in dire straits, and had to prove their loyalty to the Turks by helping to fortify the walls of Jerusalem. In the summer of 1799, as soon as it was possible to do so, Jerusalem's Jewish community sent several rabbis as emissaries to different countries to seek much-needed financial help. Among them were Rabbi Yona Sa'adia Navon, my father's great-grandfather, and Rabbi Yona Moshe Navon, his cousin, and later Chief Rabbi from 1836–40."

The ironic part of this tragedy is that at the very same time the Turks were accusing Jews in the Holy Land of being disloyal spies and soldiers for the French Emperor, over in Russia, Jews were being accused of spying for and supporting the Turks! It was in connection with such accusations that the Baal Hatanya was imprisoned on two occasions.

A parallel to this type of slander in current affairs is the campaign being waged by the Palestinians, Israel's sworn enemies, to petition the United Nations and governments around the world for support in their assertion that the Jewish State should be dismantled, based on various utterly false accusations.

In brief, Pharaoh's age-old call for anti-Semitism—on the basis of a charge of disloyalty and a perceived threat to the security of the state—has accompanied us throughout history. It all bears out the traditional saying, *"ma'ase avot siman labanim,"* meaning that the history of our forefathers is a prototype of our own.

### *"Hakodosh Baruch Hu Matzileinu Miyadam"* The Holy One, Blessed Be He, Saved Us from Their Hands...

Our history is filled with incidents—many known and many unknown—where we were saved by the Almighty at the last moment from total destruction.

A study of the history of the Second World War reveals instances in which our very existence was threatened, yet we were inexplicably saved. One such moment was the situation on the beaches of Dunkirk, in June 1940:

The Allied armies had collapsed, mainly because of the Belgian king's cowardly surrender to Germany on March 28, 1940 (a date I cannot forget, for on that day I arrived in the United States as a young boy). The English army, called the "British Expeditionary Force," was scrambling to go home. Over 300,000 men and their equipment crowded the beaches of Dunkirk, just south of the Belgian border, waiting for large and small craft to ferry them back to England.

The Germans, stunned, stood nearby, ready to swoop down and wipe out the English forces. But General Rundstedt, the German Chief of Staff, had to get instructions from Hitler himself to start the attack. The order never came. Nobody, to this day, can understand why Hitler hesitated to destroy the only military barrier between himself and victory over England—for without those men, England could not have defended herself. And so, in a miraculous phenomenon unheard of in naval history, the entire British Army was saved by an armada of large and small ships of all sorts and descriptions.

On those ships was riding not only the fate of the civilized world, but also that of the Jews of Britain and of Eretz Yisrael. The hope for a Jewish homeland, promised by Britain in 1917, would have been snuffed out if those brave English boys had not made it home. It was the kind of historic salvation which can only come from *Hakodosh Baruch Hu* Himself.

### ...And Saved Us from Their Atomic Weapons

I recently came across another great miracle of salvation which occurred during World War II, to which we were all totally oblivious while it was unfolding. In a recently published book, *Heisenberg's War*, the author describes the desperate scramble of both Germans and Allies to win the race for producing the first atom bomb. Hitler had forced all the great Jewish minds among the leading physicists of Germany to emigrate, most of whom came to the United States. Not only Einstein, but a host of other brilliant scientists arrived as refugees in the U.S. But there were those who remained, dedicated Nazis and admirers of Hitler, who worked feverishly to solve the scientific and technical problems involved in creating a workable atomic bomb. This would be the ultimate "secret weapon" with which Hitler would wipe out the entire civilized world.

Especially after the Nazis' crushing defeat at Stalingrad and in North Africa, Hitler egged his scientists on to produce a secret weapon that would offset the losses on the battlefields. Because of their close connection to the German physicists, and the information they gained through very clever intelligence, the Jewish refugees were up-to-date on German advances, and were able to convince President Roosevelt to launch a monumental program to produce an atom bomb ahead of Hitler. Roosevelt accepted their recommendations, which is how billions of dollars were set aside for this fantastic project.

If one looks through the list of the scientists involved, they were mostly Jews—starting with Oppenheimer, Teller, Niels Bohr, Fermi, Lise Meitner, Szilard and many others. Their zeal to help the Allies win over the Hitlerite evil motivated and inspired them to do the unthinkable: to harness the unknown, unexplored, vast force locked in the secret chambers of the atom!

Meanwhile, Germany slowed down its efforts to build the bomb, either because they did not have the resources or because, as some theorize today, some of her own scientists—including the leading German expert in nuclear science, Nobel Prize winner Werner Heisenberg—somehow sabotaged those monumental efforts. Hitler lost his enthusiasm for the project, and it was shelved. The world, and the Jews in it, were saved in that moment from total destruction.

This, in my mind, was a miracle of no lesser proportion than the many other miracles of salvation in our history. So, during the seder, we can sing in deep gratitude: *"Vayifr'keinu mitzoreinu, ki l'olam chasdo,"* "And He delivered us from our oppressors, for His kindness is everlasting."

## From Out of Disorder, Order (Seder): Chad Gadya, One Little Goat

The word "seder," which is not originally a Hebrew word, but Aramaic, has come to mean the night when we read the Haggadah. It means to "put things in order." This meaning is learned from such verses as Leviticus 1:7–8: "Aaron's sons shall place fire on the altar, and arrange (*archu*) wood on the fire. Aaron's sons shall then arrange the cut pieces (of the sacrifice)... on top of the wood which is on the altar fire." The Targum translates "archu" as "*vi'sadrun,*" which has the same root as the word "seder." In other words, "seder" means to put things into their proper order, neatly arranged.

When we look objectively at the Haggadah we must admit that it represents a mass of seemingly unconnected passages and portions, jumping from one subject and style to another. There certainly seems to be no logical order nor symmetry. Its sections do not appear to be "neatly arranged," nor "put into their proper order." Why then the name "seder," if what we really encounter is a state of "no-seder"?

I think the true answer only comes at the very end of the seder, in the popular song *Chad Gadya*:

If we look at each of the ten situations the song mentions separately, there is no way of knowing that they are connected to each other in any kind of order or logical sequence. What is so special about an ox drinking water? Similarly, there is nothing seemingly significant in a stick being burnt by fire, or a dog biting a cat. It is only when the author puts them all together that we discern a logical sequence, in which all of the insignificant steps in the "ladder" add up to one goal: Utopia, and the Messianic Era, when G-d finally smites the Angel of Death, and total peace reigns on earth. To reach that goal, we had to follow the seemingly unconnected steps linking the kid, the cat, the dog, the stick, and so forth. The same applies to the Hagaddah as a whole.

The lesson, I think, is that even seemingly disconnected incidents in our history—involving Jewish communities totally isolated from one another, the ups and downs in our fortunes, Golden Ages here, meager times elsewhere, migrations to this or that country, good children, bad children, loyalty, disloyalty through assimilation and so on—all move toward one destiny: the final, full redemption of the Jewish people.

And that is the message of Pesach, as embodied in the fifth cup of wine, the cup of the Prophet Elijah, the "Cup of *Geulah*."

# The Publication of Three Outstanding Books:

## Ohel Hayim Catalogue Volume 3

The amassing and building of a library is more than just a book lover's hobby. It is, in fact, our 613th Mitzvah. The *Sefer HaChinuch* lists as the last of all Mitzvot the command to maintain in every Jewish home a library in which Torah scholars can study and write books.

In past centuries such a library was a necessity to preserve and defend as much as possible our Jewish heritage from the attacks of the Church. But today, the need is equally great, because of the importance of collecting and gathering our sacred books which have been dispersed in so many countries that have suffered persecutions. It is therefore extremely important to catalogue or take inventory of those books each library holds. The more elaborate and detailed such a catalogue is, the greater the value and benefit to collectors and students. Catalogues are especially needed by libraries that can make use of them as reference works for students everywhere.

A catalogue has another mission: providing a clear definition and character to the collection it represents. By studying a catalogue you learn about the owner of the library and his aspirations and interests. Therefore, each catalogue represents another character. Unfortunately there are not many catalogues in existence. In my own case I was inspired by *Ohel David*, the 1932 catalogue of the Sir David Sasson Library in England, which introduced the practice of featuring of a few facsimile reproductions of some selected pages which Sir David placed in the back of each of the two volumes. I decided that in the case of manuscripts, one page of each and every work should be shown in facsimile form to give the student an idea of the script and style used by the author.

One feature by which a catalogue can be judged is the number of indexes listing towns, authors, year of authorship, owner, censors, etc. The first volume of *Ohel Hayim* covered kabbalistic manuscripts, written over several centuries and throughout many different countries, and contained 18 indexes and one facsimile reproduction for each work, not at the end of the book, as in the case of *Ohel David*, but always opposite the description of the manuscript. The volume contains 325 pages.

Volume Two of *Ohel Hayim* covers several hundred biblical manuscripts, ranging from the 10th to the 19th century, with a heavy component of Yemenite manuscripts, which are typical for their "super-linear" punctuation (*niqqud elyon*). This means that the vowels are written above, not below the letters. It contains 449 pages and has 44 indexes—an amazingly high number. A facsimile reproduction follows each manuscript description.

Now I can announce the publication of Volume Three of the *Ohel Hayim* catalogue. While the previous two volumes were edited by top Israeli scholars, the third volume was edited by Professor Shimon Iakerson, a Russian librarian from St. Petersburg. Volume Three contains 337 pages. Part One describes incunabula—books printed before 1500—and Part Two describes books printed before 1600.

Several plates show facsimiles of the most characteristic prints. Here the most important features described are the *shaar* (title page) and the colophon, the paragraphs on the final page, which usually gives interesting historical and biographical information.

In all volumes of *Ohel Hayim* I have written an introduction in English and Hebrew. In addition, a research director for our foundation, Professor E. Hurwitz, has written introductions. The joy in seeing such a magnificent catalogue, printed beautifully in Israel on deluxe paper, gives the student a sense of exhilaration and pride in the many generations who owned these books. It is estimated that books from the 16th century may have passed through the possession of 20 to 30 generations. Think of all the suffering that these owners went through to study from these works—and defend them from enemy attacks.

I am particularly proud of the books from the mentioned periods, during which pope after pope issued orders to seize every Hebrew book and deliver them all to the Church for burning on pain of death or—in the case of Christian owners—of excommunication. The survival of these ancient books shows that Jews were willing to risk their lives to print and thereby preserve our sacred heritage. I certainly hope that many libraries, students, and collectors will take advantage of this highly educational and inspiring catalogue.

## *The Return of Cultural Treasures* by Professor Jeanette Greenfield

Some years ago, an Australian Jewish scholar, Professor Jeanette Greenfield, wrote a book on cultural treasures that for one reason or another were stolen and removed from their country of origin. She described how many countries, including Greece and Iceland, have successfully reclaimed such treasures. In some cases such efforts were blocked. When I saw the book I was surprised that she wrote nothing about the fate of stolen Jewish cultural treasure. Over the past years I have cooperated with Professor Greenfield in making up for the omission from her first book. The result is now in: She has just published her second edition in which a very substantial chapter is devoted to the stolen Hebrew manuscripts held by the Vatican and my campaign to recover them through the Committee for the Recovery of Jewish Manuscripts of which I am the chairman.

It is a fascinating book, fully describing the history of Vatican book burning and anti-Semitic edicts from 1243 to 1797. In the process, hundreds of thousands of precious Hebrew books were burned or cannibalized—their parchment pages used as book bindings. The obsession of the Catholic Church in destroying Hebrew books was of course the result of the Christian drive to eradicate Judaism. The Church knew that without books Judaism would cease to exist. This obsession always reminds me of a Shakespeare play, *The Tempest*, where a deformed and demented slave, Caliban, conspires to destroy his master by way of burning his books:

> [T]hou mayst brain him
> Having first seized his books. . .
> Remember first to possess his books;
> for without them he's but a sot, as I am. . .
> Burn but his books.

The fury of the Church was tremendous in seeing Jews from earliest childhood fully literate and learned in comparison with the totally ignorant, unlearned Christian masses. They were very much inspired by envy in their obsession with eradicating Judaism.

Professor Greenfield describes in detail the efforts of the Committee to Recover Hebrew Manuscripts that survived the spiritual and cultural genocide perpetrated by the Vatican. She strongly rebuffs the attempts of a handful to defend the Vatican and, instead, joins in the chorus of voices calling for the return of the manuscripts to be placed in the National Library in Jerusalem. She also invokes the spirit of Nostra Astate—by which the Church undertook to seek atonement for the centuries of unspeakable crimes against Jews—by demanding such a small gesture of conciliation as returning these stolen, sacred works to their rightful owners—the Jewish people.

Professor Greenfield is collaborating with me and other interested persons to produce a TV documentary on the history of the Vatican Hebrew manuscripts and the attempts to recover them. I am personally very grateful to Professor Greenfield for prominently mentioning my own efforts to bring this important campaign to the urgent attention of Christian and Jewish officials and scholars and for giving me credit for the progress made to date in this effort.

The book is highly recommended as a fascinating course in the history of our national treasures and the fight to recover them. The case of Hebrew treasures is unique. Take for example the case of the theft in 1911 of the famous painting, "Mona Lisa," by Leonardo da Vinci and similar thefts that took place because the thief loved the painting or work of art to such an extent that he could not tolerate it being held by others. But in the case of the Vatican thieves, they wanted to destroy the owners of the treasures by withholding their most needed tools for their continuity as a special people.

## The Temple Scroll—Revised Edition

When the Dead Sea scrolls were discovered in the late 1940s and early 1950s, it was known in Israel that the most important and longest scroll was hidden by an Arab named Kando, in Bethlehem. Until the Six-Day War, the scroll was inaccessible to Jews. On the first or second day of the Six-Day War, Yigal Yadin, the great warrior/scholar, took a jeep with a few armed soldiers and drove down to Bethlehem to visit Kando. He could have forced him to surrender the scroll, but he paid a reasonable price for the great prize. He also immediately set about publishing the scroll, which he named the "Temple Scroll," because it describes the Temple of a messianic time. It is also unique in that it is written in the first person, as if G-d Himself is speaking. It was first thought that it was a "different" version of the Torah, but it was soon found that it was a collection of laws stipulated by the Dead Sea community. I myself was among the very first to publish findings showing that the community that had produced this immense scroll was that of the Sadduccees, not the Essenes. I also found that these Sadduccees were much more *machmir* (stringent) in their observance of the Mitzvot than the Perushim (Pharisees) who produced the Mishnah.

Although Yadin's work was a herculean accomplishment, later technology has made it possible to make additional, better readings of the text. And now Professor Elisha Qimron, with my help, has published an entirely new addition of the Temple Scroll which throws light on passages that previously could not be properly understood. As the scroll contains many laws, it serves as the best material for making comparisons between the Sadduccean and Pharisean laws (*halachot*). The Megillat Taanit , a pre-Mishnaic work, mentions a holiday that was instituted by the sages of the Mishnah for the day when the laws of the Sadduccees were burned. It is likely that this refers to a work similar to the Temple Scroll.

If I may be immodest for a moment, I would like to share with you the gracious words of Professor Qimron in his introduction: "This work would never have been realized without the encouragement and support of Dr. Manfred R. Lehmann. Dr. Lehmann, besides his many other pursuits, is also a fine scholar who has contributed much to the study of the Dead Sea scrolls in general and to the Temple Scroll in particular. He has published no less than 20 scientific articles on Dead Sea Scrolls. This publication is made in memory of the son of Dr. and Mrs. Lehmann, Chaim Menachem (Jamie) 1950–1982."

This work will be widely admired and studied, and I am proud to have played a role in producing it.

I hope that my readers will share in the joy that has inspired me in seeing the publication of these three outstanding contributions to Jewish scholarship and pride.

# The Rambam as Revealed Through His *Teshuvot* (Responsa)

In 1862 a remarkable society of scholars was founded in Europe, dedicated to the publication of precious medieval Hebrew manuscripts which had not been printed before. The society was appropriately called *Mekitsei Nirdamim* (Rousers of the Slumberers). The Society has just celebrated its 130th year, and can look back to the publication of innumerable outstanding works without which we would be greatly impoverished today.

The Society is headed by a board of scholars from various countries. Some of the past board members were: Chief Rabbi Nathan M. Adler, of London; Rabbi S. D. Luzzato, of Rome; Rabbi S. Ganzfried, of Ungvar; Dr. Haim Brody, of Prague and Jerusalem; A. Berliner, of Berlin; S. Y. Agnon, of Jerusalem; and Prof. E. Uhrbach, of Jerusalem. My late father subscribed to their publications while I was still very young, and I remember the radiance on his face whenever a package came to our home with a new *sefer* published by Mekitsei Nirdamim.

You can well imagine how honored I felt when, a few years ago, I was called to become a member of the Board of Mekitsei Nirdamim, after I contributed a study of a manuscript, dated around 1313, with the rulings of R. Meir of Rutenberg, which the Society published.

The Society, which has been headquartered in Jerusalem since 1934, has just published a very important work: *280 Teshuvot (Responsa) of the Rambam*, in four volumes. The Rambam (1135–1204) wrote most of these *Teshuvot* in Judeo-Arabic, and therefore they were published in Arabic as well as in their Hebrew translation. These *Teshuvot* are a fabulous source of personal encounters with the Rambam, through which we can ascertain a much more direct, intimate portrait of the master than through any of his other works. We all know his major works: his *Commentary on the Mishnah*, *Moreh Nevuchim*, *Mishneh Torah*, *Sefer HaMitzvot*, as well as his writings on logic, medicine, astronomy, music and many more subjects. But nowhere does one feel so directly in his presence as when one reads the exchanges between him and his petitioners from all corners of the world of that time. What comes out is the portrait of an immensely warm, caring leader, often lenient in his decisions, but more often than not, brusquely direct and sharp. Most of his decisions and adjudications are brief, consisting of just a few words. Even when they are lengthy, they are never as long and intricate as the *Teshuvot* of later rabbis. All of his *Teshuvot* were intended to instruct the entire Jewish people with the highest authority.

Here are a number of the *sheylot* (questions) placed before the Rambam, and his replies:

Several cases involve people who lent money to businessmen who sailed to India to buy silk, but their ship sank and they drowned. The creditors, with their promissory notes in hand, went to the orphans to collect the debts. In case after case of such voyages to India, the Rambam does not once inject a word about his own personal tragedy which befell him when his brother drowned, and all his goods were lost, when his ship sank. His brother had provided the Rambam with a comfortable living. After this tragedy the Rambam had to eke out a living by working at the Royal Palace in Cairo as a physician.

From several cases we see that many Jews owned precious books, which they considered among their most valuable possessions. A book is sometimes called *ktab* in Arabic, or *sefer* in Hebrew, but in the cases before the Rambam the Arabic word *metsachaf* is used, which in my opinion should be rendered *mitzchaf* in Hebrew, meaning a very voluminous, heavy, handwritten book, a term also used to refer to very large Biblical manuscripts, many of which were written at the academy of the Ben Asher dynasty in Tiberias.

In the *Teshuvot* we find the names of cities and countries where the Jews traveled for business or family affairs, and from where the inquiries came: Baghdad, Aleppo, Alexandria, Sicily, Tunis, Iraq, Syria and India. These Egyptian towns are mentioned: Cairo, Alexandria, Fustat, Mahalla, Tanis, Minyat Zifta, Dimanhur and Bilbais.

There are other historic glimpses we can obtain from the *Teshuvot*: As mentioned above, several of them refer to pirates who captured vessels and merchandise. We often forget that this was an ever-present danger lurking over every merchant seafarer for centuries until relatively recent times. Legal implications arose from the capture of Jewish women who were later redeemed, and the need to determine the status of stolen goods offered for sale by the pirates, etc.

Several inquiries concern commerce. For example, what is the law if a loan is given in a form of currency which later is devalued. The Rambam's answer: At the time of the loan it should be clearly stipulated whether the lender will be satisfied to receive his money back in the same currency, or whether repayment should be made in its equivalent, at whatever the rate of exchange is at the time the loan is returned.

Some cases reflect the pettiness of the petitioners, as in a case of two cantors, who initially were good friends and fair partners in their services to their community, but who later had a falling-out. Thereafter, one refused to sing in the presence of the other. The Rambam took the question very seriously, and admonished the community elders to issue their own decision as to who should sing for them, and when.

In another case, he was told that every Shabbat the head of a synagogue would deliver a sermon with his comments on the weekly Torah portion. On one Shabbat, a member of the synagogue, a learned man, suddenly cried out that what the speaker had said was nonsense, and no one should listen to such worthless words. The question was: Should this man be punished for the interruption and embarrassment he caused? The Rambam answered that unless the head of the community insisted on pressing for legal action, "it is best to close your eyes to the incident and ignore it." But, as in several of his written decisions, he concluded with the words "Safeguard the honor of the Torah, because the Torah and the mitzvot are a light unto us!"

One inquiry concerns a *shochet* who was found to be lax in his religious observances, and in fact was caught with stolen meat. May he continue to act as a butcher for his community? The Rambam replied: "It is public knowledge among gentiles that we only entrust our most honored members, whether our judges or our emissaries before G-d, with slaughtering for us. In fact, the nations envy us for maintaining such high standards. Therefore, a man of such low standing must not be allowed to slaughter for you in public, unless he performs total repentance. Otherwise there will be a profaning of G-d. However, he may slaughter for any one of you in private."

One inquirer asked whether it is permitted to decorate a synagogue with designs, and whether a synagogue may have windows. The Rambam answered that decorations and designs are only a distraction when one prays—and he adds a very personal note, "I close my eyes when I pray." As for the second part of the query, he writes that windows are desirable, because we can imagine seeing through them all the way to Jerusalem!

It appears from some *Teshuvot* that the Rambam had an aversion to liturgical *piyutim* added to the regular synagogue service. "Some of these poems were written by poets and not by *talmidei chachamim*, and their content is often alien to the meaning of the prayers. They divert the worshippers' attention so that sometimes they begin chatting and laughing in the middle of the chanting, since they do not consider these poems part of the service."

He admonished his petitioners to maintain the strictest decorum during synagogue services. For the Shabbat and festival services, especially for *mussaf*, he preferred that the cantor immediately commence the *amidah* with a loud voice, thereby obviating the congregation's own silent prayer, because he found that people usually took only the silent prayer seriously, and they started chatting and chuckling during the loud repetition. "However, during weekday services the repetition of the *amidah* should take place after the silent *amidah*." Decorum during services and full concentration during prayer were his guiding principles.

When he was asked which kind of ink should be used for writing a *Sefer Torah*, he recalled how he himself had produced the ink when he wrote his own *Sefer Torah*. (In *Mishneh Torah* he also recalls how he wrote his own Torah—a mitzvah he evidently was especially proud to have performed.) One of his longest *Teshuvot* contains a detailed description of how to measure the lines in a Torah so that they comply with each of the scribal laws. Again, all this is based on his own personal experience. He even reports that the exact length of his Torah scroll, excluding the margins at the beginning and end, was 1362 finger-breadths (a detail not mentioned in *Mishneh Torah*)!

When a questioner asked him about a certain book authored by a Karaite sage, he brusquely answered: "You must destroy this book, and purge its memory from you. This will be a great mitzvah, as it is written, 'You shall not mention the name of an alien god.'" One of the Rambam's great historic accomplishments, together with Saadiah Gaon, was to put a total stop to the Karaite heresy, which, after his death, dwindled to a very insignificant number of followers.

The Rambam was faced with problems caused not only by his Moslem neighbors, but also by the Christians who occupied Eretz Yisrael after the Crusades. He was, therefore, well-versed in Christianity. His references to Jesus and Mohammed were purged from all early printed editions of *Mishneh Torah* produced in Europe. I have a 1509 edition, however, printed in Constantinople, which was not censored.

The Rambam's greatest elaboration on Christianity is found in his famous *Iggeret Teman* (Epistle to Yemen), written to his loyal followers in Yemen, which evidently escaped the attention of the Christian censors. In it he writes that "Jesus was a Jew, even though his father was a *Goy*. Only his mother was Jewish." The Rambam did not accept the Christian Gospels' contorted and contradictory genealogies alleging that Jesus' father was a Jew named Joseph. Instead, Jews have always known that Mary, an unmarried woman, had a baby fathered by a Roman pagan soldier.

The Rambam in his *Teshuvot* gives a correct account of the two types of Christianity: the one that Jesus and his contemporaries practiced, and the one that was created later, without much Jewish content. Interestingly, in one of his *Teshuvot* the Rambam permits teaching the Bible to a Christian, but not to a Moslem, because Christians believe that the Jewish Bible was G-d-given, while the Moslems declare it to be a corruption of the Koran. Therefore it is easier for a Christian to realize the errors in his religion and return to the truth of Judaism than it is for a Moslem.

One petitioner asked whether one should sit or stand during the reading of the Ten Commandments, in view of the fact that the *Minim* declare the Ten Commandments to have greater sanctity than the rest of the Torah. The Rambam decided in favor of sitting, because to stand would "lead to harming our faith;" we must not allow any portion of the Torah to appear superior to any other. He adds that *Minim* are not only Karaites, who deny the Oral Torah, but any who deny that the Torah, in its entirety, was given by G-d at Mt. Sinai. Thus, Christians can also be counted among the *Minim*, since they deny the Oral Torah. The Rambam added an interesting admonition: "Don't let your conduct be guided by a desire to comply with everyone else. If your neighbors are all sick, you would not infect yourself to become sick like them, but you would try to heal the sick."

In an interesting response to Rabbi Ovadiah, a righteous convert—probably the famous Norman Christian convert by that name known from our literature—the Rambam wrote that a convert, like any Jew, may use all the names for G-d: "our Father," "our King," "the G-d of our forefather Abraham," because a convert has taken the G-d of the Jews as his own. However, he should not say "who has taken *us* out of Egypt," or "who has performed miracles for *our* forefathers," and the like, because that would be historically incorrect.

One petitioner was confused as to whether Moslems are considered idol worshippers. The Rambam explained: "The Moslems are not at all idol worshippers. Every vestige of pagan religion has been purged from their hearts, and they acknowledge One G-d, although in ancient days their shrine [in Mecca] was a pagan one. But that is irrelevant today. However, they commit other errors, which I am afraid to commit to writing." In his *Iggeret Teman* the Rambam goes so far as to say that the Moshiach will come when Islam is widely spread throughout the world.

The Rambam was rigorously uncompromising where the laws of *taharat hamishpacha* (family purity) were concerned. In one long *Teshuva* he spoke out harshly against those who had relented in the observance of our purity laws, and adopted the Karaite practice of only having water poured on women (in modern terms, taking a shower), rather than immersing in a *mikvah* at the end of their *niddah* period. He ordered all rabbis to announce in their synagogues that whoever violates the laws of women's purity, and fails to use a *mikvah*, will be dealt with harshly. Such women are to be divorced, and they forfeit their prenuptial property rights under their *ketuba*. Also, such transgressors—the husbands as well as the wives—are to be placed under a *cherem* of the gravest sort. Of all his *Teshuvot*, this is the longest, which shows how serious such a violation is.

This proclamation was issued in 1176, when the Rambam was a mere 41 years old! The Rambam's historic greatness is demonstrated by the fact that he actually single-handedly was able to eliminate these transgressions, and thereby he brought the entire Jewish people back to full observance of Jewish law (and in the process, separated them from the Karaites).

One questioner asks if it is proper and permissible to transport the remains of a departed person to Eretz Yisrael for burial, citing a case in which a man had taken his father's and mother's remains to be buried in Jerusalem. Did he do the right thing? The Rambam replied: "What this man did was *tov me'od,* very good, and the great men among Israel's sages did likewise." Here we get an inkling of the Rambam's own decision to be buried in Eretz Yisrael. This is worth pondering when we visit his grave in Tiberias.

The heavy burdens of his medical and communal duties are apparent in some of his letters: "Please excuse me for answering your letter with such brevity, because I am overworked, my body is feeble. I am not even able to read all the letters I receive, let alone answering them, except when they contain a point of important wisdom."

Of course, the bulk of the petitions concern family problems, commercial matters and inheritance questions. His answers on such topics reflect his legislation in his *Mishneh Torah*.

These few brief excerpts taken from the 280 *Teshuvot* give us an idea of the Rambam's unmatched greatness, a sampling of the enormous sweep of his expertise in every facet of learning and human experience, enabling him to answer each question with decisiveness and precision. His historic accomplishment in securing complete adherence to Torah law was accomplished through the much used medium of letter writing. The Jews had their own postal system, which made correspondence possible over distances of thousands of miles, and it is our good fortune that the Rambam remained at the center of this world-wide network of Torah teaching, legislation and human experience.

Truly, "from Moshe to Moshe, there was none like Moshe!"

Dr. Lehmann and the Lubavitcher Rebbe, discussing the importance of collecting and publishing ancient Hebrew manuscripts.

# Encounter With The Rambam

In February 1978, I visited Cairo as a member of the first official group of American Jews to come to Egypt as the guests of the Egyptian Government. During this visit we met with the late President Anwar Sadat and his (then) Vice President Hosni Mubarak. However, what remains very much the most overwhelming memory from that trip was my personal unexpected encounter with the Rambam. On my own I had the good fortune of making the unexpected find of the Rambam's own Beth Hamidrash in the midst of the oldest and most inaccessible part of Cairo. But let my diary from 13 years ago tell the fascinating story:

The year 1978 marks the 800th anniversary of the completion of the most important rabbinic work produced since the editing of the Talmud. It was in the year 1178 that the *Mishneh Torah*, or *Yad Hachazakah* was completed in Cairo, by Rabbi Moshe ben Maimon, also known as the Rambam or Maimonides. This work, which codifies all the laws of the Talmud, has remained a source of constant inspiration to Talmudic students and scholars till this very day, and influences the daily life of every Jew.

Little did I think that during this significant year I would have a personal rendezvous, so to speak, with the Rambam himself. But that is how I feel about my discovery of the Rambam's Beth Hamidrash in one of the oldest parts of Cairo. This discovery came about as part of a visit to Cairo which took place earlier this year.

My visit was intended to establish contact with the Jewish community of Cairo, and with any remnant of institutions, community buildings, or libraries. To my great disappointment I soon discovered that there is very little left of Jewish life in Cairo. Of 17 existing synagogues, only one, the so-called Adly Pasha Synagogue, is in use—for services Friday night and Shabbat morning, attended by perhaps 15 elderly and poor Jews, although the enormous synagogue could easily accommodate 2000 persons! Only 164 Jews live in Cairo today, and of these only 13 are under the age of 20. Another synagogue, the Ben Ezra Synagogue, is only open for visits by tourists, and is a "must" on most organized sightseeing trips. The ancient building holds some very old Torah scrolls and some famous old wooden doors to the Ark, with a Biblical verse inscribed in the wood. By chance, I discovered underneath the synagogue, at the end of a no-longer-used tunnel, a well-preserved *mikvah*! When I later mentioned this to officials in the Community Office, they admitted that they had not known of its existence.

Next, I visited the Community Office where I inspected the archive of marriage registrations going back to the last century. The officials, however, are themselves unable to read the cursive Hebrew script, which, in fact, I also found very difficult to decipher. At the end of my visit the officials presented me with a set of the locally used *Ketuba*—a set of 3 documents, one in Aramaic, one in Arabic, and one in French. (This actually came in handy, when, at the end of my visit, I was called upon to perform a marriage ceremony for an elderly couple who had been waiting for 2 years to have a Jewish ceremony performed.)

During this visit, I also heard about the poor condition of the El Basatin cemetery, where Jewish and Karaite graves alike are being desecrated. To make matters worse, the Government is threatening destruction of a portion of the cemetery to make room for a housing project and a highway. I decided to pay a visit to this cemetery, and did so with special police permission, which is necessary for such a visit. In fact, the police chief personally chauffeured me there, which I considered a very generous gesture.

The condition of the graves was as I had been warned. Many graves were torn, empty, stones removed. But far worse was that many compounds of graves, owned by old Jewish families, were now inhabited by Arab squatters who had moved in with their families and cattle., It was a sad sight to see the mausoleum of Rav Chaim Cappuci, a *talmid* of the Ari who lived in the 17th century, vandalized by these squatters. When I later met with President Sadat, this matter was brought to his attention, and he promised to look into ways to safeguard the cemetery.

At one point I noticed a small piece of paper on the ground near one grave. I picked it up. It bore the image of the Rambam; in fact, it was the receipt of a donation given to the Rambam Synagogue—some 50 years ago. This receipt fascinated me, of course. I became curious as to the existence today of this synagogue, and I commenced an intense search for it.

But where to begin? I was lucky when I was told by a foreign diplomat about a Jewish area, Hart al Yahud, where such a synagogue was likely to be found. I asked my taxi driver to take me there and to accompany me through the myriad of narrow alleys which make up the slums of Old Cairo. Everywhere I went I asked, "Where is there a Jewish mosque?" "Where is the mosque of Abu Musa ibn Maimun?" (for this was his Arabic name). I received only cold stares in answer. In fact, I was becoming more than a little uneasy about going around, alone, in the murkiest part of Cairo and announcing to one and all that I am looking for something Jewish. For the Arabs make no distinction between Jew and Israeli—"Yahud" means the same to them. Who knows what would have happened if I had run into a Palestinian Arab.

Finally, an old Arab took me by the hand and promised that for five pounds he would take me to my destination. My heart raced! I agreed to his *baksheesh* deal. Soon we stood before an ancient synagogue, but it was the synagogue of Rabbi Chaim Cappuci, whose grave I had visited only two days before. Arab squatters had turned the Ark into their bedroom. . . . I told my "guide" of my disappointment.

Well, for another five pounds I would *really* find Abu Musa's synagogue. And so it was. A few minutes later we had wound through some more dark alleys, deep in mud, climbing over dung heaps and past donkeys. I stood before a gate which had the clear inscription: *Beth Haknesset shel Rabbenu Moshe ben Maimon.* I knocked at the door. Would it be opened? After a long while a black dervish opened the door and took me inside.

There was a synagogue, all right, but it was missing a roof and large sections of the walls. The sun and wind had turned the Ark and benches into withered, warped pieces of wood. But I had the feeling that this was not a very old synagogue, since some marble plaques bore modern dates. The dervish must have read my mind, and motioned me to follow him. We crossed the courtyard and descended some steps into a very old building, through a pointed narrow door. This door led me down to another narrow arch, over which I immediately recognized a miniature portrait of the Rambam. I went down some more steps, and I suddenly found myself inside a chamber which transported me to a different world!

The thick stone walls attested to very old age. There, before me, was a room of about 30 by 20 feet, covered with carpets. On one side was a niche, behind a partition, which no doubt had held a bed in ancient times. The main area was flanked by wooden benches, placed so that they faced the person sitting in the center—the Rambam. On the wall was a large marble plaque reading: *Ze hamakom hakadosh shel Morenu v'rabenu Harav Hagadol Maoz u'Migdal Rabbi Moshe ben Maimon Ha-Rambam.* A few "traditional" portraits of the Rambam were hanging on the walls.

That was all. The rest was atmosphere. . . . A small amount of light came into the dark cellar from narrow windows in the dome-shaped opening in the ceiling. There was both darkness and light. The Middle Ages were all around me. And the spirit of the Rambam. He could have left a few minutes ago on his famous donkey ride to the Sultan whom he attended as the court physician, while this very room was filling up with petitioners and congregants who would occupy his time when he came back late in the evening, tired from the long trip. . . and only late in the night would he have time to repose and to study. . . and to write! It was here that the *Mishneh Torah* and all the other classical works were composed and penned. Jewish *halachah* was codified in this room; Jewish philosophy was formulated, too. Here! Not in some mythical, remote place. Not in some make-believe large academy, not in some legendary palace. Just in this little murky cellar, the Beth Hamidrash, which, despite its small size, contained all the majesty and grandeur of the Rambam, simply because he left his personal mark upon it, which has survived the 774 years since his death.

As I stood silently immersed in my thoughts and turned to the *mincha* prayer, the black dervish and my Arab taxi driver stood open-mouthed, themselves affected by the solemn moment.

As I returned to my hotel I wondered whether I would ever again find this sacred place, or whether, like in the dream scene in *Brigadoon*, the place would disintegrate into the mist of the far-off past. But that same evening I had the chance to propose to Boutrous Ghali, Acting Foreign Minister of Egypt, the resumption of the study of Abu Musa, with joint Jewish and Egyptian help and funds, and turning the synagogue into a national shrine accessible to Jews and non-Jews from all over the world. He showed interest, but so far nothing has happened. Whether something comes of this or not, I hope that soon many Jews can share with me the rare experience of being, if just for a fleeting moment, one with a grandiose past which makes the present richer.

Dr. Lehmann with President Anwar Sadat in Cairo, February 1978. Dr. Lehmann challenged the Islamic concept of "peace with infidels" which makes "peace" agreements problematic.

# "Libelli Fata Sua Habent"
# Books Have Their Own Fate

The Latin saying goes, "*libelli fata sua habent*," books have their own Fate. This corresponds to a Jewish saying from the Zohar, "*hakol taluy b'mazal afilu Sefer Torah sheb'heychal*," everything depends on Fate, even the *Sefer Torah* in the Temple.

As a book lover, I can testify to the truth of this statement. Very often I experience that a scholarly work finds its way to me because of my love for books. For example:

A number of works from R. Shlomo Chelmer—the great Talmudist who lived 250 years ago, famous for his work *Markevet haMishneh*, a commentary on the Rambam—were considered lost in the Holocaust. Then, one of his original handwritten manuscripts, which before the War had been in the possession of the Rebbe of Radomsk—a collection of 32 responsa entitled *Lev Shlomo*—surfaced and was bought by me. I promptly had it published. (By the way, his erudition disproves the popular notion that the people of Chelm were fools, for, much to the contrary, it was a city of great talmidei chachamim.)

Of course, I also was keen to search for more of his works that might have survived the Holocaust. One day, a well-known dealer in Judaica got a call to go to Des Moines, Iowa, to look at a silver *besomim* box which was reputed to be very valuable. On his way, his train stopped in Chicago and he chanced to meet a Jew who told him that he knew of a manuscript by R. Shlomo Chelmer. The dealer interrupted his trip, searched for the manuscript, bought it and sold it to me. It was a long-lost commentary on the *haftarot* for the whole year, a very precious work. I promptly had it published as well. I have had many similar experiences.

One of the most fantastic tales of books having a Fate of their own is embodied in what happened to the world-renowned Jewish libraries in Leningrad, where the most fabulous treasures of the ancient *Genizah* manuscripts from Cairo had been stored in the last century. The collection was amassed largely by the Russian scholars Firkovitch and Antonin. They are vastly greater treasures than all the *Genizah* manuscripts housed in Cambridge, New York, and Jerusalem combined. During the Communist rule, very few scholars had access to them, and then, only to very limited items. For example, in 1926, the non-Jewish, German Bible scholar, Paul Kahle, was permitted to examine one of the oldest existing dated Hebrew Bible manuscripts, generally referred to as "Leningrad B19a," written by the famous scribe Shmuel ben Yacov in 1010.

As known, Leningrad was the target of the most ferocious German siege of

World War II. During the winter of 1941–42—the severest winter on record—German troops circled Russia's second largest city, partly from the frozen-over Baltic Sea, and partly from the equally frozen-over Ladoga Lake. For two years, the Russians heroically held out against all odds. They ended up eating horses, cats and rats, and endured the most severe privations. But they did not give up, although the city was practically razed by German bombardments. It had been Hitler's dream to capture Leningrad in the north and Stalingrad in the south, especially as these two cities bore the names of his most hated enemies, Lenin and Stalin.

But what happened to the priceless Hebrew manuscripts? Would anyone worry about them when daily their very lives were subject to being sacrificed? The miracle was—as revealed after the war—that the Hebrew manuscripts were saved. They had been transported to the Russian interior, beyond the Ural mountains, out of reach of the hated enemy.

Who performed this miracle? Now we know it was a modest non-Jewish Russian woman named Klavdia Borisovna Starkova. Before the war, she had fortunately chosen Hebrew as her field of study, and consequently she was in a position to recognize the enormous value of the Hebrew books, and arrange for their timely removal from Leningrad.

I was, of course, intrigued by this woman, who certainly is one of the world's righteous Gentiles. Recently her 75th birthday was celebrated, and I was able to obtain some interesting biographical and scholarly data about her.

She was born in 1915 to a bourgeois family belonging to the Czarist Russian intelligentsia. After graduating preparatory school in 1930, she pursued her higher education in the field of languages, and in 1933 chose Semitic languages and literature as her specialty at the Leningrad State University. At that time a number of prominent Jewish scholars, renowned as instructors of Hebrew and Arabic—Mikhail Sokolov, Andrei Borisov, Israel Frank-Kamenetsky, Viktor Beliaev, Nikolay Yushmanov, Ignaty Krachokovsky, Nikolai Rosenthal and Alexander Riftin—were still alive. I mention their names because most of them perished in the various Stalinist purges, and it behooves us to render their memory our respect.

After a few years, Klavdia wrote a paper for her doctor's dissertation entitled "The Leningrad Fragments of the Poems of Rabbi Yehuda haLevy"—about the writings of the great Jewish medieval bard, born in Toledo in 1080, who was trampled by an Arab horseman and died at the gates of Jerusalem in 1140. Klavdia finished her dissertation in the fateful year 1941, when the war broke out and she was forced to abandon her studies and take up fighting as a member of Leningrad's air-defence command. It was during this terrible period that she managed to rescue the Hebrew manuscript libraries. Only after years of horrors, during which she suffered cold and hunger, could she return to her studies in 1945.

Then Klavdia commenced work on the poems of another Jewish giant of the Spanish period, Shlomo ibn Gabriol, the author of the *Adon Olam* poem sung in every synagogue in the world even today.

In recent years she has devoted her considerable talent to studying the Dead Sea Scrolls, and she has several publications to her credit.

It is time that this heroic Russian scholar and woman of valor, who can truly be called the "Angel" of Leningrad's Hebrew libraries, receives our boundless thanks. We can join all of her colleagues in wishing her a long, long life, with continued productive scholarly activity. The Fate of an important part of our sacred literature was in her hands, and as a tool of Providence she carried out her sacred mission, thus contributing to our Jewish spiritual survival.

Another case illustrating how Providence guards over the Fate of our sacred Hebrew books comes from an unlikely place—Finland.

Centuries ago Finland was part of Sweden. But in 1808, during the Napoleonic period, Russia wrested Finland from Sweden, and it remained an autonomous "Grand Duchy of the Russian Empire" until 1917, when it achieved its independence under Marshall Mannerheim.

Finland had been set aside as a retirement site for pensioned Jewish troops who managed to survive, with their Jewish identities intact, the ordeals of 25 years of enforced military service as "Cantonist" soldiers, victims of a policy instituted by Czar Nicolai I as a means of eradicating Judaism.

Only Jews who were physically and spiritually very strong could withstand the unbelievable pressures and privations of such long isolation from their Jewish roots, especially since they were snapped up by the government from as young as 8 years old to be conscripted into the military. Perhaps not surprisingly their descendants even today are among the world's strongest and proudest Jews.

I once visited their synagogue in the Finnish capital of Helsinki (Helsingfors in Swedish), where I noticed something very unusual. There was a large wreath hanging on the wall, presented by Finland's great war hero, Marshall Mannerheim, when he visited the synagogue to honor the memory of seven Jewish soldiers who had fallen fighting for the Finnish Army—on the side of Hitler! Finland was the only country under Hitler's sway where, because of Mannerheim's intervention, not only were the Jews not persecuted, but they were actually kept in the Finnish army fighting with the Germans on the Russian front! How tragic was the sight of that wreath! But it was a tribute to the heroism of descendants of strong Jewish soldiers of the past.

For some reason the Russian Czarist government selected the Helsinki University library to become its "copyright library," where specimens of all books, including Hebrew books, published between 1828 and 1917 were deposited. This meant that immense numbers of Hebrew books, as soon as they were printed, had to be deposited in the Helsinki library—where they gathered dust for all these years, since they were never touched again.

Only a few years ago this treasure trove of Hebrew books was discovered. They were catalogued and found to number over 5,000 items; some of them had previously been totally unknown, since never before had they been sold or distributed in the open market. These books include Bibles, prayer books, and rabbinic literature on the Mishnah, Talmud, Midrash, Rambam, philosophy, and more. Many periodicals and Yiddish books were also found! The books were amazingly well preserved, and many of them did not even have their pages cut open. What a treasure! Little work has been done yet on investigating these marvels preserved by special Fate, but surely a number of unexpected, important discoveries will be made through their study.

Of course, everyone is also aware of the other recent discoveries of "lost" Hebrew works, amazingly brought back to us by Providential protection, the Cairo *Genizah* and the Dead Sea Scrolls. The unusual Fate of these collections has miraculously preserved them for us after thousands of years!

Yes, truly *"libelli fata sua habent,"* books have a Fate of their own—especially our precious Hebrew books—and for this we must be deeply grateful.

# Assuring Perpetual Jewish Learning: The Halberstadt Archive of 1713–1847

The Jewish people have been the custodians of that precious, divine gift—the Torah—for over 3,600 years. And during all these years the Jewish people have understood how to perpetuate the intensive learning of the Torah, despite the greatest handicaps and crises. There were moments in our history when Torah learning was threatened with total extinction. And yet, at the moment of greatest crisis, one man would arise to single-handedly save the perpetuation of Torah learning.

Fortunately, we have historical records relating the deeds of those great individuals. One such person was Behrend Lehmann, 1661–1730, the greatest of the court Jews of the 17th and 18th centuries. I have in my possession an archive documenting the herculean effort of that great Jew to secure Torah learning at a time when, after the Thirty Years War, unspeakable pogroms had nearly wiped out the Jewish people in Poland, where the centers of Torah learning had been located. This archive shows the foresight and feeling of profound responsibility that this rich community leader felt in facing history's call for his services—services that only he could perform.

Lehmann was the *Hof-Faktor*, or court financier, for the extravagant king of Saxony, August the Strong, as he is known in the history books. Lehmann not only helped finance the king's extravagant lifestyle and military campaigns, but also succeeded in procuring for his royal master the Crown of Poland which in those days was awarded by the Polish nobility to the highest bidder. Lehmann had to raise the astronomical sum of 10 million *thaler* to compete successfully with the rulers of England, France and Sweden.

In 1697, August was crowned king of Poland. He did not forget Lehmann, whom he now elevated to "Polish Resident"—equal to an ambassadorial title. The king offered to fulfill Lehmann's three wishes. These were: 1) the rebuilding the synagogue in Halberstadt, Lehmann's native town; 2) the reprinting of the Babylonian Talmud of which practically no more copies could be found; and 3) the establishing of Klaus—in modern terms, a *kollel*.

All three wishes became the greatest blessings of the time. The magnificent synagogue in Halberstadt in Central Germany stood until 1938 when, in the Kristallnacht, German hoodlums destroyed it. The Lehmann Talmud was a magnificent edition which was praised profusely by the rabbinical leaders of the Sefardic and Ashkenazic communities of the time; and the Klaus was a seminal institution of learning, where selected scholars were given stipends to sit and learn without any economic worries.

For 235 years the Lehmann Klaus was the mainstay of Torah learning in Germany and Western Europe. Lehmann brought with him from Poland leading Torah scholars who helped create a center of learning in the small German town. Lehmann applied his amazing financial ingenuity entirely to perpetuate his foundation which was in charge of the *kollel*. My archive contains extremely interesting contracts and documents which reflect the legal trappings used to make the *kollel* viable into perpetuity.

On 27 Nissan, 1714, the 32 leaders of the Halberstadt community signed a contract with Behrend Lehmann that acknowledged receipt of an amount of 6,000 *thaler* toward the construction cost of the new synagogue. This amount was to be regarded as a loan—which however was immediately waived. The "loan" carried an interest of 6 percent per annum, to be paid in perpetuity to the "Yoshvei Beth Hamidrash"—the Klaus scholars. This rate of interest was to be reduced to 5 percent in the year 1740 "unless Moshiach comes by then" (*be'ikuv bi'at Meshichaynu chalilah*).

The contract, demonstrating Lehmann's great concern for uninterrupted Torah learning, took into consideration the tragic, frequently occurring interruptions of Jewish community life through local riots, pograms and expulsions. The contract therefore provides that no interruption in learning should be permitted—"*Kedey shelo yibbatel Talmud Torah chas veshalom.*" But in case of some catastrophe—If a year or years unusual circumstance occur by political events or reasons which cannot be written down, all that the mouth may pronounce and the heart think of (*Im shehaya chas veshalom shanah o shanim shelo kedarkan o mikoach makkat medinah o shum sibbah asher lo nitan lichtov kol mah sh'hapeh yuchal ledabber ve'halev lachshov*)—then the community undertakes to pay the amount due as interest to other communities but only for Torah learning. And as soon as the crisis has passed and the Jews of Halberstadt can return to their town, Torah-learning in the Klaus must resume immediately, and the amounts due will again be paid to the Halberstadt Klaus scholars.

In further support of the Halberstadt scholars, Lehmann also extended a loan to the community of Berlin for the construction of the first synagogue built by royal permission. Lehmann "lent" them 3,000 *thaler* with a similar proviso: The loan was waived but interest of 6 percent would go to the Halberstadt Klaus scholars, to be lowered to 5 percent in the year 1740. This synagogue—the famous Heiterreutergasse Synagogue—was one of Germany's most beautiful Jewish edifices and was also destroyed by the German mob in 1938.

We have many contemporary eyewitness accounts of Behrend Lehmann. For example, one Swedish traveler described how Lehmann came to the printing shop to inspect the printing of the Talmud in a magnificent coach driven by six horses, with six lackeys and coachmen attending him. This account shows that the great community leader gave his personal attention to every detail. Lehmann's financial business extended to most European commercial centers. He left family members in charge of his various branches. In this he set an example for the Rothschild family

100 years later which placed five sons in its major branches to start the fabled Rothschild banking empire.

Lehmann's love for Torah was of historical value. While he himself was not noted as a scholar—as some of the other famous court Jews were—his father and grandfather had been noted, pious scholars. Behrend inherited from them a love of Torah and an outstanding sense of responsibility to use his great political and financial influence strictly to enhance Torah learning and to improve the political plight of his Jewish brothers. No wonder that he was held in greatest esteem by all generations after him. In my own case, my family originated in Halberstadt and my late father educated his sons to see in Behrend Lehmann a role model: *Torah u'Gudulah be'Makom Echad* (Torah and Greatness in One Place). The name of the Halberstadt synagogue, Kehal Adat Yeshurun, was the name that my father gave to the synagogue that he saved from Hamburg and moved to Stockholm after the Kristallnacht. It is still in daily use.

There can be no doubt that without Behrend Lehmann, Judaism would have died out in Germany. But by importing great Polish Torah scholars and establishing the Klaus, Germany revived as a Torah center. Some of the "graduates" of the Halberstadt Klaus were the leaders of German Jewry. Among them was Rabbi Ezriel Hildesheimer, the founder of the Berliner Rabbinerseminar—the Orthodox Rabbinical Seminary which spawned great educators, among them, Rabbi Josef Carlebach, the head of the Hamburg Jewish Day School "Talmud Torah" which became the model for all day schools in the United States. Thus in a sense, American Jewry is a direct heir to the Judaism of Behrend Lehmann's foundation.

There is a sequel in my archive to the initial foundation contracts. After the community had paid the interest to the Klaus scholars for over 120 years, they moved to reduce the interest rate; they claimed they could only afford to pay 4 percent. The archive contains various documents showing how the community approached leading rabbinical personalities of the time including the last German *av bet din* (chief of the rabbinical court), R. Yukev Ettlinger, of Altona, to get permission for this reduction, which he refused to grant. The community ultimately turned to the state government with the same request, but were sharply rebuked and rebuffed for the "constant discord" with which Jewish communities are beset. At this point the community unilaterally went ahead and reduced the interest payment by 1 percent. There follow heart-rending complaints by two scholars in the Klaus, Zevel Eger and Gershon Yehoshafat, who demonstrated they could simply not make ends meet unless the interest payments were reinstated as per contract. At this point the archive ends: a treasure of documents evidencing Jewish history, dated 1713, 1714, 1730, 1770, 1788, 1789, 1790, 1791–1795 and 1836–1847.

It is interesting to observe that Gershon Yehoshafat—who later became rabbi of Frankfurt am Main—had a brother named Issachar Ber Yehoshafat, who was a book dealer. After a while he became a "news monger," but found that business for a Jew in the field was bound to fail. So he converted and changed his name to Reuter.

He was knighted as "von Reuter" and moved to England where the famous news empire of Reuters was founded!

The towering personality of Behrend Lehmann and his accomplishments are ever inspiring for every generation. In the letter in my archive of 1841, R. Ettlinger fittingly called him *"oto tzaddik asher zichro lo yassuf mi-zaro"* (that tzaddik whose memory will not disappear from his descendants). In a sense we are all his descendants and it is incumbent on us to honor his memory.

Dr. Lehmann with Cardinal Stickler, Librarian Emeritus of the Vatican, holding a disputation in Cambridge, Massachusetts about the Hebrew manuscripts wrongfully held by the Church. The Cardinal broke off the "disputation" and walked out of the Harvard University hall where the meeting took place.

# The Vatican

Our greatest adversary over the past 2,000 years has been the Vatican, representing the Christian Church with its rabid hatred for Judaism and anything Jewish. In an effort to eradicate Judaism—that stubborn religion which sees no basis for believing in Jesus—the church has used many murderous means. The burnings of Jews in many countries has been only one avenue. A spiritual genocide was also attempted over several centuries by confiscating and burning our precious holy books. After thus destroying hundreds of thousands of sacred Jewish books, there is still a residue of some 800 Hebrew manuscripts in the Vatican. For ten years I have led a campaign to recover at least these survivors of spiritual genocide and have campaigned for their return to their legitimate owners, the Jewish people.

## The Story of the Hebrew Manuscripts in the Vatican Library

Much has been written recently about the Jewish claim to some precious, ancient Hebrew manuscripts lying in the Vatican Library. These Jewish treasures came to the attention of American Jews when in 1987 a selection of 57 of them traveled to various American cities on an exhibit, arranged as a fundraiser by the Reform congregations of the United States.

These exhibits, which began in Miami, were introduced by publicity handouts that glorified the "cultural cross-fertilization" of Christians and Jews during the Middle Ages to which these precious manuscripts allegedly testify. This line was immediately attacked as a falsification of history by those who knew the tragic background of the manuscripts. The Church had for 600 years carried out a ferocious spiritual genocide against Judaism by seizing and burning hundreds of thousands of Hebrew books in order to thwart the continuation of Jewish education. Only a handful—some 800 by the latest count—still survive in the Vatican besides some hundreds of charred fragments salvaged from the pyres of the book burnings.

A group of concerned Jews, knowledgeable in Jewish history, formed the Committee for the Recovery of Jewish Manuscripts and placed ads wherever the Vatican exhibition went asking the Pope to return to the rightful owners—the Jewish people—these surviving Jewish treasures in the spirit of the "Nostra Aetate" of Pope John XXIII. The Committee requested that these manuscripts be housed in the National Library in Jerusalem, the center of research on Hebrew literature.

The Vatican totally stonewalled the request. But after two years, the Vatican sent its Librarian Emeritus, Cardinal Stickler—an Austrian and good friend of Kurt Waldheim—to lecture at Harvard, the last stop of the exhibit. He made the astounding claim that the Vatican got these Hebrew works, not by seizing them from Jews, but as gifts from Italian noblemen and that the "Renaissance" Popes of the 16th century were lovers of Hebrew books.

I, as chairman of the Committee to show the falsehood of his claims, presented him with a copy of the Bull of Pope Clement VIII dated 1592—in the midst of the Renaissance period—which in the most ferocious anti-Semitic language condemned the Talmud and other Hebrew writings as "obscene," "blasphemous" and "abominable"— all to be ordered seized and burned. The good Pope also forbade non-Jews to own, give as gifts or print Hebrew books on pain of torture and excommunication. The embarrassed cardinal had no answer and stalked out of the meeting room.

The campaign of this Committee has had the support of such American personalities as Seymour Reich, Elie Weisel, Rabbi Emanuel Rackman and others. Since the time of the manuscript exhibition in America, the Committee has further researched the origin of the Vatican manuscripts. The Israel Government, through its Institute of Manuscripts, published a report written by two prominent Professors, Aloni and Loewenberg, showing that the largest part of the 800 works originated in a part of Germany where they were seized after a pogrom. One of the Catholic rulers in Germany presented them to the Vatican.

This finding is consistent with the sordid story of the persecution of Jews by the Vatican throughout history.

We found that the burnings of Hebrew books were initiated by Pope Gregory IX. He persuaded French King Louis IX to burn some 12,000 copies of the Talmud in Paris in 1243. He was followed by Pope after Pope. The most ferocious haters of Judaism and Jewish books among them were Innocent IV (1243-1254), Clement IV (1256-1268), John XXII (1316-1334), Paul IV (1555-1559), Pius V (1566-1572) and Clement VIII (1592-1605). They almost succeeded in stamping out Jewish books entirely. Yet Jews continued to pen holy books without letup, and once the printing press was invented, the Church found it impossible to destroy entire printed editions of the Talmud and our other sacred books. Gutenberg, the German who invented the printing press around 1450, is certainly one of our great heroes, since he helped us to victory over our Catholic enemies, who had hoped to blot out our Judaism.

We also found that a part of the seized Hebrew books were not burned but turned over to a special building in Rome reserved for renegade Jews, who were ordered to search for passages in the Talmud that the Church could use to combat Judaism in the public disputations that took place from time to time between rabbis and Jewish converts.

When the first attempts were made to negotiate an agreement between the Vatican and the State of Israel, I proposed that the question of the return of the Hebrew manuscripts to the Jewish people should be put on the agenda. To my pleasant surprise this proposal was met with great approval by Shimon Peres, then foreign minister; Shulamit Aloni, then minister of education; and Deputy Foreign Minister Yossi Beilin. Their letters of approval make interesting exhibits in our file.

I cannot disclose the status of the negotiations but can report that action is being taken in Rome.

When the Pope recently visited New York the question of the manuscripts was supposed to be taken up with him when he met with American Jewish leaders, but the meeting did not allow any substantive discussions. Chief Rabbi Lau of Israel on a visit to the Vatican did take up the question at my suggestion. We must hope that sooner or later we will have positive results, because if the Church is really intent on atoning for the past sins against the Jewish people, the return of the surviving manuscripts is one of the few concrete gestures the Vatican is capable of making.

A symbolic beginning of the process would be for the Vatican to annul the ferocious Bull of Pope Clement VIII, which is until this day on the books. The ban against the Talmud and other religious Hebrew writings must be lifted, just as the Vatican recently lifted the ban on the writings of the astronomer Galileo! Are we not entitled to the same atonement as the memory of a scientist who died 300 years ago? Time will show if the Church is really serious about atoning for its sins against the Jews.

# Unsung Jewish Martyrs—Victims of the Church

If you ask the average person which were the greatest tragedies in the long history of the Jewish people for which the Church should seek atonement, you will probably get as an answer: the Inquisition, leading to the expulsion from Spain in 1492, and the Holocaust in Christian lands in this century. But in fact there were countless other atrocities committed against us in different lands and in different centuries for which the Church bears a heavy burden of guilt. Here are just a few events of suffering inflicted upon us by the Church for which no desire for atonement has yet been voiced.

### *The Brothers Chaim and Joshua Reizes (1728)*

In the early 18th century Poland was totally dominated by the Catholic Church, and more specifically, by the Jesuits. In the city of Lwow (Lemberg) the Church had installed an Inquisition which set out to do all in its power to wipe out Judaism by bringing about forced conversions by torture, and executing those who resisted their rule of terror. Their one success, the conversion of a Jew by the name of Jan Filipowicz, felt remorse after the fact and returned to his Judaism. This infuriated the Jesuits who seized and tortured him to get a confession as to who had influenced him to abandon Christianity. When no confession was forthcoming they turned to the Jewish leaders of the city and arrested them just before Pesach in 1728. Rabbi Chaim Reizes, a giant in learning and piety and head of the yeshiva, and his younger brother Joshua were imprisoned. Both were tortured cruelly for 40 days without yielding a confession. Rabbi Joshua died from this ordeal, but the men of the Church in their fury were not satisfied; they tied his body to the tails of a team of horses and had it dragged through the streets of Lwow. Then they took Rabbi Chaim to the execution site. Till the last moments the priests tried to lure him into a conversion by promising him his freedom. He refused. The Church recorded its failure in the Latin words, *"Sed nihil evicit in obstinato pectore"* (he could not convince his obstinate soul). Before a large, cheering crowd they proceeded to execute the great Rabbi in the most cruel manner, by first cutting off his hands, feet and tongue, and finally cutting out his heart from his living body. Like Rabbi Akiva long before him and countless martyrs in our history, he gathered his last strength for the words "Shema Yisroel. . ." Then his remains were burned at the stake.

The Jews of Lwow composed a special prayer in commemoration of these two beloved martyrs. I have just acquired an old prayer book from Lwow, handwritten on parchment, containing this heartrending prayer, said in Lwow till recent times, together with the weekly *"Av Harachamim."* The martyrdom and greatness of the two Reizes brothers is expressed in a two-page long poem, also giving the author's name as Rabbi Aryeh Leib ben R. Yitzchak. Today, the Jewish community of Lwow has vanished in the Holocaust, but my manuscript still bears witness to the crime inflicted by the Church on those pious Jews of yore.

### *Antonio José Da Silva*

Hundreds of years after 1492, the ravages of the Inquisition continued unhindered under the sway of the Catholic Church. Brazil, which from 1598 had also been exposed to the excesses of the Inquisition, was still being terrorized in the early 18th century. Countless "Conversos" or "New Christians" who had hoped for refuge in Brazil from their Portuguese homeland were burned at the stake in the dreaded autos-da-fé. And yet, thousands of "Conversos" still practiced secretly the Jewish religion, even though they no longer had any formal Jewish education and depended on family-kept traditions. The last Brazilian victim burnt at the stake was the famous playwright Antonio José da Silva, born in Rio de Janeiro in 1705. His father was a well-to-do lawyer and poet, who, together with his wife, Lourença Coutinho, was of Jewish origin. Antonio José's mother was the first to be arrested for the "crime of Judaism" and taken to Lisbon to be interrogated and tortured by the "Holy Office." As an outstanding expression of love and respect, both her husband and son moved across the ocean to be near her in her ordeal, which lasted for many years. Antonio José enrolled in the University of Coimbra and soon became known as an outstanding and popular playwright and lawyer. The Church became suspicious of him when they discovered that his plays contained attacks on the Inquisition. He was arrested and tortured to the point that he ultimately emerged a cripple in 1726. Yet he never uttered, even under the most severe torture, any other name but that of G-d Almighty—never a Christian name. In 1734 he married Leonor de Carvalho, also of Jewish origin.

His plays gained wide popularity, including one entitled *O Judeo*, the Jew. (He has been known in Brazilian literature ever since as Antonio José da Silva O Judeo). In 1737, just as the family celebrated the birth of a daughter, the playwright, his mother and wife were again arrested by the Inquisition, after a black slave girl, herself under threat of arrest for "lewd living," denounced them for keeping the Sabbath and the fast days of Yom Kippur and the Fast of Esther. Although no independent witnesses could be found to testify against him, he was secretly observed while in the dungeon, and was found to desist from eating on Jewish fast days. That was enough for the Church to condemn him to death! And so, on October 19th, 1739, the famous playwright and author, exuding the faith of his ancestors, cheerfully climbed up to the stake at the public auto-da-fé and was garotted and burnt to death, an eternally remembered Jewish martyr.

Not only bodies of Jews were burnt by the Church; our spiritual heritage, our sacred books were also burnt. One Pope after the other issued ferocious attacks on our literature. The most extreme was that issued in 1593 by Pope Clement VIII. It is important for our assessment of the position of the Church today to know the contents of that Bull. I quote briefly from the 4-page Latin document which, in my opinion, is required reading for anyone dreaming about Catholic-Jewish dialogue today: "Deeming it both fatal to ourselves and perilous for the Christian people to tolerate and overlook the Jews' wickedness, we again condemn that godless work known as the Talmud, as well as other similar rejected and detestable writings and books. We forbid *in perpetuity* in any way to read, possess, buy, sell or publish any and all of the books and codices of that godless and often censured Talmud and other utterly worthless, cabalistic and abominable books, as well as any works, commentaries, treatises, volumes and writings in the Hebrew language or in any other tongue whatsoever. . . . If they possess any books at the present time, they are altogether required to surrender, deliver and consign them in Rome immediately, within ten days, to the Office of the Holy Roman and Universal Inquisition. Without any further order from us, *the books are to be burnt*. This applies to all books also in places where the Jews dwell, not only in their synagogues and public places, but also in their private places, homes and offices."

The punishment for violating this Papal order is confiscation of all goods, bodily torture and, in the case of Christians holding Jewish books, excommunication. For good measure, the Pope also added this afterthought: "Should anyone dare to disobey this order, let him know that he will incur the wrath of Almighty God and of Peter and Paul, His Blessed Apostles." Under this and the Bulls of preceding popes, literally hundreds of thousands of our most precious and sacred books were burnt over the course of centuries—all in an ongoing spiritual genocide aimed at wiping out Judaism by denying us our tools for educating our young and old—our sacred books.

The *mesirat nefesh*—self-sacrifice for the glory of G-d—which inspired so many of our heroes to willingly accept a martyr's death, also inspired our forefathers to defy these vicious Papal Bulls: hundreds of Hebrew books were printed right under the noses of the Church's eagle-eyed spies and henchmen. I myself own close to 400 Hebrew books printed between 1500 and 1599, besides some 40 printed before the year 1500, most of them in Italy, the main domain of the Popes.

How does this affect us today? The amazing fact is that all these Papal bans on Jewish books *still stand today!* One of the greatest experts on Vatican relations with Jews, and especially the Vatican's stand on Hebrew books, writes me:

"I have checked and double-checked: the Papal Bulls ordaining the destruction of Hebrew books have never been withdrawn. To me that is more relevant than a Papal visit to a synagogue or bleeps and mutterings by Cardinals and third parties."

The continued validity of all the vicious and ferocious anti-Semitic Papal orders stems, of course, from the fact that, to faithful Catholics, Popes are supposed to be infallible.

After my reports on the Catholic-Jewish Colloquium in Baltimore in May, I have received a number of letters from Catholic clergymen criticizing one or another point made by me. These letters are true eye-openers, and all imply that I am the kind of Jew who obstructs "a respectful, intelligent encounter" (Monsignor John M. Oesterreicher, a *meshumad*), or an "intense theological dialogue between Catholics and Jews" (Dr. Eugene J. Fisher of the National Conference of Catholic Bishops). In fact, Msgr. Oesterreicher calls me a "Jewish triumphalist" and "the same psychological type as anti-Semites" (I will not venture into the "psychological type" who becomes a renegade Jew!).

We must remember that these and other representatives of the Catholic Church in large American cities with large Jewish populations are more or less doing a public relations job for the Vatican. The real face of the Church, however, is to be found in the secluded halls of the Curia in Rome, where no annulment of the Papal Bulls has yet been issued.

As a parallel, Israel has understandably refused to engage in any dialogue with the PLO until its Covenant, which calls for the destruction of Israel, is withdrawn. Until such time, any statement of peaceful intentions, etc. is rightfully discarded as only a P.R. gesture designed to mislead public opinion as to the true objectives of the PLO. In the same vein, how can anyone believe that a dialogue with the Church can take place, while "in perpetuity" the Jewish culture is declared "godless, utterly worthless, blasphemous, detestable, obscene, lewd?" Those who have knowledge of these Papal Bulls have a right to ask whether the much-publicized "Nostra Aetate" should not have been preceded by a public cancellation of all these hateful Papal Bulls.

My Catholic critics have brought to light several other highly significant points which otherwise would have remained brushed under the carpet:

> 1. While I understood the Baltimore Colloquium, in the words of the Most Reverend William H. Keeler, Archbishop of Baltimore, to call attention to the anti-Christian stand of Islam, and thereby calling for a direct Israeli dialogue with Christian Arabs, the Archbishop has now modified his stand. He implies that it is the Jews' fault, not the "nationalist Muslims" that so many Christians Arabs are leaving Israel. He calls the legal purchase of the so-called St. John's Hospice in the Old City a "very painful situation." He clearly wants to avoid having criticized the "nationalist Muslims" in any way, even though they fight against all "infidels," whether Christian or Jew.
> 2. Dr. Fisher is not convinced that Catholic scholars, as I wrote, are directed to see in every Biblical study a search for the coming of Jesus. For several decades I have worked on the Dead Sea Scrolls and know from personal experience how the Catholics in charge of the Scrolls—De Vaux, Benoit, Strungnell and others—were strictly guided by concern for

safeguarding Christian doctrine about Christianity's alleged originality, not by pure scholarship.

3. The undimmed rejection of the Talmud, just as in the Middle Ages, comes out in three letters received from Msgr. Oesterreicher. He and his Judeo-Catholic Institute in New Jersey are a worthy successor to the Neophytes in Rome of old: an institution for renegade Jews who were ordered to research the Talmud for anti-Christian statements which could be used in dialogues with rabbis. He even goes so far as to repeat the medieval anti-Jewish statements known to us so well: "I warn against public airing (of the call for the return of the Vatican Hebrew Manuscripts) in the media. It might well lead to a harmful chain of arguments and counter-arguments about anti-Christian passages in the Talmud." There is no reference to the Jesus he has in mind in the Talmud, even in the censored portions (called "*hashmatot ha-shas*"). Jewish tradition knows of a man called Jesus who lived about 100 B.C.E. in the days of R. Yehuda ben Tabbai, but it was probably not the same man. The Jesus whom Christians have in mind was probably not significant enough among authentic Jews to warrant mention in the Talmud.

4. Msgr. Oesterreicher revives the old canard that the "Pharisees" were in some way bad people. Only the late Christological glosses interpolated into the Gospels give such an impression. The Pharisees, the *"Perushim"* to us, were the heroic and magnificent guardians of Judaism and the Oral Law. Recent Dead Sea Scroll discoveries—I refer especially to the outstanding work of Professor Lawrence Schiffman of N.Y.U.—prove that the Pharisees were the authentic proponents of the Oral Law already in the days of the Hasmonean rulers, or some 300 years before their rulings were recorded in the Mishnah. We consider it a badge of honor to be called a "Pharisee."

5. What is more worrisome is that while the statement coming out of the Baltimore Colloquium called for the resumption of diplomatic relations between the Vatican and Israel, Msgr. Oesterreicher—no doubt on higher authority—backtracks and denies this: "The diplomatic relations are a matter for the government (he writes it with a small "g"—probably because a capital "G" would imply diplomatic legitimacy) of Israel and the Secretariat of State to deal with."

Finally, both Dr. Fisher and the Archbishop insist that Cardinal Cassidy did in fact quote the first verse in Tehillim (Psalms) 85, which refers to the return of Jews to their Land, and that he did not skip this *pasuk*, as Dr. Josef Burg had pointed out. As I had only reported what Dr. Burg had said in Baltimore, I called him on the phone. He stood by his previous statement, but thought that maybe the acoustics in the St. Mary Academy were at fault. It is gratifying that Cardinal Cassidy, Archbishop Keeler and Dr. Fisher have all vociferously assured me that the good Cardinal did in fact quote the all-important verse. That should lay to rest the doubt about the Vatican's acceptance of the Biblical promise that the Jews would indeed return to their Land. (By the way, Mohammed said exactly the same thing in the Koran—Sura 17, verse 105.) If this mishap—although of least significance in the context of all the other points which have come up—has caused the Cardinal discomfort, I am, and I am sure Dr. Burg is too, sorry.

What is more important, however, is the memory of the brothers Reizes, the martyrs in Lwow, and Antonio José da Silva O Judeo, the martyr of Rio de Janeiro. When will we hear about atoning for the crimes committed again them and all our other martyrs? And when will we hear that the anti-Semitic Papal Bulls have been canceled? Or is all we can expect to hear "bleeps and mutterings by Cardinals and third parties"?

# Sainthood for Pope Pius XII?

The press has begun to lay the groundwork for the consideration of sainthood—an honor reserved for Catholics showing extraordinary martyrdom—for a Pope who is still very much in everyone's memory: Pope Pius XII, the Holocaust Pope! *Time Magazine*, for example, reported that he is being considered for sainthood, despite the fact that "one Jewish leader says no"—referring to Rabbi Marvin Hier of the Simon Wiesenthal Center. This statement can easily be used for anti-Semitic purposes, as if to say that only Jews are hostile to Pius XII, whereas the rest of the world would welcome his sainthood with open arms. It also implies that only "one Jewish leader" is opposed to him, not the whole Jewish people.

Before these distortions of history become the accepted norm—considering the all-powerful influence of the media on the unthinking, uneducated masses—I find it necessary to review the whole sordid chapter of the Vatican's role in the Holocaust. The severe criticism of Pius XII did not come only from "one Jewish leader," but even from a Catholic historian who was given full access to the Vatican archives (which are still closed to us!). When one studies the facts presented by Father John F. Morley, an objective observer must ask himself: What kind of martyrdom did Pius XII exhibit during the Holocaust that would entitle him to sainthood? If he is declared a saint, wouldn't all the other saints of the past feel uncomfortable, since respect for sainthood would thereby be considerably lessened?

Certainly, the memory of our own six million martyrs would be desecrated if Pius XII, who might have saved a good part of them from death, is declared a saint!

It would be truly astonishing if the current Vatican, after claiming that under the Second Vatican Council its attitude to Jews has changed, would again identify itself with the questionable attitude of Pius XII. I therefore place before my readers an article featured almost four years ago in the *Algemeiner Journal* (November 3, 1989), entitled "The Vatican and the Holocaust":

It is timely to look at the historic record—through the eyes of a Catholic historian who had access to highly sensitive diplomatic material inside the Vatican archives.

*Vatican Diplomacy and the Jews During the Holocaust, 1939–1943,* written by Father John F. Morley, a member of the Ecumenical Commission of the Archdiocese of Newark, is based on the Vatican's own diplomatic records, to which he had access. He explains the time span covered by his book as follows: "The first date chosen, 1939, marked the beginning of the papacy of Pius XII, as well as the outbreak of the War. The study ceased at the end of 1943 because the Vatican records, published to the present, extend only to that date, and also because the majority of Jews of Europe had already been killed by then."

In other words, Father Morley concentrates on the actions and motivations of

Pope Pius XII, yet stops short of the worst crescendo of the barbaric Nazi Final Solution, which took place in 1944 and early 1945. Unfortunately, his conclusions about the first four years of the Pius XII era are grim enough to leave no doubt about the Vatican's attitude during the most tragic of all the Holocaust years.

Father Morley gives us an important insight into the pyramid of the Vatican's global organization, which consisted of the Pope, his Secretary of State, and the Nuncios. He goes through country after country under Nazi domination, reviewing the contacts between this organization and the local rulers, who, with the full knowledge of the Vatican, carried out the extermination of millions of Jews.

The two countries which prided themselves as true Catholic States, where the Pope's word was law, were Slovakia and Croatia. Here, more than anywhere else, strong condemnation of the anti-Jewish measures could have been expected. Here the Pope could easily have resorted to ecclesiastic remedies, in the form of sanctions and excommunications of those involved in these crimes. Yet, despite unceasing appeals for intervention, the Pope chose to use diplomacy here as everywhere else, instead of ecclesiastic sanctions. The diplomatic tack he chose was one of utter prudence and reserve, always guided, as Father Morley states repeatedly, by an ardent desire to do nothing which might annoy Germany, a country where Pius XII had been Nuncio for 17 years prior to 1939.

Father Morley explains this by pointing to "the autocratic tendencies of Pius XII, and his total interest in Germany." A characteristic epistle from the Pope, dated April 30, 1943, addressed to the Bishop of Berlin, reads:

"Our paternal love and solicitude are greater today toward non-Aryan or semi-Aryan Catholics, children of the Church like the others, when their outward existence is collapsing and they are going through mortal distress. Unhappily, in the present circumstances, *we cannot offer them effective help* other than through our prayers."

This message was the basis of the famous Hochhut play *The Deputy*, with its devastating criticism of the Holocaust Pope.

The astounding feature of this and other communications is that the Pope basically showed some degree of concern only for baptized Jews, for whom he had to demonstrate the same love as for born Catholics.

For example, according to Father Morley, in Slovakia, a country then ruled by Dr. Tiso, a Catholic Bishop, the Vatican's charge d'affaires, Burzio, limited his concern to those Jews who had been baptized.

In Rumania, the efforts of Cassulo, the Papal Nuncio, "on behalf of the Jews, concerned almost exclusively those who had been baptized as Catholic."

The Nuncio in Germany, Orsenigo, when told about the new anti-Jewish laws, expressed worry not about the Jews themselves, but about their Catholic spouses in cases of mixed marriage. A Vatican-hatched scheme to save 300 "non-Aryans" by arranging Brazilian visas for them was only intended for baptized Jews. The scheme never materialized.

In France, when the Vichy Government informed the Vatican's Assistant Secretary of State, Giovanni Montini (who later became Pope Paul VI), about the new anti-Jewish laws, the latter only expressed concern that the laws might obstruct mixed marriages.

In the case of Poland, Morley documents dispatch after dispatch, received during 1942 at the Vatican, detailing all the atrocities and extermination schemes of the Nazis. The Pope was probably better informed of the inferno going on in Poland at that time than anyone else outside of Nazi Germany. Yet his only reaction to the avalanche of telegrams sent to him by Jewish leaders in all parts of the free world was to ask his Nuncios to "answer *orally* that the Holy See is doing what it can."

The Pope hid behind general, complicated phrases, which could not be clearly identified, and therefore could not upset anyone. Even after the Allies had liberated Italy, President Roosevelt's envoy, Harold H. Tittmann, expressed his exasperation with the Pope in his report of a meeting with him: "The Holy See was unable to publicly denounce particular atrocities, but it had frequently condemned atrocities in general. He said that he thought that it was plain to everyone that he was referring to the Poles, Jews and hostages when he declared that hundreds of thousands of persons had been killed or tortured through no fault of their own, sometimes only because of their race or nationality."

While the Pope professed to be unable to do more than to pray, Father Morley does not excuse his inaction, since there were innumerable opportunities for the Pope to critically influence Germany's policies. For example, when 1,259 Jews were deported from Rome, the German Ambassador watched nervously for the Pope's reaction. In a dispatch to Berlin, he congratulated himself that the only feeble reaction had been a visit by the Vatican Secretary of State, Maglione, who uttered some noncommittal words on the subject of the deportation, but was keen on keeping even those words off the record, ending his conversation: "If you think it more opportune not to mention our conversation, so be it."

While the Pope again and again said that he left it up to the Bishops to react to local excesses by the Nazis, he carefully orchestrated an attitude of reserve through his Secretary of State. The only time he personally showed great indignation is repeated several times in Father Morley's book: On March 24, 1942, the Vatican received a communication from the Chief Rabbi of Budapest, according to which "the Germans were planning on sending several thousand Slovak Jewish girls as prostitutes for their front-line soldiers in Russia. The Pope himself was so disturbed at this news that he instructed Maglione to protest to Sidor (the Slovak Minister to the Holy See) and to attempt to dissuade his Government from allowing such a horror." The Pope also ordered Burzio, his charge d'affaires in Bratislava, to do likewise. This incident offers amazing insight into the psychological make-up of Pius XII: evidently his libido was more active than his sense of indignation in the face of mass murder.

Contrary to Pope John Paul II's recent statement, Father Morley's condemnation of the Pope and the Holy See for its failure during the Holocaust is unequivocal: "It must be concluded that Vatican diplomacy failed the Jews during the Holocaust by not doing all that was possible for it to do on their behalf. It also failed itself, because in neglecting the needs of the Jews, and pursuing a goal of reserve rather than humanitarian concern, it betrayed the ideals that it had set for itself. The Nuncios, the Secretary of State, and most of all, the Pope, share the responsibility for this dual failure."

We must, however, delve further into the perplexing attitude of the Vatican during the Holocaust to find its true, basic motivations, so that we may draw some conclusions from this history. It is simply not enough to blame the omissions of the Vatican on Pope Pius XII's personal pro-German bias. There were, as I have found, two basic motivations, fully documented by Father Morley, both of which are still very much alive today: 1) theological anti-Semitism, and 2) theological anti-Zionism.

Father Morley describes the Vatican's anti-Jewish attitude as follows: "[Some of the Nuncios] felt that certain aspects of the anti-Jewish legislation would be beneficial in minimizing Jewish influence in countries where it was considered harmful to Christian society. Such an opinion. . . has an historical echo in the age-old Christian view of the Jews as 'the witness people.' According to this theory, the Jews rejected and killed Jesus, and by so doing, incurred the anger of G-d. Because they were deicidists, the Jews were destined by G-d to suffer. One aspect of their suffering was to be their low status in Christian society, with all kinds of legislation to that effect. It was thought that this servile posture would serve as a testimony to Jewish inferiority and Christian superiority in the mind of G-d."

The Nuncios were "not reluctant to use moral and physical pressures and threats to attempt to convince the Jews of the veracity and superiority of Christianity." That is why they accepted the baptism of Jews, even under the force of threat and deportation, and concentrated whatever efforts they cared to exert on behalf of such converts.

When it comes to theological anti-Zionism, the material offered by Father Morley is simply amazing. Archbishop Angelo Roncalli—later known as the "Good Pope John XXIII"—as well as Secretary of State Maglione and his principal assistant, Mgr. Domenico Tardini, are all quoted as warning against any steps which may encourage Jews to found, after the war, a Jewish state in Palestine: "Palestine is by this time more sacred for Catholics than. . . for Jews."

Morley explains their attitude further: "If Palestine were to become predominantly Jewish, then Catholic piety would be offended and Catholics would be understandably anxious as to whether they could continue to peacefully enjoy their historic rights over the holy places."

The most amazing formulation of this antagonism is expressed by Maglione, the Vatican Secretary of State, the man who, more than anyone else under the Pope, was responsible for implementing a policy, year after year, of turning a deaf ear to Jewish suffering: "It is true that at one time Palestine was inhabited by Jews, but how can the principle of bringing back people to this land where they were until nineteen centuries ago, be historically accepted? It would not seem difficult, in case there is a desire to create a 'Jewish Home,' to find other territories which would be better suited for that purpose, while Palestine, under Jewish majority, would give rise to new and grave international problems, would displease Catholics throughout the entire world, would provoke justifiable protest of the Holy See, and *would badly correspond to the charitable concern that the same Holy See has had and continues to have for the Jews.*"

Roncalli, the "Good Pope"(!), added that he "felt uneasy about the attempts of Jews to reach Palestine, as if they were trying to reconstruct a Jewish kingdom. . . . [It would not be] proper that the *charitable activity of the Holy See* should be used in this way to help in the realization of any messianic dream that the Jews might have."

In short, we deduce from Father Morley's elaborations that the Vatican's motivations during the War were, on the one hand, the belief that the Holocaust represented divine justice against the Jews, and, on the other, an attempt to prevent a Jewish State from being established in Palestine after the War.

Now, almost 50 years later, the same currents within the Vatican are apparent. They are well formulated by Brother Marcel-Jacques Dubois, O.P., a Dominican philosopher from France, now head of the Philosophy Department at the Hebrew University in Jerusalem (*Encyclopedia Judaica, Year Book 1974,* p. 167). The Diaspora is considered to be a consequence of the crucifixion, a punishment for deicide, and Zionism must therefore be regarded as an arrogant presumption, in opposition to the will of G-d, Who has punished His people, condemning them to exile and wandering. Now that the Messiah has come, the Church—"Verus Israel"—has taken the place of the old Israel. "The Jewish people no longer have any reason to exist; so the Jews as a nation may now vanish and, in any case, have no right to occupy the historic land of Israel."

As horrifying as these conservative Catholic theses are, they become even more horrifying and tragic when one thinks back to the naive and unsuspecting Jewish leaders—from Geneva, London and New York—who sent petition after petition during the War to the Vatican, appealing to the supposed sense of humanity of the Church, never sensing that the Church's aims were directed in an entirely different direction.

One can also understand how, against the background of such negative attitudes to the Jewish people, the Catholic clergy must have woken up, with a sense of total theological shock, to find the Jewish people reborn, stronger than ever, and reestablished in that very State which the Church had written off forever for the Jews, and long ago had usurped for itself.

Against the background of such clear historic evidence, it is obvious that during the Holocaust the Vatican was motivated by its age-old animosity toward Judaism and by its long-standing goal of converting Jews to Christianity, coupled with a fear of the establishment of a Jewish State. Unfortunately, this anti-Jewish prejudice still surfaces from time to time, despite the good intentions of the Church to change its attitude to Jews under the encyclical "Nostra Aetate," initiated by Pope John XXIII.

We all remember the deliberate slight of Pope Paul VI, when, after a visit to Israel, he sent a thank you letter addressed to "Mr. Shazar, Tel Aviv," without using his Presidential title, or any mention of Israel or Jerusalem. (In contrast, when the predecessor of the current Pope, John Paul I, assumed office, he wrote a letter properly addressed to "President Ephraim Katzir, Jerusalem, Israel," which must have been very much against the liking of the Curia. A few days later, however, he was dead, having died under mysterious circumstances, which to this day have not been cleared up.)

The current Pope has again and again demonstrated his disregard for Jewish sensitivities by his repeated meetings with Kurt Waldheim and Yasir Arafat, his refusal to recognize Israel, his refusal to allow a discussion of the return of precious Hebrew manuscripts seized by the Church from Jewish communities, and by his inactivity during the recent Auschwitz crisis, etc. When he says he does not recognize Israel because her borders are not yet settled, he is obviously avoiding the true reason: the theological objections to a reborn Jewish State, as we have observed above. He did not even allow an American cardinal to visit Israel's President and Prime Minister during a visit there!

The benign and conciliatory voices of American cardinals in cities with large Jewish and Protestant populations can therefore not always be accepted as the genuine voice of the Vatican. For that voice, the words, actions and inactions of the Pope himself, and the Curia around him, must be watched. For example, when some Catholic bishops in the United States recently put forward a plan for "settlement" of the Arab-Israel problem, they claimed that they had the security of Israel in mind. But at the same time, the Pope in Rome declared himself in favor of a Palestinian State, which we all know would be a mortal peril to the survival of Israel.

Our only hope, however, is that younger elements inside the Vatican, who have a different philosophy from the Curia of old, may one day change the attitude of the Church to Jews and to Israel, in a spirit of appreciation and respect.

But as to the Holocaust years, history has pronounced a negative judgement on Pope Pius XII, which no media blitz can eradicate or dilute: He was hardly saint material, from anyone's point of view.

## Worst Anti-Semitic Outrage in 1,000 Years Perpetrated by the Church

About a thousand years have passed since the Vatican demonstrated its plans for Jews in Jerusalem: When the Crusaders reached Jerusalem and captured the city—after having massacred numerous Jewish communities on their way—the princes and knights of the Church promptly killed every Jew in sight. The Christians herded the Jews into a synagogue, and—as was later copied hundreds of times by Hitler—set it on fire. This crime was indicative of what place they would reserve to Jews in the Jewish capital.

Now, 1,000 years later, they have again manifested their passion for barring Jews from Jerusalem and barring Jerusalem from Jews. It happened when Arafat came to Bethlehem, after a series of actions by the Vatican.

As was publicized, Leah Rabin—who had shown her contempt for the Jewish religion by wearing no head covering at her husband's funeral, as is the Jewish custom—visited the pope. In a show of respect for the Christian religion, she wore a very chaste, large hat. (She had previously shown her respect for the Moslem religion by declaring that she would prefer that her grandchildren marry Moslems rather than religious Jews.) In either an intended or unintended faux pas, she declared that the Pope had told her that Jerusalem is the capital of Israel. This statement was not only denied the very next day by the Vatican, but the pope immediately dispatched his cardinal in charge of inter-religious relations, Archbishop Tauran, to Jerusalem. While for show he visited the Chief Rabbi, the President and the Prime Minister, Tauran carried out the Pope's order to dismantle the Jewish claim to Jerusalem without waiting for any of the "final negotiations" under the Oslo agreement.

And this is how it happened: The Christian Orthodox Patriarch Deodorus I handed over to Arafat the keys and custody of all Christian churches in Jerusalem, including the Church of the Sepulcher. This was done in the presence of the Catholic, Anglican and Greek Orthodox archbishops. And he made the following statement to the beaming PLO terror chief: "I am heir of Sophronius and I am handing the keys to Christian holy sites in Jerusalem to the heir of Omar ibn al-Khattab." Sophronius was the last representative of the Byzantine empire to rule over Jerusalem, who, after the capture of the city by Omar in 638, signed a surrender treaty with the Moslem leader in which Jews would be banned from living in Jerusalem. The name "Jerusalem" did not appear in the Omar-Sophronius treaty. Only the Roman pagan name, Aelia Capitolina—introduced by Emperor Hadrian—was used.

Arafat has from time to time alluded to his ambition to be another Omar, just as the late President Anwar Sadat said in his Knesset speech, "Let us invoke the spirit of Omar." Although unnoticed during Sadat's life, any reference to Omar simply means, "Jerusalem must be Judenrein."

This utter perfidy performed by the Church has a two-fold purpose: 1) It wants to show the world that Israel cannot be trusted with the shrines of other religions, despite her impeccable record in assuring freedom of worship and religion and protection of all holy shrines and despite the murderous record of Moslems as custodians—they destroyed churches in Lebanon, and all the synagogues in the Old City; 2) By giving away the Christian section of Jerusalem to the Moslems, the Church weakens the political influence of Israel over Jerusalem and, G-d forbid, destroys it.

As I wrote in a recent column, for the Vatican, keeping Jerusalem out of Jewish hands is essential for maintaining the Christian religion, because according to the Gospels, the Jews must remain punished and banned from the Holy City as long as they do not recognize the (Jewish) "founder" of the Christian religion—although their religion was founded by yet another Jew, Paul, who did not know Jesus.

I also reported last year that the Israeli press revealed that Peres, even before the Oslo agreement, had made an agreement with the Vatican that the Christians would be given the over-all control of our capital—to be "sub-divided" into Christian, Moslem and Jewish sectors. Peres has been totally silent in the face of the latest Vatican outrage: no protest; no retaliation at this insult and political attack on Israeli sovereignty. Is Peres a participant in this horrible offense against Jewish honor, history and claim?

Coming on top of the recent lopsided, 128-1 U.N. vote against Jewish sovereignty over Jerusalem, the Peres government's failure to oppose by all available means this intrusion into Jewish sovereignty is what is responsible for the fatal erosion of our position in Jerusalem.

Those Jews who lined up in New York to shake hands with Arafat were not only shaking the hands of a man with countless murders of Jews on his conscience, but—probably unknown to most of them or conveniently forgotten—they were shaking the hands of someone who has also hurled the most outrageous insults and curses against Jews since Hitler.

Some time ago, a telephone conversation by Arafat with someone in Paris was monitored and recorded. The gist of his statements was: "The Jews—damn their fathers! The dogs, filth and dirt! Trash is always trash! The rotten Jews—I will settle accounts with them in the future!"

There may be those who will say that Arafat has changed his feelings and is now only harboring gentlemanly sentiments about Jews. No such luck! His speeches in Arabic—shielded from Jewish viewers by Peres and Israeli government censorship—reveal that he is hell-bent on fulfilling his decision to "settle accounts" with Jews. He praises anyone who has killed Jews in suicide attacks; he vows to take away our Land and capital.

Like the leopard who does not change its spots, Arafat has had no change of heart. Only Peres and his likes have had a change of heart. They seem to have abandoned Jewish honor, security and future.

*The New York Times* continues to display its extreme anti-Jewish bias in its reporting. When it came to the Bethlehem take-over by the PLO, *The Times* ignored reports of widespread Christian calls to boycott the ceremony because of the PLO's sordid record of destruction of Christian churches in Lebanon and murders of Christian nuns, priests and worshippers. *The Times* ignored signs that the PLO had placed in Bethlehem in the past, written on the PLO flag, reading: "Today we kill the Saturday children (Jews), tomorrow we will kill the Sunday children (Christians)." Any newspaper that fails to report such important news is obviously one-sided and biased.

Instead, *The Times* saw the Bethlehem take-over only as a great victory for the Moslems. When it comes to Rabin's assassination, here are some invectives used: *The Times* wrote that Yigal Amir was "fired by those who spew violent religious ideology." Would they talk of Catholics or Protestants "spewing religious ideology?" They only reserve that utterly ugly term for the Jewish religion. Last Sunday *The Times* characterized the assassination as a "racist act!" What could possibly have been racist about it? Are not all Jews involved in these events of the same race?

We see again the spectacle of Americans and Israelis running, hat in hand, to elicit some kind of "word" from the arch-schemer, Hafez Assad of Syria. Leading them is American Secretary of State Warren Christopher, who was Jimmy Carter's close disciple. As a member of the Carter administration, he should have learned a lesson about the treachery of the Syrian dictator and should not lead Israel, America's faithful ally, into the Syrian trap. The best testimony we have comes, posthumously, from the late Egyptian President Anwar Sadat, whose memoirs were published under the title *Those I have Known*.

There he mocked Jimmy Carter for putting any faith in the double crosses of Assad: "Carter did not know how to handle the Syrians. He imagined they would be as good as their word and was taken aback when he found that the word of a Syrian was in fact a thousand and one words and that what they agreed to one day they rejected the next."

Bearing this treacherous character in mind, what can Israel expect from the so-called "peace" negotiations, other than that the Syrians will gain everything and Israel will lose everything? No wonder that all leading generals have now lined up against the Peres government, including Gen. Yitzchak Mordechai, commander of the Northern front; Gen. Dan Shomron, hero of the Entebbe raid; Gen. Peled, intelligence chief; Gen. Avigdor Kahalani, hero of the Yom Kippur War; and many more.

Gen. Arik Sharon has declared his support for Bibi Netanyahu and it is likely that Dovid Levy will also re-join the Likud party. When Israel's very survival is in danger—and Peres even offers to give up Israel's vital deterrent, its atomic power—the call for unity must override all other considerations.

# A Confrontation With The Vatican

The American Jewish community has, for close to two years, been agitated about the exhibition of Hebrew manuscripts from the Vatican Library, which have been traveling from city to city since September 1987. The controversy about these precious manuscripts arose from the fact that all available history books testify that the Church, for over 600 years, by order of the Popes, seized and destroyed Hebrew books in communities under jurisdiction of the Church. How then did these manuscripts making up the Vatican exhibition come into the possession of the Church?

The arguments set forth by the Vatican and the promoters of the exhibition have been that these manuscripts were gifted and donated to the Church by well-meaning Italian aristocrats and a Swedish queen, and that in fact the Church did not confiscate any Hebrew books. In fact, they propose that there was wholesome "cultural cross-fertilization" between the Church and the Jews, and that the Church was only interested in Hebrew manuscripts from the point of view of "Renaissance humanism" and "a reverence for the Hebrew language as one of the languages of Divine revelation." They stress the fact that there was "a millennium of cultural and intellectual exchange between Christians and Jews."

This controversy has taken the form of newspaper ads in most of the cities visited by the Vatican exhibit, radio talk shows, public discussions, etc. It was followed by a coast-to-coast campaign for petitions addressed to the papal nuncio in Washington, the Pope's personal representative in this country, for the return of the manuscripts to their original owners, the Jewish people. Thousands of concerned Jews signed these petitions.

It was only a question of when the Vatican would react to the Jewish concerns. This happened on April 24, when the Vatican dispatched their librarian emeritus, Alfons Maria Cardinal Stickler, to Cambridge to deliver an address to a meeting called for the opening of the Vatican manuscripts exhibit at Harvard.

The Committee for the Return of Jewish Manuscripts, of which I am the chairman, welcomed this opportunity to engage in meaningful dialogue with such a distinguished representative of the Vatican, and therefore sent a delagation to attend the Harvard meeting. To our disappointment, however, the organizers of the meeting called for the meeting to close immediately after the cardinal had read his paper and did not allow any questions to be posed. I, however, took the opportunity to express, on behalf of our Committee, our disappointment that the customary question-and-answer session had been *verboten*. In the loud calls which ensued, the cardinal beckoned to me to approach him on the podium for a private conversation. I decided to converse with him in German, his native tongue as an Austrian, in order to allow him better freedom of expression.

Now, a rather startling conversation took place. I had with me fascimile copies of some papal bulls—issued by the very Popes whom he, just moments before, had called "Renaissance humanists" and lovers of Hebrew books—in which the Talmud and ancillary Hebrew books are called obscene, blasphemous, impudent and therefore banned and to be burned! Faced with this contradiction, the good cardinal called out, "That is a lie! That never happened! The Church never seized any Hebrew books!" Stunned, I concluded that he was no different than those who today claim that the Holocaust never took place. When I asked him with whom we should conduct a dialogue on these questions, he was incensed and shouted, "Nobody will want to discuss this with you! These are all lies!"

Disheartened, a large group who had witnessed this confrontation nevertheless counseled me to have a talk with Cardinal Law of Boston, who had also attended the Stickler lecture. This cardinal had already been previously interviewed by the Jewish advocate of Boston and had expressed conciliatory sentiments. I felt, therefore, happy that Cardinal Law took over my conversation with Cardinal Stickler, who meanwhile abruptly left the poduim. Cardinal Law proposed that our Committee seek an audience with the papal numcio, The Most Reverend Pio Laghi in Washington, and even volunteered to notify the nuncio so that the ground would be prepared for a meeting with him. Cardinal Law's friendly attitude therefore left the confrontation with Cardinal Stickler on a promising note.

The argument made by defenders of the Vatican is that most museums and libraries also have stolen books and art, and furthermore that the Vatican safeguarded the Hebrew books, when otherwise they might have been destroyed. The answer to these arguments is of course that while lovers of books and art may have stolen objects elsewhere, nobody, however, seized books for the purpose of destroying their owners! Because that was the intention of the Church—by depriving the Jews of their precious books, they wanted to prevent Jewish education and practice, and thereby call Judaism to an end as a religion. And as to having safeguarded our books, we appreciate that. But the time has come—now that a Jewish State of Israel has been reborn and Jerusalem again has been restored as the world center of Jewish scholarship and devotion—for our sacred manuscripts to be returned to the National Library in Jerusalem.

The return of these Jewish treasures would be a fine gesture of goodwill on the part of the Pope, which would exact no price from him, either in theological or political terms.

It now remains to be seen how the papal nuncio will react to the delegation made up of leading Jewish scholars and community leaders, when the meeting with our Committee takes place. Let us hope that this time the strong Jewish concerns will be answered in a constructive way.

# Do We Not Deserve the Same Consideration as Galileo?

Three hundred and fifty years ago, the Inquisition of the Catholic Church was able to break the spirit and conviction of Galileo, the astronomer and physicist, who had dared to proclaim that the earth circles around the sun, and not, as the Church held, the other way around. But unlike the hundreds of thousands of Jewish martyrs whom the cruel Inquisition could not break and who were burned at the stake for their religion, Galileo cowardly kneeled before the Inquisitor and recanted his views as false and erroneous, and publicly embraced the backward views of the Church. Galileo was placed under "house arrest" for the rest of his life, and his writings were banned by the Vatican Censor.

Now, 350 years later, the "infallible" Pope has been forced to admit that it was the Church which erred, and that Galileo, after all, was right. The Vatican officially rescinded its "condemnation" of Galileo in an elaborate ceremony in the Pontifical Academy of Science, where the Pope spoke publicly before the world's TV cameras.

Mind you, Galileo only received a relative rap on the fingers from the Church, without a "Papal Bull" or other solemn declaration being issued against him, since he so meekly recanted his Copernican views. Yet legally, the mere "condemnation" of his views required an official act to cancel the ban against him. Compare that to the countless Papal Bulls issued over the centuries condemning Jews, Judaism and the Talmud, which *till this day have not been withdrawn or cancelled*. Would you like to hear some examples of the hate-filled edicts still outstanding against us?

Excerpt from a Papal Bull of Pope Paul III, 1542: "It is our desire that the Jews be converted to the Catholic faith. The Church must keep those Jews who have converted (called neophytes) far away from members of their former religion, lest they regress to their original pernicious practices. Clerics are urged to arrange marriages for the neophytes with Christians by birth." (Note: This is also the strategy of "Jews for Jesus" and other missionary groups: grab a Jew, fix him up with a Christian girl, and encourage them to marry so that their children are sure to be lost to the Jewish people forever.)

"If neophytes fail to correct themselves following a priestly admonition, and are discovered to be living as Jews and to have returned to their vomit, then the clerics should proceed against them in accord with the regulations of the Sacred Law, just as against perfidious heretics."

Excerpt from a Papal Bull by Pope Paul IV (1555-59), forcing the Jews into Ghettos: "There can exist nothing more absurd and unseemly than the Jews. As long as they persist in their errors, as a result of their behavior they are servants, while

Christians are free men. All their synagogues are to be destroyed except one. They should wear a badge of yellow color. From now on, and for all times, their quarters must be separated from Christians."

Excerpt from a Papal Bull by Pope Pius V, in 1566: "The Hebrew race merits to be cast down head first. Its priesthood is lost, its laws stripped of their authority. It is driven asunder from its land, to wander through the world for so many generations, hated, the object of opprobrium. They are given to soothsaying, incantations, magic, superstition and evil practices. Therefore, we decree that every Jew must depart from our Republic within three months, and that their goods become the property of the Roman Church."

Pope Clement VIII, 1593: "The vile and obdurate perfidy of the Hebrews does not even acknowledge the great mercy of the Holy Mother Church that has patiently awaited their conversion. But we now believe that such a nation must be totally expelled from the midst of the majority of our population. But in order that they not be driven too far from the path of salvation promised to the remnant of Israel, but to such closer states where they can be readily restrained, they must be enticed from their mental darkness to an acknowledgement of the true faith of the Holy Roman Church. Any Jew found here after this decree has gone into effect shall be punished by condemning him to the slave ship for as long as he shall live."

Excerpt from the Bull against the Talmud by Pope Clement VIII: "We Christians must not overlook the Jews' wickedness. We decree and condemn that godless work known as the Talmud, and other similar rejected and detestable writings and books. We forbid in all perpetuity all Jews, communities and individuals, from daring in any way to read, possess, buy, sell or publish any books or codices of the godless and often censured Talmud, and those other utterly worthless, cabalistic and abominable books that are forbidden and condemned, as well as any commentaries, treatises and writings in the Hebrew language or in any other languages which are lewd and obscene works. Anybody, Jew or non-Jew, possessing any of such books must deliver them to Rome within ten days to the office of the Holy Roman and Universal Inquisition, the books to be burned. Anybody violating this decree is subject to confiscation of all goods and bodily torture."

None of these outrageous and hate-crazed rantings against Jews, Judaism and our literature, have ever been rescinded or cancelled. When I inquired with the National Conference of Catholic Bishops about this unacceptable situation, which totally violates the tenets and spirit of the "Nostra Aetate" of 25 years ago, I received an answer from Dr. Eugene Fisher, the public relations spokesman for the Catholics: "There is no need for an 'official annulment and withdrawal' of the anti-Jewish Church legislation of previous ages. That has already been officially accomplished by the Second Vatican Council." This answer flies in the face of what happens when the Vatican *really* wants to atone for past errors—as in the case of Galileo. There, 13 years of investigation was carried out, leading to the official retraction. I repeat the question: Do we not deserve the same consideration as Galileo?

On the subject of the Second Vatican Council, raised by the good Dr. Fisher, I recommend the reading of the day-to-day account of what happened during that 4-1/2 year process, from June 1962 until December 1965. The declaration "On the Jews and Non-Christians" led to anti-Semitic attacks of the crudest sort by many Cardinals, and excruciating and agonizing discussions, with compromise after compromise necessary until a consensus could be reached. A large portion of the "Church Princes" meeting in Rome were simply unable to force themselves to say anything exonerating the Jews. To them, the Jews must remain forever condemned, and the Church's single-minded purpose must remain to force them into conversion.

Any reference to past persecutions and massacres of Jews by the Church was met by stunned objections, and in the end, the sponsors of the Declaration were defeated. They could not even get approval for identifying the hundreds of years of crimes against the Jews, including the Church's role and silence during the Holocaust, as "persecution" (Latin: *persecutio*). They had to settle for the meaningless expression "harassment" (Latin: *vexatio*), and for including the condemnation of anti-Semitism together with condemnation of *all* "injustices."

The final Declaration, therefore, is a greatly watered-down document, which cannot by any means give Jews full satisfaction, especially as it strongly alludes to a call for conversion of all Jews: "Just as the Church repudiated *all* injustices inflicted on *any* man, so she likewise deplores and condemns hatred and harassment of the Jews. *The union of the Jewish people with the Church* is a part of the Christian hope. Indeed, *the Church awaits the entrance of this people into the fullness of the people of G-d established by Christ*." (Mind you, we Jews are called "this people," and the Christians are called "the people of G-d.")

To think that in the mind of the Church all they did to us during centuries of the worst crimes imaginable was nothing more than "harassment!" Can one expect true atonement from such people? No wonder that the anti-Jewish edicts and Bulls remain on their books. We evidently cannot expect to share the fate of Galileo. Dr. Fisher's assertion that the Second Vatican Council "accomplished" the annulment and cancellation of the anti-Jewish legislation therefore does not hold water.

Jewish leaders who are professionals in dealing with the Catholic Church, seem to have overlooked the enormous obstacles to any relationship between Jews and the Church—these anti-Jewish measures which have never been withdrawn. This is a serious omission which should be addressed before they proceed further in their inter-faith activities. It is also a matter for Israel's Government to consider before discussing normalization of diplomatic relations between Israel and the Vatican.

The ink was hardly dry on the Declaration of the Second Vatican Council, with its call for the conversion of world Jewry, when a world-wide appeal was made in 1985 for funding a convent at Auschwitz for Carmelite nuns. The appeal said the convent would be presented as a gift to the Pope after his visit to Poland. The convent's purpose would be "the conversion of strayed brothers," referring to the Jews.

When Jews found out about the convent, an outcry of protest was heard. Years of bitter recrimination and nasty reaction from the Polish clergy ensued. It soon became apparent that the Church planned the convent to serve as a memorial for two alleged Christian martyrs of Auschwitz: Father Kolbe and Edith Stein. The convent would thus become a "gift" to the Pope, as he had singled out these two individuals for sainthood. This was, of course, another blow to Jewish sensitivities: While we had 6 million martyrs from our faith during the Holocaust, the Church could only find two individuals whom they thought would qualify: Father Kolbe, a known Polish anti-Semite, who by some accounts only accidentally ended up in Auschwitz, and Edith Stein, a confused Jewish girl, who at one point had converted to Christianity.

The rest is history, which most people already know. The many efforts to move the controversial convent away from Auschwitz, although attempted innumerable times, have not resulted in any action. When the Church saw that its original designs for the convent as a strictly Catholic-Polish memorial at Auschwitz would not succeed, they switched plans. They proposed to establish at Auschwitz a "Center of Information, Meetings, Dialogue, Education and Prayer," a plan met with little enthusiasm by Jews, as the memorial would retain its Christian nature, erected on a site drenched in Jewish blood. It seems to have been overlooked that such a Center would serve the same purpose as the convent—"the conversion of strayed brothers."

Sir Siegmund Sternberg, a British Jew who has maintained good relations with the Church, and who has also worked toward the removal of the convent, received a letter dated September 30, 1989, from the highly controversial Polish Cardinal Glemp, in which he contrasted the "moderating voice" of Sir Siegmund, a Reform Jew, with the "shrill voices" of such idealistic and dedicated Orthodox militants as Rabbi Avi Weiss of Riverdale. Glemp proposed to Sir Siegmund: "The best solution would be to work on a new Center."

Sir Siegmund has no doubt done much in his attempt to have the convent removed. Although he has not succeeded in this, he has nonetheless gotten high praise from the former Chief Rabbi of Great Britain, Lord Jakobovits, who in a personal letter to me wrote: "He (Sir Siegmund) is a dear friend of mine (even if there are items on which we disagree), and he has enormous achievements to his credit, building bridges of understanding with other faiths, notably the Roman Catholics, and lately embracing Eastern Europe."

Sir Siegmund also wrote directly to me, stating that the proposed "Center of Information, Meetings, Dialogue, Education and Prayer" is not his own creation, but was agreed to at a Jewish-Christian meeting in Geneva on July 22, 1986. *I apologize if in another column I erroneously put the blame for this on Sir Siegmund.* Therefore, anyone objecting to such a Center should not blame Sir Siegmund!

Now that three years have passed, world Jewry is deeply suspicious of the ultimate purpose of that "Center." Reform Jews are the only ones pressing for theological dialogue with the Church, which can only lead to missionary activities and a challenge to Judaism. Mainstream Jews maintain the *halachic* prohibition, promulgated by Rabbi J.B. Soloveitchik in 1964, against such interfaith dialogue. That is the reason why in a previous column I criticized Sir Siegmund's recent attempt not only to support the Center, but also to invite Sister Teresa, the anti-Semitic Carmelite head of the convent, to assume a leadership role in the proposed Center. When, to top it all off, Sister Teresa refused his request, and he begged her "to pray" to change her mind, I found it a demeaning act, insensitive to the memory of our martyrs at Auschwitz, and to the entire tragic history of Christian-Jewish relations.

The above sampling of unrevoked Papal Bulls—forerunners of Hitler's atrocities against Jews—tells us what the Catholic Church must do before we can take their claim that they like to perform "atonement" seriously. They must revoke those hateful anti-Jewish edicts, by official acts of the Pope, similar to his revocation of the condemnation of Galileo!

# "Rome Reborn"—
# A Thoroughly De-Judaized Vatican Exhibition

During my stay in Washington for President Clinton's inauguration, I managed an extended visit to the Library of Congress, where the magnificent, newly-refurbished "Great Hall" is being used to house a Vatican exhibition of manuscripts entitled "Rome Reborn—the Vatican Library Renaissance Culture."

I was, of course, most curious to see what the Vatican is putting on display, as this is the first exhibition of Vatican manuscripts since the sadly remembered exhibition "A Visual Testimony: Judaica from the Vatican Library." That exhibition was inaugurated by the Pope himself when it opened on November 11, 1987, in Miami, Florida, from where it travelled from city to city across the United States. An anguished outcry was heard from concerned Jews all over the world, because the manuscripts displayed had been seized and confiscated by the Church over the centuries with the intention to burn them, and thereby—as they hoped—to eradicate Judaism. The few such manuscripts left in the Vatican Library—estimated to be about 800—are a dismal remnant of the hundreds of thousands seized and burnt by Pope after Pope. A grass-roots movement arose in many countries, calling on the Vatican to return these sacred manuscripts to their rightful owners, the Jewish people. That campaign goes on unabated and is increasing in strength.

The Church initially stonewalled our grievances, putting forth such untenable arguments as the explanation that the sacred Jewish manuscripts were, in fact, gifts presented by Italian noblemen, and that the Popes, especially in the 16th century, were "Renaissance Humanists" who loved the Hebrew language. These arguments have, of course, been refuted, but it is interesting to note the ramifications of this campaign on the current exhibition.

In presenting the "Vatican Judaica" exhibition of 1987, its organizers—Vatican experts and Reform Jews—claimed that the Humanist Renaissance Popes held the ideal "that every man of culture should be *trium linguarum gnarus*," meaning, he should know Latin, Greek and Hebrew, the "sacred languages" of the Bible, and that the Vatican Library had embraced the trilingual ideal. By contrast, the new exhibition has trimmed this statement down, saying that the Humanists believed that Greek and Latin were needed—with no mention of Hebrew!

The publicity hand-outs at the 1987 exhibition spoke glowingly of the Vatican Hebrew manuscripts, saying that they testified to "a millennium of cultural and intellectual exchanges between Christians and Jews," and to "cross-fertilization" between the two religions. However, the campaign for the return of Vatican manuscripts helped educate and enlighten the public as to the utter fallacy of such distorted statements, for the Church's attitude toward Judaism had in fact been one of unremitting hostility, bent on spiritual genocide. Vicious Papal Bulls, issued by one Pope after another, absolutely prohibited any Jew or non-Jew from even owning a single Hebrew manuscript. Therefore it is inconceivable that any Pope would "collect" Hebrew manuscripts for "the love of the Hebrew language."

It is obvious that the Vatican has learned its lesson: The same Father Leonard E. Boyle, O.P., who organized the 1987 exhibition, has also been selected to organize the present exhibition of Vatican manuscripts—only now he has changed his methods.

His new scheme became crystal clear as I visited one display after the other, examining each exhibit with a fine-tooth comb. I discovered that this time, what the exhibition does *not* show is more important than what it does show. A total cleansing has taken place: *not one Hebrew manuscript* is on display!

The catalogue of the Washington exhibition fleetingly mentions where some of the Vatican's possessions came from, citing, for example, that one source was "the Palatine Library from Heidelberg, with some 2000 Latin and 430 Greek manuscripts, the gift of Maximilian of Bavaria when he captured Heidelberg." Conveniently omitted, though, is any mention of the few hundred Hebrew manuscripts that were also taken from Heidelberg, which had been wrested from a massacred Jewish community in that part of Germany and which thereby ended up in the Vatican.

While in the past the Vatican claimed that some Hebrew manuscripts were a gift from Sweden's Queen Christina, the new catalogue omits mention of her Hebrew manuscripts, and only mentions "2000 Latin manuscripts of Queen Christina of Sweden, purchased from her heirs." That must have been a neat trick, since, as everybody knows, Queen Christina never married, and died a spinster in Rome. She therefore had, of course, no "heirs." She did, however, plunder the Library of Prague, a city her father captured during the 30 Year War, and amassed Hebrew manuscripts in that fashion. Those are the manuscripts she took to the Vatican.

It is easy to surmise why the good Father Boyle went out of his way to cover up the true facts of the matter: He is trying to avoid another showdown with concerned Jews, who would justifiably protest, on the one hand, the glorification of the Vatican with stolen sacred Jewish possessions, and demand, on the other, the return of these treasures to their rightful owners, the Jewish people.

Another objectionable point made in the new exhibition catalogue is the statement that Pope Gregory XIII, at the end of the 16th century, "opened a further institution for 'Neophytes,' an establishment for the education of converts from Judaism." The truth is that this was one of the Church's most sinister and ferocious attempts to combat Judaism: Renegade Jews were taken there and ordered to search in Hebrew books to find arguments against Judaism, and to provide reasons for banning the Talmud. It was, therefore, not a place for "educating" converts, but for renegade Jews to teach the Church how to combat Judaism!

Another example of the agenda of the Church's "ethnic cleansing" at work here: The exhibition is divided into different sections, such as "Mathematics," "Humanism," "Archaeology," "Music," and "Medicine and Biology." The section called "A Wider World" displays manuscripts in Arabic, Chinese, Coptic, Ethiopian, Russian, Armenian, and Greek—but none in Hebrew.

A polyglot Bible, printed in Genoa in 1516, is displayed with translations of the Hebrew Bible into Latin, Greek, Aramaic and Arabic, but, of course, this is not a Jewish book. Further, this book is probably not even the property of the Vatican, but of the Library of Congress; it was exhibited some years ago by the Library of Congress because it contains the earliest reference to Christopher Columbus having been born in Genoa.

Prominent mention is made in the exhibition of "Christian catacombs" underneath ancient Rome, where archaeologists are said to have found "a whole lost world of early Christian symbolism." Not a word is said to indicate that a significant part of the Roman catacombs contain not Christian, but Jewish relics, tombstones and symbols.

These catacombs are subterraneous chambers running for miles under the surface of Rome. At a time when it was dangerous to openly profess one's adherence to Judaism, Jews would bury their dead in these underground alcoves, raising countless beautifully decorated marble plaques over them. Many are decorated with such symbols as the *shofar*, *lulav* and *etrog* and the holy ark. Secret services were also probably held in the catacombs.

Until recently, Jewish scholars were barred from working in these catacombs, and the official line of the Church was that these were Christian, not Jewish, shrines. However, Mrs. Tulia Zevi, president of the Association of Italian Jews, should be given credit for obtaining, after many frustrating years of negotiations with Italian authorities, the rights to the Jewish catacombs. We must hope that enough funding will be made available from Jewish sources to research and publish accounts of the untold historic monuments which are buried below Rome's street level.

The Church's attempt to hide or deny the presence of important ancient Jewish relics in the Rome area can be understood as based on the theological problems they present for Christianity. The Church is embarrassed by the fact that Jews made up a significant part of Rome's population, and that it was Jewish rabbis who exerted the influence needed to veer the pagan Roman rulers away from idol worship and start them on a search for a monotheistic religion. The Church would like to pretend that it was the Christian population of Rome—even though it was infinitesimally small compared to the much older Jewish population living there—which influenced the pagan Roman Empire to abandon its paganism.

The truth is very different: It was the example of the Jewish religious and moral superiority that, for centuries, first annoyed and then impressed the Greek-Roman pagan world.

For centuries they tried to obliterate this small, irritating, superior people.

When they saw that nothing would repress the Jews—not the constant battles with the Maccabees, the destruction of the Temple, the outlawing of the Jewish religion and the breaking of the Bar Kochba revolt—the Romans came to the conclusion that "if you can't beat 'em, join 'em!"

By the time Emperor Constantine came to power in the 4th century C.E., the Roman Empire stood at a crossroad: Should they adopt Judaism as the official state religion? It might have been tempting, and even flattering to the Jewish leadership at the time, to accommodate Rome. But our leaders were not ready to compromise the Torah's laws dealing with ritual purity and impurity, family relations, dietary laws, circumcision, etc. So, instead, the Christians jumped in, and, with open arms, waived all commandments and restrictions, offering their watered-down religion with a healthy dose of pagan components to the Romans. That is how Christianity, not Judaism, became the religion of the Roman Empire, with disastrous consequences for the Jewish people, who were promptly persecuted and hounded by the new Christian masters. The result was endless suffering for the Jews throughout the ages.

Another important archaeological discovery, which has embarrassed the Church for decades, is the unexpected find of the ruins of a very large synagogue at the excavations carried out in Ostia Antica. This town, now far inland, was in Roman days a flourishing commercial seaport. The city was dominated by Jewish merchants who carried on a worldwide trade from there. The magnificent synagogue bespeaks a large and affluent Jewish community.

When my family and I passed through the Leonardo da Vinci Airport some 30 years ago, our driver took us, to our delight, to the synagogue excavations, and over the years I have watched more and more being unearthed. The holy ark is still standing, flanked by "Corinthian" pillars. Some of them bear engraved symbols of a shofar and other Jewish objects. A *matza* bakery was also discovered next to the synagogue.

When these ruins were first discovered, the Church did everything to suppress news of the discovery—for it proved the predominance of Jews in an important Roman city, again embarrassing the Church and discrediting its presentation of history. We are fortunate that a Socialist member of Parliament, who did not care for the Church, made the discovery public.

Coming back to the Vatican exhibition at the Library of Congress, I was just about ready to give up my search for at least *one* Jewish manuscript, when I made a startling discovery. It was in the "Music" section, where ancient manuscripts of Church chants, some called "antiphoners," some "graduals," from the Gregorian and Renaissance periods, were displayed. Suddenly, I spotted a strange manuscript: The legend said it was written by one Elezar Genet of Carpentras, and represented the melody for singing Jeremiah's Lamentations! (Carpentras is the famous ancient Jewish community in Provence, which has survived all persecutions and expulsions and still exists today.) Obviously this was a synagogue manuscript, containing the *niggun* or *trop* for singing *Eicha* on Tisha B'Av.

I photographed the two pages opened to the public, and the next day showed them to Cantor Yossi Malovany, who is not only a world-renowned cantor, but also a brilliant musicologist. He immediately recognized the niggun as an authentic synagogal melody, no longer in use, now known only from scholarly sources. I fervently hope that Dr. James H. Billington, the head of the Library of Congress, will give permission to photograph the entire manuscript, as it will be a most important contribution to our knowledge of synagogue music of past centuries. Of course, I also pray and hope that Father Boyle, upon realizing that his "Judenrein" policy for the exhibition was actually—probably unbeknownst to him—broken, will not withdraw this precious manuscript from the display!

In spite of the exhibition's obvious distortions, it does remind us of an important lesson: that our vigilance for the sake of salvaging our precious and sacred manuscripts must continue, and that our outstanding heritage must be recovered wherever possible.

Professor William Foxwell Albright (1891-1971), who had seminal influence on Lehmann through his revolutionary innovations in Bible study and archaeology.

# Dead Sea Scrolls

Of all the archaeological discoveries, the Dead Sea Scrolls, first found in 1947, have had the greatest impact, not only on Jews but also on non-Jews. The near miraculous preservation of Hebrew texts, both Biblical and non-Biblical, after 2,000 years proves the strength of Jewish tradition and the correctness of our ancient texts. Many more keys to our early past are still hidden in these scrolls. My pioneering work, starting in the 1950s, opened the avenue from our Oral Torah to the earliest scrolls. Other archaeological discoveries are also of paramount importance in helping appreciate our unbroken history and culture.

## The Dead Sea Scrolls in the Jewish Tradition

June 2, 1993, marked a very memorable occasion, when I was privileged to deliver the annual Memorial Lecture in memory of our son Jamie *z"l*, to a standing-room only audience at Fifth Avenue Synagogue. My wife and I were overcome by the enormous outpouring of interest in these Memorial Lectures, which—as Rabbi Roth of the Fifth Avenue Synagogue said—have become the highlight of Jewish cultural life in New York. Since many who could not attend have expressed interest in the subject, I will herewith give some of the main points covered.

In my talk I stressed that we must be proud of the rich heritage represented by hundreds of written scrolls, some 2000 years old, which document our forefathers' piety, values and aspirations. We should allow no one take our Jewish patrimony away from us, as was attempted in the early stages of the Dead Sea Scroll scholarship.

Christian scholars had quickly jumped to the conclusion that the Scrolls were the product of a little known group, the Essenes. No authentic Jewish sources have ever mentioned this "sect," which, according to Josephus, Philo and Pliny, existed alongside two other "sects," the Sadducees (Tzedukim) and the Pharisees (Perushim). The Essenes were pictured as a rebel group, opposed to the "legalistic" religion of the Pharisees and their "vain ceremonies." The Essenes were pictured as being on a strictly spiritual level—for the most part they were celibate and lived as hermit-like recluses. In other words, they were divorced from normative Judaism and isolated. As such, the Essenes could not be suspected as having been the source of Christianity, nor of having influenced the early Jewish-Christians. In this manner these researchers tried to maintain the myth of Christianity's "originality."

In my opinion, no Essenes, as so described, ever existed. However, our rabbinic sources mention a host of groups within Judaism, separated mainly by the degree of their observance of the mitzvot: Beit Shamai, more stringent than Beth Hillel, the Chasidim Harishonim, Vatikim, Tzenuim, etc., even more stringent than Beit Shamai. But in reality there was no "split" between them and the normative Pharisaic school. In fact, the Talmud tells us that although they differed in regard to many laws, once the *halacha* was established, they all followed the same rules, they intermarried with one another, used the same implements, etc.

There were, of course, those whom our rabbis condemned, e.g., the Baitusim, who tried to upset our calendar and our observance of the holidays. But even the Tzedukim, although they conflicted with the Prushim, who rejected their writings, did not leave the people, and their *kohanim* still served in the Temple.

This is where the Dead Sea Scrolls benefit us, for the halachic texts (especially the Temple Scroll, the Damascus Document, the MMT text) all show an extreme degree of stringency and strictness in the observance of mitzvot, especially those related to the concepts of purity and impurity, the Temple service, the sanctity of Jerusalem, etc.

It would seem that Hillel beseeched them not to divorce themselves from the Jewish people: "*al tifrosh min hatzibur*" (Do not separate from the congregation.). However, they answered (in MMT) "*peirashnu mi'rov ha'am*" (we have separated ourselves from the majority of the people). That was their undoing, and soon, after some disputations between them and the rabbis (reported in MMT as well as in the Talmud), their halachic writings, such as found in the Scrolls, were condemned to destruction. This, according to Megilat Taanit, happened on Tamuz 14, which for a while remained a joyous day in the Jewish calendar. But they returned to the fold of the Jewish people.

One unusual Scroll is the "Copper Scroll," written on thin copper foil, not on parchment or papyrus as the others were. It contains a strange inventory, listing huge hoards of gold and other precious items, worth about $30 million in current value, with 64 hiding places where they were concealed. Could this refer to a real treasure, or was it a fable? Christian scholars, unaware of the halachic background involved, preferred to call the Scroll a fantasy, no such treasure was ever accumulated. One Polish Catholic priest, Milik, to whom the Copper Scroll was officially assigned for publication, fumbled totally in his interpretation, mistranslating the most elementary terms.

In 1964 I published a new interpretation: Based on several passages in the Talmud, I concluded that the Scroll simply listed gifts to the Temple and other taxes which Jews continued to offer, even though the Temple was destroyed and the Romans had prohibited them from entering Jerusalem. Under such circumstances, the *halacha* requires that the gifts are to be redeemed, and their counter-value hidden away, in the Dead Sea area and in similar places. I listed the Hebrew terms actually contained in the Scroll which I re-translated totally. It took 29 years before my interpretation was accepted the world over, and Milik's mistranslations condemned as faulty.

Still, the question remained: What ever happened to those treasures? For this, too, I have found a solution, and my method of discovery may be described as a detective's coup:

I have in my possession a large Roman coin, issued by the little-known Emperor Nerva, who ruled from 90-92 C.E. This unusually large coin bears the Latin legend *"Fisci Judaici Calumnia Sublata"* (The insult of the Jewish tax has been lifted). Until now, the universal interpretation of this inscription was that the Romans had levied a discriminatory tax on the Jews, but that Nerva cancelled it, and issued this large coin in celebration of his kindness. Nonsense, I said, who could believe that Rome would celebrate having been good to Jews by striking such a large commemorative coin? In fact, three Roman Emperors, Vespasian, Titus and Domitian, issued coins marked "Judea Capta" or "Judea Devicta," celebrating Jerusalem's destruction. Would Rome now issue coins for having helped the Jews? Impossible.

Rather, I say that Nerva discovered that the Jews had continued, clandestinely, to collect their regular Jewish taxes right under the noses of the Roman oppressors. The Romans, of course, put a stop to the practice, since it was "insulting" to Rome. Nerva and his soldiers no doubt helped themselves to these treasures, and therefore no trace of them remains today.

The Copper Scroll therefore provides proof that even decades after the *churban* the Jews were confident that the *Beit Hamikdash* would be rebuilt at any time, and were planning for that time when they would be able to complete the delivery of their gifts and taxes to Jerusalem.

As we all know, several books written after the close of the *Tanach* were not included in our Bible. Among them is the Book of Ben Sira, a wisdom-book written about 300 B.C.E. Although it was not included in the Tanach, it is quoted countless times in the Talmud and the Midrashim. For a very long time the original text of the book was lost, and only the Greek and Syrian translations were known. But then 100 years ago, a Hebrew text of Ben Sira's work was found in the famous Cairo Genizah.

However, there was still some doubt as to whether this newly discovered text may have been only a re-translation from the Greek. In 1950 I predicted that some original Hebrew Ben Sira texts would be found in the Dead Sea Caves. My prediction was fulfilled. Small fragments of Ben Sira's book were found in what is called Cave No. 2.

After that, we all experienced another startling sensation uncovered at Masada: Yigal Yadin, the great archaeologist-scholar-general, found long pieces of the Ben Sira work in the ruins of the fortress where 1000 staunch Jewish men and women had committed suicide. Since Masada fell in 73, any text found there therefore had to be from a time preceding that date, and the Masada Ben Sira—in script like all the other Dead Sea Scrolls—contained the original Hebrew text, almost the same as the document found in Cairo 100 years ago.

The book of Ben Sira is the link between Biblical days, the Dead Sea literature and the Talmud. I have found countless parallels between Ben Sira and the Dead Sea texts, and have delivered a lecture on the subject at the Hebrew University as part of the World Congress of Jewish Studies.

In sum, the Dead Sea Scrolls prove to a surprising degree how reliable and faithful Jewish tradition is. For over 2000 years, Jews copied the same Biblical texts, and were concerned with the same mitzvot, some more leniently, some more strictly. But no one ever did away with the Jewish traditions or the divine commandments, except for the Christians, who therefore were promptly counted out of our people.

I hope that more and more Jewish scholars and experts will take a serious interest in the Dead Sea texts which still have not been translated and interpreted. The thousands of papers and books on the subject published till now were worthless, since they did not see the literature as authentic Jewish literature, which can only be understood based on our rabbinic sources. That task is now up to our Jewish scholars.

As we study the Dead Sea Scrolls, we vividly relive and revive the lives, ideals and practices of our forefathers. We preserve their memory in awe and respect in a manner akin to what we have been doing now for eleven years, keeping alive and preserving the memory of our son Jamie *z"l*, along with his hopes and aspirations.

May such memories be a blessing for us all.

# Last Gasp for Christological Dead Sea Scroll Interpretations

When the Dead Sea Scrolls were discovered in 1947, they were first identified and provisionally dated by Professor E. Sukenik of the Hebrew University, who, at great peril to himself, was able to hold meetings with Arabs in the Old City in November 1947 and obtained some of the most important Scrolls. He then submitted samples to my teacher, the great Orientalist, Professor William Foxwell Albright at Johns Hopkins University, who confirmed Sukenik's identification. Albright dated them in the Maccabean period of the first and second centuries B.C.E. Israeli scholars swiftly interpreted and published all major scrolls, including those which Sukenik's son, Professor Yigal Yadin, was able to purchase some years later from the Church of St. Mark of Jerusalem.

Although the original Scrolls had been found by Bedouins in the desert near the Dead Sea, most of the Scrolls were later found by teams of professional archaeologists. At that time, before 1967, the Dead Sea area was occupied by Jordan, and as a result, no Jewish scholar was admitted to study the material coming from such important caves as Cave No. 4, although all this was clearly Jewish patrimony and heritage. Thousands of publications based on the Scrolls followed, written mostly by Christian scholars in all countries of the world. They were, understandably, thirsting for any scrap of data that could be related to their Gospels, either by confirming or disproving any of the basic tenets of Christianity. Equally understandable is the fear and trembling which these Christian scholars—many of whom are professional Catholic or Protestant clergymen—feel in the face of the possibility that the entire fabric of their religion would be disproved once and for all.

As a result, an all-Christian (mostly Catholic) Committee was formed to work up the thousands of fragments and scraps of writings which had been found in caves after the major Scrolls, had landed in Israeli hands. The controversy which followed is well known: Jewish scholars and publicists-after 40 years of a virtual monopoly by Catholics—clamored for the opening up of the material for any qualified scholar, whether Jewish or Christian. The story has made headlines ever since, especially as a court case developed over the rights to publish certain Dead Sea Scrolls texts.

From the beginning I have had the privilege of access to texts before other Jewish scholars in general took a special interest in the scrolls. It has been already over 40 years since I publicly stated for the first time that the Scrolls, originating with extremely pious and learned Jewish communities of 2,000 years ago and stemming from one of the most productive periods in Jewish scholarship, necessarily had enormous relevance to our understanding of some of the rabbinic writings contained in the Talmud and Midrash, and vice versa. The scrolls cannot be understood without a knowledge of their background, rooted in the rabbinic literature. Mine was a lone voice at the time, and except for the late Professor Yigal Yadin's early wholehearted approval of my thesis, my 30 to 40 scholarly publications gained general acceptance only in recent years.

Today we can point to a number of qualified Jewish scholars—among them Professor Larry Schiffmann of New York, Baumgarten of Baltimore and others—who concentrate on the halachic aspects of the Scrolls. This means that until now the scholars uneducated in Jewish *halachah* and literature wasted decades on nit-picking existing or non-existing hints at theological and denominational concepts and doctrines known to them from their own religions, but which were irrelevant to the people of Qumran themselves, while only now significant and worthwhile analyses of the Scroll material are being published. Therefore, today no self-respecting scholar would publish a work on the Scrolls without making ample reference to the Talmud, the Midrashim and other rabbinic sources. Studies based on Jewish sources have shown that the men who wrote the Scrolls were extremely pious Jews, who were concerned with *halachah* in every aspect of their lives—whether Shabbat laws, laws on purity and impurity, oaths, laws on the Temple service, or on other aspects of Jewish law.

I sometimes feel pity for those Christian scholars who have spent a lifetime on the Scrolls without really gaining any understanding of them. Tons of their books, filled with the barren monotony of Christian theology, can just as well be consigned to the wastebasket, even though they are no doubt well meant.

One book, which represents the last gasps of studies bereft of knowledge of halachic sources, is the 1992 study *Responses to 101 Questions on the Dead Sea Scrolls* by Joseph A. Fitzmyer, a Jesuit Priest at the Catholic University of America, and a representative of the Vatican in the field of Bible studies.

I would start my review of the book by adding a 102nd question: why is the Hebrew text on the title page of the book upside down? However, Professor Fitzmyer should not feel too unhappy about that gaffe, because quite frequently non-Jewish publications—ranging from *The New York Times* to the *London Times* to the *Daily Telegraph* of London to *Vanity Fair* magazine, etc.—have published pictures of the Dead Sea text upside down.

My 103rd question would be: why does the index not contain one single rabbinic reference, while listing some 160 quotations from the Gospels and other Christian writings?

Now as the to the 101 questions, I counted 32 of them addressed to Christians and Christian concerns, with little or no practical interest to Jews. These Christological questions circle around the Christian concept of a Messiah, of the Kingdom of G-d, crucifixion, celibacy, communal meals, John the Baptist, Son of Man, Son of G-d, etc.

A Jewish scholar knows, of course, that what signifies or characterizes a

Jewish community is not its philosophical concepts, but its practice of Mitzvot and its adherence to the *halachah* of the Oral Law. Therefore, to us it was a major discovery when Jewish scholars found direct textual parallels and links with passages from the Mishnah, which help us identify the men of Qumran as Sadducees, not Essenes.

Christians have a great love for Essenes. However, they are never mentioned in any of the rabbinic sources. They are mentioned in Josephus, the renegade Jew who wrote for the Romans and whose writings have been heavily tampered with over the centuries by Christians. There are also references to the Essenes in the writings of Roman historians. But they probably never existed.

The Essenes, if they ever did exist, are pictured as hermits, probably celibate, living in the desert and opposing the Jewish authorities in Jerusalem. That description suits the Christians because they are anxious to wipe out any link between the early Christians and Judaism, so that it should not be said that Christianity was influenced by Judaism but was, instead, some kind of revolutionary, totally novel religion. Since they picture the Essenes as isolated from the normative Jews of Jerusalem, they do not mind linking the Essenes to the early Christians.

The book by Fitzmyer, of course, follows this pro-Essene line, which is slightly more comfortable to Christians than any theory would be that linked any other Jewish sect to the early Christians. However, Christians can no longer escape the conclusion that early Christianity had it roots in Jewish concepts and institutions. Its originality had to be given up long ago. Even Jesus himself, whose Jewishness was denied for almost 2,000 years, is now generally recognized as a Jew.

As to the impact of the Dead Sea Scrolls on their religion, an account that characterizes the mood among Christians who have studied the Scrolls is related about John Allegro, a British Scroll scholar, who when his colleague, John Strungell, planned to study for the clergy, told Strungell, "When you finish your studies there may not be Christianity left to come back to." Allegro himself, after studying the Scrolls, said "good-bye to Christianity."

Here is a good example of the hopelessness of interpretations offered by Christian scholars lacking knowledge of Jewish literature. In one instance, they caused a sensation when they claimed to have found a reference in the Scrolls to the concept of the "Son of G-d." (This "discovery" was suppressed for some years by the Vatican because it would have robbed the Gospels of the originality of the "Son of G-d" as a strictly Christian concept.)

The text read, in Aramaic, "*Bar Elyon*." Now anyone with knowledge of common Hebrew terms would see in this a parallel to "*Bar Mitzvah*," "*Bar Samcha* (one who can be relied on)," "*Bar Daat* (one who has knowledge)." Just as, for example, Bar Mitzvah means someone who is legally mature, a "*Bar Elyon*" —*elyon* meaning "heavenly" —is someone who is inspired by the divine but certainly not "Son of G-d." Besides, on every Shabbat we read a section from the Zohar where we express our disbelief at any "*Bar Elahin*" —angels or divinely-inspired people.

In order to clear the Catholics who manned the official Dead Sea Scroll Committee of the charge of anti-Semitism, Fitzmyer gives some rather forced explanations as to why no Jews were admitted until recently to work on his Committee. He claims that because of the political situation no Dead Sea Scroll material could reach the Israeli side of the division of Jerusalem. He does not seem to have heard of mail or fax communications, which easily could have supplied the Israelis with the necessary material to do their work on interpreting the Scrolls.

Fitzmeyer's book has some useful descriptions of the history of the discovery of the Scrolls and also includes a useful brief inventory of the Scrolls. But if we want to know what kind of Judaism the Qumranites practiced, we must look for Jewish scholars to give us the answers.

# On The Dead Sea Scrolls—
# The Mysterious MMT Scroll

The Dead Sea Scrolls have again made news the world over. Two weeks ago, at a Press Conference at the New York Hilton Hotel, the publication of the "unauthorized" Dead Sea Scrolls was launched with all the fanfare of the world premiere of a new film. Mr. Hershel Shanks, head of the Biblical Archaeological Society, announced that the "monopoly" of the Committee in charge of the publication of the Scrolls had been broken, in that several hitherto unpublished Dead Sea texts had been spirited out of Jerusalem and published ahead of schedule. In his opinion, the publication of these texts might otherwise have taken several more years.

I have more than a passing interest in this event. First, it was our Foundation which financed the publication of this volume. Next, the volume is dedicated to the memory of our son Jamie z"l. All this is mentioned in the introduction to the book, although it was not mentioned in any of the press notices.

But beyond this, my involvement with the Dead Sea Scrolls goes back to 1947 when my revered teacher, the late Professor William Foxwell Albright identified and dated the first Dead Sea Texts to become known. He placed them in the first or second century Before the Common Era. A portion of the Scrolls from Cave I ended up in Israel, and were quickly and expertly published: the Isaiah Scroll, the Habakuk Pesher (Commentary), the Ordinance of the Community, the War Scroll, the Genesis Apocryphon and, later, the Temple Scroll were placed before the public in amazingly expert and professional editions, with the Hebrew text reproduced and English translations given.

Other Scrolls, especially those from Caves 2, 3, 4 and 11, remained in Jordanian hands. Jordan appointed an "inter-confessional" (that means, no Jews allowed) committee of alleged scholars to prepare the deciphering and publication of their material. Years and years passed with very little appearing. Then, in 1967, Israel liberated Jerusalem along with the Rockefeller Museum, where the Scrolls were kept. Amazingly, Israel respected the Jordan-appointed Christian Committee consisting of Catholics and Protestants, although it was apparent that, in many cases, they lacked even rudimentary knowledge of the Jewish literature of the time represented by the Scrolls. Israel allowed them to continue their work. Of course, they made gross mistakes in their translations and identifications. A typical example is the so-called Copper Scroll, which these Christian scholars totally misunderstood and mistranslated.

Fortunately, things have changed. The Catholic heads of the Committee—all of whom, whether De Vaux, Benoit or Strungnell, were rabid anti-Semites and haters of the State of Israel—are gone. Young Jewish scholars in Israel and the U.S.A. have been given major assignments of publication rights.

*The New York Times* has shown ongoing interest in accelerating the publication of the remaining Scrolls. One Scroll on which *The New York Times* has focused is the so-called MMT Scroll, which *The Times* claimed is being held back, because it will prove embarrassing to Jews and Christians alike. *The Times* is totally wrong. First, the MMT (*Miqtsat Ma'asey haTorah*) is not being held back. Professor Sussman of the Hebrew University already published an analysis of the Scroll many years ago, although the actual Scroll text has not yet been published. Second, the Jews have absolutely nothing to worry about concerning this or any other Scroll. It is the Christians who will be embarrassed for reasons soon to follow. Third, the publication of the full text is about to take place, in the hands of a very capable Israeli scholar, Professor E. Qimron of Beer Sheva University.

Through my close collaboration with Professor Qimron—our Foundation is funding the publication of a new, improved version of the Temple Scroll through Professor Qimron—I have in my possession the full text of MMT. Because of the intensive interest in this Scroll and its unique nature and standing in the field of *Halachah*, I find it appropriate, in advance of publication of the full text, to place before the public some parts of the Scroll to illustrate its importance.

The Scroll represents a Letter or Epistle sent by the sages of the Qumran Community to sages elsewhere, probably the sages in the Sanhedrin in Jerusalem. The Qumran sages clearly represent the views of the Sadducees (Tzedukim) quoted in the Talmud. MMT is written in the style of a polemic; it strongly defends the version of *Halachot* in which the Qumranites believed, which differs in many cases from the normative *Halachah*.

"Ma'asey" here means "Laws." This meaning is attested in the Talmud (Baba Metsia 30b): *Maaseh zeh ha-Din* ("Ma'aseh" means Law). Christians, ignorant of Judaism and Jewish literature, have consistently mistranslated this term as "works" throughout the Christian Bible. For example, in the Epistle by Paul to the Galatians, Paul rants against the "works of the law." The writers did not realize that he was talking against the *Ma'asey haTorah*, indeed against MMT, which should correctly have been translated "the laws of the Torah." It, of course, has nothing to do with "works." This is another instance where we see clearly that Christianity and the Dead Sea Scrolls are totally opposed to one another and have nothing in common.

MMT is a close parallel to dialogues or disputations between Sadducees and Pharisees (Perushim) as reported in the Talmud, for example, in Masekhta Yadayim 4:6,7,8. Because the text is badly damaged, only some 130 lines can be read. These cover the following laws:

    1. Prohibition against Temple gifts by Gentiles

    2. *Halachah* about the cooking of offerings (too incomplete for identification)

3. *Halachah* about sacrifices by Gentiles (too fragmentary)
4. Cereal offerings must be left overnight
5. Purity of those offering the Red Heifer
6. *Halachot* concerning the purity of animal skins
7. The place of slaughtering and offering of sacrifices (too fragmentary)
8. The slaughter of pregnant animals
9. Forbidden sexual unions
10. Banning of the blind and deaf from the Temple
11. The purity of "the liquid streams": liquids poured from pure to impure vessels (*motskot*)
12. Prohibition against dogs in Jerusalem
13. The fruits of the Fourth Year to be given to the Priests
14. The cattle tithe to be given to the Priests
15. Impurity of lepers
16. Impurity of human bones
17. Prohibition against marriage between Priests and Israelites

A frequent phrase is "*anahnu omrim*" or "*anahnu hoshvim*" to indicate that there is a dispute with the opinion of the sages in Jerusalem. About the opposite side, the text says: *atem yod'im*. Here is a typical case of such disagreement: The tithe of cattle (*ma'aser behemah*) is by the MMT legislation to be handed to the Priests only: *ma'aser behemah veha-tson la-kohanim*. Contrast the Mishnah Tractate Zebahim 5:8: *Veha-ma'aser le-khol adam* (Rashi: *ma'aser behemah*), the tithe of cattle is given to any person.

In another *halachah*, MMT legislates that all of the city of Jerusalem is considered a "holy Camp": *Yerushalayim hiah mahane ha-kodesh*. It follows that the severest restrictions affecting a sacred area apply to the whole city. In a parallel *halachah* found in the "Unauthorized" Dead Sea Scrolls published two weeks ago, we find that this restriction went so far as to even prohibit co-habitation between husband and wife inside Jerusalem.

By contrast, our own *halachah* limits the sacred status only to the Temple itself, not the rest of Jerusalem (Tractate Makkot 14:6).

In all cases, the MMT author is more severe than the accepted *halachah*. This is very significant in answer to those—like the writers in *The New York Times*—who constantly refer to MMT as a link between Christianity and "Rabbinic" Judaism. These writers are clearly poorly informed—last week they even featured a Hebrew text upside-down in the Sunday edition of *The New York Times*. They even try to create the impression that "Rabbinic" Judaism and Christianity started at the same time, the time of the writing of the Dead Sea Scrolls! If they only check the Scrolls themselves, they would realize the extreme error: the Dead Sea community represents a "maximalist" form of the observance of the Mitzvot, and a community committed to intensive study of the *halachot*. They clearly followed an Oral Law—contrary to the popular belief that the Sadducees only followed the Written

Law, as did later the Karaites. Their extremism disqualified them, however, from acceptance by the Sanhedrin, perhaps akin to the rejection, in most cases, of the severe views of Beth Shammai. Judaism as we practice it today is, therefore, the same as our forefathers practiced from the beginning of time, 3500 years ago. Our faith has weathered attacks by countless sects and heresies. Already in the days of the First Temple, the Talmud reports, there were 55 different sects. Later, we had the Sadducees, the Essenes, the Baitusimites, the Christians, the Karaites—they all withered away and disappeared, only Judaism survived.

As to the Christians, they were exactly the opposite of the "maximalists" of the Scroll community: they rejected all *Halachoth*, especially under Paul, who turned his back on the Jews, and catered strictly to the pagans. So how can the Scrolls form any kind of bridge or link between Jews and Christians? The Scroll community stressed scholarship and study, just as Jews have always done. (See, for example, Psalms Chapter 119.) By contrast, Christianity was a religion of the uneducated. Even Jesus himself is described as an unlearned man in the Gospels: see John 7:15 "Jesus did not learn letters." What chance of acceptance did Christianity have among the Jews who were steeped in learning, according to our age-old tradition?

We can now see why Christian scholars delayed the publication of MMT, which so clearly contrasts the high scholarly and religious level of the Jews of Qumran as against the uneducated, shallow followers of Jesus, who turned to pagan concepts in order to attract converts among the Gentiles. Any attempt to place Christianity into the tree of Judaism now fails, in the face of the evidence of MMT.

Let us close with the actual words of MMT, where the yearning for Israel's redemption is movingly expressed, in terms of declaring theirs to be "the end of the days."

"We recognize that a part of the Blessings and Curses written in the Book of Moses have been fulfilled, and that these are the final days in which Israel will do penitence and will no more turn back. While the wicked will do their wicked deeds, consider the fate of the Jewish kings: those who observed the Torah were saved from any misfortune; those who pursued the Torah were absolved of sin. Remember David, the man of kindness: he, too, was saved from many misfortunes, and his sins were forgiven. We, too, have written unto you a part of the Laws of the Torah [*Miqtsat Ma'asey ha-Torah*] which we consider good for you and for your nation. . . in order that you may rejoice in the end of days, when you accept part of our sayings. This will be counted unto you as righteousness when you practice the good and just path. Then it will be good for you and for Israel."

Here then is another fundamental difference between the men of Qumran and early Christians: the writers of MMT were inspired by a love for all of Israel, while the Christian Bible is full of venom and hostility to and rejection of anyone outside of their group. Thus MMT is a worthy follower of the Mishnaic testimony about the Schools of Hillel and Shammai (Tractate Yebamoth 13b): "Although these declared ineligible what the others declared eligible, the men of the School of Shammai nevertheless did not refrain from marrying women from the families of the School of Hillel, nor the men of the School of Hillel from marrying women from the families of the School of Shammai. Similarly, in respect of all questions of ritual purity and impurity, where these declared clean what the others declared unclean, neither of them abstained from preparing pure food for each other." And the Gemara adds (14b): "To teach you that they exercised love and comradeship to one another, as is written 'Therefore love the truth and peace.'" The latter verse is found in Zecharia 8:19, in the midst of the most beautiful prophetic description of a panorama of Messianic brotherhood, bliss and peace for the Jewish people in the end of days. It expresses aptly the sentiments and the prayers which we all feel at the High Holiday season and the Feast of Sukkoth, especially at this turbulent juncture in Israel's history.

# The 10 Greatest Archaeological Discoveries

Archaeology has become an indispensable tool for understanding the Tenach and the lands of the Tenach. In the last century all Bible "science" was based on analysis of the text itself, called the "School of Higher Criticism." Since many of the so-called scholars who employed this method—mainly those in Germany—had hostile biases against Judaism and Jews, their conclusions were therefore quite destructive.

But with the beginning of this century, things changed completely. My own teacher, the late Professor William Foxwell Albright, at Johns Hopkins University, pioneered in applying archaeology instead of texts to understand the Bible. And it is through archaeology that we have made amazing discoveries that have thrown hitherto unknown light on biblical accounts and the world of the Bible. If you ask a number of people to enumerate 10 of the most important archaeological discoveries, you will get a variety of answers. I have selected those that I believe have the most immediate relevance to the Jewish concept of our history.

### *1. Rosetta Stone*

When Napoleon invaded Egypt in the end of the 18th century, he was enlightened enough to take with him an army of scholars. Among them was François Champollion, who concentrated on deciphering the ancient Egyptian hieroglyphics. These picture signs had baffled the world for centuries. Then luck struck, and in a place called Rosetta, in the Nile Delta, Champollion found the key to the mystery.

The black stone that he found is divided into three sections, each written in a different script: Greek, ancient hieroglyphics, and Demotic, the cursive version of the hieroglyphics. Champollion logically concluded that this was one single text, repeated three times.

He then compared the Greek names in the upper part of the stone with outstanding words in the hieroglyphic text: the names Cleopatra and Ptolmy, which had a kartouche—a frame—around them indicating the special importance of these words. Once Champollion could read those two words he soon broke the "code" of the rest, and so established the first dictionary of Egyptian signs that stood for whole concepts. From then on, Egyptology became a rapidly spreading science that unraveled the entire spectrum of thousands of years of Egyptian history, which is so closely related to ancient Jewish history.

### *2. Cuneiform Texts*

At the same time that Egyptian hieroglyphics were being deciphered, scholars were finding the key to the cuneiform texts used throughout the kingdoms of Babylonia, the Hittites, Assyria and Persia. While the Egyptian language did not vary much throughout the millennia—just as their architecture and art hardly changed—the languages using cuneiform letters varied a great deal. But the most important basic texts discovered about 100 years ago were the Hammurabi Code and the Gilgamesh Epic. Hammurabi, probably identical with Amrafel in the Torah, was a great codifier. His Code is well preserved, and its laws and types of punishments have been compared by some to the Seven Noachide Laws.

The Gilgamesh Epic describes the creation and flood stories, with a man named Utnapishtim taking on the role of the biblical Noah. The flood story is found in many countries and periods in history, even China. Obviously this discovery was relevant to the study of the Bible.

### 3. Mesha Stone

About 130 years ago, a large stone slab was found in what is today Jordan, written in Moabite, a language very similar to Hebrew. Although the Arabs who found the stone decided to break it up into small pieces to increase sales, an impression of the intact stone has been made that gives us the whole text. This amazing stone tells the story of the kings of the Kingdom of Israel, called "Beth Omri" in the stone. Of course, as all nations have done throughout history—except for the Jews!—the inscribers of the stone tailor history to glorify themselves. Thus their god, Kemosh, is described as more powerful than the G-d of the Jews. But the stone confirms important details in the Bible.

### 4. Tel el Amarna Tablets

Although Egyptian history was monolithic throughout the millennia, a revolutionary change took place under a young king of the New Kingdom's 18th dynasty. His name: Amenophis IV. He dismantled the polytheistic religion of his forefathers and recognized only one god, Aten, the sun disk, as the supreme ruler of the universe. Amenophis changed his name to "Akh-n-Aten" and moved his capital from Thebes to Akhetaten, today's Tel el Amarna. There, some 120 years ago, archaeologists found a huge number of cuneiform tablets representing the official correspondence between Egyptian kings, mainly Amenophis III and his son Akh-n-Aten, and the governors of Canaanite towns, which were in reality Egyptian colonies at the time. Names such Urusalima—Jerusalem—appear in these letters.

But the main surprise is that a people called the Habirus are mentioned who invade Canaan from the desert and who threaten the Egyptian colonies. Luckily for the Habirus, Akh-n-Aten was a poetically and religiously inclined king without a taste for warfare. He therefore did not offer any help to his governors to defend themselves against the Habirus. This happened around the year 1375 B.C.E. If we equate the Habirus with the Hebrews, this gives us a date for the Exodus. Consequently, Ramses II, who ruled about 200 years later, could not have been the Pharaoh of the Exodus. The monotheism of Akh-n-Aten would have been influenced by the Jews, including Moses, who lived in the royal court for some time.

## 5. *Elephantine Papyri*

At the turn of the century a hoard of papyri written in Aramaic were found in Egypt on the island of Elephantine, near what is today the Assuan Dam. These amazing texts, most of them well preserved, describe the conditions of a Jewish military colony that had been assigned the duty of defending the border of the Persian empire against invading Nubians—Ethiopians—around 480 B.C.E. Because the Jews there descended from Samaria, the kingdom of Israel, their observance of the Torah was not what we today would call Orthodox. They built themselves a Temple but amalgamated it with some pagan Egyptian or Persian religious practices. They did keep Pesach very strictly, as reflected in the famous Passover Papryus that describes the removal of Chametz before Pesach through special permission of the Persian ruler in Shushan. Commercial contracts, bills of divorce and other documents shed light on the legal practices of these Jews living during the Second Commonwealth.

## 6. *Ras Shamra or Ugaritic Texts*

In 1929, farmers in Syria discovered tablets bearing cuneiform-like signs in a location called Ras Shamra. These texts were soon deciphered as old Canaanite epics and religious texts. The cuneiform signs, instead of numbering some 3,000 used in Babylonia and Assyria, were limited to about 28 signs, each representing one letter of the alphabet. The texts reflect religious beliefs that mirror some of the pagan practices described in the Bible, especially as they center on the gods of Baal or Elyon, the goddess Anat or Ashera, and god of death, Mavet. This then was the religion that our patriarchs met when they entered Canaan. Some historical names are useful for us, too. For example, the name Daniel refers to a mighty ancient king in Canaanite history. This explains the occurrence of this name in the Book of Ezekiel (Chapter 14) and has nothing to do with the prophet Daniel of a much later age.

## 7. *Dead Sea Scrolls*

The greatest discovery of all—at least for us Jews—is of course the Dead Sea Scrolls, discovered near Qumran in 1948. Entire libraries can be written about them, and have in fact been written. I was probably the first Jewish scholar who applied parallels from the rabbinical and midrashic literature to these texts. My publications, which number over 20, are now contained in the bibliographies in many scholarly books being published. The one main phenomenon that to me is most striking is the faithfulness with which Biblical texts were copied and handed over throughout 2,000 years of our history. Any child today can read the Qumran texts of 200 B.C.E and see that they are practically the same as our Tenach today. Even the letters have changed very little over this enormous span of history. We can rightly be proud of this unmatched record of religious piety and reliability. The Qumran texts will occupy scholars for many generations to come.

### *8. Genizah*

In the second half of the 19th century, hundreds of thousands of discarded Jewish documents were found—mainly in the El Basatin cemetery outside Cairo—some in the famous Ben Ezra Synagogue. These texts are now housed in leading libraries in St. Petersburg, Cambridge and New York. Commercial texts, *halachic* (Jewish legal) responsa, liturgical poems, business and private correspondence and many more categories of writings are contained in this indescribable treasure of Jewish culture, religion and literature. Scholars for many years to come will work and publish in this field.

### *9. Beth David Stones*

The latest important archaeological discovery is the stones from the ancient town of Dan, written by an Aramean king, and referring a few times to "Beth David." The full impact of this discovery has not yet been made, but it already sheds light on the powerful Davidic dynasty of the Kings of Judah.

### *10. Priestly Blessing*

The earliest biblical text outside the Bible was found in one of the hills of Jerusalem a few years ago—a small silver scroll that at first did not yield any writing. But the genius of one specialist, Mrs. Yardena, brought a sensation: The little scroll held the Priestly Blessing from the Torah, which we use daily. Written in the 7th century B.C.E, it is the earliest biblical text, outside the Bible, ever found. It gives us hope that many more and even older Biblical texts will be found.

I hope you will agree that this vast spectrum of archaeological discoveries has revolutionized our knowledge of the world of the Bible. They have brought so many personalities and events closer to us and prove the historicity of our traditions.

As more and more Jewish scholars apply themselves to this field, we will be blessed with unimaginable discoveries that will enormously enrich and strengthen our outlook as faithful, believing Jews.

# Zionism

From the moment the Jews were expelled from their Land, Jews have prayed for their return to Eretz Yisrael and for the coming of Moshiach, who would usher in the ultimate peace and security for the Jewish people. The first stirrings came in the Middle Ages, followed by the Shabatai Tzvi movement in the 17th century. Then came the followers of the Ba'al Hatanya and of the Gaon of Vilna who settled in Eretz Yisrael about 200 years ago. Political Zionism came 100 years later, and culminated in the establishment of the Jewish State in 1948. Some of the outstanding achievements of Israel are briefly described.

## Zionism Before Zionism

As we approach Nissan, the month of Redemption, it is timely to examine the history of redemption in our own times. Here are some common misconceptions:

When did Zionism begin? Around 1880.
Who was the first Zionist? Theodor Herzl.
When did the first *aliya* take place? In 1881 with the first Biluim.
Who introduced Hebrew as an everyday language? Eliezer ben Yehuda.

All wrong. "Zionism," although known by other names, started in earnest in the middle of the 18th century, and became intense in the beginning, not the end of the 19th century.

One can even go further back to the middle of the 17th century when the famous "false Messiah" Shabatai Tzvi electrified all of European Jewry with his messianic claims, which overnight raised hopes for a Messianic era. Jews even sold their belongings and headed for Palestine and Turkey to see their *Mashiach*. This dream-like exaltation, just as suddenly as it had begun, turned into traumatic disappointment and frustration when Shabatai Tzvi was revealed to be a fraud. He died as a Moslem convert. But the hope had been kindled. And more than that, for the first time, an international movement among Jews had been forged—both Eastern and Western Jews had joined in one gigantic enterprise: to physically leave the Diaspora and move back to the Holy Land. For many, it was difficult to abandon such a marvellous era in Jewish history. They continued to come to Jerusalem, Tiberias, Hebron and Safed, the nuclei of the small Jewish population in Palestine.

In 1700 Rabbi Yehuda HaChasid, together with a group of some 500 followers, came to Eretz Yisrael from Russia, perhaps in the hopes of finding a revived, legitimate Shabatai Tzvi. They built a large synagogue in Jerusalem. But it was only after the appearance of the Baal Shem Tov that a real drive for settlement in Eretz Yisrael took place. In 1747 Rav Avraham-Gershon from Kotov and his followers made an *aliya*, followed year after year by more followers of the founder of Hassidism, culminating in the "Great *Aliya*" headed by Rav Menachem Mendel of Vitebsk in 1777, which was inspired by the Baal Hatanya, Rav Schneur Zalman of Liadi, who himself had been frustrated in his own plan to migrate to Eretz Yisrael. The Hassidim thereby established a firm foothold in the Holy Land.

Another great movement, called *Hazon Zion*, developed shortly thereafter. The Gaon of Vilna, who had all his life been inspired by an abiding love for Eretz Yisrael, instilled in his many disciples and followers an overwhelming desire to organize not only an *aliya* on a large scale, but also the resettlement of the Land in preparation for the coming of *Mashiach*. The Gaon himself was the catalyst for a decisive migration movement. He embarked on the long and hazardous voyage, but also had to turn back in frustration like the Baal Hatanya. However, his disciples excelled in their zeal and skill in organizing and carrying out a large migration to Safed and Jerusalem. Interestingly, an entire town in White Russia, Shklov, populated by the disciples of the Gaon, had been gripped by the desire to migrate to Eretz Yisrael and thus became the mainstay of the movement of the *Talmidei Ha-Gra* who settled in the Holy Land beginning in 1809. They were soon called the *Perushim* because they had given up the comfort of their lives in Russia, and gladly undertook the dangers of the hazardous trip, as well as the hardships and privations of life in Eretz Yisrael at that time.

The towering personality among the Perushim was without doubt Rav Menachem Mendel mi-Shklov. Others with great merit for the success of this historic undertaking were Rav Benjamin Rivlin, Rav Yehoshua Zeitlin, Rav Neta Notkin, and R. Hillel mi-Shklov. (The famous Rivlin family in Israel is descended from their famous ancestor of that early period. The name Rivlin, was originally Riveles, after a righteous ancestress Rivka or Rivele. Often in Eastern Europe family names derive from pious women—for example the Maharsha's full name was Rav Shmuel Edels, after his mother, whose name was Edel. In our own day, Isaac Bashevis Singer, is named after an ancestress by name of Bas Sheva. I knew a family hailing from the Mir, whose children were called Bashevis, after their famous mother Bas Sheva, whom I myself was privileged to have known.)

Both the Hassidim and the Perushim found horrendous problems on arrival: there was ongoing political and military turmoil in the Ottoman Empire, with this or that Pasha revolting against the Sultan in Constantinople, resulting in lawlessness and bloodshed in Eretz Yisrael. On top of this there was heavy internal strife: the Sefardim, who had lived uninterruptedly in the Land for centuries, did not always take kindly to the new Ashkenazic arrivals. After a while, the sharp strife between Misnagdim and Hassidim in Eastern Europe was also transferred to Eretz Yisrael.

When one reads the rich correspondence between the leaders of the Hassidic groups to their home communities, one can read about unfortunate conflicts and harassment of one community by the other. However, the great leaders of the generation did great deeds in healing the rift, especially Rav Menachem Mendel of Shklov.

In 1827 another historic event took place: Sir Moses Montefiore arrived on the first of his seven trips to the Holy Land. This towering personality, born in Italy but raised in England, revolutionized the development of the Jewish communities in the Land. He was able to heal the main rift between the Sefardim and the Ashkenazic Jews. He infused large funds for their well being, and ultimately bought the first land outside the Old City to create an agricultural foundation for future Jewish settlements, and to make the Jewish inhabitants of the Land independent of the contributions which came from the Diaspora. The windmills that today we find here and there in Jerusalem were established by him, as was the section called Yemin Moshe, named after Sir Moses. Until recently it housed the beautiful carriage which had taken Sir Moses and Lady Judith on their fabled voyages.

The Land was also shaken by the occurrence of terrible earthquakes, like the one in 1837 in Safed when thousands were killed or made homeless. There were also outbreaks of the most dangerous epidemics, such as the plague, which claimed countless Jewish victims. Another scourge was the onslaught of the missionaries, coming from England. This brings us to the underlying motivations of these migrations:

There is no doubt that both the Hassidic and Misnagdish migrations were propelled forward by the conviction that the coming of *Mashiach* was calculated to take place in the year 1840—or 5600 in the Jewish calendar. Based on the Zohar, the coming of *Mashiach* would take place in the beginning of the last 400 years of the six thousand years of Creation. This was also borne out by a multitude of *gematriya*-like calculations: For example, in the verse in Shir Hashirim, *Kol ha-Tor nishma be'artzenu* (The voice of the turtle-dove is heard in our Land), the word *Tor* has the numerical value of 600. In the international political arena too, world-shaking events had taken place. First the American Revolution of 1776 had shown the world that the tyranny of monarchs can be shaken off. This was followed by the French Revolution of 1789, which also demonstrated that freedom could be brought about by human actions. Finally came Napoleon, hailed by some Jews as the closest thing to a Messiah he gave freedom to Jews wherever he conquered lands, and even instituted a Sanhedrin for France's Jews. All these dramatic events clearly heralded the beginning of a new world order. It would also seem that the Christian world had very similar expectations.

As a result by the middle of the 19th century there was a veritable flood of Christian pilgrims and missionaries coming to Jerusalem from England, Sweden, and Russia. They all established churches and missionary posts which, in part, can still be observed to this day. The English sent a baptized Jew, Alexander, as the first Anglican Bishop to Jerusalem, along with other missionaries. The most aggressive and cunning one was a man called David Wolff who did everything in his power to con innocent Jews, especially children, to be caught in the web of the Mission. One of the weapons the missionaries used was to establish a hospital where poor and sick Jews would be tended free of charge. While the Sefardim, with proper foresight, issued a strict *cherem* against anyone stepping into the missionary hospital, the Misnagdim were more open minded about it, which occasionally resulted in problems. I have in my library a 555 page report on their activities, published in 1839, not only in the Holy Land, but also among the Jews in Europe. The book is full of derogatory remarks about Jews—evidently intended to be read only by fellow Christians—and contains an implied call to target especially poor, helpless Jews as likely victims for their proselytizing.

The missionaries hovered over the Jews in anticipation like vultures around a dying animal. They warned the Jews that no Messiah would in fact come in the year 1840, and that therefore, the Jewish religion should be foresworn. Of course, although *Mashiach* did not come in 1840, the Jews were steadfast enough in their faith, understanding that the Divine Plan was for events to evolve differently. As the Gaon of Vilna had preached again and again, we were facing the *atchalta di'geula*, the beginning of the Redemption. And that, in his opinion, meant that the physical reconstruction and building of the Land had to be accomplished *before* the coming of *Mashiach*, through human hands, and not by supernatural miracles. There is evidence that the Gaon did not necessarily foresee that all Jews had to do *teshuva* as a precondition before *Mashiach's* arrival. If we examine the 150 years since that fateful year 1840, we can marvel at the many anticipatory developments, beyond human comprehension, which, step by step, have lead to the creation of a Jewish State in fulfillment of the most blessed promises of the Prophets. The Perushim had organized their economic support through a well-built network of contribution centers in Europe, mainly in Amsterdam, where the Lehren family for many years were in control of all payments going to Eretz Yisrael. The Perushim, in collaboration with the Hassidim, were able to build one new settlement after the other. With these funds they not only supported the many outstanding yeshivot and built synagogues—including the large Hurba synagogue in Jerusalem which the Arabs had destroyed—but also founded agricultural settlements for the employment of Jewish workers. Thus they founded Petach Tikva in 1870.

When the politically recruited Zionists arrived in Eretz Yisrael after 1881, a Jewish infrastructure already existed. The Biluim, the early Zionist settlers, found Jewish employers who could give them work. Jews had already broken out of the medieval areas of habitation, and were ready to expand into the rest of the Land.

Divine Providence had performed a miraculous program of preparing for the great influx which was to come in the 20th century, culminating in the Jewish State as it exists today. The real milestone in all this was the "messianic" year 1840, as correctly predicted by our saintly sages of 200 years ago, to whom the credit for modern Zionism should go. The Perushim also strove toward the revival of the

Hebrew language. The first Jew in modern times to introduce Hebrew as the only language spoken in daily use was Rav Elijah, a disciple of the Gaon, also called the *Baal Lashon Hakodesh*, who arrived in Eretz Yisrael in 1809. He would only converse with those who answered him in Hebrew. This happened 50 years before Eliezer ben Yehuda was born and 90 years before he came to Eretz Yisrael. Therefore, Rav Elijah Baal Lashon Hakodesh, not Eliezer ben Yehuda, was the father of spoken Hebrew in modern times. The letters and documents written by the Perushim, of which I have collected quite a number, are written in very beautiful Hebrew.

I recently made the amazing discovery of an actual contemporary portrait of a group of Perushim. In my favorite book store in London, Henry Sotheran off Piccadilly, I recently bought a collection of drawings by David Roberts, the famous English artist who visited the Orient in the early 19th century and left behind beautiful depictions of Palestine of that period. As I looked closely at one of them, dated 1839, I saw an amazing scene: In his painting of the harbor at Jaffa, Roberts portrayed a group of European Jews talking to Arabs, evidently about the cost of a caravan which would take them to Jerusalem. The Jews wear wide-brimmed hats, are bearded, and are dressed in long coats—just as one would imagine a Misnaged of the period to look. I was also reminded of the travel account of W. M. Thompson of England describing a visit in 1834 to a synagogue in Jerusalem, where he describes the Jews as wearing "broad brimmed hats." That year, 1839, was a crucial year in the migration of the followers of the Hazon Zion movement of the Vilna Gaon's disciples. I was happy to have found what is probably the only contemporary portrait of Perushim at the end of their journey, which sometimes took ten months.

The Gaon of Vilna's favorite saying about Eretz Yisrael was that only two mitzvot totally envelop the Jew performing them: dwelling in a *sukka,* and living in Eretz Yisrael. Both have something else in common as well—just as a *sukka* is not kosher unless you build it anew (*ta'ase ve'lo min ha'asuy*), Eretz Yisrael must be built up by each one of us. He found both concepts combined in the verse of Psalms 76:3, "*Va'yehi beshalom suko u'meonato b'Tzion*"—"And His *sukka* shall be in Jerusalem, and His dwelling place in Zion." These were said to be the last words he spoke before passing away on Sukkot in 1797.

As we sit down at the seder to celebrate the Feast of our Redemption, we can discern the outline of a Divine pattern of Redemption for us and the generations to come.

# Who Are the Palestinians? The Giant Arab Propaganda Fraud

Under the hail of propaganda clichés attempting to "prove" Arab rights, the world has been totally misled about certain basic historical facts. Here are some pertinent questions that are being ignored:

1. Are there any Palestinians?
2. When did Arabs enter the Holy Land and how many were there?
3. For how long was the Land totally emptied of population?
4. What are the countries of origin of the "Palestinians?"
5. Which colonial power falsified immigration figures?
6. How many foreign invasions swept various foreign populations in and out of Eretz Yisrael through 2,600 years of history?

Theodor Herzl, after personally visiting Eretz Yisrael 100 years ago, came to realize that the Land was desolate, its agriculture long destroyed and with only small population pockets in a handful of towns and villages. He realized that this land was no longer "flowing with milk and honey" as in biblical days, and had in fact reached the level of utter desolation and desert-like aridity, as described in Leviticus Chapter 26 and Deuteronomy Chapter 28. After conferring with local Arabs, he came to the conclusion that this "land without people" should go back to the "people without land," who are the only legitimate survivors of the original owners, namely, the Jewish people.

In ancient days, every conqueror would either massacre the local population or displace it with people imported from other areas. Thus when the Assyrians captured the Northern Kingdom (Israel) they promptly deported the Jews and replaced them with Samaritans and other foreign groups. When Nebuchadnezzar captured Jerusalem in 576 B.C.E., he deported the Jews to Babylonia, whence they returned some 70 years later. In 70 C.E., and again in 135 C.E., Rome captured Judea and took a large part of the Jews to Rome and other parts of the Roman Empire. Yet many Jewish communities in Eretz Yisrael remained in their native land. As we will see, only Jews either remained in or returned to their ancient homeland. All other nations disappeared, never to return. In fact, it is not possible even to trace and identify them anymore. The Land fell into disuse and was described by travelers as "almost abandoned lands," "unoccupied," "uninhabited."

Those few people who could be found were migrants, who constantly moved from place to place. Few had steady homesteads and these were exploited and squeezed by a few rich landowners who often brought in farmers from other countries to work for them. The result was that a large portion of the Land went out of population and hundreds of villages were depopulated. By 1865 an observer concluded that "Palestine will be desolated and given up to nomads." The people who roamed the country in the 19th century had connection with the troops who had captured the Land centuries before the Moslems. They were no longer indigenous to the Land.

In 1878 the first Circassians arrived from Southern Russia as well as the Bosnians who had been placed under Austrian rule by the Bismarck treaty for Bosnia and had to flee Christian rule. Egyptian soldiers' families were settled in Beisan, Nablus, Irbid, Acco and Jaffa. Moorish settlers and Kurds settled in Safed.

In short, there was never a mention of a land called "Palestine" or a people called "Palestinians." These names were invented only in the late 19th century to oppose the new influx of returning Jewish settlers. It is a total rewrite of history for political interests.

Local, scattered tribes made their appearance here and there and are recognizable to this day by certain local characteristics. The Arabs in Hebron represent a special local tribe who probably entered the area only some 250 years ago. They are known to be more bloodthirsty than other tribes. In 1839, Moses Montefiore and his wife were almost killed by a hate-crazed Arab mob when they visited the Machpelah. The massacre of Hebron Jews on a Friday in 1929 followed the same tradition. These were the Arabs who, in March 1994, were being whipped up by the local Moslem clergy with continuous cries of *"Atbach el Yahud* (slaughter the Jews)" in preparation for a pogrom on a Friday.

It has been shown that the influx of Arabs or Arab-speaking tribes into Eretz Yisrael largely followed the successful appearance of Jewish settlers. Envy and lust for Jewish bounty were the driving force. In 1858, Hebron Arabs claimed the right "from time immemorial in their families, to enter Jewish homes and take toll and to plunder at any time, without giving account to anyone."

Who displaced whom? The often raised claim that Jews displaced Arabs from their land is historically incorrect. In fact, there were hardly any Arabs to speak of in the Land up to the 19th century. The improvement in living standards achieved by the Jews made it attractive for Arabs from a host of countries to emigrate and then claim land that they said had been theirs for generations. This is totally untenable.

From the 1930s when the colonial officials of Britain began keeping track of Moslem immigrants, there is documentation on the growing influx of Arabs from neighboring countries. They were classified as "aliens," not "natives."

As the Arab population grew, their leaders incited them to attack Jewish settlements and to remove Jews from their land—not the other way around. In this they were supported by the British colonial power which wanted to balance the influence of Jews and Arabs alike. Old Arab families, especially the Husseini, Nashashibi and Khalidi clans—which still exercise a tight grip on the Arab masses—supported the attacks on Jews, as they are doing to this day.

These leaders, and rich effendis, broke up the chance for peaceful co-existence with Zionism, which some Arab rulers had embraced after World War I. That is a great tragedy from which Israel and the Arabs themselves suffer greatly today.

In sum, we must remember that historically there is no Palestine nor a Palestinian people in existence today. These names were conveniently chosen by political leaders to give legitimacy to their claims. A thorough investigation of these claims should be conducted to eliminate the mass of misinformation and deception that has flooded the media. The hundreds of official reports from the colonial records, which are available for scrutiny, should be examined to trace the origins of this mislabeling of entire peoples.

Nowadays you hear so much about the alleged Moslem claims to Jerusalem. This is total innovation. No such claim was ever made by Mohammed, founder of Islam. In fact, in his Koran, Jerusalem is not mentioned one single time but is mentioned some 800 times in the Bible (Tenach).

Mohammed had this to say about the Land of Israel: "Allah said to the Children of Israel, Dwell ye in the Land, and *when the day of final reckoning comes, I will bring you back from among all the peoples.*"

There is also historical proof for Mohammed's disinterest in Jerusalem. In the beginning of his campaign to win Jewish proselytes, Mohammed temporarily ordered the *qibla* (direction in prayer) to be toward Jerusalem, as a lure to Jewish candidates for conversion to Islam, who were accustomed to pray facing Jerusalem. But when he realized that the Jews were not interested in his new religion, he put out a strict prohibition against facing Jerusalem, and ordered that worshippers face only Mecca and Medina in Saudi Arabia, the sacred towns of Islam. This prohibition was issued on February 12, 624, shortly before Mohammed died. No wonder that throughout all the centuries of non-Arab tribes and nations sweeping in and out of the Land of Israel, no affinity with Jerusalem existed. The Arab claim therefore must be totally re-examined and reassessed in the light of the facts of history.

What happened to the first Arab invaders? Moslem scholar Professor Philip Hitti has stated that the small number of Arab invaders who had been imported by the Arabian conquerors was wiped out by disease. Thus the myth of the "Palestinian Arab descending from the Arab conquerors" appears to be factually incorrect. The Arab conquerors ruled almost entirely over Christian and Jewish subjects. Apart from the Bedouin nomads, in the earliest days the only Arabs west of the Jordan—not all of whom were Moslems themselves—were garrisons.

Professor Bernard Lewis, the famous expert on Islam, wrote, "A vast variety of people—different race, languages and religions, *among whom the Arabs only formed a minority* [emphasis added]—were conquerors looking for booty to be seized from Jews and Christians.

"Not only was there no country of 'Palestine,' there was never a 'Palestinian' people and never a 'Palestinian' rule. The first Arabian use of the word 'Arab' means Bedouin or raiders or highway robbers. They made up the original followers of Mohammed. In the Koran, the term 'Arab' is only used in this sense, never of townsfolk of Mecca or Medina."

In sum, it is obvious that the entire world has fallen prey to a giant conning operation, perpetrated by oil interests, anti-Semites and ferocious, hate-crazed tribes. An enlightening campaign must be carried out to remove these unfair, incorrect allegations, which—like the propaganda of Josef Göbbels of Hitler's Germany—was based on the "Big Lie." Only when the truth becomes known can peace be introduced into the Middle East.

As the centuries passed, one invasion after another swept over the Land, removing all vestiges of previous populations and bringing about a total mixture of peoples. Here are the principal invasions which totally obliterated "original" populations:

614 C.E. Persian invasion and capture of the Land
628 C.E. Reconquest by Byzantine Empire
633 C.E. Conquest by Arabs
660 C.E. Omayyad rulers take over and rule until 750
878 C.E. Turks capture the Land, introducing rule of the Tulunides
904 C.E. Abbassids of Baghdad reconquer the Land
906 C.E. Invasion of Carcassians
914 C.E. Egyptians rule
970 C.E. Byzantine invasion
1070-1080 C.E. Seljuk Turks conquer the Land
1099 C.E. Crusaders conquer Jerusalem; massacre of Jews and Arabs
1187 C.E. Saladin, a Kurd, captures Jerusalem
1244 C.E. The Kharzmians, Genghis Khan, invade the Land. Jerusalem's population is slaughtered
1260 C.E. Mongol invasion, Jerusalem sacked
1516 C.E. Ottomans conquer the Land

It is obvious from the list of invasions, conquest and subjugations that no people survived intact from the bloodletting. Only the Jews, always remembering their native Land, returned to claim it. None of the original races remained. Obviously there is no historical foundation to any claim of "thousands of years" of Arab presence in the Land. Some of the peoples and races that came and went, to this day, were the Tudomans, Persians, Afghans, Motawila, Kurds, Circassians, Algerians, Albanians and hundreds of Bedouin tribes. In the process, the land was despoiled—stripped of trees and arable land—and ended in total waste and desert.

By mid-19th century, the entire land was depopulated. Travelers left behind dozens of accounts of the lack of population and the disappearance of hundreds of villages. Various travelers had this to report about the Land: "a desolate country," "a ruined country," "wretched desolation and neglect."

Only the Jews continued saying to this day, "Next year in Jerusalem."

# Whose Land Is It Anyway?
# Who Has The Right to Give It Away?

Lately we have heard revolting reports that this or that member of the Rabin Government proposes to offer the Arabs parts of Eretz Yisrael. Shimon Peres, Shulamit Aloni, Yossi Sarid—they are falling all over each other in their rush to offer Jerusalem, the Golan Heights and Gaza to the Arabs. But who has given them the legal, moral and historic right to give away Jewish land?

Let it be remembered once and for all: the land of Israel belongs to all the people of Israel—including those in Israel, those in the Diaspora, those who lived before us and those who will live after us! Think of the 2000 years of suffering that Jews in all corners of the world have endured—praying, dreaming and languishing for the day when the land of Israel, when Jerusalem would be ours again. Think of the millions who were herded into the gas chambers singing *Ani Maamin*. Think of the generations of settlers who gave their health and their very lives to gain a foothold in our ancient land. Think of the tens of thousands of martyrs who died in the various wars since independence. Think of the millions of Diaspora Jews who gave their time and wealth to help reestablish the Jewish State and keep it strong.

Now, with the Almighty's help, we have been given back our land—for us to safekeep for the past, present and future generations. How, then, can some opportunistic, callous politician come along and decide that the land can be handed out to our enemies? Let them show us the legal, moral and historic right that they have to do so, before they irreparably damage the security of our land and the survival of our people.

The Rabin Government must understand that any decision about the land must have the approval of the Jews in the Diaspora. We were told that we are full partners in the building of the land and that we all share the responsibility for the land and its people. Let us invoke the rights arising from that partnership, the rights of a full partner. We cannot be left out of any decision affecting the future of the land!

In the Diaspora, as well as in Israel, for generations we have sung the words of *Hatikva*: "to be a free people in our land, the land of Tzion and Jerusalem."

With the rapid deterioration of Israel's position, brought about by the Rabin Government's flawed stance in the peace negotiations, what is needed now is not just an emotional outcry. What is needed is an urgent and concrete last-minute call for mobilizing the Jewish masses to immediate and hard-hitting action in order to ensure a strong, secure, intact land of Israel. In groups and as individuals we must all strongly protest against the irresponsible disregard those in Jerusalem have shown for the wishes and opinions of Israel's Diaspora partners, and we must make it clear in Washington that we disagree with Rabin's initiatives, so that President Clinton once and for all will understand that those around him who preach "peace at any price" are not speaking for the rank-and-file American Jews who voted for him last November.

One of the most salutary and beneficial results arising from the current crisis—and from the apparent impotence of such "establishment" organizations as AIPAC and the President's Conference—is that a new and powerful world-wide group of totally committed Jews has been formed. It is called the World Committee for Israel, and it marks the first time in modern history that the Sephardic and Ashkenazic communities have linked hands and formed a single united front for Israel.

In the past, the powerful Sephardic forces—representing communities originating in Aleppo (Syria), Morocco, Tunisia, Egypt and Algeria—have had their own parochial groupings, centering mainly around the Shas Party in Israel. Seeing that the crisis now facing Israel goes beyond party lines, they have decided to let bygones be bygones, and forge an alliance with equally committed Ashkenazic Jews. Together they form a formidable force in the United States, Europe and Israel. Party labels are no longer important, whether one is a member of Shas, Likud, Mizrachi, Agudah, etc. The main goal is to bring the message to Jerusalem and Washington that Jews—not politicians or minority extremists—want and demand an intact, strong and secure Israel and Jerusalem.

The names of the founding members of the World Committee for Israel, together with the manifesto setting forth their aims, will soon be officially issued.

In 1846 the United States declared war on Mexico, fighting fiercely for about two years, even invading Mexico and occupying the capital, Mexico City. Then, at the Guadeloupe Hidalgo, the United States forced the Mexicans to sign a treaty under which Mexico had to yield California, Nevada, Utah, most of Arizona and New Mexico, and parts of Colorado and Wyoming. These vast territories, making up most of the southwestern United States, were the fruits of a war of aggression. The return of these lands was never carried out, nor was it ever even considered. Yet peace has reigned for the past 147 years—without the United States having to give up the land it had confiscated. America has thus proven that the concept of "land for peace" is totally alien to America's history and sense of political morality, even when that land is the fruit of a war of aggression.

Nevertheless, the same American Government is pressing Israel to adopt a "land for peace" policy, although in Israel's case the land was acquired not as a result of aggression, but as a result of a defensive war against the unprovoked aggression perpetrated against her.

The previous Israeli Government under Yitzchak Shamir staunchly rejected the idea of "land for peace," and integrity and justice were on Shamir's side. The spineless accession to the concept of "land for peace" has only happened under the current leftist Government.

Under the present depressing circumstances created by the leftists in Israel, it is refreshing to read George Shultz's just published block-buster memoirs, *Turmoil and Triumph*, containing almost 1200 pages of highly informative notes on the dramatic years of the Reagan Administration.

When George Shultz took over the job of U.S. Secretary of State from Alexander Haig in 1982, friends of Israel were deeply worried—for Shultz had been the Chief Executive of the Bechtel Corporation, known for its vast business dealings with Saudi Arabia, and it was feared that he would have a strongly pro-Arab tilt. We were pleasantly surprised when Shultz turned out to be one of Israel's best friends to come along in a long time.

This change was brought about largely because of Shultz's personal exposure to the treachery and sabotage of leading Arabs, especially by President Assad of Syria, who personally sabotaged Shultz's laboriously worked-out peace agreement between Israel and Lebanon. Such peace was an anathema to Assad, who was plotting the invasion and takeover of Lebanon in order to turn that Christian-dominated nation into a Moslem-Syrian province. Since in Syria's textbooks Israel is marked as "Southern Syria," any peace between the neighboring Jewish and Christian states would be an obstacle to Assad's grandiose dreams for military domination of the area.

We have similar testimony regarding the deceit and unreliability of Syria's President from none other than the late Egyptian President Anwar Sadat. In his book *Those I Have Known*, Sadat wrote about how confused and uninformed President Jimmy Carter was: "President Assad of Syria baffled and bewildered him. He imagined the Syrians would be as good as their word, and was taken aback when he found that the word of a Syrian was in fact a thousand-and-one words."

In spite of his terrible lesson in Arab double-dealings, Shultz made many attempts to start peace negotiations between Israel and her Arab neighbors. But he was convinced that Israel should not have to give up any land, rather, she should allow the Palestinians self-administration within their districts.

Mr. Shamir displayed iron-clad opposition to international conferences, or bringing the Soviet Union or the United Nations into any peace process. Even as Prime Minister, Shamir consulted Menachem Begin on all important foreign policy matters, and Begin meticulously held to the letter of the Camp David agreement—which called for "a full five years of experience with autonomy before Palestinians and Israelis could address the final status." Shultz, of course, realized the wisdom of this policy, especially after the violent intifada had broken out, ruining the chances of reaching a peaceful coexistence expeditiously.

Against this background it is totally and irresponsibly reckless of men like today's Shimon Peres to call for "final settlement" now, even before trying out a period of coexistence through the implementation of an interim agreement.

We have an old saying, *"maasei avot siman l'banim,"* meaning, that what happens to the children of Israel was anticipated by what happened to their forefathers. Another saying, "there is nothing new under the sun," from King Solomon, also applies to today's peace process—for an exact parallel to current events is found in annals of our long and glorious history, and our understanding of it will help us find the proper answer for our own times as well.

Over three thousand years ago, in the days of the Judges, the Jews were challenged by Amon (today's Jordan), who claimed and demanded that "Israel occupied our land when she left Egypt. . . so now please return it through a peace (b'shalom)" (Judges 11:13). The Amonite's idea of "peace" was for the Jews to relinquish the entire land they demanded. Today such a one-sided demand is called by the Arabs "peace with justice." Yiftach, the Jewish leader of that time, pointed out to the leaders of Amon that the land they were claiming had never belonged to them 300 years earlier, but to the Amorites, who had turned down a peace offering from the Jews—choosing instead to attack the Jewish people, who had merely wanted to cross their territory to reach the Promised Land.

Fortunately for the Jews, they won the war that followed, and thereby gained the land of the Amorites east of the Jordan River. "And now," continued Yiftach (verse 23), "regarding what G-d has given us, the land of the Amorites, how can you ask to take it from us? Be satisfied with the land which your gods gave you!"

However, Amon did not accept this declaration, but persisted in its aggression against the Jews. In the ensuing battle Yiftach was victorious over the Amonites, inflicting "an exceedingly great defeat that humbled the Amonites before the Jews" (verse 33).

The parallel is obvious: The land which the Palestinians now claim was never theirs. Back in 1948 no one had even heard of a "Palestinian" people. Then the land was occupied by Jordan, after an illegal invasion which violated the U.N. Partition Plan. In 1967 Israel offered Jordan peace, but Jordan refused and attacked Israel. The Arab war of aggression was successfully repulsed, resulting in the territory on the West Bank coming under Jewish sovereignty. For the Palestinians to now come and claim the land which had been held by Jordan is exactly like the Amonites claiming land which had belonged to the Amorites.

The attacks carried out by the Amorites just after the Exodus from Egypt and by the Amonites 300 years later were wars of aggression. Just as in those days, Israel in our times has successfully repulsed the same kind of wars of aggression. The subsequent claims for land by the defeated enemy parallel the claims of our ancient adversaries.

Today, just as in ancient times, the plans of our enemies will, with the Almighty's help, be thwarted—but our own active participation in opposing them is an urgent requirement.

# Bosnia—Motherland Of "Palestinians"

The current turmoil in former Yugoslavia cannot be understood without knowledge of the region's long history of Balkan wars, ethnic strife, religious persecution and violence. The curious aspect about all this is the existence of a Moslem pocket in the heart of Europe, and how Bosnia came to be the origin of many of today's "Palestinians."

Bosnia, in ancient times, was a Roman province called Illyricum; Christianity was introduced in the Middle Ages. For centuries Bosnia was a football between Hungary, Turkey and Serbia, which fought each other in unending bloody wars. In 1386 Turkey invaded Bosnia. In line with the tenets of Islam, the entire population was forced into conversion. The Pope in Rome preached in favor of war against the Turks, with little immediate effect. But from 1691 on, when Turkey was expelled from Transylvania, Turkey lost one area after another, until in 1878, at the Congress of Berlin, dominated by Otto von Bismarck of Germany, Turkey lost Bosnia to Austria. The result was a stream of Moslem refugees pouring out of Bosnia looking for haven in the Ottoman Empire, because—just as today—the Christian Serbs who had been suppressed brutally by the Moslems were out to take bloody vengeance on the Moslem Bosnians in an effort to settle very old accounts.

This migration of Moslem refugees marked a very important historic milestone in the history of Palestine. The Ottoman rulers adopted a policy of Moslem colonization. In 1878, an Ottoman law granted lands in Palestine to the Moslem refugees from Bosnia. In the Carmel region, in the Galilee, in the Plain of Sharon and in Caesarea, lands were distributed to the Moslem refugees from Bosnia and Herzegovina. The refugees were further attracted by 12-year tax exemptions and exemption from military service.

The same colonization policy as for Bosnian Moslem refugees was also directed toward Moslem refugees from Russia—particularly from Georgia, the Crimea and the Caucasus, called Circassians and Turkmenians—leading to their settling in Abu Gosh, near Jerusalem, and in the Golan Heights. Refugees from Algeria and Egypt were also settled in Jaffa, Gaza, Jericho and the Golan.

Thus, the often-repeated Arab claim that the Palestinians are the descendents of the ancient Canaanites is just a lie. A hundred years ago many of them lived in Europe and other countries outside Palestine. The Jews, however, have had an uninterrupted presence in the Land of Israel during the 3500 years of our history. Clearly, our claim has much more validity and strength. It is not too late for this historic truth to come out and dispel the heavy clouds of vicious propaganda and lies.

The close ties between Palestinian and Bosnian Muslims—also called "Bushnaks," their Arabic, Turkish name—was shown in World War II: The infamous mufti Hajj Amin el-Husseini, uncle of today's PLO member Faisal el-Husseini, set up an "Islamic Legion" consisting of Bushnaks to fight for Hitler. They wanted to help their Palestinian cousins by killing as many Jews as possible so that none would be left to emigrate to the land of Israel after the war.

Now that Bosnia is independent again, it should not take long before her fiercely militant Moslem President, Alija Izetbegovic, will invite the Bosnian Palestinians to return to their motherland!

# Ben-Gurion: Without Chasidim There Might Not Have Been a State of Israel

The first time I saw David Ben-Gurion, he was a fiery orator at the 20th Zionist Congress, held in Zurich in 1937. He supported Weizmann's "Ja-zager" (yes-sayers), who championed the division of Palestine under the Peel Report. Then, at 51, his hair was cropped short; his characteristic white mane grew only later. Posing for a photograph taken on that occasion, I, as young student, stood next to the round-faced Ben-Gurion, who had just good-humoredly signed my autograph book. Nothing yet indicated he would become the great Jewish leader in war and peace, piloting the young State of Israel to its existence.

The next time I saw Ben-Gurion he was riding up Broadway in an open car, in an unforgettable ticker-tape parade, preceded by Jewish sailors proudly holding aloft Israeli flags, fluttering in the wind. That was in 1950, and the Jews of New York were delirious with happiness at this great manifestation of love for Israel by such huge masses of cheering onlookers.

The last time I saw him was in 1964. My family was spending some weeks at Haifa's Dan Carmel Hotel. One Shabbat, the chef, in anticipation of Mr. and Mrs. Ben-Gurion's visit, outdid himself in preparing a most lavish and beautiful smorgasbord. There he stood in his shining white uniform, expecting the Prime Minister's praise and appreciation. However, when David and Paula Ben-Gurion entered the dining room, the chef's utter disappointment was clearly visible, for Ben-Gurion brusquely walked by the laboriously prepared table without even so much as turning his eyes toward it. The open-shirted, former proletarian turned statesman had no interest in such *narishkeiten*. Moments later, however, his wife Paula was heard saying to their waiter, in Yiddish, *"far meinem Duvid'l darft ir geben a fett shtickel fish."*

The illustrious couple made a formidable pair; both were outspoken and strong willed. Now they lie together in their twin grave in S'dei Boker, in Ben-Gurion's beloved Negev.

Ben-Gurion was a great Bible scholar. His comments on the *Tanach* have been published, and they display profound expertise. He was not observant, yet he, like Golda Meir of the same generation, had deep respect for the Torah and for Torah observers.

Further, his famous agreement with Rav Maimon of Mizrachi assured that many important institutions in the new nation, including marriage, divorce and conversion, would be subject to rabbinic jurisdiction, and *kashrut* in public establishments and in the armed forces, was guaranteed. Ben-Gurion allowed Rav Maimon, a great scholar and patriot, to add a passage in Israel's Declaration of Independence expressing thanks to the "Rock of Israel" for the establishment of the Jewish State. (This should be a timely reminder to today's detractors from the Jewish religion, such as Shulamit Aloni and her Reform backers!)

There was another religious leader whom Ben Gurion greatly respected: Agudah leader Rav Yitzchak (Itche) Meir Levin, a Gerer Chosid and long time Cabinet Member.

Recently I acquired a historic letter written by Ben-Gurion, as Prime Minister, to Rav Levin, on December 4, 1955. In it he writes:

"With us, in our village in Poland, there were numerous Gerer Chasidim, many of whom had embraced Zionism. One of them was among the first *chalutzim* of the Second *Aliyah*, Reb Simcha Aizik, of blessed memory, who was harassed by some Chasidim who looked upon him as upon an *apikores*, although he remained strictly observant and religious all his life. If Reb Simcha Aizik and his *chaveirim* had listened to those Chasidim and would not have joined the Zionist enterprise, there would be grounds for great doubt whether a State would ever have been established."

This letter focuses light on the outstanding record of love for the Jewish land prominently displayed by the Chasidim of Gur, starting in the century before political Zionism flourished. Many Chasidic leaders encouraged their followers to settle in the Jewish land. One of them was Reb Yehuda Leib, the *Admur* of Gur, grandson of the famous author of *Chidushei Harim*. He lived from 1847 to 1905, and came to be known as the "Sefat Emet," after his celebrated *sefer*. He also wrote several *teshuvot* on the subject of *aliyah*, and held that settling in Eretz Yisrael is a mitzvah, although it should not be done just for the sake of economic betterment. In the latter case it is still a mitzvah, but one "*shelo lishma*."

In the second half of the 19th century, the Chasidic world of eastern Europe was deeply stirred up by the appeals coming from Germany, where a fund for the support of the Eretz Yisrael *yishuv* had been established by such Orthodox rabbinic leaders as Yukev Ettlinger, Ezrial Hildesheimer, S.R. Hirsch, I. Bamberger and others. Jointly with the Lehren-Rubens Committee in Amsterdam, they performed magnificently, not only raising funds from practically every Jewish community in Europe, but also by alerting Jews everywhere to the thought of settling in the Jewish land.

Initially, most Chasidic rebbes supported the idea which inspired this effort. It was only when the *Chovevei Tzion* (Lovers of Zion) movement became politicized and dominated by irreligious elements, that some Chasidic rebbes distanced themselves from it. Many others joined Mizrachi, the religious Zionists. A number of prominent Zionists, including Theodore Herzl and Nahum Sokolow, personally made strenuous attempts to win over the Sefat Emet and other Chasidic leaders to the Zionist movement, but without success.

Yet the idea of settling in the Jewish land and working on its soil had gripped many Chasidim, and evidently also Reb Simcha Aizik, whom Ben-Gurion mentioned in his 1955 letter. Just about the time of the Sefat Emet's death in 1905, the

Second Aliyah took place, ultimately bringing 40,000 young Jewish men and women to Eretz Yisrael, including many Gerer Chasidim who had been inspired by the love for the Jewish land exuded by the old Gerer Rebbe.

Realizing the value of a well organized party, many rebbes, *roshei yeshivot* and *rabbanim* from eastern Europe, and many Orthodox leaders from western Europe, founded their own party, the Agudah. At Agudah's first Knessiah Gedolah in Kattowitz in 1912, eastern Chasidim and Mitnagdim and western rabbis meshed together well. In attendance were Rav Chaim Brisker from Lithuania, a multitude of Chasidic rebbes from Poland and Galicia, and German leaders, including Jacob Rosenheim, who survived World War II.

The successor to the Sefat Emet was his son Reb Yehuda Aryeh Leib, also known as the "Imrei Emet," born in 1866. He fulfilled his father's dream of going to the Holy Land. His first trip took place in 1921, followed by more trips in 1924, 1927, 1932 and 1935. He would visit the *Kotel* as often as possible, to be near the *Shechina*. During these trips he inspired his followers to contribute to the building of the Jewish land, and they founded Bene Brak and Kfar Chasidim, as well as a large number of other communities and institutions.

In 1937 the Gerer Rebbe attended the third Knessia Gedola of the Agudah, in Marienbad, Czechoslovakia. My family had come from Sweden to spend the summer there. My father, z"l, and I were present at a few meetings, and I was impressed with the great number of rebbes and rabbanim I saw there. But the highlight of our trip to Marienbad came as we took a walk through the city park one day, and the Gerer Rebbe, surrounded by many of his followers, came there for a walk, too. I remember the Rebbe's very substantial figure, his long white beard and *peyot*. He seemed emerged in deep, deep thought, with his worried-looking, serious eyes. As I remember, my father took me to the Rebbe for his blessing. That, of course, was a great *zechut*, and left a very profound impression on me, especially as I had never in my 15 years seen a Chosid before.

Much has been written about the erudition and piety of the Imrei Emet, but no doubt his greatest historic contribution was his leadership in inspiring countless Chasidim to settle in Israel, thereby helping to build the Jewish land. He also called on Jews to invest in Israel. The Chasidim who followed his lead were spared the agonies of the Holocaust, which began soon after the 1937 Marienbad Congress.

Because of the early pioneering involvement of the Gerer Chasidim in Eretz Yisroel, it is no wonder that each of the succeeding Gerer Rebbes has been the spokesman and leader of Moetzet Gedolei Hatorah, Agudah's guiding council, in both religious and political matters.

The Imrei Emet appealed to his affluent devotees as follows: "I believe that if some 500 well-to-do families from our circles were now to settle in Eretz Yisrael, we would conquer the Holy Land both materially and spiritually." This predictive pronouncement was unfortunately not followed.

Although the Imrei Emet was a staunch fighter for the Agudah, he was a man of peace. On one visit to Eretz Yisrael, when he found controversies between the Chief Rabbi, Rav Abraham Kook, and elderly rabbanim, Reb Yosef Chaim Sonnenfeld and Reb Yerucham Diskin, he did everything he could to make peace between them. He understood that Rav Kook, as Chief Rabbi for all Jews, had to "draw the unobservant near with his right hand." He also agreed with Rav Kook that "one strictly observant Jew who settles in the land carries more weight than a thousand free-thinking settlers." By promoting mutual respect, the Gerer Rebbe brought about peace. He emphasized this in a lengthy letter to his followers in Europe, discussing how unity is more important than petty controversy.

When the War broke out in 1939, the Rebbe miraculously escaped the clutches of the Germans and arrived in Eretz Yisrael. He settled in Jerusalem and lived through the fighting of the War of Independence. To those who worried about the outcome of the War, he said reassuringly: "The end will be good. Do not fear. The gentiles will yet flee from our people." He died after Shevuot, in 1949, and was buried in the courtyard of his yeshiva, as there still was no way for Jews to approach Mt. Olives in those days. Thousands of Chasidim—who thanks to his inspirational love for the land had come to live there—joined his funeral, along with dignitaries and visitors from many lands.

Looking back on the long association of the Gerer Chasidim with the return to the land of Israel, it becomes clear that Ben-Gurion was right: If it had not been for the Second *Aliyah* in the days before World War I, in which Gerer Chasidim participated prominently, no basis for the ultimate Jewish State would have been built. In fact, there might never have been such a State.

The hand of Divine Providence is clearly visible in the history of the Gerer Chasidim and their contribution to Israel.

# General Schwarzkopf Says: Don't Give Back The Golan Heights

We all admired the dynamic personality and rhetoric of General (Stormin') Norman Schwarzkopf, the commander of the Allied Forces during the Gulf War. Daily, his briefings over TV were classics in relaxed, but professional, descriptions of intricate military operations. Last Wednesday night my wife and I had the opportunity of hearing him in person when he addressed a mainly Jewish audience in the Jackie Gleason Theater in Miami Beach. About 2000 people crowded the auditorium and gave him a resounding ovation and applause at many occasions during his witty and hard-hitting talk. Here are some of the most important points he made:

About Israel he had this to say: "I admire Israel because she is a democracy; I admire Israel because I love the underdog, I always loved the underdog, and as a military man I cannot help but admire Israel's military successes. But let me tell you that I have never admired Israel more than I did during Operation Desert Storm because Israel had 40 reasons to enter the war—that is how many Scuds were fired at Israel. Sometimes it is said that Israel does not have the interest of the world at heart, and only has its own interest at heart, but this is not true. The Desert War proved the opposite: Israel was under tremendous pressure to enter the war, but for the good of everyone in the Coalition, Israel showed great forbearance for the common good, and because of that I am convinced today that we have the greatest opportunity today for peace, greater than at any time in my lifetime."

He singled out one of Israel's famous military inventions for special praise: the pilotless small planes, the VUA, which the American Army is using for aerial surveillance. He told us that the plane was so successful that in some cases Iraqi troops surrendered to the pilotless plane! What the General probably did not know was that in Israel's military history there have been several instances when Arabs surrendered to invisible armies and arms. An old Palmach leader once told me that in Safed, the old city of Kabbalists, the Arabs surrendered during the War of Independence and afterwards told the utterly surprised Israelis that they had heard the noise of a giant (non-existent) Jewish army approaching with vastly superior arms. Or think of the gun which is still displayed near the Central Hotel in Jerusalem, the famous "Davidka" which, with its enormous noise, although without much fire power, overwhelmed Arab armies.

On the question of the Golan Heights, General Schwarzkopf made the most significant political statement for the benefit of Israel, and I quote his words: "If I were in charge of the Golan Heights, I would only argue from a position of strength.

I would not consider giving them up unless I had absolutely satisfactory assurances that the security of my country is protected. I would make that determination entirely on the basis of very, very strong assurances." He implied, of course, that such assurances cannot be expected from either Syrians nor any other power! Coming from the highest Allied field officer, who has close knowledge of the Arabs and their mentality and military capabilities, this is surely a most important and telling utterance, which no doubt will carry much weight in Jerusalem as well as, hopefully, in Washington.

One questioner asked the General: "When Kuwait executed Palestinians and deported hundreds of thousands of them, no one said anything. So why is Israel condemned for deporting 12 known terrorists?" The General replied: "The Palestinians are a terrible problem for the Arabs in the entire region. They are a destabilizing element and that is the reason that all Arabs are very anxious to solve their problem. This is the reason for the general support among the Arabs for the peace process. But, of course, we cannot expect instantaneous results, and nobody does." In other words, the Arabs would like to get rid of their Palestinians by unloading them on Israel.

Of course, he had to justify somehow that despite the "victory" in the Desert Storm war, Saddam Hussein is still in place. This can be compared to President Roosevelt and General Eisenhower leaving Hitler in charge of Europe after World War II! General Schwarzkopf professed certainty that Saddam is totally powerless, having lost his entire nuclear and chemical arsenal, and that he has lost face in the Arab world. "Saddam Hussein is irrelevant! I know nothing worse than being irrelevant!" Perhaps it was on this point that the General was less convincing than on any other point he made during his talk. He came back again and again to the prospect of the peace process and commented: "If Saddam Hussein had any influence whatsoever in the Arab world, do you think there would be a peace process today?"

Dr. Lehmann with the late Prime Minister Menachem Begin, in New York, 1979.
The meeting took place after the Camp David agreement.

# Entebbe Rescue Operation 20th Anniversary

We have just lived through a clear divine miracle—the liberation of Israel from the control of the leftists and atheists. If we look back on our history, we can point to many, many miracles—situations where our survival hung by a hair. The greatest miracle of all is, of course, our very survival after 4,000 years.

Since the beginning of time, we have been surrounded by enemies whose main aims have been to eliminate that trustee for truth, justice, and morality—the Jewish people. Our continued existence bothers them to no end, because we have put them to shame. Compared with the Jews, they must be shamefaced because of their shortcomings. So instead of trying to reach the intellectual, moral, and ethical heights of the Jews, they try to eliminate us and the humiliation of being compared to us.

We must therefore never forget the miracles that saved us and helped us overcome the non-stop onslaught by our adversaries. To be ever-thankful for these results is to be *makkir tov*—appreciate the good—which G-d is giving us. The miracle of the victory in the War of Liberation in 1948-49, the Six Day War, the Yom Kippur War . . . we can never thank G-d enough for these salvations.

And one miracle that we must never forget is that of the Entebbe rescue operation which took place on July 4, 1976. As it is likely that this dramatic and heroic event will be commemorated in the media this year—the 20th anniversary of the rescue—I offer herewith my account of my own involvement in this event, even though I have mentioned it briefly in past columns.

In 1972, Uganda—a lush, fertile land with a highly capable population—was the scene of a military takeover. An obscure parachute officer, Idi Amin, took over a democratic government, which the British colonial power had left behind, and ruled his country as a dictator.

Although nominally a Christian, he "converted" to Islam in order to get financial and political support from the oil rich Arab sheikdoms. His "conversion" brought with it bloodbaths against the black Christians on a large scale. For this he relied on his new friend, Yasser Arafat, who installed his PLO training camps in Uganda, from where PLO-trained thugs massacred hundreds of thousands of Christians. Idi Amin became an outcast in the civilized world, but he still had some warm feelings for Israel, where he had been trained as a parachutist. The Israeli military attaché, Col. Bar Lev, lived in Kampala, Uganda, in a beautiful home where I visited him sometimes.

The plot that the PLO and Idi Amin hatched came suddenly to the foreground in the last days of June 1976. An Air France plane was hijacked by PLO terrorists on its way from Tel Aviv to Paris and was flown, at gunpoint, to Entebbe, Uganda's airport.

The world was at first uncertain whether the hijacking was directed against France for its role in Lebanon. But soon enough the demands became known: The hijackers demanded the release from Israeli and Kenyan jails of a number of terrorists captured in past operations. (It later turned out that Kenya had no prisoners. They had been turned over to Israel long before.)

The threat to kill hostages, one by one, was broadcast around the world. Family members in Israel marched around Prime Minister Rabin's office demanding that Israel lift its old policy of not giving in to terrorist demands. The deadline for beginning the killings naturally heightened the tension in Israel, and the pressure on Rabin to do something became unbearable. (In his autobiography he wrote that Peres had nothing to do with the decision to try a rescue operation; yet, after its success, Peres tried to take the credit away from Rabin.)

While planning various alternatives, Rabin decided to find "our man in East Africa" who could negotiate with Idi Amin for the release of the hostages. And that man was myself: An Agudah member in the government, Rav Shlomo Lorentz, knew of my connections in East Africa and reached me in Nairobi by telephone Friday afternoon, July 2, a few hours before Shabbat. His message: Rabin needs someone who can establish personal liaison with Amin and make an offer leading to the release of the hostages. I was of course bewildered. It was true that I had met Idi Amin a few times, but I doubted that I could establish the link that Rabin wanted. All I could do was try. I could see before myself the hundreds of suffering hostages facing death and the thousands of Israelis who clamored for action.

Suddenly I remembered a high-ranking Ugandan officer whom I knew and who might be helpful, even in Amin's absence from Kampala, the capital. The Organization of African Unity (OAU) was holding a conference on the island of Mauritius in the Indian Ocean. Amin was there and was being feted like a conquering hero for having humbled a powerful white nation—Israel. After various attempts, I reached the Ugandan officer, Col. Marjan. To my surprise he acted as if he had been waiting for my call: "Ransoming the hostages? That is exactly what the Field Marshall has been waiting for!" (Idi Amin was called Field Marshall among his people—not bad for a soldier who had never risen above the rank of sergeant!)

I quickly reported back to Israel that contact had been established. I asked for instructions. Instead, Rav Lorentz reported back that I had "carte blanche": "You can offer them any deal—Israel will back you. Just act fast because the deadline for killing the hostages is near." After a few more phone conversations with Col. Marjan, the details of my meeting with Idi Amin, the giant Ugandan, were set. I would take a flight on Sunday, July 4 from Nairobi to Entebbe, from where—after a 1-hour meeting with the "Field Marshall," I would continue to fly to Lagos, Nigeria, to report on my meeting at Entebbe to Rabin's security people.

Rav Lorentz was delighted with the encouraging news. He told me that he always consults with the gedolei Yisrael on important decisions. In this case, he told me, he had consulted Rav Greineman in Bnei Brak, kinsman of the late Chofetz Chaim. Rav Greineman sent me the message that I should not be overly optimistic in my reports to the Rabin government, as it might discourage them from undertaking other avenues for the rescue . . . .

Next, Lorentz advised me that Rabin was sending a Mossad man named David to brief me the next day in Nairobi.

That Friday night there were more Jews in the local synagogue than I had ever witnessed. Clearly they were Israelis who had come to help with a rescue operation. One local prominent Israeli contractor came to visit me. He showed me that it had been his firm that had designed and built the Entebbe Airport terminal, so he had all the plans and blueprints for every bolt and nut in the airport. . . .

All my local friends came to dissuade me from keeping a date with the Ugandan dictator. There was no guarantee that I would come out alive from my trip. But I would not let anyone dissuade me from my plan, which could mean the saving of hundreds of Jewish lives. I did not tell my wife, who was in New York, about my undertaking, in order not to upset her. I did inform my late son, Jamie, so that I would have a line of communication with my family. Later my wife told me she would not have dissuaded me from going. I give her much credit for being so idealistic in the face of danger to Jewish lives.

The next day in shul we said with fervor the prayer for the well-being of President Jomo Kenyatta, whose cooperation was vital. I waited in my hotel room for the appearance of David. Some Africans were visiting me when David entered my room. I asked him to wait a few minutes before my friends left, but his answer was: "When Jewish lives are to be saved, you do not stand on ceremonies. Send them away!"

He then gave me a list of instructions: 1) Find out if our people are still alive; 2) Find out exactly where they are being kept; 3) Try to meet at least one Jew and assure him that we are all working hard for the hostages' release. (At his point he sat down, and cried. It showed me the strength of true Jewish compassion. I must confess that I, too, at that point cried together with the sturdy Mossad man. It was such a moving moment.); 4) As to the negotiations, offer Amin any amount he wants. It will be made available.

"We know that Amin can settle the whole affair in five minutes. But warn him, if one Jew is hurt, he will not get one cent!" David said. "We know the number of Amin's secret Swiss bank account; paying him the ransom money will pose no problem. But Israel cannot afford to release one single terrorist!"

As quietly as David had entered my room, he disappeared again.

That night I heard on Israel short-wave radio the voice of Menachem Begin, calling for the release of the PLO hostages—as requested by the terrorists. I was of course stunned: How could Begin make such a statement? But later it became apparent that this was a ruse to lull the Ugandans into complacency, making them think they had won the battle. . . .

Sunday morning, July 4: In the United States the nation was celebrating the 200th anniversary of the birth of the nation, and here in Kenya, in the darkest part of Africa, I was getting ready to meet face-to-face the feared African dictator, to save Jewish lives. . . .

As I was getting ready to go to Nairobi's airport for my Entebbe-bound plane, my phone rang. It was Jamie calling from New York. There was overwhelming emotion in his voice: "Daddy, do not go. Our people are already back in Tel Aviv!" I was stunned. How had it all changed? How had they been rescued? Jamie filled me in with news reports: "The rescuers had come, taken away the Jewish hostages, and left. . ." In a flash, I could see a repeat of the biblical rescue operation in Shchem 3,000 years before: "Dinah's brothers took their sister and left. . . ."

I decided to drive out to the airport despite the news. Maybe some assistance was needed; perhaps those wounded and killed had to be looked after. At least a few would need to put on Tefillin. . . .

As I came to the airport, I saw a giant Israeli hospital plane parked. It had been estimated that some 50 persons would be killed or wounded in the operation. Soon I heard the truth: Only one officer was killed, Yonni Netanyahu, whose name became synonymous with heroism and Jewish courage.

Later my Kenyan friends told me that the head of the Kenyan Telephone Company, William Gitau, had simply cut the telephone links between Uganda and the outside world, preventing any of the news about the rescue operation from going out of Uganda.

Back in my hotel I had a call from Rav Lorentz to exchange *mazel tov* wishes. He thanked me profusely for my role in the drama. *Only one call I never got: Rabin never called off my Entebbe mission!* Had Jamie not notified me, I would have flown to Entebbe and would have been torn limb from limb by Idi Amin in his fury, like the poor Mrs. Dora Bloch, who had been rushed to the Kampala hospital—and there was torn apart by Amin. I never understood Rabin's evaluation of a Jewish life. Was I expendable?

Arafat and his PLO also let out their fury and frustration: On New Year's Eve, 1981, a PLO terrorist blew up the Jewish-owned Norfolk Hotel, with 16 people killed and 85 maimed. The PLO terrorist escaped to Saudi Arabia. Kenya's request for his extradition was never answered. Idi Amin lives as an honored guest in Saudi Arabia until this day.

The world reaction to Jewish heroism was characteristic: Kurt Waldheim, then the secretary-general of the United Nations, deplored Israel's invasion of the sovereign territory of Uganda, a U.N. member state. The world should have noticed right then and there that Waldheim was a pathological anti-Semite and Nazi. Israel's ambassador to the United Nations, Chaim Herzog, delivered one of his finest oratories defending Israel's action.

Years later I met Bibi Netanyahu in Kenya. He told me, "If your plan had been allowed to proceed, my bother Yonni would still be alive today." In honor of Bibi, and in memory of Yonni, the Entebbe rescue operation should be commemorated—as a message to the world that Israeli strength and Jewish heroism are back again. A warning to our enemies.

Dr. Lehmann with President Daniel arap Moi of Kenya, at the opening of a telephone exchange in Nakuru. Lehmann also contributed to the establishment of diplomatic relations between Kenya and Israel.

# Arabs

Next to the Vatican, our most dangerous enemies are the Arabs of today. They have turned their religion—which originally was benign to the Jews—into a blood thirst against every Jew in the world, but particularly those in Israel. They have never deviated from their resolve to evict—through violent means—the Jews from every inch of the soil of Israel. The double-faced and deceptive statements of the Arabs are analyzed in this section.

## Arafat's Secret Speech in Stockholm

*Total Collapse of Israel Pending; Millions of Jews to Leave*
*"We Plan to Eliminate Israel and Establish Purely Palestinian State"*

Yasser Arafat has just delivered his most outrageous and revealing speech before a secret meeting in Stockholm of all the Arab ambassadors. The meeting took place on January 30, 1996, the birthdate of the late Swedish Prime Minister Olaf Palme, a friend of the PLO. A leaked report was sent to me from a reliable source.

The day was celebrated with a 250,000-crown prize handed to leftist Jewish youngsters of the Peace Now and the Labor Young Leadership—jointly with the Fatah Youth—for their promotion of "peace" between Jews and Arabs. Yossi Beilin was also in Stockholm for the occasion.

Arafat spoke in a closed meeting to the Arab diplomats, but his speech was leaked through secret channels. His topic was "The Impending Total Collapse of Israel." He stated that at least half of the Russian immigrants to Israel are Christians or Moslems. When the civil war, which can be expected, will break out in Israel, the Russian immigrants will fight for a united Palestinian state. He stated that he has proof that the "so-called Ethiopian Jews" really are Moslems. He announced that both Peres and Beilin would support a Palestinian state as long as some degree of religious freedom would be guaranteed to its Jewish inhabitants. However, the Jews are expected to give up their dwellings and will emigrate to the United States.

"We Palestinians will take over everything, including all of Jerusalem," Arafat declared. "Peres and Beilin have already promised us half of Jerusalem. The Golan Heights have already been given away—subject to just a few details."

Arafat said that as soon as the Golan Heights are returned, at least a million rich Jews will leave Israel.

"All the rich Jews who will get compensation will travel to America," he said.

Arafat then revealed his plan for the Palestinian takeover of Israel:

"We of the PLO will now concentrate all our efforts on splitting Israel psychologically into two camps. Within five years we will have six to seven million Arabs living on the West Bank and in Jerusalem. All Palestinian Arabs will be welcomed back by us. If the Jews can import all kinds of Ethiopians, Russians, Uzbekians and Ukranians as Jews, then we can import all kinds of Arabs to us! (Three and half million Arabs will thus be brought to Palestine.) You understand that we plan to eliminate the State of Israel and establish a purely Palestinian State. We will make life unbearable for Jews by psychological warfare and population explosion; Jews will not want to live among us Arabs!

"I have no use for Jews; they are and remain Jews! We now need all the help we can get from you in our battle for a united Palestine under total Arab-Moslem domination!"

This horrendous revelation of true intentions flies in the face of Arafat's repeated promises to abrogate the dreaded PLO covenant. It is now obvious that he has no such intention, but expects Peres and Beilin to cave in again and surrender Israel to a Palestinian state, in fulfillment of the PLO covenant.

Peres faces a national election: How can he survive the impact of a double-cross by Arafat—his "peace partner? Will not Israelis rise and throw out the party that opened the Pandora's box of PLO aggression? And will the duped American Jews continue to support this "peace process?"

Arafat also revealed in Stockholm that Swedish Prime Minister Ingvar Larson has been approved as a mediator in the negotiations about the future of Jerusalem. The Swedish prime minister also met with Yossi Beilin in Stockholm, during Arafat's visit, and discussed Jerusalem's future.

Beilin's meeting with Larson must be seen against the background of his and Peres' assurances a few days earlier to the OU conference in Jerusalem that Jerusalem is not negotiable and that the status quo will be maintained. Will this brazen double-talk and deception be tolerated by Israelis? Does President Clinton know what Arafat's real intentions are? And does he really care?

We are outraged by the callous disregard that the leftist government in Jerusalem has shown the last four years for the outcries of concerned Jews over the sacrificing of Israel's security, water resources, strategic positions and sacred sites in exchange for the totally uncertain chance-taking with "peace." Meanwhile, the outcries of a vast number of Christian groups are clearly growing, as they see their reliance on Jewish self-interest vanish. In other words, while Christians took for granted that Israel would safeguard its minimal and basic needs, as every nation in history has done, they now find that Israel is history's lone exception: Without provocation or need, Israel—the strongest military power in the Middle East and the victor in all wars against the Arabs—is acting like a meek, vanquished nation, surrendering its most basic interests. Christians never thought this development could be possible; but with this realization, the Christians have gathered in ever greater numbers to protest what is going on and to demand a change in Israel's foreign policy course. Will the leftists in Jerusalem turn a deaf ear to these millions of Christians?

A few weeks ago, a large gathering, representing some 50 Christian human rights groups and millions of Americans, met for several days in Washington to plan action. The groups, coming together as the Coalition for the Defense of Human Rights under Islamization, placed special emphasis in their meeting on the need to expel the Syrian occupiers from Lebanon and to ensure the freedom of the Christians in Southern Lebanon, who have been Israel's loyal allies for many years. They are all united in the knowledge that the Arabs are the invaders, who for the past 1,000 years, have robbed Christians of their land, property, culture and independence. They know that among peoples of the Middle East, only the Jews have regained their ancient independence—hence, their admiration for Israel.

The resulting resolution of the Coalition contains the following passages:

> 1. The Coalition for the Defense of Human Rights under Islamization is concerned about the fate of the Lebanese Christians in general, and the Christian population in South Lebanon in particular.
> 2. The Coalition rejects any attempts to legitimize Syria's domination over Lebanon and the political, military, legal and economic repression of its Christian community as a reward for any political arrangement.

On Friday, January 22, a delegation of the National Alliance of Lebanese Americans met at the State Department with Dennis Ross, the United States' top Middle East negotiator, to discuss the fate of Lebanon in the framework of the Syrian-Israeli negotiations. Ross promised that Lebanon will not be a part of a Syrian-Israeli deal.

Lobbying was conducted in Congress in the days following these meetings—mainly by Christian Israel PAC and the World Lebanese Organization.

Rev. Jan Willem van der Houven, head of the International Christian Embassy in Jerusalem, recently completed a two-week, grassroots tour, with successful addresses to pro-Israel Christian audiences in Tennessee, Massachusetts, Washington, D.C., California and Texas. He has also undertaken to help Moshe Feiglin, the courageous Israeli civil rights activist, who, as head of the non-partisan civil rights group, Zo Artzeinu, is now being indicted by the leftist Israeli government—with the threat of a long jail term—under the accusation of "sedition."

The International Christian Embassy in Jerusalem issued a lengthy statement after the assassination of Rabin, which contained this passage: "Although peace is the desire of all Israelis, the debate over giving away land for peace will continue to cause deep divisions in Israeli society. It is the prayer of the Christian Embassy that the great legacy of Mr. Rabin, as a military commander who oversaw the miraculous unification of Jerusalem during the 1967 war, will strengthen the resolve of those who desire to see Israeli sovereignty remain over an undivided Jerusalem."

# Arafat's Ferocious Stockholm Speech Makes Major Impact on Public Opinion

On January 30, 1996, when Arafat thought his secrecy was safeguarded, he revealed in a speech before Arab diplomats in Stockholm his plans for Israel and the Jewish people. A few days later the contents of his speech were featured in the *Algemeiner Journal*. The rest of the media hesitated at first to publish what was such a vicious reflection of the murderous intentions of the PLO since its inception. Then, after checking the story out, one paper after the other published this story, which was called "explosive" by David Bar-Ilan, executive editor of the prestigious *Jerusalem Post*. The free Israeli radio station, Channel 7, featured the story a few times. Even leftist *Haaretz* featured it, albeit on Page 7 at the bottom. The U.S. correspondent for *Haaretz* read from the speech on a CNN interview program.

In this country the story spread fast. *The Wall Street Journal* published a sharply critical editorial headlined, "Arafat's Complicity," which quoted from the Stockholm speech and commented, "There is no reason to doubt the authenticity of the reports given other statements Mr. Arafat has made to Arab audiences." *The Washington Times, Miami Herald, Kansas City Star, Palm Beach Post* and many others had prominent editorials on the Stockholm speech. *The Wall Street Journal* drew a direct line between the speech and Arafat's praising the "martyr" suicide bombers before huge crowds that vowed war against Israel. Here are the main points in Arafat's speech which every thinking person sees as a clear disqualification of the PLO terror chief from being accepted as "peace partner" and whose statements are not to be trusted in the least:

1. Israel's collapse is imminent.
2. There will be civil war in Israel and the Russian and Ethiopian immigrants, who are mostly Christians and Moslems, will join the Palestinian fighters against Israel.
3. Peres and Beilin have already promised him "half" of Jerusalem, but the PLO wants it all and will take over the entire country.
4. The Golan Heights have already been given away by Israel.
5. Over 1 million Jews will initially leave the country.
6. The PLO will bring in 3½ to 5 million Arabs, from various origins, who will be called "Palestinians." Five to six million Arabs will populate the Land, every inch of which will be a totally Moslem state.
7. The PLO will practice psychological warfare against the Jews in order to divide them into two opposing camps.

6. "I want to have nothing to do with Jews; they are and remain Jews."
7. "I call on all Arabs to help with the struggle for a United Palestine under total Moslem Arab domination."

Shortly after this speech came the torrent of suicide murders, with the blood of more than 60 Jews drenching the streets of Israel. The same Arafat appeared on television and mumbled, amid crocodile tears, some words of how much he deplored violence, because it was bad for the Palestinians and for the peace. The height of hypocrisy.

With the murderous Stockholm speech widely known, how can Peres ignore its impact? Is he blind—unable to judge anymore—biased by unknown pressures? Here is the real truth: The speech was speedily faxed to Peres through an important political personality. The exact hour on February 6 when the fax arrived in Israel is well known. Yet, when asked about the speech, Peres denied that he ever got it. In his desperation he is using "deniability" as his way out of a compelling impasse. The general public is of course asking: "How can the head of the Israeli government continue talking about the 'peace process' with a man who aims at Israel's destruction?"

The medieval Moslem theologian, al-Ghazali, spoke very clearly about the permissibility of using lies and deception instead of the truth: "Know that a lie is not wrong in itself. Ignorance sometimes is an advantage, and if a lie causes this kind of ignorance it will be allowed. It is sometimes a duty to lie. If a lie is the only way to reach a good result, it is allowable. A lie is lawful when it is the only path to duty. We must lie when truth leads to unpleasant results." (Quoted from *The Arab Mind*, by John Laffin, London, 1975).

A perfect practitioner of this doctrine is Yasser Arafat, who cons the whole world into accepting him as a "peace partner" while all along he plots *jihad*—holy war, violence.

When I was a guest at the White House on September 15, I had a fine chat with the President. This was before the second White House ceremony with Arafat. I warned the President not to dishonor the hallowed grounds of the White House and the high prestige of the presidency by inviting Arafat.

Now the inevitable has happened: Arafat dishonored the word he gave the President last September, and now—as it defies belief—Clinton is going to Egypt to shake hands again with this con man and terrorist. All this is explained as a political necessity in an election year. But is such expediency really acceptable to the American people? There must be a limit to the embarrassments and insults that an American President is expected to swallow. Is there no sense of honor and ethics left? According to the Hamas Covenant, both the PLO and Hamas are identical—as "father and son, as brother and brother." Since I published the main points of the 34-page Hamas Covenant in the *Algemeiner Journal* last week, I sent a copy of it to the

President, so that he may be forewarned of what he is likely to face after yet another handshake.

Of course, since the Arab doctrine justifies lies, deception and hiding of facts, it is not surprising that this doctrine is being practiced in order to cover up the complicity of Arafat with the terrorist attacks on Jews—in the language of the *Wall Street Journal*. But after three years of on-going conning and lying, shouldn't this ploy be stopped once and for all?

Two weeks ago a friend called me from London. Had I ever heard of the pigskin taboo among Moslems? he asked. After he gave me some hints, I proceeded to research the matter with one of the most knowledgeable experts on Islam in the world, Professor Moshe Sharon, whom I met some time ago in Jerusalem. Yes, he immediately exclaimed, when the British had colonies in Moslem countries, especially in the Sudan and Pakistan, and they were plagued by suicide terrorists, they introduced a simple remedy: They announced that every terrorist would be buried in pigskin bags. The effect: Anybody exposed to an unclean animal, such as a pig, will not be admitted to Paradise. The conclusion: If Israel announces that the suicide bombers will not be handed over to their families but buried inside pigskin bags by the Israeli authorities, the result will be loss of incentive to try to reach Paradise. The suicide missions would lose their attraction. There should be no "social" inhibitions against using this simple device.

Well, I passed the suggestion to the *Jerusalem Post*, which promptly featured it in one of its editorials. There has been wide discussion in Israeli society about my "pigskin" solution.

Sometimes quite simple solutions, if psychologically effective, can bring about great results.

President Clinton with Dr. Lehmann in the White House dining room, December 15, 1995, discussing the problems arising from the "peace" process.

# Islam in America

The public, and especially the Jewish public, has in recent years abhorred the anti-Semitic rhetoric and diatribe that has flowed from the mouths of black leaders. Starting with Jesse Jackson's venomous reference to New York as "Hymietown," this flatulence has grown into a flood of crude and gross hate-filled litanies, which have not been heard since the heydays of Hitler. The question is, where does that hate propaganda come from?

On a larger scale, the extreme hostility by Moslem Arabs against Israel and Jews is most clearly personified in the Hamas Constitution, which calls for the killing of Jews wherever they can be found.

To discover the generator that drives this hatred, it is enlightening to examine the literature that Moslem hate groups have published, as well as the inside documents distributed in the Moslem community.

A publisher of characteristic literature is the Qoranic Open University, Inc. USA, which recently published a book titled *Target Islam*, which is nothing more than 265 pages preaching unbridled hatred against Jews and Zionists. In the tradition of the old Russian forgery, *Protocols of the Elders of Zion*—which is still the "Bible" to some Moslem Arabs today—*Target Islam* pins every ill on earth on a "Jewish conspiracy" to rule the world.

While praising the "benevolence of Moslems and their desire to live in peace and harmony with their fellow creatures in G-d's creation," the book states that it is "Zionist hatred that is plotting against mankind." The Zionists are spreading "malicious fabrications against Moslems" in order to "destroy the good work of the Moslems and divide them from friendship with their Christian brethren." Yet it talks of the "exposure of decadence in the high ranks of the Christian ministry" as the reason for the rapid rise in conversion to Islam in the United States.

Among the events that *Target Islam* attributes to the Zionists is the Gulf War, which it says was orchestrated by the Zionists, "because their purpose is to physically destroy as much Moslem life and property as possible using whatever and whomever." It even attributes to the Jews the fighting in Kashmir, the province claimed by both India and Pakistan: "In Kashmir, Israel directly supplies weapons and training to the Indian soldiers, who rape, torture and pillage the people and property of Kashmir."

The fighting between Bosnians and Serbs is described as "the struggle of Moslem brothers against the Serbian aggressor." The World Trade Center bombing and revelations of terrorist plans by the Brooklyn Moslem bombers are described as a case of mistaken identity: "In New York a group of Moslems were being trained by an FBI plant, whom they believed would lead them to Bosnia to participate in the struggle there. . . . Imagine their surprise when they were arrested along with their training materials and charged with plotting to blow up the Holland Tunnel along with other targets in New York City." The book explains the increasing suspicion directed toward Moslems in this country as being the result of Zionists worried about the "growing influence of Moslems in the Western world. Thus the Zionists have taken great pains to implicate Moslems in terrorist conspiracies, especially in the late manufactured New York incidents." The accusation against Sheikh Uram A. Rahman, who was sentenced in Egypt for terror acts before he fled to this country, are called "false propaganda."

But the main targets of the author's hatred are the Task Force on Terrorism and Unconventional Warfare of the House of Representatives and the Anti-Defamation League. The former has been a tremendously successful research team in the office of Rep. Bill McCollum (R-Fla.), with the research mainly conducted by Joseph Bodansky, whom the Moslems call "a Mossad spy."

The ADL is pictured as running paramilitary camps "that are equipped as small armies that are put together expressly to train members for terrorist and paramilitary activities to guard the security of their Jewish state, Israel. . . including the horrendous slaughter committed by one of its trained members in the massacre of Moslem worshippers at the Hebron Mosque in Palestine." In other words, Dr. Goldstein was, according to this story, a paramilitary anti-terrorist trained in this country by the ADL. (Mr. Abraham Foxman, take note!)

The general description of Jews is presented as follows: "The Jews are condemned by Allah for their actions, as written in the Holy Koran. They are described as liars, cheats and conspirators with hearts harder than rocks; and not only that, but a large number of them were turned into apes and swine, as punishment for their conspiracy to violate the command of G-d. They, the disobedient Jews, are sentenced to a life of misery and homelessness and debasement for their acts."

Israel, according to *Target Islam*, "is the stolen homeland of the Palestinians. Israelites in their disobedience to their Creator, forsook all rights to any 'promised land' wherever that might have been." This passage is clearly aimed at blunting the strong argument made by Mohammed himself in the Koran (Sura 17:104) that G-d promised the land to the "Children of Israel," which I have often cited in these columns.

The World Trade Center bombing is very much on the mind of the author of the book. He concludes his analysis of the bombing with this statement: "The World Trade Center bombing was a design of the Mossad to lessen the rush of world opinion turning against the Zionist Jews because of their expulsion of 364 Moslems from Israel. The bombing was supposed to divert the attention of the world from that event and to create hate and fear in the American public against Moslems in general. That is why the bomb blew up at an off hour with minimum damage to life and property."

As to fundamentalism itself, the author concludes that "the Zionists have created this term 'fundamentalism' to make the unsuspecting feel that their prejudice is now against the general body of Moslems."

The book then turns to a favored subject going back to the Russian forgery *The Protocols of the Wise Men of Zion*, namely, the Rothschilds. They claim that the Rothschild's International Bank eventually led to the creation of the Federal Reserve Bank, over which the U.S. government has no control. (Mr. Greenspan, chairman of the Federal Reserve, take note!) The Rothschilds, whom the world admires for their public spirited, philanthropic enterprises in most countries of the world, are pictured as "a dark crew of financial pirates who would cut a man's throat to get a dollar out of his pocket. They prey on the people of America."

The author denies that Arabs are anti-Semites, because in his opinion the Jews are not Semites, but descendants of Mongols who founded the Khazar empire in 740 C.E. The descendants of the Mongolian Khazars, says the book, "are most commonly known as Russian or Polish Jews. . . . They have no claim to Palestine."

It is interesting that all enemies of Jews and Israel have one thing in common: They deny the Holocaust. The Moslems in America do not wish to be outdone by the neo-Nazis and parrot the line of the Holocaust deniers: "There is no one who can substantiate the six million count of Jewish deaths in World War II, which is claimed by the Zionists." *Target Islam* proclaims that, rather than dying from atrocities or the gas chambers, Jews died "from the extremely poor conditions in the concentration camps and due to starvation." The book goes on and on with accusations against the Jews, in some instances using misquotations from the Talmud—all in the tradition of the ancient anti-Semitism of the Church and ultimately of Hitler and Streicher, editor of *Der Stürmer*. It also reproduces the old Nazi accusation that the Jews control the media.

The author's special ire is reserved for the successful Task Force on Terrorism and Unconventional Warfare, carried on for some years by the staff in Rep. Bill McCollum's office. They must therefore feel profound glee that Rep. Newt Gingrich, the incoming Speaker of the House, recently disbanded all caucuses in the House of Representatives. As unbelievable as it sounds, the Task Force on Terrorism was a victim of that same banishment of caucuses. That would not only spell glorious victory for the Moslems and Moslem terrorists around the world, but would expose every American man, woman and child to terror acts that cannot be detected or foretold without the thorough monitoring that the task force carried out. *You should therefore write to your congressman, especially if he is a Republican, to maintain the work of the Task Force on Terrorism in one form or another and to maintain its thoroughly trained staff.* The existence of the task force is needed now more than ever, as demonstrated by the recent excellent TV documentary by Steve Emerson, "Jihad in America." This documentary was an eye-opener to millions of Americans, with its flood of eye-witness, first-hand video tapes of Moslem leaders egging on their followers to terror acts, especially against Jews.

In June 1993, the Arabic United Association for Studies and Research published a 47-page study, which gives the impression of being serious research judging by its large number of footnotes, documentation that is absent in *Target Islam*. However, the line of argument is practically synonymous in both books.

The main thrust of *Islam Under Siege* is directed against the Task Force on Terrorism and Unconventional Warfare, chaired in Congress by Rep. Bill McCollum. The book tries to discredit this prestigious task force by calling its findings prejudiced and exaggerated. The book also distances itself from the most cherished American philosophy—the "Judeo-Christian heritage." Instead, the author recognizes "primarily the products of an Islamic history and bases his world view on that identity."

The author has a long list of writers, scholars and organizations whom he wishes to discredit, such as Professor Bernard Lewis, columnist Richard Grenier of the *Washington Post*, Mortimer B. Zuckermann, publisher of *U.S. News & World Report*, Amos Perlmutter, editor of *Journal of Strategic Studies*, ads in the name of FLAME, the ADL and a large number of popular magazines and journals. He attacks Rabin and Chaim Herzog and other Jewish leaders. His main aim is to whitewash Hamas and the PLO and to deny any Arab culpability in the World Trade Center bombing. About Hamas he says, "Hamas is always careful to avoid killing innocents." (Tell that to the victims of the Tel Aviv bus attack.)

Interestingly, the author of *Islam Under Siege* admits that "Islam is plagued by two general ills: a) the extremist tendencies of the movement; and b) a significant failure to address issues of concern to Western nations and secularists. Mainstream Islamists should not be held accountable for the actions of extremists. . . ." This sudden about-face smacks very much of the customary Arab deception in order to confuse their enemies. Therefore, beware!

The Islamic Society of North America (ISNA) held a convention September 2-5 in Chicago. Its extensive program book is quite revealing as to the sophisticated methods that have been adopted by this society to indoctrinate the young with traditional Moslem concepts and to prepare them for a Moslem society in America.

Every effort was made at this convention, as evidenced by the program book, to make as good an impression as possible on non-Moslem observers. The instructions are therefore given to participants to "keep your appearance as neat as possible, keep your rooms neat and orderly, keep bathrooms clean."

The very professionally worked out convention program calls for each hour of the convention to be filled with specific lectures and workshops—very much like the standard American conventions. Here are some of the programs:

"Vision for the Future: Addressing the Hopes and Dreams for the Future of the Moslem Nation"

"Moslem World Issues, Palestine and Algeria: Discussion of the Peace Talks in the Middle East and the Crushing of the Democratically Elected Leadership in Algeria, Bosnia and Kashmir; What Lessons and Parallels We Can Draw From These Situations to Our Positions Here in North America."

"Identity Crisis Among Moslems: *Passing Our Hates and Prejudices to Our Children*" [italics mine]. Education plays a central role in these conventions, as we see from this incredible statement, promoting a practice not sanctioned in any other society—passing hatred and prejudices from generation to generation!

"Spreading the Moslem Message Throughout the Campuses: Moslem Students, Their Role Here and Abroad; A Lecture About the Student Movement and its Role and Contribution to Islamic Work in North America and in the Islamic World."

"Interfaith Workshop and Dialogue Cooperation Between Moslems and Peoples of Other Faiths." The Convention assumed that Moslems were interested in respect for other religions. Judaism was represented by a Dr. Howard Sulkin of Spartus College. If you read the program side by side with the quotations from *Target Islam* cited above, you realize the discrepancies.

"Protecting Your Community From Anti-Moslem Acts and Dealing with the FBI" [!] Arab fear of the FBI was amply demonstrated in this workshop. Again, a comparison between the two publications is enlightening.

The convention organizers clearly aimed at prime-time publicity: "Before you know it, our activities will go from campuses to CNN and public schools, *Insh-Allah* (G-d willing)."

The convention also dealt with standard concerns, such as financial problems, investment possibilities, etc.

The professional approach of this convention, as compared to the crude, crass hostility and intransigence displayed in Target Islam, shows the two faces of Islam—the public facade and the private. For example, compare what Arafat tells CNN with what he said in Arabic in Johannesburg about his *Jihad* (Holy War) plans!

Deception is a tactic widely used by the Arabs. But to understand Islam, it is incumbent on us to learn as much as possible about its tenets, nature and tactics.

# PLO Covenant Update:
# A Phony Abrogation in the Offing

How many times has Arafat given his pledge to President Clinton, to the world press, that he will abrogate the dreaded PLO covenant. He has broken every promise with impunity.

Now Peres has clearly said—if there is anything clear in what Peres ever says—that Arafat must fulfill his promise, or the "peace process" will come to a stop. But the hollowness of that statement is already becoming clear.

The day of the Palestinian election Peres stated, according to newspaper accounts, that Arafat and the new Palestinian Council should "take action within two months to strike out a clause in the Palestinian covenant that calls for the destruction of Israel."

"A clause?" Only one clause? That is where the fraud shows itself: There are 32 clauses in the Covenant, of which 31 call for the destruction of Israel, the end of Zionism, deportation of Jews, etc. On top of it, the Covenant defines "Palestine" as the entire British Mandate Palestine—which includes today's Jordan, which was part of the British Mandate. King Hussein is therefore as interested as Israel in removing such dangerous clauses—all of them!

Peres and Arafat consequently seem to have come up with a phony plan to fool President Clinton and the rest of the world: Arafat will pick any one of the 32 paragraphs at random and ceremoniously "abrogate" it while keeping all the others in full force and effect. Peres will then declare himself "satisfied" and the matter will be forgotten. Arafat and his followers will have themselves a good laugh, but will it be so easy to fool the world?

The recent election among Palestinians was given a devastating criticism by Peace Watch, the highly respected neutral monitoring organization. Even before the election, they issued a report with a long list of election-related arrests, bribing of candidates to withdraw and threats to the lives of candidates forcing them to withdraw.

These massive abuses took place before the election. Jimmy Carter, the ever-smiling friend of Arabs, only monitored election day itself and had only one complaint: An Israeli soldier made video tapes of the voting. Carter whitewashed the election completely!

Peres, on the day after the election, invited 483 deported extremists and murderers, such as George Habash and Nayef Hawatmeh, to return to Israel. This outrage, putting Jewish lives at risk, is matched only by the outrageous barring of Rabbi

Avraham Hecht as a "security risk." Will Peres' idea of Israel joining the Arab League now be realized?

For many decades the valiant soldiers of Christian Southern Lebanon have shed blood in the defense of Northern Israel, by placing the Army of Southern Lebanon within the security zone along the Israeli border. The army is under the command of Gen. Antoine Lahad, a Maronite Christian. It is this army that has thwarted many Hizbollah attacks on Jewish towns in the north. They have been ambushed and attacked by the Moslem terrorists, which are paid for by Syria and Iran.

Now, as pawns in the Washington-sponsored campaign to conclude a peace with Syria "at any price," these courageous Christians risk being thrown to the Syrian wolves, who stand ready to carry out a genocide against them. The Labor government gave indications that in a "peace" accord with Syria, the Syrians would be in charge of the Lebanese Christians, which has caused a wave of furor and fear in the worldwide Lebanese "diaspora," with millions living in the United States, South America, France, and other countries.

Their protests have been raised through press releases, advertisements, etc. There seems to have been a cautiously positive reaction from Jerusalem: After the Syrian puppet government in Beirut staged a show trial in absentia of Gen. Lahad and 300 of his officers for "treason against Lebanon," Peres extended a symbolic gesture of support for the Christians, meeting him in Jerusalem. Unfortunately, what Peres' promises are worth is not very much, based on his long record of breaking them. *The Jerusalem Post* editorially raised serious doubts about the reliability of Peres' promises to the Christians. After all, in January 1995, the leftist government assured the Christians that Bethlehem would be spared from the PLO—only to break that promise after Rabin's assassination. Another broken promise by Peres will surely unleash another round of Christian outcries

On January 13 the Vatican made a veiled threat against Israel, warning in a statement by the Pope that "peace in the Middle East could disappear if the status of Jerusalem is not resolved in a way that preserves its uniqueness as a holy city open to all." The Pope urged that "Jerusalem be declared an international city for religious worship." This shows that nothing has changed in all the 47 years since the first U.N. Partition Plan was issued, with the support of Count Folke Bernadotte, for the internationalization of Jerusalem.

Today the Pope disregards the torrents of Jewish blood shed in the recapture of the Jewish capital, under Gen. Yitzchak Rabin, in 1967, after being attacked by Hussein of Jordan. He disregards the fact that at no time in its 2,000-year history has Jerusalem been "open to all." His theological aim remains: Jerusalem must not be in Jewish hands. Jews must be punished! It is now up to a staunchly Zionist Jewish government to oppose the onslaughts on Jerusalem by the Vatican, by the PLO and our own internal enemies, to assert the historically fully justified Jewish claim to the Jewish capital, undivided, under 100 percent Jewish sovereignty. But sadly there is no such staunchly Zionist government in sight. I attended a meeting not so long ago with Mr. Leon Levy, the new chairman of the Conference of Presidents of Major American Jewish Organizations. We pleaded with Mr. Levy that the Presidents' Conference should come out with a strong statement in support of the Jewish claim to Jerusalem. I am still waiting for such action—although it may, G-d forbid, come too late. What will history then say?

Meanwhile, behind the back of the Jewish public, and in his usual style of stealth and deceit, the gray eminence of the left, Yossi Beilin, has met with Israel's archenemy, Feisal el-Husseini, kinsman of the infamous Mufti Haj Amin el-Husseini. The secret meeting, which took place in Europe, took up plans for the future disposition of Jerusalem. I shudder to think what their plans are

A movement in Israel totally committed to the teachings of Martin Luther King was put on trial for "sedition" just when, throughout America, Martin Luther King Day was being celebrated from the president down to every child in the country. Dr. King, following in turn the teachings of Mahatma Ghandi of India, taught peaceful civil disobedience to champion the cause of civil rights. His campaign led to full recognition of the civil rights of all in the United States.

Meanwhile, in Israel the opposite is taking place. The popular Zu Artzeinu movement, totally disavowing any form of violence, practiced Dr. King's teachings by peacefully demonstrating against the Labor government and its policies of surrendering vital land to the Palestinians. These demonstrations took place in Jerusalem and on the roads leading to Jerusalem. The reaction by the police of the leftist government was brutal. Mounted police charged into masses of innocent, unarmed civilians, children and elders—trampling them with their horses, dragging them to the police station, and other outrages.

Now after Rabin's assassination, another philosophy has taken over: total annihilation of the opposition. Measures that the late Prime Minister Rabin surely would not have tolerated are now dominating the domestic scene in Israel. And now, for an event that took place before the Rabin assassination, the Peres government is putting on trial three leaders of Zu Artzeinu under an old law that the British used mainly against Arab terrorists. They are accused of sedition, which carries long-term jail sentences.

The leader of the peaceful movement is Moshe Feiglin, a computer technician living in Ginot Shomron with his American-born wife and four children. It is of course the hope of the leftists that Feiglin will not be able to afford a high-level lawyer who could defend his civil rights. Therefore, he is coming to the United States the week of January 29 to brief the vast number of American Jews to whom these violations of civil rights are abhorrent. Among the cities that Mr. Feiglin will visit are New York, Washington, Florida, Boston, and he will carry with him video cassettes taken during the demonstrations and the police brutality that followed. It must be hoped that this blemish on the traditional Jewish defense of freedom will be removed and that the charges against these civil rights champions will be dropped.

The model of strong, patriotic Jewish youth has in the past been exemplified by the valiant Hesder boys, immersed in Jewish learning and at the same time committed to the defense of Israel. These skullcapped soldiers were always the pride of all Jews. Now, after the "peace process" has infiltrated the youth in Israel, a totally different type of youngster has emerged with headquarters—not in Jerusalem—but in Goa, India, by the "Tel Aviv Beach," center of the drug culture.

In a five-page, fully illustrated report in the Israeli press, the sordid tale is revealed: Thousands upon thousands of young Israelis are converging on Goa, on the western coast of India, to engage in drug orgies—sometimes lasting for over one week. A popular song by these Israelis runs, "I am drugged up, the world is dead, the world is dead." Looking at the faces of these drug-crazed youngsters—many of them just released from military service—they remind you of the faces seen at the "peace rallies." For them, the world is dead, so there is no room for the traditional Jewish *tzelem Elokim* (G-dly image) nor for a patriotic defense of Israel, which seems irrelevant to them.

It is paradoxical that Goa, of all places, has become the doom for so many Jewish youngsters. Goa was, till recently, a Portuguese enclave in India. During the Middle Ages many secret Jews escaped from Portugal's Inquisition to Goa to find safety. But the Inquisition followed them, and I have seen records of trials of Jews by the Inquisition in Goa ending in autos-de-fé burnings. I have also met Portuguese refugees who fled Goa after the Indian invasion of their territory—and they are all proud of their Jewish roots. So while Goa was a symbol of Jewish perseverance in the face of Christian onslaught, today, under the leftists in Jerusalem, Goa has become just the opposite: a surrender to every un-Jewish trend and practice.

Crown Prince Hassan of Jordan with Dr. Lehmann, discussing the only Dead Sea Scroll still held in Amman, the "Copper Scroll." The others are in Jerusalem.

# Africans Were Enslaved by Arabs—
# And Freed by Jews

An important development has taken place in response to the reckless charges by black demagogues. These demagogues are repeating again and again the lie that slavery was carried on and financed by Jews. In reaction to this fiction, black Christian leaders from the Sudan, Mauritania and other Moslem-dominated countries have publicized the slave trade still carried on today by Moslem Arabs. Black newspapers have given these revelations much space, while followers of demagogues are stonewalling these reports.

Here are two instances which totally refute the anti-Jewish charges. Slavery was abolished, not supported, by Jews! In 1807, the British Parliament passed an Emancipation Bill to abolish slavery in the British Empire. But slave owners paid no attention—freeing slaves would cause them economic losses. But then, lo and behold, two prominent Jews came to the slaves' rescue. Nathan Rothschild and his brother-in-law Moses Montifiore agreed in 1835 to extend a loan for the huge amount of Pounds Sterling 15,000,000 to be used to compensate slave owners for their losses in freeing their slaves. It was this loan which made the abolition of slavery in the British Empire possible. Emancipation of American slaves by Abraham Lincoln followed a few decades later.

In the Diaries of Montifiore I found some moving passages as to his personal feelings when he signed the loan agreement. It happened to take place on the eve of *Tisha b'Av*, the day when the destruction of the Jerusalem Temple is commemorated. Immediately after finishing the meeting for the loan to abolish slavery, Montifiore proceeded to his synagogue to start the fast. An observer had this to say: "Few financiers perhaps would feel inclined, after all the excitement incidental to the successful contracting of a loan for Pounds Sterling 15,000,000 to comply with so exacting a religious observance as a fast of 24 hours duration. Nevertheless, Montifiore would not on this occasion, any more than on any other, allow worldly interest to prevail over religious duties. The loan for the abolition of slavery reminded him of the words of the Prophet Isaiah, and attuned his mind to reflection on the former glory of Zion and its present state of sorrow." In other words, freeing of slaves was the fulfillment of a Jewish concept of freedom for all men! Which other nation brought such noble thoughts to the problem of slavery?

Another anti-Semitic charge concerns Aaron Lopez, the great patriot of the American Revolution, whom the demagogues single out as "proof" of Jewish slave traders. True, Lopez did use some of his ships to transport slaves. But who was Aaron Lopez? He was a Christian who came direct from Portugal to this country in the mid-1700s. He had been a merchant in his native country. Only after he was here did he convert to Judaism. As all former Christians of the Iberian Peninsula, he practiced what his Christian ancestors had practiced for centuries. These were not Jewish practices. In fact, 90% of all European Jews languished in ghettos during the slave trade period and did not have access to any trade, let alone slave trade.

Even if demagogues are not interested in facts, we should certainly educate ourselves to the historical truth, especially our young people who are exposed to hate propaganda over the airwaves and on college campuses.

# The Slave Trade—An Arab Invention

We have now heard ad nauseam from anti-Semitic, bogus "scholars," such as Leonard Jeffries, that Jews were the main slave traders.

Last week, *The New York Post* quoted Basil Wilson, a Provost at City University, who spoke at a recent black-Jewish relations conference, that "there is not yet a body of knowledge to refute Leonard Jeffries' contention that Jews played a prominent role in the slave trade."

Accordingly, it is high time to furnish the world with that "body of knowledge," to once and for all put an end to that anti-Semitic canard and insult to the Jewish people. Since I am a student of black Africa and a frequent visitor there over the past 40 years, I feel qualified to speak up with the facts.

The slave trade was invented by the Moslem Arabs, who single-handedly carried on this ferocious practice for 1000 years before the first European became involved with slaves. The enslavement of blacks began when the Arabs, in their expansionist drive to conquer the world for Islam, captured large parts of Africa and immediately exacted, as a form of tribute from the vanquished black African kings, large contingents of slaves to be surrendered to Arab countries.

The first known such arrangement took place in the year 641, just a few decades after the Moslem drive for conquest began. An excellent source for the historic facts is the book *The Arabs as Master Slavers*, by British historian John Laffin (SBS Publishing Inc., 14 West Forest Avenue, Englewood, N.J. 07631). He writes: "The slave trade was first begun in Africa by the Arabs; they were the procurers and suppliers. Soon after the Arabs began to conquer North Africa, the first record was made of their desire for African slaves. An agreement was signed with Nubia, after the conquest of Egypt in the year 641. Some Arab conquerors imposed on various African rulers an annual tribute of several thousand slaves. Thus the Arabs had many centuries of experience in slave trading, long before the European entrepreneurs entered the scene. The Arabs knew every trick of the trade—how to ambush Negroes, how to deceive them, where to find their hiding places."

When European powers, inspired by the Biblical aversion to slave trading, tried to stop the Arab practice and even sent gunboats and military expeditions deep into African jungles to punish kings and princes for engaging in slavery, the Arabs nevertheless kept right on slaving. The Arabs provided an ever-hungry market for slaves, they promoted and supported wars between chiefs, and by power of their guns controlled huge areas from which to extract slaves.

The largest slave market, even today, is the Kingdom of Saudi Arabia. Several U.N. missions have tried to stop the practice, but it goes on unabated. In fact, prices for various categories of slaves are circulated openly: a girl under 15 years old costs

$300-600; a man under 40, $60-225; an old woman $60. King ibn Saud had 3,000 slaves of his own. In recent years countless thousands of African girls were first sent by the Arab slave traders to work in night clubs in Beirut and Damascus, where they were chosen, without their knowledge, by the more important Arab slave traders. From there they ended up in harems, brothels and other markets in Arabia.

Throughout the history of Arab slave trading, Arabs often used their male black slaves as guards or soldiers, but the richer ones used them as eunuchs in their harems, after subjecting them to brutal castration operations. (It is interesting that in Mozart's opera *The Abduction from the Sareglio*, a black Negro slave is the eunuch in charge of guarding the harem.) Girl slaves, on the other hand, were mainly used to gratify the sexual appetites of their Arab owners.

The well-known hatred for Arabs still shown by black Africans is rooted in centuries-old memories of the barbarism of the Arab slave traders. In a study of slavery, a Ghanaian scholar, Professor L.H. Ofosu-Appiah, comments as follows:

"On the eastern coast of Africa and in the Sudan, the Arab raiders started enslaving Negroes during the period of Islam's empire building. The difference between the methods of the Arabs and those of the later European traders was that the Arabs actually went on slave raiding expeditions and herded slaves to the coast. They travelled as far as the Congo forest and Lake Victoria. Wherever they went they burned down villages and carried off human beings to cart their ivory to the coast.

"For years the Arabs were the only slaving nation which settled in Africa and depopulated it. When Arab leaders cannot understand the hostility of some Africans to their regimes, it may be worth while to remind them that their dominant role in enslaving Africans is a festering sore which cannot be easily cured."

Those African-Americans who show sympathy with the Arabs seem to be indifferent to the savage fate of their own ancestors at the hands of the Arabs.

It was only in the 15th century that Europeans, spearheaded by Portugal, arrived along Africa's coast. These navigators, backed by their nations' military power, built a string of forts along the West African coast. The Portuguese were followed by other nations: the Danes, the Germans (also known as Brandenburgers), and the Dutch built these forts, which usually included a compound into which the Africans would march black prisoners taken in tribal wars. The Europeans never set foot in the African countryside to capture slaves, as the Arabs did. They played a passive role—the Africans themselves did the job for them.

I have seen some of these forts. In Ghana there still exists a Portuguese fort called Elmina, built 500 years ago. A Danish one, called Christianborg Castle, was built in the 18th century. Each of them has a compound into which black prisoners were marched by their black captors. The ships of the respective European nation would then come and sail away with them. After arriving in London, Amsterdam or Copenhagen, some of these slaves were resold and sent to the Americas. But after a few centuries the call for the abolition of slavery was heard in European Parliaments, and by the 1830s slavery was abolished in Europe. The United States followed suit in 1860, which caused the Civil War. Yet the Arabs, as mentioned above, paid no attention to these human rights efforts, and continued their slave trade with same degree of brutality as during the previous 1200 years!

It is obvious from this account of history that Jews could play no role whatsoever in the basic slave trade. Firstly, most of them were languishing in the European ghettos for most of the time the slave trade was thriving, with no opportunity at all to engage in international trade. Secondly, the few Jews who were possibly involved in the trade for a very limited time in the 18th century, were for the most part Christians by birth, who at some time in their lives converted to Judaism, but who had learned their attitude toward slavery from their Christian parents.

One example, which the likes of Leonard Jeffries cite, is Aaron Lopez of Newport, Rhode Island. Lopez was a Christian, born in Portugal. He came to Newport in the 18th century and converted to Judaism. His involvement in trade was of limited duration, because as an American patriot he was punished by the British colonial powers, who stripped him of his business, so that he died a poor man. While his business was still flourishing he traded in general merchandise and, only occasionally, in slaves. In fact, I own an original Bill of Landing from Aaron Lopez, dated May 31, 1771, for one of his ships. Its manifest lists general cargo, including quantities of kosher meats—"Ninety-four kegs of Jew beef, one quarter barrel of kosher meats and tongues, four kegs of kosher fats, one keg of smoked kosher beef"—but not one slave!

Why is it that Jeffries and Co. do not point out that when emancipation and freedom came to the slaves, it was due to Jews and Jewish teachings? One Philadelphia Jew, in 1800, was among the first to call for the emancipation of American slaves. The concept of liberty and freedom, and the proposition that "all men are created equal" comes directly out of the Jewish Bible. (When this country was founded, the Founding Fathers considered making Hebrew the official language, because liberty was so intimately identified with the Jewish Bible.)

More recently, it was Jews who founded and for decades headed the National Association for the Advancement of Colored People (NAACP), and there were Jewish human rights martyrs who died fighting anti-black racism in Selma and elsewhere. Only a totally self-centered, hate-blinded person can ignore these historic facts.

In summation, the anti-Semitic attack on Jews as alleged slave traders falls flat on its face. It is a total non-starter.

# Personalities

To be a Jew in the fullest sense of the word, means to be exposed to the great geniuses and personalities which our nation has produced. No other nation today can point to such a towering array of illustrious men and women who have helped shape world history. This section only touches upon a few selected personalities and could be extended endlessly to our everlasting pride. In our own generation, Rabbi J. B. Soloveitchik—called "The Rov" for short—had the most profound impact on modern Judaism. I was privileged to know him closely. I have included great personalities in politics, literature, music, science and finance. I have also listed non-Jewish personalities whose contact with the Jewish people influenced our history: Churchill, Albright and Rembrandt.

## Encounters With Lubavitch

Just before Rosh Hashanah I was privileged to be received by the Lubavitcher Rebbe, z"l, in his office in Brooklyn. But before I report on this memorable meeting, I should like to tell you of some previous encounters with Lubavitch over the past close to 60 years.

In the early '30s, the Orthodox community in Stockholm, Sweden, engaged a young Russian Chabadnik as rabbi, shochet and mohel. His name: Yakov Yisrael Zuber, a chosid of Lubavitch, a native of Georgia, southern Russia, who had worked underground in Soviet Russia. My late father persuaded him to take on one more assignment, that of a private teacher in our home. And so, in 1933, at the age of 11, I started learning Gemara with Rav Zuber, the first chosid I had ever met, and continued my private lessons with him for several years.

When I reached my Bar Mitzvah, Rav Zuber worked with me on my "Pilpul"—on the subject of *Hessech Hada'as B'tefillin*—the law of Tefillin in case of diversion of attention. I mention this because the term *Hessech Hada'as B'tefillin* played a great role during my subsequent meeting with the Lubavitcher Rebbe.

Later, during the Holocaust, Rav Zuber played an important role as a Posek, specializing in the plight of the many "Agunoth" resulting from the tragedies in war-ravaged Europe. When the war was over, Rav Zuber emigrated with his family to the USA, but met a tragic death in Boston, where he was the victim of a yet unsolved murder.

To honor his memory, I published his writings in Israel, in a sefer entitled

*Zichron Yaakov,* mainly a collection of his Responsa during and after the war, with a special section on Agunoth.

In March, 1940, the following historic event took place: the then Lubavitcher Rebbe, Rav Joseph Yitzchok Schneerson, *zt"l*, passed through Stockholm, my native city. This came about because, quite miraculously, he had been freed from the German occupation of Poland, through the political intervention of President Franklin D. Roosevelt. He was now on his way to the USA, and had taken the boat to Sweden. From Stockholm the Rebbe had to take the train to Gothenburg, Sweden's leading port city, from where a ship would take him to New York. I found myself in a group of local Jews, led of course by Rav Zuber, who helped the Rebbe to the railway station to see him off before his long and hazardous journey. I shall never forget the sight of the Rebbe standing at the open window of his railway compartment, looking out at us and far beyond. . . .His face, with deep, burning black eyes, is as clearly engraved in my memory as if I had seen him five minutes ago. It was evident that in his eyes were mirrored his deep worries about the Jews he had left behind under German occupation, and his deep concern for the future of European Jewry facing terrible persecution and tragedy in the future. I have never again seen such expressive and penetrating eyes.

My father, who was of German origin and who had never before had any contact with chassidim, neverthelesss expressed his appreciation of what Lubavitch stood for, by paying for one of the earliest volumes containing the "Sichoth" of the Rebbe.

One of the Rebbe's earliest supporters in Crown Heights was my late father-in-law, Mr. "Feish" Moskovitz, himself a Satmarer and Belzer Chosid, who had settled in the beautiful home at 1400 President Street in 1941. (This house is now occupied by a prominent supporter of the Rebbe, Rabbi Chitrik, whom I first met when he came from Russia and was a Hebrew teacher in Sao Paulo, Brazil.) At that time there were so few observant Jews in Crown Heights that when my father-in-law put up a Sukkah, his Jewish neighbors complained to the police. The police promptly showed up and told Mr. Moskovitz that he had to dismantle the Sukkah in ten days! His support for the Lubavitcher Rebbe was of pioneering importance.

Many years later I joined the thousands of mourners who followed the Rebbe's hearse down Eastern Parkway after his death in 1950.

Shortly after the present Rebbe had assumed the leadership of world Chabad, I noticed the immediate impact he had on Jews in all corners of the world. One day, while on a plane to Africa, I met Rav Josef Weinberg, one of the Rebbe's most trusted and active followers. I asked him where he was heading, and he answered, "I am flying to Dakar, Senegal, in West Africa." Why? The Rebbe had heard that there was a Jew in Dakar, a very distant place in Africa, who did not have any Tefillin, and so he sent Rabbi Weinberger there to bring this Jew a pair of Tefillin! This made a very deep impression on me, especially when I compared this attitude with that of certain other chassidic rebbes who had nothing but scorn and contempt for anyone not belonging to their group.

At this point I must relate a remarkable personal experience which very few know about. In 1953 my wife and I went in for an oil-drilling program guided by the late Dr. Jacob Griffel, an ardent follower of the Rebbe. Dr. Griffel had been in the oil industry in his native Rumania and was considered an expert in evaluating oil properties. He was also known to me as a colorful and heroic Holocaust figure, for it was he, stationed in Istanbul for rescue operations, who tried to help Joel Brandt's mission to succeed. This was the famous rescue project which had Eichmann's approval and which would have saved hundreds of thousands of Hungarian Jews, but which was thwarted by the British. Griffel was involved in helping Brandt, albeit without success. He is mentioned in Ben Hecht's epic book, *Perfidy*.

Among the properties which Dr. Griffel had negotiated was one in Oklahoma, in Sholem Aleichem County. Maybe we were attracted to the project because of this unlikely but fascinating name, in Oklahoma, of all states. Anyway, we had many holes drilled, but one after the other turned out to be dry. After five dry holes we made a calculation that it was time to suspend further drillings which evidently all seemed to be without prospect for finding oil. However, Dr. Griffel urged us to wait till he could consult the Rebbe.

After a few days he came to us saying that the Rebbe had recommended that we continue drilling and even indicated the exact location where we would be likely to strike oil! To my great regret and embarrassments I must admit that we ignored the Rebbe's advice and gave up our drilling lease.

Would you believe that today the Sholem Aleichem field is one of the richest oil-producing areas in the country? Had we followed the Rebbe's advice the field could have been ours. What we did not know was that the Rebbe had studied engineering at the Sorbonne University in Paris and therefore was quite capable of reading and professionally evaluating the so-called electrologs which our dry holes had yielded.

I had another occasion to marvel at the unbelievably detailed knowledge which the Rebbe had in areas where we would not expect him to be so familiar. Over twenty years ago, a distant relative in Israel had been unjustly made the scapegoat for an offense committed by someone in government. As a true hero, he willingly accepted the "rap" without betraying any confidences. One of the consequences was that he lost his license to practice law. At this point, my mother-in-law, Mrs. Moskovitz, a true Jewish princess with saintly qualities who had open access to Rebbes in many parts of the world, joined me in a private meeting with the Rebbe. Since the then-president of Israel, Shazar, was himself a Chabadnik, we appealed to the Rebbe for his intervention on our relative's behalf. I was stunned at the Rebbe's close personal knowledge of the case. A few days later I received a personal 3-page letter signed by the Rebbe in which he minutely and wisely analyzed the situation involved. My relative was later fully exonerated.

During the recent government crisis, I appealed at an early stage to the Rebbe to make his influence felt within the ranks of the Agudah so they would refuse to join a Peres government which I judged would pose a grave danger to Israel's survival. The Rebbe answered promptly by hinting that the decisions would be made by the Agudah Council of Sages—which in fact a few weeks later produced Rav Verdiger's defection from the Peres camp, thereby delivering a death blow to Pere's ambitions. No doubt the Rebbe was responsible for this fateful and timely change of the tide.

# Rabbi J. B. Soloveitchik, z"l, 90 Years Old
## His Father's and Grandfather's Testimony

It is startling to think that the Rov passed his 90th year! All those who have had the privilege of meeting him throughout his long life have only the recollection of a young, vigorous man, and it is only right that this be the image which we should always preserve in our memory.

I first had the privilege of meeting the Rov when he was a mere 37, in 1940, the first of many meetings and close encounters. That year, in Boston, the Rov was surrounded by a small group of yeshiva students who had recently arrived from Europe. It was his hope to establish there a permanent yeshiva, with that group as an initial nucleus. This plan was never realized, perhaps in part because shortly afterward, his father, Reb Moshe, of blessed memory, passed away, and the Rov was destined to take his place at Yeshivat Rabbenu Yitzchak Elchanan in New York. He did, however, succeed, together with his unforgettable wife, Rebbetzin Tonya Soloveitchik, in establishing a Day School, the Maimonides School, first in Dorchester and later in Brookline, which has prospered and grown over the years and which is a worthy monument to their joint sacrifices for Jewish education and scholarship.

I have written about my experiences with the Rov in a past article, but today I wish to present a most historic portrayal of the Rov—by his own father! I had the great good fortune to acquire some years ago the original 6-page letter which Reb Moshe wrote about his son in 1935, in which he also quotes what the Rov's grandfather, the famed Reb Chaim of Brisk, had to say about him. Both portrayals have, over the years, proven totally accurate, and even prophetic.

The letter, dated Elul 19, 5695 (1935), was addressed to Mr. Jacob Joshua Bauminger, secretary to the Religious Council of Tel Aviv, whose committee was to decide on the choice of the next Chief Rabbi of Tel Aviv, after the death of Chief Rabbi S. Ahronson. The main contenders for the post were Rabbi Soloveitchik of Boston and Rav Amiel of Antwerp. Rabbi Soloveitchik had visited Eretz Yisrael shortly before the letter was written—his only visit ever to the Jewish Land. As we all know, the vote, two months later, fell on Rav Amiel, and it was through this historic decision that Providence saved the Rov for America. Orthodoxy in America was thereby totally reshaped, for which we must be profoundly grateful. A revealing feature in the letter is the news that the Rov, over 50 years ago, had written a complete work on all parts of the Rambam. This work has not yet been published!

Here is the translation of Reb Moshe's letter:

"Although I do not know you personally, I have heard your name, which permits me to turn to you. Since my son, the true Gaon, Rav Yosef Dov Halevi

Soloveitchik, Chief Rabbi of Greater Boston here in America, travelled this summer to Eretz Yisrael and stayed there several months, and he is an official candidate for the position of the Tel Aviv Rabbinate, which is now on the agenda, I am writing to you regarding this matter.

"He is not in need of descriptions, praise or recommendation, because, as I have noted in the newspapers of Eretz Yisrael, his Torah and wisdom preceded and publicized him, and he is already recognized as one of the great men of our generation. But in my opinion, this alone does not sufficiently gauge his true dimensions and weight. Also, a brief recognition cannot be compared with a long-term recognition, and who is better equipped to make that assessment than myself, his father, who has known him from birth till now.

"Normally, a father cannot legally testify about a son, but it is different in the case of something that is evident and clear for all eyes to see. So I do not come as a witness, because the sun in the sky does not need a witness. I merely come to point out with my finger his personality and qualifications. He is a unique species which requires preparation to understand. A gem for the Jewish people. From childhood on he proved an enormous genius which only rarely appears.

"My father and master, the saintly teacher of all Israel, of blessed memory, prophetically pronounced that my son was born for greatness and would grow into a giant tree—because, while he still lived, he saw a handwritten work by him of *divrei Torah*, and his excitement over his words cannot be described. Reb Chaim confirmed that his grandson's words were the true Torah.

"His later development in Torah and scholarship progressed with giant and rapid steps. That is how he advanced until today, when he stands a giant with whom all of Israel prides itself. In previous generations it was believed that Torah and worldly sciences could not be combined, but in this generation, we do encounter this. In the case of my son, this combination has an unusual dimension. If he is unique in the worldly wisdoms, there can be no doubt that he is unique in the understanding of the Torah. His knowledge is such that his opinion is decisive in all parts of Jewish law, whether in minor or critical cases. Already, some years ago, the head of the Beth Din in Kovno wrote that the *halachah* is as he decides in every case. And now that he is growing older, his mind matures even more.

"He knows the whole Torah, from beginning to end, with a profound and clear knowledge. He has learned everything—that which is applicable in our days and that which is not applicable anymore, like *Zeraim, Kodashim, Taharot*, or the fixing of the new moon. His mind is like a cemented well that does not let a drop escape. He is a great and original innovator in his learning. He has written a work on all parts of the *Mishneh Torah* of the Rambam which will soon be published. His words open up the eyes and gladden the hearts, as when the Torah was given at Mt. Sinai. Through his original interpretations everyone is convinced that his words represent the truth. He is like an active spring which pours forth water without interruption. He absorbs and emits Torah all the time, both in its outer and inner meaning.

"He was a genius as a child, and now the whole Torah is engraved in his heart and he is qualified to teach and to judge in any legal matter, like one who is fully qualified by the Sanhedrin. But he does not only master one subject. He has also acquired deep knowledge of the wisdoms at the periphery of the Torah. He obtained his Doctor's degree from the University of Berlin, with highest distinction, and the University professors were enthusiastic about his unmatched genius and the width and breadth of his understanding. He has produced very original theories in these academic subjects, as the outstanding genius of our times, and has printed some works in German all in a perfectly religious spirit.

"His fear of G-d precedes his wisdom. His whole being is filled with the fear of G-d—he is a *tzadik* and full of piety in his conduct. He is like a live '*Mussar Sefer*,' and can serve as an example and model in his Torah, wisdom and piety. He is a born leader of Jewish leaders. He is active in communal matters, and has accomplished great things in this field. His character is filled with excellent qualities and he always shows courtesy to his fellow man. He is modest and incorruptible. He receives everyone with a pleasant demeanor and has deep understanding for each person through his psychological insight.

"G-d has blessed him with a phenomenal speaking talent. His speeches are full of pearls of wisdom, and he can speak fluently in various languages: Hebrew, Yiddish, German, English. He has a vast knowledge of Jewish history and literature (*Chochmat Yisrael*). He speaks with an authority which comes from competence and the ability to express himself lucidly. He captures his audience and commands their love and respect.

"I would like now to come to the subject which moves me to write to you. A city like Tel Aviv has many factions. It must have a leader who speaks in popular language and in terms that all can understand, someone who can influence all parties. All of the Jewish nation looks up to Tel Aviv and takes note of what happens there. Of course, its Rabbi must be the greatest man in our generation, someone truly outstanding and exceptional, whose influence can also reach the Diaspora.

"My opinion, and the opinion of all who know my son, this giant of a man, is that he is the only one fit for this position. He is the only one who can be the central support of all, from one extreme to the other; he can unite all camps. Who can compare himself to him as the true shepherd of our brethren, the Jews of Tel Aviv? He is the man who personifies all that is required—a giant in Torah, a senior authority and a genius in all the other wisdoms. He is the most gifted among the Jewish people of today, a man with enormous influence, with the greatest energy and success. He is the man who will capture the Land spiritually and materially. His home will be the setting of the councils of the wise, and he will influence all parties. Some will derive Torah from him, others will derive worldly wisdom. But all will flock to him and be captivated by his speeches, out of love, honor and respect, as practical experience has already shown.

"I have heard that some say that he is too young. Firstly, this is not so. He is, thank G-d, between 30 and 40 years old—an age which in previous generations produced great geniuses and scholars, true leaders of their generations, who were chosen to hold the greatest and most honored positions in the Jewish nation. Their opinions were decisive in everything that affected the Jewish people. Those much older in years would bow to their authority with love, respect and honor. On the contrary, this in itself is his greatness, that at this age he is already counted as an elder among elders. After all, 'Who is old? He who has acquired wisdom.' Reb Eliezer ben Azarya was elected Head of the Academy at a time when there were much older people to choose from, strictly because of his wisdom, and it was he who said 'I am *like* a 70-year-old,' and he had the benefit of ten previous generations, going back to Ezra, in his family lineage. In every generation it has been the wisdom of a scholar, not his age, which was definitive. That is how the assembly of Jewish people was built. At a moment when Reb Yochanan ben Zakai was allowed only one wish, he ignored all the attractions of the world, even the Temple itself, and only asked for Yavne and its scholars. That is how the Jewish people's existence is assured.

"My son is the greatest among the wise: all laws of the Torah have been weighed and measured by him with deep understanding and profundity.

"I take the liberty of asking you, and through you the others on the Committee, to evaluate your decision in a balanced manner. Then you will surely arrive at the conclusion that he is the only one who will bring honor to Tel Aviv in particular, and to the Land of Israel in general.

"May you be inscribed in the Book of the Righteous, speedily, for a long and good life.

"With friendship and respect,

*Moshe Halevi Soloveitchik"*

# Rembrandt—Painter of Jews

You don't have to be a *mayven* to recognize a painting by Rembrandt. The most typical Rembrandt paintings are rendered in hues of dark brown and yellow, with a touch of red. There is usually one area on the canvas which is highlighted, as if by a spotlight. The areas around that spot recede into shades of darker colors. Rembrandt's portraits do not show the sparkling, dancing eyes of a Franz Hals, nor do his limbs have the pink flesh-color of a Rubens. His portraits often depict very sad, old eyes, and the bodies do not follow any exact pattern of nature. (In this he may have been influenced by El Greco, who lived a hundred years before, many of whose paintings are housed next to the synagogue in Toledo, Spain). Rembrandt's interiors do not show the almost geometric lines of a Vermeer, but concentrate on the interaction of his models. Yet he revolutionized the art of painting, in a complete departure from anything that was accepted at his time. And Rembrandt's life and work were closely intertwined with the Jews of his period.

When Rembrandt Van Rijn was born in 1606, his native Holland was in the midst of a protracted war of liberation from the yoke of Spain. The Dutch provinces of Spain had revolted in 1579, and by the time Rembrandt was born, both sides were ready for a truce which would give the "low countries" independence and freedom of religion.

This happened a little over a century after the cruel expulsion of the Jews from Spain in 1492, and from Portugal in 1497. The memory of the Jewish religion and the burning love for it still smoldered in the heart of every forced convert. The news of an island of freedom which beckoned in Holland was a strong magnet for thousands who found their way to the gates of Amsterdam and the other open Dutch towns, where they could cast off the dreaded charade of Christianity.

Once these sturdy Jews had returned to the proud religion of their forefathers, they also excelled in all branches of human endeavor, stimulating talents which had lain dormant in them for many years. It did not take long before the Spanish-Portuguse Jews of Holland excelled in commerce, diplomacy, the arts, sciences, philosophy and medicine. This is the world which stirred and inspired Rembrandt!

Had the independence of Holland come but a few decades later, Judaism among the Marranos might have been weakened to the point where a return to the ancestral religion might not have taken place. Thus, the Dutch war of independence at that particular time was one of those miracles in our history which clearly demonstrates G-d's direct intervention for our survival—similar to the capture of Constantinople by the Turks, just four decades before the Spanish exiles found a haven in the hospitable Ottoman Empire.

The forced converts, called "new Christians," who had fled Portugal for Brazil, were, after more than 100 years, understandably getting more and more remote from the wells of their ancestral learning and practices. So, when the Dutch captured northeastern Brazil in 1624, renamed it "Nova Holanda" and introduced freedom of religion for the first time, the forced converts cheerfully and happily shed the detested cloak of Christianity and embraced Judaism with full force. They founded the congregation Tzur Yisrael in Recife, maintaining close religious and communal ties to the Spanish-Portugese Jews of Holland. Had the Dutch come just a little later, Judaism in Brazil might by then have been totally purged by the Inquisition, with no one left to return to Judaism. The timing of their liberation was therefore another truly miraculous intervention by Providence in favor of Jewish survival.

When the Dutch had to abandon Brazil in 1654, thousands of practicing Jews emigrated, as Jews, to New Amsterdam (today's New York) and many Caribbean areas, where they founded strong, viable and lasting Jewish communities. None of that, not even the founding of the Jewish presence in North America, would have been possible except through the timing of the miracle of Dutch Brazil.

The Jewish genius which blossomed in Holland produced an unprecedented number of aristocratic Jews, who could easily compete in social splendor with their Dutch neighbors. Rembrandt had established his studio and home right in their midst, and he evidently relished using many of them as his models for portraits and Biblical scenes. In fact, it has been estimated that about twenty percent of all portraits by Rembrandt depict Jewish subjects.

Rembrandt's etching of Menasseh ben Israel, his next-door neighbor, is well known. He was the scholar, philosopher and diplomat who maintained close relations with Queen Christina of Sweden, Oliver Cromwell of England, and other leading figures of his time. Impressed with his writings, Oliver Cromwell re-admitted the Jews into England after some 350 years of exile.

Ephraim Bueno, a physician and Hebrew poet, was the subject of a famous portrait by Rembrandt. Baruch Spinoza, too, may even have been painted by the renowned artist into one of his group paintings. Several anonymous Jews, including Jewish merchants, Oriental Jews, a Jewish bride, etc., were painted by him.

It is likely that Chacham Saul Levy Morteira, a very colorful and erudite leader of the Jewish community, is portrayed in one of Rembrandt's paintings. Chacham Morteira was born in Portugal, and upon arriving in safe shelter in Holland, developed as a profound Talmudic scholar as well as a philosopher, whose voluminous work in Portuguese was only recently translated and published by my good friend Professor Herman Salomon.

Rembrandt's portraits of Spanish-Portuguese Jews, recently escaped from their native lands, reveal another important historical fact: Despite the more than one hundred years these Jews had languished under the cruel yoke of Christianity, they were not changed, either internally nor externally. Only their immensely sad eyes bespeak the suffering they went through in the lands of the Inquisition.

Rembrandt's broad erudition in the Bible is displayed in his many paintings and etchings on Biblical themes. He also exhibited a good knowledge of Hebrew, in that several paintings contain Hebrew sentences. His famous painting of Moses shows the full Hebrew text of the Second Tablet. The painting of Belshazar's banquet shows the Hebrew letters which, according to the Book of Daniel, spelled "*mene mene teqel ufarsin.*" In a detail of his painting "Judas Returning the Thirty Pieces of Silver," I found an open Hebrew book and the ends of a garment's *tzitzit*.

Rembrandt was typical of Holland's population in his admiration for the Hebrew Bible with its tales of liberation from oppression and servitude. Dutch playwrights of the time produced many plays on Biblical themes. Rembrandt was therefore not so much interested in the Creation story of the world—as was, for example, Michelangelo, who lived about the same time—but with the human events and fate of such Biblical personalities as Adam and Eve, Cain and Abel, Noah, Abraham, Isaac, Jacob, Joseph, Daniel, etc.

Some of Rembrandt's Biblical scenes have come down to us in the form of drawings and etchings. One famous etching shows Haman leading Mordechai on the King's horse through the streets of Shushan.

Other Biblical scenes painted by Rembrandt are "Samson's Wedding," "Samson Threatening His Father-In-Law," "Hannah and Samuel at the Temple at Shiloh" (again, with a rich Hebrew text in the background), "Tobit and His Wife," "The Blinding of Samson," "Manoah's Sacrifice," "Potiphar's Wife Accusing Joseph," "Jacob Blessing His Grandchildren," "Jacob Wrestling with the Angel" and "David Playing the Harp Before Saul."

Even when depicting Jesus, Rembrandt veered away from the usual artificial and unnatural presentations favored by the Church, and painted him as any of the Jews he had met in his life.

At one point in his life, Rembrandt was economically successful. His works were in great demand, and he produced an amazing number of paintings, drawings and etchings in very short order. Yet he had much misfortune in his private life. His beloved wife Saskia died in 1642. Their children, with the exception of one son, Titus, died early. When financial disaster struck, Rembrandt had to sell his large collection of art objects.

When he died in 1669, he had lost most of his possessions, with the exception of one book—the Bible he had owned since childhood.

One art historian spoke of Rembrandt's life as follows: "Never before or since Rembrandt wrought his great work has there appeared upon the stage of life an artist whose works provided such inspiring testimony to the content and power of the narratives of the Holy Writ."

To this we can add that no artist has handed us such vivid portrayals of Jews of centuries ago, giving us a correct depiction of our forefathers in their daily life, their synagogue attendance and their professions. But beyond this, Rembrandt reproduced their faces in moments of anguish and of joy, in poverty and affluence. Rembrandt served our history well, as a true friend and admirer of the Jews and of Judaism. He deserves to be remembered as a righteous gentile.

# Winston Churchill—Hero, Villain or Pawn of Providence?

Few people in this century have gained as much admiration and love as Winston Churchill, whose life spanned almost a century. Few people know that his American-born mother, who exerted a great influence on him—Lady Randolph Churchill, nee Jerome, originally Jacobson—was of Jewish origin.

As a young man, before the turn of the century, Churchill fought in the Boer War in South Africa. In World War I he was a prominent, albeit not very successful, Cabinet Minister. But his career came to its full and history-making bloom during World War II.

For a long time, in the 1930's, his was the only voice warning against the danger Hitler posed to the free world. Hitler's aggression was creeping along, gingerly feeling out the West's resolve to resist him. In 1935 his troops marched, with impunity, into the Rhineland, which was supposed to be demilitarized under the Versailles terms of 1919. The Western world said nothing. (In parenthesis we should note that the "Western world" in those days was strictly England and France. The United States was not a factor at all, after having opted for "splendid isolation" in the years following Woodrow Wilson. Russia, although powerful, was totally engrossed in Stalin's purges of the military, which killed off dozens of top generals and party leaders for imagined treasonable acts.)

Hitler, who was able to convince the world that his aim was only to save the world from "Bolshevism," was in his heyday. Absolutely no one blocked his way. He next took over the Saargebiet, bordering on France, which had been separated from Germany under the Versailles Treaty, and likewise, miniscule Memel on the Baltic. In March, 1938, he engineered the "Anschluss" of Austria into Germany. This left Czechoslovakia, figuratively, in the jaws or pincers of German might from all sides. Half a year later Hitler was ready to gobble up that country too, at first pretending that he only wanted to liberate his fellow Germans in the Sudeten mountains, all along the Czech border. The pressure built up day after day, with Hitler ranting at mass rallies, broadcast all over Europe, that he would not tolerate the "mistreatment" of the Sudeten Germans, but wanted them back in the fold of the German people: *"Ein Volk, ein Land, ein Führer"* was the motto screamed daily by the throngs.

In October, 1938, the infamous Munich Pact was engineered by Neville Chamberlain, Britain's Prime Minister, along with French Prime Minister Daladier, Mussolini and Hitler. Czechoslovakia was to be carved up, and the Sudetenland handed over to Germany. The Czechs themselves were not even consulted at this sell-out.

Hitler, of course, assured the world that this was his "last demand."

At this point, Winston Churchill, a Conservative "back bencher" in the London Parliament, raised his voice in warning against Hitler's obvious plans to conquer the world, but Chamberlain persisted in his policy of appeasement. Churchill knew this road would lead to disaster; Hitler tried to silence Churchill by calling him a "warmonger." In 1939, Hitler turned his aggression against Poland, at first demanding the "return" of Danzig, a Baltic town. On September 1 of that year, the fatal act took place: he invaded Poland and launched World War II.

Chamberlain maintained his Premiership. But by May 10, when Hitler invaded France, Holland and Belgium, the British people had had enough of Chamberlain's appeasement policy. Churchill became Britain's Prime Minister, and in his first speech in Parliament he said: "I can offer you nothing but toil, blood and sweat." In June, 1940, France fell. Russia had become an ally of Hitler. England stood alone.

In July, 1940, Hitler offered Britain peace: Germany would dominate Europe and get back its former overseas colonies, but Britain could retain its Empire and Navy. Churchill turned him down with contempt. The rest is history.

Now a 36-year-old English writer, John Charmley, has published a widely-noted, highly controversial book, *Churchill, the End of Glory*, in which he holds that at that point, Churchill should indeed have accepted Hitler's offer. It would have saved the British Empire, saved England's economy and would have freed England from being a satellite of the U.S., he postulates.

As can be expected, this thesis has unleashed a fierce debate in England, with the press carrying such headlines as "Churchill—Hero or Villain?" "What If...?" "Sir Winston Still Stands upon His Pedestal," "If Hitler and Churchill had Divided up the World," "Britain Was Right About Hitler, Says Germany," etc.

It is obvious that a man born in 1955 does not have a ghost of a chance of savoring the grandeur of Churchill's performance, the hope he gave to billions of people around the world and the concept of freedom he personified. A German historian, Ranke, once said that the writing of history should be dedicated to recreating events *"wie es eigentlich gewesen ist"* (as it actually happened). Only those who lived through the Churchill era know "how it actually happened." A young Monday morning quarterback cannot judge.

My late father, who lived through World War II in isolated but neutral Sweden, used to say a prayer every day—I found the text, long after his death, in his *siddur* for the welfare and success of Churchill and Roosevelt. These two alone, a formidable pair of fighters, stood between hope for freedom of the Jewish and other oppressed peoples, and disaster. To think, now, that Churchill should have trusted Hitler's word in July, 1940, is utterly preposterous:

Hitler broke every word he ever gave to any country. He signed a non-aggression pact with Denmark, only to invade that country on April 8, 1940. The same happened with country after country. On June 21, 1941, he proceeded to invade Russia, his erstwhile solemn ally. What nonsense to think that Britain would have been treated any differently. How could the return of the few pre-1914 colonies have satisfied Hitler? The colonies, in Africa, consisted of Cameroon, Tanganyika (now Tanzania), South West Africa (now Namibia) and tiny Togo, plus some specks in the Pacific Ocean (the Marshall Islands, Caroline Island, etc.). Surely, Hitler would have grabbed not only for Britain's overseas colonies, but also for South America, where he had built up a network of Nazi agents.

But a reading of the John Charmley book gives an entirely different perception of world history. The book relates the tension between President Roosevelt and Churchill regarding the overall Allied strategy. While Roosevelt and General George Marshall, his Chief of Staff, were mainly intent on liberating Europe from the west, Churchill skilfully and successfully promoted giving the Mediterranean priority. He wanted to attack Hitler's Europe through its "soft underbelly," Greece and Italy. It was for this reason that the Allies embarked on the invasion of North Africa in November, 1942, and were able to pursue and defeat General Erwin Rommel's Afrika Corps, the formidable German Army supported by Italy, which already stood at the gates of Alexandria, poised to invade Palestine and—like Napoleon, 140 years earlier—embark on the road to India.

This turn of events had providential consequences for Jewish history. Only by concentrating on the Mediterranean and North Africa did the Allies prevent the greatest disaster which could have befallen the Jewish people: Palestine, at that time a British Mandate, would have fallen into Nazi hands, and its population would, G-d forbid, have shared the fate of their European brethren. It would have ended the beginnings of the messianic trend toward a Jewish State.

In 1942, the Wannsee Conference took place on the outskirts of Berlin: the "final solution" to the "Jewish question" was sealed by Hitler, Himmler, Eichmann and their fellow butchers. Wannsee led to Auschwitz and all the other death camps. But 1942 also saw Erwin Rommel 60 miles from Alexandria, the last bulwark in his road to Jerusalem. What happened at that point in the history of the Jewish people?

In Eretz Yisrael, fast days and non-stop prayers were launched by the greatest rabbis and kabbalists. I even heard that a small plane was chartered to circle the Land, while rabbis inside the plane recited urgent prayers.

And what was the reaction to Auschwitz in America? Aside from actions by the rabbis of the Agudah and of the Vaad Hatzalah, there was relative inaction. Such "leaders" as Stephen Wise, the Reform rabbi and founder of the American Jewish Congress, blocked protests which concerned Jewish groups wished to place before President Roosevelt. A few weeks ago, my friend Motty Retter published a report in London's *Jewish Chronicle*, charging that Stephen Wise even blocked an attempt by British Jews to call on the British Parliament to make a public protest against the atrocities committed against Jews in Europe.

The prayers of the Jews in Eretz Yisrael were heard. Rommel was defeated at the last moment at Alamein; his armies were swept away from North Africa, and Eretz Yisrael and its Jews were saved. But, on the other hand, the silence over the fate of the Jews in Europe, the absence of the kind of fasts and public prayers which had saved Eretz Yisrael, resulted in the crematoria in Auschwitz being stoked day and night.

Auschwitz or Rommel? This may be a daring assessment of how this dilemma was answered, but I am persuaded that I must express my own assessment of the lesson of our history.

Churchill was clearly a pawn of Providence in helping to bring about the fulfillment of our messianic dream of 2000 years. So to us, regardless of what "revisionists" of history have to say, Churchill remains a hero.

# William Foxwell Albright (1891–1971)
# A Righteous Gentile

William F. Albright was a legend in his own lifetime. During his extraordinarily fruitful life he produced some 1,100 books and articles. He was awarded thirty honorary doctor's degrees. Institutes are named after him. In addition, his character and outstanding personal attributes were equally important in contributing to his reputation. Can a biographical profile do justice to such a great man?

Albright was born in Chile to Methodist missionary parents hailing from Iowa. His love for Oriental languages and history began at a very early age. He earned a scholarship at Johns Hopkins University, when he had already mastered Hebrew, Akkadian (Babylonian), Spanish, French, German, Latin and Greek. After World War I, he arrived in Jerusalem in 1920 and made his home in the American School of Oriental Research, now called the William F. Albright Institute of Archaeology.

He conducted several important archaeological excavations at sites with deep Biblical significance, among them those at Tell el-Ful, the palace of King Saul, and Tell Beit Mirsim, believed to be Biblical Dvir. He also excavated at Bethel and at Beth-Zur. In his excavations he innovated excavation and dating techniques, especially sequence dating of ancient pottery and stratigraphical dating.

On returning to the USA at the outbreak of World War II, he assumed the post of head of the Oriental Seminary at Johns Hopkins University, where I was privileged to be his student 1941–1946. I will never forget my first encounter with him when he turned to me and said, "How do you like a Sheketz like me speaking Hebrew?" His classes were never attended by more than a handful of students, at maximum. In fact, in my class in Egyptian, I was the only student! His seminars, once every week, did attract students and scholars from other institutions who were inspired by his lectures.

The significant feature in Albright's nature was his extreme modesty. He had almost no ego, and therefore never insisted on claiming credit for having innovated certain theories or discoveries. He was always ready to change and abrogate long-held views, if he was convinced that someone else had better solutions.

His good "middot" were exemplary. Thus during the war he received for review a book, in Swedish, by a scholar on the life of Saul. He did not know Swedish, but felt an obligation to the author to produce the review. He therefore learned Swedish for the sole purpose of being able to read and review the Swedish scholar's work.

He was a great friend of the Jews and Jewish scholars. He earned a very modest salary, $6,000 per year, and had offers of much higher fees from other institutions, among them the prestigious Rockefeller Institute at the University of Chicago. But, as he confided to me, he knew that if he were to leave Johns Hopkins, the Board would introduce a "quota system" for Jewish students which he was vehemently opposed to. So he made a personal sacrifice for the protection of academic freedom for Jewish students.

Thus in 1944, during a trip to California, I visited George Steindorff, the aged Jewish Egyptologist, who lived very frugally as a refugee from his native Leipzig. He was one of the many Jewish victims of the Nazi regime. To my surprise Steindorff, whose books I had already devoured as a young boy, told me that he could not survive without the financial help which Albright was sending him every month. Considering Albright's low salary, it was amazing that he sacrificed a part thereof to assist this suffering Jewish scholar.

Albright was beloved by the Jewish communities of Israel and the USA. In Baltimore, he was often invited as a guest of honor at banquets for Yeshivot and Hebrew schools, and impressed everyone with his speeches in fluent Ivrit. This made more for the propagation of Hebrew education than many speeches made by Jewish educators.

His books on archaeology were epoch-making in introducing the "archaeological school" to Bible studies. The previous "school of higher criticism" by some Germans known as anti-Semites—especially Wellhausen and Delitzach—were aiming at destroying the truth of the Bible, by delegating totally different dates to its composition. Their favorite dating system was to declare most of the books of the Bible to have been written long after the Babylonian exile, or even in the Hellenistic period. Albright was able to prove, on archaeological evidence, that the events related in the Bible really took place during the indicated ages. Thus the story of Abraham was shown to have happened during the patriarchal age. The songs of Moses (Haazinu), and Deborah, the Oracles of Bilaam were shown to correspond to the indicated Biblical age. The destruction of Jericho and of Hazor fit into the Biblical account. The discovery in 1929 of the Ugaritic language, a Canaanite dialect, and the vast literature written in that language, showed that Biblical Hebrew was of very old age. Dr. Albright's major works are *From Stone Age to Christianity* and *Biblical Archaeology*.

Albright was an extremely kind and friendly person. My late father met him during my own graduation exercise at Johns Hopkins in 1946 and struck up a very fine friendship. I have some 30 letters and postcards from Albright which he sent me in the years after I left Hopkins. In all of them he encouraged me to continue my interest in Biblical history. This included the inspiration I got from him in connection with the Dead Sea Scrolls. I was present when E. Sukenik, father of Yigal Yadin, presented to Albright the first specimens of the Scrolls for dating purposes. After comparing them with the oldest Hebrew text known up to then, the so-called Nash Papyrus of about 200 BCE, Albright immediately announced that the Scrolls hailed from the Hasmonen period, or about 160 BCE. This dating was immediately accepted by all scholars, even though later discoveries showed material of some earlier and some later dates.

Another occasion when I met Albright concerned the Ner Israel Rabbinical College in Baltimore. Rabbis Weinberg and Neuberger asked me to enlist Albright's recommendation at the Maryland Department of Education for granting a charter to the Yeshiva for giving Graduate Degrees. After I explained my mission to him, he readily agreed to help, on condition that he would spend a week at the Yeshiva to gauge its academic standing. After spending the week, Albright declared "that the academic effort of the Yeshiva students is by far greater than that at any university." The charter was granted.

The last time I spoke with Albright was in 1970, during the hijack of the plane on which Rav I. Hutner was a highjack victim in Jordan. Rabbi Moshe Sherer turned to me to ask if Albright, who had spent so many years in the Orient and was fluent in Arabic, could be of help in freeing the hostages. Albright thought a while, then told me that while he would love to help, he knew that his reputation among Arabs was very low as they considered him practically an Israeli.

I also made sure that my children Jamie *z"l* and Barbara would meet Albright. I took them to Baltimore especially for the meeting, and I am hopeful that this left a lasting memory with them. In my own case, I can say that, with two other personalities, Albright was the greatest influence on my cultural life. May his memory be blessed, as he was truly one of the "Righteous Gentiles."

# Eugene V. Rostow—An Unsung Hero

In 1967, when the United Nations Security Council wrangled with a Resolution in the wake of the Six Day War, the post of Undersecretary of State for Political Affairs was held by Eugene V. Rostow. He can be called the father of Resolution 242, which took almost 6 months to formulate and agree upon. Arabs today try to convince the world that this was an "ambiguous resolution" which they can interpret at will. However, since the meaning of the Resolution is now pivotal in the negotiations going on in Washington, let us consult Eugene Rostow himself for the truth in the matter.

Already in Madrid we heard daily from the Arabs and the Americans that 242 means "land for peace." Consequently, one Arab spokesman after the other kept hammering away at the idea that Israel must give up "every inch" of occupied land before peace can be discussed. It was left to Benjamin Netanyahu, the skillful spokesman of Israel, to remind the world that, under 242, Israel never had to give up all land occupied, and that in fact, she had already given up 91% of that land by returning the Sinai to Egypt. The remaining 9% would make Israel again a tiny stretch of land with a width of 10 miles along the coast, which, of course, would be impossible to defend. This would be in contradiction with the same 242 which also specified that Israel must have secure and defensible borders.

In a recent article in the *New Republic*, Eugene Rostow offers the truthful record and meaning of 242, which should be the definitive and final source of information. After listening to his testimony, all discussion should end. His word is fully authoritative and should dispel all confusion—except to those who say, "I have made up my mind; don't confuse me with the facts."

I quote from the Rostow article: "Israel is allowed to administer the territories it occupied in 1967 until a 'just and lasting peace in the Middle East' is achieved. When such a peace is made, Israel is required to withdraw its armed forces from 'territories' it occupied during the Six Day War—*not from 'the' territories nor from 'all' the territories, but from some of the territories.*" He related that attempted proposals that include the word "the" before "territories" were defeated in the United Nations. "Speaker after speaker made it explicit that Israel was not to be forced back to the 'fragile' and 'vulnerable' Armistice Demarcation Lines (which marked the 1967 borders), but should retire, once peace was made, to what Resolution 242 called 'secure and recognized' boundaries. In negotiating such agreements, the parties should take into account, among other factors, security considerations and access to international waterways of the region."

Rostow is also an invaluable witness to the legal status of the "settlements" which, too, the Arabs and Americans keep challenging. Rostow, who was also a

Professor of Law at Yale University, states that "The British Mandate (of Palestine) recognized the right of the Jewish people to 'close settlements' in the *whole* Mandated territory. It was provided that Britain could postpone or withhold Jewish settlement in what is now Jordan. This was done in 1922 (when the Eastern Province of Palestine was temporarily separated from the rest of Palestine). But the Jewish right to settlement in Palestine *west* of the Jordan River, that is in Israel, the West Bank, Jerusalem and the Gaza Strip, was made *unassailable. That right has never been terminated and cannot be terminated* except by a recognized peace between Israel and its neighbors."

Hence, former President Ronald Reagan was legally right when he declared in 1982: "I have personally followed and supported Israel's heroic struggle for survival since the founding of the State of Israel thirty-four years ago: In the pre-1967 borders, Israel was barely ten miles wide at its narrowest point. The bulk of Israel's population lived within artillery range of hostile Arab armies. *I am not about to ask Israel to live that way again.*"

Eugene V. Rostow has earned an honored place in history, not only for the role he, together with the late Ambassador Arthur Goldberg, played in formulating and getting approval for the clear-cut version of Resolution 242, but also for speaking out now at a crucial moment in history, when Israel's detractors are plotting to falsify and distort history for their own perverted aims. It is time to show proper gratitude, honor and respect for Eugene Rostow!

# The Jew in Benjamin Disraeli, The Earl of Beaconsfeld

My late father had certain heroes whom he idolized and about whom he often related stories to me during my youthful years. He would read every book and biography relating to their lives. These heroes included Don Isaac Abarbanel; Behrend Lehmann, the 17th century great Court Jew of Halberstadt and possibly one of our ancestors; the Rothschilds; the Sassoons; Sir Rufus Isaacs; the Viceroy of India, and—Disraeli.

Benjamin Disraeli has therefore fascinated me for a very long time. My impression of him was the common one: the skilled British Prime Minister who won the Suez Canal for Queen Victoria, and although a baptized Jew, was attacked throughout his political career by anti-Semites who reveled in the nasty caricatures of him which regularly appeared in the British press.

It is only now that I have gained an insight into his colorful personality, his great artistic talents as a writer, his boundless pride in his Jewish ancestry, and his knowledge of everything Jewish, whether ritual, historical or Messianic. A recently published book has enriched my acquaintance with Disraeli immeasurably. I recommend it to everyone as a source of true pride and gratitude—for in my opinion, we would probably have no Jewish State today if Disraeli had not lived. The book is *Disraeli*, by Stanley Weintraub, published by Penguin Books.

Disraeli's family originated in a small Italian town, Cento. Since "Cento" means "One hundred," Jews used to call it "Meah," Hebrew for 100. Disraeli was the son of Isaac d'Israeli, a highly literate but individualistic Jew who had built up a large library and engaged in literary activities.

On December 28, 1804, Isaac d'Israeli made a *Brit Milah*, ritual circumcision, for his new-born son, Benjamin, in the d'Israeli home. The special chair—the "*Kisseh shel Eliyahu*"—on which the *sandak*, who holds the baby, sits, was brought over from the old Bevis Marks Synagogue, which Disraeli's grandfather joined when he came to England from Italy in 1748. Disraeli's uncle, David Abarbanel Lindo, was the *mohel* who performed the *brit*. Disraeli would muse that his ancestors must have fled Spain because of the Inquisition and "found a refuge in the more tolerant territories of the Venetian Republic." Some of the most famous Sephardic and Italian Jewish names figure in his family tree: De'Rossi, Furtado, Villa Real, Calimani, de Gabay, Shiprut, Basevi.

His father, Isaac, the poet and writer, was at one point elected "warden" of the Bevis Marks synagogue, but rejected the honor. He was then, according to the rules of the congregation, fined forty pounds for refusing an honor. This caused his rift with the Jewish community. When his father, Benjamin the Elder, died and left him an important heritage, Isaac Disraeli resigned from the synagogue in 1817, just as his son Benjamin's Bar Mitzvah was nearing. He already had a private tutor preparing him for the great event, although it could not take place in a synagogue because of his father's idiosyncrasy and querulous nature. On July 11, 1817, just a few months before Benjamin's Bar Mitzvah, his father, long non-observant, took him (as he later wrote he only "half-consented") to an Anglican Church to be baptized. It was around the time that another great European, Heinrich Heine, the great German-Jewish poet, was baptized to Christianity. It reminds me of the story that one of Heine's friends in later years confronted him with the question: "Chayim [his Jewish name], do you really believe in Jesus?" Heine answered: "Have you ever met one Jew who believed in another Jew?" Disraeli would certainly have given the same answer!

In 1830 Disraeli embarked on a trip to the Middle East. When he passed Gibraltar, he wrote to his father singling out "Jews, with gabardines and skull caps." His encounter with Jerusalem made a profound impression on him. In a book resulting from the trip he clearly expressed his desire to restore Jerusalem to the Jews. The leading character in the book says: "My wish is a national existence which we have not. My wish is the Land of Promise and Jerusalem and the Temple, all we forfeited, all we have yearned after, all for which we have fought, our beauteous country, our holy creed, our simple manners, and our ancient customs."

Several of his later books, especially *Tancred*, were literally manifestos of his love for Judaism, for the restoration of the Jewish people to its soil. These books profoundly influenced the Christian world of England, and, no doubt, to a great extent helped formulate England's desire for control of the Holy Land. At the same time, Sir Moses Montefiore, his great and immediate neighbor on Park Lane (Disraeli occupied the stately mansion at 95, Montefiore the town house at 99 Park Lane) conducted his many trips to the Holy Land to render political and financial help to the growing Jewish community there. The two—Disraeli and Montefiore, backed by their intimate friends and partners, the Rothschilds, thus performed a truly historic role: they prepared the return of Eretz Yisrael to the Jewish people!

Meanwhile, in the Yeshivot in Lithuania and Poland, Kabbalists had reckoned that the Mashiach would come in 1840. How right they were! That was the pivotal year in which all the components for the beginning of the Messianic age, through truly miraculous circumstances, had fallen into place! In studying this chapter in history, we must be overwhelmed by the realization how divine Providence worked—yet totally unbeknownst to the Jewish people itself!

Disraeli was an intimate friend—both financially, socially and politically—of the Rothschilds. In fact, he once considered marrying a Rothschild daughter and only shrank back because it would undermine his career. He was hounded enough as a Jew, and could not "afford" to identify himself openly with the Jewish religion. He was attracted to Baron Lionel de Rothschild, in part because like himself, a Rothschild was an "outsider" in English society.

When his propaganda for the restoration of Palestine to the Jews resulted in the Anglican Church sending, as the first Bishop in Jerusalem, a converted former rabbi from Posen, Germany, Disraeli defined the mission as "consisting of the Bishop's own family, the English and Prussian consuls, and five Jews whom they have converted at twenty piastres a week, but I know they are going to strike for wages."

Entry into the House of Parliament of England was barred to Jews, through the technicality that every member had to give an oath by Jesus.

Year after year a "Jew Bill" was introduced to eliminate this oath, and admit Jews into Commons. Year after year Disraeli would support the bill, yet it would be defeated in the Upper House, the House of Lords. Disraeli's great zeal to accomplish the admission of Jews, was mainly intended to facilitate Lionel de Rothchild's entry, since he had been elected to the House. When after countless attempts the oath was finally abolished, Rothschild nevertheless refused to take his seat in a House that had shown so much hostility to him and his fellow Jews.

Disraeli mocked Christians and their anti-Semitism by saying: "Half of Christendom worships a Jewess, and the other half, a Jew." He referred to the Mary worship of the Catholics, and the Jesus worship of the Protestants.

England was always and constantly aware of his Jewishness, whether in politics or in literature. A review of one of his books said: "To the Hebrew fraternity it will be particularly acceptable, for the author goes much farther than he has done in his previous works toward exalting the character, talents, and religion of the Jews." When his father died he sold all of his rich library—except his Jewish books. These included books by Menasseh ben Israel and Moses Mendelssohn, both of whom no doubt had influenced Isaac Disraeli.

Disraeli displays detailed knowledge of Jewish customs, possibly observed in the houses of the Montefiores or Rothschilds. Thus in *Tancred* he gives detailed descriptions of the Shabbat including the Kiddush, of Sukkot and other customs. Like Heine, who pined for the warmth of his Jewish youth, Disraeli felt great nostalgia for Judaism and Jewish life.

His dreams of restoring Eretz Yisrael as a Jewish state to his people, is recorded in the memories of a friend, who recalled that "Disraeli spoke with great apparent earnestness about restoring the Jews to their own land and outlined details of his plan. The Holy Land has ample natural resources—all that we needed was labor and protection for the laborer. The very land might be bought from Turkey, money would be forthcoming: the Rothschilds and leading Hebrew capitalists would all help. All that was necessary was to establish colonies, with rights over the soil, and security from ill treatment. He added that these ideas were extensively entertained among the Jewish nation. The man who would carry them out would be the next Messiah. He saw only a single obstacle: arising from the existence of two races among the Hebrews of whom one, those who settled along the shores of the Mediterranean, look down on the other, refusing even to associate with them. Don Isaac Abarbanel, 'Sephardim' I think he called the superior race."

I have no doubt that Disraeli gained all this knowledge from his next door neighbor for 40 years, Moses Montefiore, who devoted much of his efforts to making peace in Eretz Yisrael between Sephardim and Ashkenazim! The fact that Jews already plan for a return to their land, which he mentions, means that he knew of the early migrations of the Chassidim and "Perushim" (Disciples of the Gaon of Vilna) which had taken place before 1840, the "Messianic" year. Maybe he saw himself as that Messiah, who could bring about the Restoration he had dreamt about since his childhood.

When Disraeli managed to give England control of the Suez Canal, through the financial help rendered by the Rothschilds, and thereby assured England's entry into the Middle East, he may have, consciously or unconsciously, intended to help the return of the Holy Land to the Jewish people, through England's assistance! Interestingly, some centuries earlier, another man of Jewish descent, Christopher Columbus, had hoped to help rebuild Jerusalem according to Biblical prophecies, through his maritime discoveries and exploration of new sailing routes.

Disraeli showed his preference for friends in whom he could find something Jewish. One of his greatest lady admirers was Mrs. Sara Brydges Willyams, with whom Disraeli exchanged hundreds of letters. He insisted that she always use her maiden name—Sarah Mendez da Costa, to indicate her descent from noble Sephardic families.

In Disraeli's political activities, it is interesting to note that he actively supported Bismarck's Germany against England's traditional foe, France. This helped Germany win the wars of 1864 and 1870, and established the German Empire. I wonder if German history books make any mention that the very existence of Germany is built on the support of a Jew?

Disraeli's disdain for the alleged originality of Christianity was expressed when he said: "Everything gentle and sublime in the religious code of the Christian Gospel, is a mere transcript from the so-called Oral Law of the Jews."

His political foe, Gladstone, led attacks on Disraeli using methods which nowadays would certainly be condemned. He published a poem which began with the lines:

> "Oh dear! Oh dear! What shall I do?
> They call me merry Ben the Jew
> The leader of the Tory crew"

Gladstone also attacked Disraeli by claiming that "he was holding British foreign policy hostage to his Jewish sympathies, and that he was more interested in relieving the anguish of Jews in Russia and Turkey than in any British interests." Of course, Gladstone was totally wrong, since the British Empire never flourished as brightly as under Disraeli's tutelage, for which Queen Victoria was especially grateful and appreciative.

But certainly he must have been aware of Montefiore's efforts to alleviate Jewish suffering in so many countries. In a sense, Disraeli and Montefiore were comrades-in-arms. Yet, although their homes were back-to-back, I have yet to find written records of their conversations or correspondence. Such records must have existed; perhaps they were destroyed, as were so many of Disraeli's and Montefiore's records.

By 1879 Disraeli had moved from Park Lane to 19 Curzon Street, where he died in April, 1881. His tomb is inside Westminster Abbey—but I am sure that his soul is in the Jewish hereafter.

Disraeli was one of the greatest Jewish personalities in history. I can well see why my father idolized him, and wished to pass that admiration on to future generations.

# The Jew in Felix Mendelssohn (1809–1847)

We all know the enthralling and charming incidental music to Shakespeare's *Midsummer Night's Dream*, including the Wedding March, which is so often played at weddings. Equally famous is the Violin Concerto in E Minor, which the world's leading violinists until this day treasure as equal to the violin concerti of Beethoven, Mozart, Brahms, Bruckner and Tchaikovsky, as well as the Scottish Symphony and the Italian Symphony.

The composer of these masterpieces was born a Jew, the grandson of the great Jewish philosopher Moses Mendelssohn. His name is Felix Mendelssohn-Bartholdy, better known as simply Felix Mendelssohn. Felix was baptized as a Lutheran Protestant as a young boy. How could this have happened, and what connection did he maintain with Jews and Judaism through his short life?

Felix Mendelssohn was born into a very tortuous period in Jewish history. The French Revolution, which broke out in 1789, inspired by the American Revolution a few years before, had kindled the flame of freedom in Europe. Napoleon, a son of that Revolution, brought with him the ideas of the French Revolution wherever he took his armies, especially in Italy and Germany. In those countries he introduced emancipation and equality for Jews as a matter of priority. Walls of ghettos crumbled and Jews suddenly were given access to European culture.

Even after the French armies were defeated and withdrew to France, the ideas of democracy and freedom stayed on. The old conservative circles in Europe, beholden to the reactionary policies of the Church and the aristocracy, were not amused by these innovations. And their animosity to the new winds of freedom extended to assimilated Jews, who had penetrated the academic and commercial life of Europe and in whom they saw the French enemy. The only consolation to many Christian anti-Semites was that through assimilation, which the emancipation had brought about, all Jews—they thought—would convert and become Christians. That would put an end to the "Jewish problem."

What actually happened? Well, many Jews did convert, but the majority remained Jews. When the converted Jews hoped to be accepted as full-fledged Christians with their Jewish pasts forgotten, they were soon shocked by the emergence of racism, which made being of "pure race," not religion, the criterion for acceptance in Christian society. By the end of the 19th century, this kind of racist anti-Semitism had planted the seeds of Hitler's ideology, and the subsequent Holocaust.

The confrontation between Judaism and European culture thus was the watershed for the Jews of Europe: Would they succumb and convert, or would they bring about an amalgam of Torah and European culture? The three outstanding personalities who had to face that dilemma in the 18th and early 19th centuries were Moses Mendelssohn of Berlin, Chacham Bernays of Hamburg, and Samson Rafael Hirsch of Frankfurt. The first two failed to bring about the continuation of their teaching; their offspring largely converted and disappeared as Jews. Hirsch, however, succeeded totally. At a recent reunion of Hirsch descendants, 3,000 people gathered—all of whom to this day are Orthodox Jews. How can this be explained? The case of Moses Mendelssohn and his grandson, Felix, provides an answer to this question.

Moses Mendelssohn (1729–1788), a hunchback born in Dessau, moved to Berlin in 1743 and there created a sensation with his sharp wit, brilliant philosophical discourses and books. He consorted with all the great minds of his day, almost all Christians. In a contest announced by the Royal Academy in 1753, papers on a philosophical subject were submitted anonymously. Among the contestants were Mendelssohn and Immanuel Kant. Mendelssohn came out Number One, while Kant came out far down on the totem pole.

Mendelssohn wrangled with the reconciliation of his own rationalism with the classical Jewish philosophers, especially Maimonides. In a seminal paper by my late son Jamie, z"l, titled "Maimonides, Mendelssohn, and the Me'asfim," a widely quoted, brilliant study, he established that Mendelssohn revealed his diversion from Orthodox Jewish thinking when he disagreed with Maimonides over the question whether doctrines of faith could be the subject of religious legislation, as in the *Mishneh Torah*.

Although Mendelssohn for many years pretended that his philosophy was in harmony with that of Maimonides, he finally had to admit that he had strayed from traditional Jewish beliefs. Freedom of belief was paramount to Mendelssohn's philosophy. Thus, even though he is remembered for his translation of the Torah into German, his influence on future generations was not constructive. This can best be seen in the upbringing of his own children.

Of his six children, four ultimately converted—except Joseph and a daughter, Recha. Moses Mendelssohn characterized each of his children, finding his son Abraham to be of mediocre intelligence, while his son Joseph was brilliant. He therefore neglected the Jewish upbringing of Abraham and concentrated all his efforts on Joseph.

A great talmudist, Rabbi Salomon Dubno, a disciple of the famous Rabbi Shlomo Chelma, had come to Berlin to be close to Moses Mendelssohn, who hired him as a tutor in his home. I recently acquired an interesting manuscript: the diary of Rabbi Dubno, in which he meticulously recorded his activities for every day that he spent in Berlin. Therein he lists the lessons he gave Joseph Mendelssohn—mostly Hebrew grammar.

No mention is made of Abraham. As a result Abraham was not armed for the onslaught of the assimilation and lure of Christianity that surrounded Jews at the time. After his father's death Abraham and his children, including Felix, converted to Lutheranism. Abraham even disparaged Judaism as an "antiquated, distorted and self-defeating religion." What a paradox that the son of one of Judaism's great thinkers would have so misunderstood his ancestors' faith! The difference between Mendelssohn and Hirsch can therefore be seen in the stress on education for one's own children: Mendelssohn neglected his own children's upbringing, while Hirsch knew that his own children's education came before that of any one else's.

The Mendelssohn family had always been saturated with culture. Many of them created "salons" in Berlin where the intelligentsia of Germany would congregate and exchange gossip and their new ideas. Moses Mendelssohn himself had a keen sense for music and stressed its pursuit in some of his writings. No wonder that Felix grew up in a home where music was an integral part of the home atmosphere. He started out as a pianist, as Mozart had done a few decades before him. Then he turned to composition. He traveled widely and was inspired wherever he went to compose on local themes. After he was received by Queen Victoria and Prince Albert in London, he spent some time in Scotland and the Hebrides Islands, far in the North of Scotland, where he was inspired to compose the famous Hebrides Overture.

Throughout his life Felix stayed in close contact with all members of his family, including his Jewish uncle, Joseph, and his cousins. Abraham and Joseph had founded the very successful Mendelssohn Bank, which flourished until the days of Hitler. Felix Mendelssohn had an especially close relationship with his uncle Joseph, who had been the most scholarly of the Mendelssohn children.

In Felix's voluminous letters there is hardly a mention of Christianity. Felix was a Jew until 1816 when he was baptized at the age of 7, while his parents remained Jews until 1822 when they, too, were baptized. Felix was almost bar mitzvah age in that year.

It is no wonder that Felix's Christianity was no more than skin deep. Lutheranism is the least ceremonial and dogmatic of Christian faiths; therefore, the transition from Reform Judaism to Lutheranism was not a great leap. Even today, Reform Judaism, which has divested itself of all basic components of observance of our commandments, is in a sense nothing more than Christianity without Jesus.

Felix Mendelssohn's father had chosen a new family name after the family's conversion: Bartholdy. But Felix refused to adopt it, in deference to his grandfather and the Jewish family tradition of which he was proud. So he compromised by allowing himself to be called Mendelssohn-Bartholdy.

Some of Felix Mendelssohn's music gives hint of his deep immersion in the Bible. His greatest oratorio, "Elijah," is filled with verses from the Bible. He composed separate choral works for Psalms 19, 100, 66, 115, 42, 95, 114 and 98, in this order. And one of his compositions was titled "Israel in Egypt."

Besides his family, Felix Mendelssohn also socialized with the well-known Jewish banker, Salomon Heine, the uncle of the famous bard, Heinrich (Chayim) Heine—also a convert of convenience—who retained his Jewish consciousness very conspicuously throughout his poems. (When a childhood friend once asked Heine if he really believed in Jesus, he answered: "Have you ever met a Jew who has faith in another Jew?")

I recently heard Mendelssohn's String Quartet in E-flat Major, Opus 12, and was struck with the Jewish-sounding themes, especially in the first movement, which could have been taken out of the Kol Nidre melody. It has been said that Felix Mendelssohn had hopes to somehow combine the rationalism of his grandfather with "Christian rationalism." Since the latter hardly exists, it is likely that he was frustrated in his search for an amalgamation of Judaism and Christianity. In short, he was frantically trying to rationalize and justify his parents' conversion, without finding a satisfactory answer.

Meanwhile, he suffered much from anti-Semitism, since the Christians—just as in the case of his contemporary, Benjamin Disraeli, who was also a convert—continued to see the Jew in him. One of his leading enemies was Richard Wagner, who pretended that there was no originality or genius in Mendelssohn's music. Anyone familiar with Mendelssohn's wonderful music, whether for orchestra, chorales or single instruments, knows that only a mind warped by hatred and anti-Semitic prejudice could make such a judgment. As we know today, Mendelssohn's music has remained more popular than Wagner's pompous, muddled and sometimes obscure music.

Mendelssohn was an extremely modest and unassuming man. Although he was aware of his talent, he always thought that his success was also due to an element of luck. In those days a composer needed a sponsor who would finance him and fund the printing of his music. Luck was required to find such a sponsor. I once saw, when I was a very young child, an inscription on a house in Germany, which I have never forgotten: *"Ohn' Glück und Gunst ist Kunst umsunst"* (Without luck and the favor of a sponsor, art is in vain.)

Mendelssohn was planning to compose an oratorio, "Moses," which, however, he never finished. In it he wrote, "O, that help might befall Israel and G-d save His chosen people." In his oratorio, "Elijah," there are also many verses invoking help for the People of Israel: "G-d's mercies on thousands fall, on all of them that love Him, and keep His commandments." It is certain that Mendelssohn knew what was meant by these "commandments"—the Jewish mitzvot, which Christianity under Paul had discarded.

Felix had a sister, Fanny, who was an accomplished pianist and composer. In the climate of those days, a female composer could not get the share of attention that she deserved. But her brother Felix was very close to her throughout his life. And when Fanny suddenly died in 1847, it was a great shock to him. A few weeks later he, too, died.

Like other great composers—Mozart, Schubert, Chopin—Mendelssohn died in his thirties. We must lament the great loss of further productions that his enormous genius might have produced if he had lived longer. But we must be justly proud and grateful for the great music that this greatest of all Jewish-born composers left behind for us. And that genius was in no small part imbued in him through the genius of his remarkable grandfather, Moses Mendelssohn, about whom some said, "From Moses to Moses to Moses there was none like Moses" (referring to Moshe Rabbeinu, Rambam and Mendelssohn).

# The Warburgs

An 820-page book on the history of one of the most interesting German-Jewish families of bankers, the Warburgs, has just been printed. Published by Random House and authored by Ron Chernow, it is of very special interest to all who still have clear memory of the powerful position in banking, as well as in Jewish community affairs, which the Warburgs occupied for over a century.

The book jacket has this to say about the Warburgs:

"A glamorously seductive clan, the Warburgs entered spheres of business, politics and society previously closed to Jews in Europe and America. Financial advisers to the Kaiser, titans of German business, they led a Shangri-la-type existence on their estate outside Hamburg. Brilliantly flamboyant, the Warburgs spawned many famous figures: a confidant of Kaiser Wilhelm II, a Nobel Prize winning scientist, the architect of the Federal Reserve system in the U.S.A., an adviser to President Roosevelt, a pioneering art historian, a gifted cellist, a knighted adviser to Prime Minister Harold Wilson of Great Britain, and America's leading philanthropist."

The book swarms with dozens and dozens of names of the various branches of the family, whose ancestry is traced back some 400 years, but the author shows ignorance of some of the profound contributions to Jewish life in Germany made by certain members of the family over a period of more than 100 years.

No doubt many of the Warburgs are worthy of being the subjects of biographies, but I have decided to be very selective as to which personality among them I should highlight. Fortunately, I have rare personal memories and documents to draw on which were not available to Mr. Chernow. Therefore I will mainly comment on the following Warburgs: Mrs. Sara Warburg (1805–1884), Max Warburg (1867–1946), and Eric Warburg (1900–1990).

## *Sara Warburg—Family Matriarch With a Unique Mitzvah Project*

Sara Warburg, the matriarch of the dynasty which meant so much in Germany and America, is pictured in the book as a strong-willed, extremely capable woman, who kept her grandsons in disciplined regime and led them on the road to becoming enormously successful. She was a driving force in the lives of Abby S., the art historian; Max, the Hamburg banker; Paul and Felix, who became bankers in New York; and Fritz, who spent part of his life in Sweden.

What the book does not mention is that Sara Warburg was the founder and head of a wonderful mitzvah-institution which cared for the postnatal needs of poor Wöchnerinnen (*kimpetuerinen* in Yiddish).

She founded the society in 1829, after witnessing the sufferings which Jews lived through during and after the war with Napoleon in 1814. Although the Jews experienced great benefits while Napoleon was in charge, since he introduced liberty and emancipation for Jews wherever he ruled, when his control was fought off there remained an aftermath of pogroms and other sufferings which ravaged and impoverished the Hamburg community.

Sara Warburg's Foundation was therefore a godsend for the many poor Jewish women of Hamburg. She based her Foundation on very well worked out organizational lines. It had a Directorate, consisting of a number of prominent Jewish ladies from Hamburg, some of them listed as medical doctors, with a male accountant and with Sara Warburg herself as the Chairlady. She set down the rules for the Foundation in a beautifully penned Constitution, written in German with Hebrew letters, its parchment pages handsomely bound into a book, which today is in my possession.

Paragraph after paragraph sets down exactly which supplies—in terms of blankets, towels, soap and other necessities—the recipient was entitled to. To my knowledge, this is one of the earliest formal Constitutions for a mitzvah-enterprise of this type.

It is no wonder that the woman who performed this important mitzvah with such conscientiousness and meticulous care was also successful in business.

### *Max Warburg—King of Hamburg*

As for her most prominent grandson, Max, I have had the privilege of observing him in person. During the years when our family lived in Hamburg, our pew in the magnificent Bornplatz Synagogue was across the aisle from the Warburgs'.

Because of this connection I can testify that author Chernow is totally off the truthful track in several of his claims: He writes that Max Warburg "was only marginally religious and attended synagogue on High Holidays, but with a book secreted in his lap to pass the time"; describes the magnificent Bornplatz Synagogue as "a large, ugly brick building," and the service there as taking place in "a weird room full of men in shawls and skullcaps, swaying and mumbling indistinctly"; and says that the Chief Rabbi stood before "a buzzing and writhing congregation."

I can bear witness that all this is pure nonsense and fantasy, totally contrary to the truth. I observed Max Warburg quite often in his seat near our family. His presence was always noticeable because his arrival created quite a stir in the synagogue—after all, at the time I remember him, around 1931–1933, Max Warburg was internationally known as the "King of Hamburg," and his contributions to benefit the Jewish community were legend.

The Bornplatz Synagogue was a beautiful building, with palatial architecture of white and black marble. Most of the congregants wore top hats to every Saturday morning service. These hats were stored in special containers in the coat-room from week to week. The decorum was absolutely superb—certainly no "swaying, mumbling, buzzing or writhing"!

Max Warburg was not very fond of the sermons of the Hungarian-born Chief Rabbi, Rabbi Salomon Spitzer, and I remember one occasion when just as the Rabbi mounted the stairs to reach the podium to deliver his sermon, Max Warburg and a companion, possibly his son Eric, demonstratively ripped off their Taleisim, pushed them into the box in front of their pew, and stalked out of the synagogue. He wanted to demonstrate his dislike for the rabbi's Hungarian accent. He preferred everything to be spoken in pure German.

While the book acknowledges the fact that Sara Warburg's son Moritz and his five sons had built and endowed the exemplary Jewish day school, the Talmud Torah Realschule, in 1908, Chernow fails to tell us that Max Warburg remained closely associated with every aspect of that school until its very end in the Nazi period. I recently wrote about the fabulous innovations in Jewish education which the Talmud Torah, through the direction of Rabbi Josef Carlebach, pioneered. His ingenious plan for integrated religious and secular studies—inspired by the example of Rabbi Esriel Hildesheimer's teachings a century before—ultimately influenced the entire day school system in the United States.

Max Warburg, who aside from being a leading German banker with thousands of clients and renowned as an intimate of Kaiser Wilhelm II, spent a good part of his time in caring for the Talmud Torah. He served as Chairman for its Board. I know, because my late father was a good friend of Max Warburg, and often exchanged letters with him in matters relating to the school.

In later years of crisis Max Warburg also had close consultations with Dr. Arthur Spier, the school's last principal. He was also in very frequent contact with Rabbi Josef Carlebach, practically the last Orthodox rabbi in Germany. Without Max Warburg's support, Rabbi Carlebach could not have carried out his tragic task of caring for Hamburg's last few thousand Jews before they were sent off for extermination near Riga.

All these historic activities are left out of Chernow's biography, and I consider it my duty to make the necessary corrections and amendments to his book.

Max Warburg had reached such a high degree of influence in Germany's financial world that even Hitler could not do without him. As a friend of Hitler's Director of the Central Bank, the shadowy and opportunistic Dr. Hjalmar Schacht, Max Warburg continued his activities as a banker. He did well until 1938, when Schacht was fired and could no longer protect Warburg.

By that time two of Max's brothers, Paul and Felix, had long migrated to the United States and founded the highly successful and influential Kuhn Loeb and Co., in association with Felix's in-laws, the Schiffs. His brother Fritz had been imprisoned by the Nazis, but ultimately he was released through high-level intervention, whereupon he promptly left for Sweden.

Max alone, an ardent German patriot, refused to leave Germany. Max became now a heroic figure, although largely unknown to the surviving world. Single-handedly, he used his powerful position during the Hitler years to negotiate with the

Nazis for all kinds of schemes to allow Jewish emigration. It was he who negotiated the "Haavarah Scheme," under which German Jews could deposit German currency and, after an interval, get a small portion thereof paid out overseas in foreign exchange.

Max had several other schemes which he thought the Germans would approve and which would have saved tens of thousands of German Jews. But as all these plans would have benefited the German economy, nobody outside of Germany was interested in them, least of all American and British Jews who, quite contrarily, pursued a strict boycott of everything German.

In the beginning of the Hitler days, aside from urging Jews to remain in Germany and continue acting as good citizens, Max Warburg also helped establish cultural organizations and associations for the representation of German Jews to the authorities. In discussing this, Chernow again leaves out an important chapter: the centrally important role played by Chaim Arlosoroff, the representative of Zionism in Germany, in the Haavarah and other schemes.

The Nazi press stepped up its hate-propaganda against the Warburg bank, and against Max in particular. Yet he ignored all the danger signs, and continued to work for the good of the German Jews. He could not conceive of these persecutions continuing. He foresaw that Hitlerism would end, and with it the German state-sponsored anti-Semitism.

Max's brothers in New York endlessly sent him pleadings to quit Germany forthwith. Finally, the Warburg bank was dissolved on orders from the Nazi Government, and Max handed over its management to trusted non-Jewish employees. It was quite by chance that Max was abroad when the Kristallnacht took place. Had he stayed he would without doubt have been arrested and sent to a concentration camp, to be held as a hostage by the Nazis.

He remained abroad, emigrating to New York, never to set foot on German soil again. Although he started banking activities in New York, he was a broken man. He realized, too late, that his trust in Germany was totally misguided.

At the age of 79, on December 26, 1946, Max Warburg died in New York. Without doubt he had been a true Jewish hero of the Holocaust—fearless and idealistic, and totally devoted to help his fellow Jews. He took risks which no one else could take. He used every avenue available to him within the Nazi regime to find ways to alleviate the cruel fate of Germany's last surviving Jews.

### *Eric Warburg*

Many years later, in 1986, I met his son Eric on a business trip to Hamburg. Eric was the only Warburg who, after a brilliant military career in the U.S. Army, decided to return to Germany and start life there anew.

He was said to have been alienated from Jews, but to my surprise, he welcomed me in Hamburg warmly and volunteered to take me to the surviving cemeteries in Hamburg and Altona.

My visit to the Portuguese cemetery in Altona was a most memorable experience: I observed the same style of tombstones, Portuguese inscriptions, and even names, as I had seen in Portuguese Jewish cemeteries in the Caribbean Islands. It again accented the very important and close religious and cultural bonds which Sephardic Jews established throughout the world with one of the world's leading trade centers in Hamburg-Altona, so soon after escaping from the Christian hell in Spain and Portugal.

My encounters with Eric Warburg—later I also visited him on business matters in his New York office—convinced me that he, too, despite his apparent assimilation, was deeply proud of the Jewish heritage personified by the Warburg dynasty in Hamburg.

Many comparisons can be made between the Rothschilds and the Warburgs: In both families, the first generation consisted of five brothers who branched out into the banking world. But the Rothschilds never made meaningful inroads into the United States, concentrating instead on London and Paris. The Warburgs made Germany and the United States their prime fields of successful activities.

Both families, however, made historic contributions to Jewish charities in Israel and in the Diaspora. These contributions, along with the Warburgs' accomplishments in so many fields of Jewish life over more than 100 years, give us ample reasons to be proud of these illustrious Jewish financiers.

# Heinrich (Chayim) Heine—
# the Great German Jewish Bard

If you want to savor the deeply nostalgic longing of a Jewish poet for his Jewish roots, you must turn to the work of Heinrich (Chayim) Heine (1797–1856), Germany's greatest poet of the Victorian age. The fact that he was a Jew, deeply rooted in all the Jewish sentiments and values, created the conflict so typical of the assimilationist times in which he lived.

Heine was born in Duesseldorf, the part of Germany that under Napoleon had been occupied by the French army. As elsewhere, when Napoleon had conquered parts of Europe, he brought with him democracy and, for the Jews, emancipation. But just as sudden as the emergence of this emancipation was, it suddenly disappeared, leaving deep wounds in the Jews of Europe, once Napoleon was defeated and exiled. The reactionary, conservative forces of the Church saw to it that anything smacking of the detested democracy and freedom would be associated with Jews and Judaism. Those were the roots planted for the next century's Holocaust. Heinrich Heine was caught between the freedom of the French period and the anti-Semitic reaction of the German conservatives.

While his poetry was recognized as the finest Germany had produced, he was politically "not correct." He had to flee Germany and settled in Paris, where he spent his last years.

While he accepted conversion in order to qualify for a university post, he regretted throughout his life the hypocrisy of this act. He once said, "I never returned to Judaism, because I never left it." In order to understand the deep love Heine had for Judaism, you must read his many poems dwelling on Jewish history, Jewish religious life, and conflict between Jews and Christians.

I am giving herewith my own free translations of some of his most beautiful and poetic expressions of his tortured soul: His style of German is unusually free, and he even creates his own expressive terms. Almost all of his poems require some commentary to reach the innermost meanings of his lines.

The most prosperous member of his family was the banker Salomon Heine, who donated a very considerable sum to build the Jewish hospital in Hamburg in honor of his wife. On the inauguration of this impressive institution, Heinrich Heine wrote a poem, of which the first verse reads:

> A hospital for poor, sick Jews
> for human beings smitten with three disadvantages
> and suffering from three-fold handicaps
> with poverty, disease and Judaism

A constant theme in his poems is his abhorrence of anti-Semitism, from which he suffered and from which his conversion could not shield him. He wrote in a poem to his cousin Betty Heine:

> The flames of the inquisition
> have swallowed up books and human beings
> while church bells peal
> pious Christian hymns

He makes occasional references to his contemporary and distant kinsman, Felix Mendelssohn, as well as to his friend and fellow convert, Karl Marx.

One of his most beloved and famous poems is titled "Princess Sabbath." Here he describes how the suffering, poor Jew is transformed on Friday night as the Sabbath starts, and takes on the role of a Prince. He describes in detail the synagogue service on Friday night, including the singing of "Lecha Dodi," which he ascribes (erroneously) to his favorite Hebrew bard, Yehuda ha Levy. (It was composed by Shlomo Alkebatz of Safed.) He glorifies the calm and spiritual elevation that every Jew feels on the Sabbath.

As a poetically humorous departure from his poem, he lounges into praising *cholent*—called *schalet* in German-Jewish. As a takeoff on Friedrich Schiller's "Ode to Joy," which Beethoven incorporated into his majestic 9th Symphony, Heine wrote:

> Schalet gift of the Almighty
> daughter of Elysium
> thus would Schiller's
> ode sound
> if he had tasted schalet even once in his lifetime

The poem ends with a beautiful description of the Havdalah ceremony, which he calls a farewell scene between the Princess Sabbath and the ordinary Jew, who has to leave his princely form until next week's Sabbath.

His most erudite and inspired Jewish poem is titled "Jehuda ben Halevy," in which he expresses his admiration for the great philosopher-poet by describing his entire education in childhood and manhood:

> His father took on his education
> who was strict and conscientious
> in teaching his son with G-d's own book,
> the Torah

As Yehuda Halevy approaches his Bar Mitzvah, Heine feels that the *trope* of the young man must have sounded like a *shalshelet*, that rare musical note only found five times in the Torah:

> The ancient text, the young boy
> recites by heart in the old musical version called trope
> and chirped the shalshelet like a bird

Soon the father introduces Halevy to the Talmud. He mentions the young man learning Aramaic, Targum Onkelos, and *halachah* (Jewish law). The Talmudic debates are described in terms of a German gymnasium exercise:

> Fencing instructions
> were taught like the dialectic of athletes
> in Babylon and Pumpeditha
> his accomplishments
> are found in the Book of Kuzari

But he also pays tribute to the Haggadah, which he calls a beautiful garden where the finest-smelling flowers and plants gladden the heart of the student. The Haggadah is contrasted with the sharpness of the study of *halachah*, and Heine uses as illustration the Mishnah in the Tractate Betza:

> The *halachah* is intoxicated
> by the disputes such as
> the question around that famous egg
> that a chicken laid on a holiday

He shares Halevy's love for Jerusalem, and expresses the great suffering he feels at the memory of Yehuda Halevy's death in front of the gates of the Jewish capital.

One of his most moving poems, which I believe has autobiographical undertones, is titled "Donna Clara." In this poem a brave, strong knight woos a Spanish noble lady. They exchange sweet expressions of love, but Donna Clara mixes every strophe with some attack on the Jews, which the knight waves off. He does not reveal his identity, but finally as the two must part, Donna Clara beseeches the knight:

> Before we part
> you must reveal your name
> which you have shielded from me so long

The knight, after gestures of respect for the noble lady, cannot hold back anymore and blurts out proudly:

> I, Señora, your beloved,
> I'm the son of the well-known
> great scholar in Scriptures
> Rabbi Israel of Saragossa

Heine's life as a disguised Jew must have inspired this poem. Yet it is apparent that Heine did not hide his Jewish identity, as the knight does in this poem. He proudly professed being a Jew, and in fact, heaped contempt on those who tried to hide their Jewishness. With such a deep love for everything Jewish, and his contempt for the shallowness of Christianity, this is not surprising.

The conflict this created in reactionary Germany is easy to understand. His most popular song, "Die Lorelei," dedicate to a mythical mermaid along the Rhine River, was set to music and is sung to this day throughout Germany and especially—as I remember from a boat ride along the Rhine River that my family took in 1931—when one actually faces the rock where the Lorelei is said to live. Even Hitler could not stamp out this song, but denied its Jewish origin by ordering the song to be called "a folk song of unknown origin."

Heine should get more attention from us. His love for Judaism can be an inspiration for our own times, when assimilation is a grave danger to our people.

# Albert Einstein—Exponent of Outstanding Jewish Traits

While it is generally recognized that Jews by and large have superior intellects, it is not always easy to define the uniqueness of the Jewish mind.

One can define it by negative factors, as e.g. what is it that anti-Semites criticize in us, and what Jewish trait gives rise to the jealousy, envy and fear on the part of the non-Jewish world. I would venture to say that most outstanding and enduring of the Jewish mind and what is most characteristic about it is the "*koach ha-chiddush,*" the originality and inventiveness of the Jewish mind. It is a term that has been coined in the Yeshiva world, where inventiveness and originality, contrary to popular belief, is the most desirable and sought-after quality of thinking and analyzing. The cradle of the Jewish mind is the world of Torah study, it is in the world of the Yeshivot over the past 2,000 years that the Jewish intellectual approach to mental problems has been molded. That is where we can examine the mental processes which go into successful Torah and Talmud studies, which form the basis of all Jewish thinking over the millennia.

The Talmudic thought pattern is totally built around the questions: Why? Wherefrom? How? Nothing is accepted on its face. Nothing is taken for granted. Nothing, no matter how sacred and lofty its source, is accepted without scrutinizing and minute examination. Every problem, every law is tackled as if it was given today and, therefore, is brand new. This process follows the Medrash dictum: "The Torah should be as new in your eyes, every day" (see Rashi, Ekev 11, 13). We may, of course, after a thorough examination come to the conclusion that this or that law was "given to Moshe at Sinai," which stops further investigation, but till we get to that point, our analysis must proceed.

One of the most amazing experiences is—as I have often heard when great Talmudic authorities deliver a "*shiur*"—when it is said "*dos is a gevaldiger chiddush*" (This is a tremendous novelty or innovation). I heard Reb Shlomo Heiman, Reb Chaim's disciple and Reb Aharon Kotler say it. Mind you, this may be said about a passage in the Rambam or some other early authority, a text 800 or 900 years old! No matter how old, the Torah can always yield something new, something never said before. That is a totally unique and characteristic quality in Torah learning.

What is the ultimate target of such penetrating analyses? It is to find underlying principles and thought patterns, akin to laws of nature which determine phenomena in the physical world. The truth of such an intellectual discovery is to find whether it will solve and explain more than one problem. The more problems a rule can explain, the closer to truth that rule is. I am reminded of a discussion between two Talmud students. One said: "My teacher is so brilliant that he has 50 answers for every question," whereupon the other, a student of Reb Chaim, said: "That is nothing, my teacher has one answer for every 50 questions." It is the universal application of an intellectual rule which defines its truthfulness.

This search for new discoveries in the pursuit of truth, is called in the Yeshiva world "*koach ha-chiddush*"—the ability to make new, inventive discoveries. Not every student always comes to realize this ability, of course, but those who do have the merit of experiencing the glorious satisfaction and triumph of seeing new vistas opening before them every time a "*chiddush*" has been discovered.

When we behold the great Jewish minds who have contributed to progress in the world, we find that they were the men who applied everything we have said so far, in their respective field of inquiry. Karl Marx, in searching for solutions of social ills, invented a totally new social and economic system where, he thought, the injustices and imbalances of societies would disappear. Sigmund Freud, in dwelling on the mysteries of the psychological make-up of the human mind, found his way to psychoanalysis as a key to unlock the innermost secrets in the human mind which, once unlocked, could be cured through analysis.

We can find success in business, too, rooted in the Jewish "*koach ha-chiddush*." Successful Jewish businessmen have often been the ones who were able to come up with entirely new, revolutionizing ideas. For example, the Reuters News bureau, today a multi-billion dollar world empire, started when an ex-Yeshiva student, Israel Ber Joshafat, in a small German town, turned his bookselling business into a newsmongering service after he discovered that newsmongering was needed. Tragically he felt that to succeed, he had to convert to Christianity. After changing his name to Reuter, he was subsequently knighted.

No one better personifies the typically Jewish genius of "*koach ha-chiddush*" than Albert Einstein, this century's greatest physicist.

He set aside everything that physics had taught since the beginning of time, which has been firmly fixed, and declared the hitherto observed laws of nature, "relative."

Having set down the unbelievably simple formula for relativity, he set out to find a universal law which could explain all phenomena in the universe.

Two books have recently been published on Einstein.

*Einstein—A Life in Science*, by Michael White & John Gribbin, gives a balanced account of Einstein's scientific achievements, with many explanations of the most intricate laws of physics, and at the same time of Einstein's life and biography. The stress, however, is on the scientific achievements, which is fully justified, since Einstein's social and family life was not always exemplary, while as a scientist he was no doubt the greatest scientific mind of many a century. The book gives prominence to Einstein's experience as a Jew and a Zionist.

*The Private Lives of Albert Einstein*, by Roger Highfield and Paul Carter, gives too many details of Einstein's disillusioning private life, at the expense of a more careful analysis of his scientific achievements.

Einstein was born March 14, 1879 in a small town in Southern Germany. There is nothing in his family tree to indicate that there were great Jewish, rabbinic minds among his ancestors, at least not for 100 years before he was born. But going back further, we would no doubt find such antecedents. As in the case of Marx and Freud, who had rabbis among their close ancestors, Einstein's mind shows traces of the typical Jewish search for unified, basic rules and principles which can explain vast problems.

He became interested in physics rather by accident. Following the Jewish custom that every family had to offer hospitality to poor students, the Einsteins, when Albert was barely 10 years old, had a guest for a meal once a week, a 21-year-old medical student named Max Talmud. In return for this hospitality, Talmud would bring with him popular books on science, which Albert would devour with great relish. In later life, Einstein would credit his career as a scientist to the encounter at an impressionable age with Max Talmud. Thus the fulfillment of a time-tested Jewish Mitzvah practiced in every country where Jews lived—of offering hospitality to poor students, helped the century's great scientist to be launched.

Max Talmud also caused Einstein to become deeply interested in philosophy. When he was 13 years old, he suddenly turned intensely interested in Judaism, and became deeply religious, although his parents had not been observant Jews. This period did not last very long, but it established his continuous concern with philosophy and the philosophical implications of his achievements in physics. Thus toward the end of his life, he came to the conclusion that "G-d does not play dice with the universe"—one of his most famous and influential statements. Although he was basically an Internationalist and pacifist, he turned intensely Zionist and champion of Jewish causes, after his confrontation with anti-Semitism.

His career as physicist and physics teacher took him to Germany, Austria and Switzerland in the years before World War I. When he was to be appointed professor in Austria he faced his first problem over his religion. The Emperor had decreed that only Christians could hold professorial appointment, Einstein, instead of hiding his religion, wrote clearly in his application that his religion was Jewish. Of course, his fame was already so great that all restrictions were waived for him.

*Einstein—A Life in Science*, gives clear and detailed definitions to his scientific work. When he coined the seemingly simple formula $E = mc^2$, to define his relativity theory, he reached the pinnacle of his scientific career. Universities in many countries were vying for him. Yet anti-Semites, egged on by Einstein's academic competitors, branded his relativity theory a "Jewish science," which should be rejected for that reason alone, and for decades he was hounded by these enemies. In some cases, the antagonism which he had encountered even led to violence.

But his fame could not be curbed. He became, in fact, an international celebrity. When he visited the U.S.A. in 1921, he was celebrated like a movie star.

He used the trip to help raise funds for Zionist causes, including the young Hebrew University. Chaim Weizman was his good friend and partner in these campaigns.

In 1922 he was awarded the Nobel Prize, which his friends said was long overdue. It was not given for his Relativity Theory, but for his other work in physics, on the photoelectric effect.

The relativity theory laid the foundation for the practical application of atomic power; it led to the big-bang theory for the creation of the world and many other breakthroughs in physics which the world now takes for granted that took many years to be tested and become accepted. Some of his theories were proven and recognized only in recent years, long after his death in 1955.

During World War II, he was, fortunately, safe in the United States. The Nazi attacks on him and his "Jewish Science" went on unabated—which of course was Divine Providence, because it robbed Hitler's Germany of the great benefits and advances which this "Jewish science" gave to the Free World. His many disciples came as refugees to the U.S.A. and fulfilled his dreams for making the U.S.A. the leading scientific nation in the world.

Having mastered the new physics launched by his Relativity Theory, Einstein turned to his life's great dream: to find the T.O.E.—the theory of everything. (In other words, to find a theory which would explain all forces in nature.) To my mind, he expressed his Jewishness the most in this search. The Talmud proposes a similar search: for the one concept which envelops all concepts of Judaism. In the Tractate Mackot 24a, the Talmud lists those who attempted to calculate the duties of man in this world—a summary of the 613 divine commandments—to the lowest common denominator: The Prophet Isaiah defined 6 basic precepts, the Prophet Micah reduced them to 3. Isaiah, also stated the matter in two precepts. Finally, Amos and Habakuk each stated them in one: Amos, in the verse "Study me so that you may live," and Habakuk in "The virtuous man lives through his faith."

A similar venture to reduce the mass of Judaism to one precept is found in case of Hillel (Talmud Shabbat 31a) with his famous saying: "Do not do unto others what you do not wish to be done unto yourself, that is the entire Torah, the rest is commentary, go study."

Certainly, one of the most unique and innovative approaches to truth and reality in human intellectual history is to think all of the complexities in man's life in this world can be reduced to one precept. Yet, Micah, Habakuk and Hillel did it. The memory of their intellectual achievement molded Jewish minds for thousands of years. Thus, it can be said that they were Einstein's teachers and forerunners.

Einstein, on the one hand was able to penetrate the deepest secrets of the universe, and on the other hand, was able to reduce knowledge to the simplest common terms. To him there had to be order, he could not fathom that there could be chaos or unpredictability in G-d's creation. Therefore, he was opposed to the quantum theory which was developed in the '20's and on. It stipulated that, at best, man can conclude the probability of physical phenomena, but not their certainty. That is when Einstein set down his conviction that "G-d does not play dice with the universe." Again, Einstein was, consciously or subconsciously, totally inspired by the Jewish philosophy of the world. The Medrash (Eycha Rabba I:50) tells us that Reb Joshua was asked by the Roman ruler for proof of G-d's existence. Reb Joshua gave a simple answer: "Why? Is the world one of '*hefker*' (chaos)?" In modern terms: (As Einstein said) "G-d does not play dice with the world. There are iron-clad rules, which clearly demonstrate that there is a Master." Einstein was guided by the same rule.

While he was convinced that a unification theory could be found, combining all physical phenomena, he was humble enough—again a Jewish trait—to admit that it would be human arrogance to think that we can fathom and explain everything in the universe. Thus Einsteins's famous credo contained these memorable lines:

> "The most beautiful and deepest experience a man can have is the sense of the mysterious. It is the underlying principle in religion as well as all serious endeavor in art and science. He who never had this experience seems to me, if not dead, then at least blind. To sense that behind anything that can be experienced, there is something that our mind cannot grasp, and whose beauty and sublimity reaches us only indirectly and as a feeble reflection, this is religiousness. In this sense I am religious. To me it suffices to wonder at these secrets and to attempt humbly to grasp with my mind a mere image of the lofty structure of all that there is."

Toward the end of his life, Einstein was offered the presidency of the young State of Israel. Although he declined, his typically Jewish trait of intellectual inquiry would have made him a fitting head of a Jewish State. By understanding him, we can understand many other great Jewish minds. In recent years, it was said about the Gaon of Vilna: One could make ten Einsteins out of one Gaon of Vilna. Thus Einstein serves as a measuring stick for the greatness of the Jewish mind. His emotional strength in overcoming anti-Semitism, and seeing his theories vindicated, again and again, serves as a vindication for all Jews, at all times.

We can see in Einstein traces of the great Jewish genius. Does this mean that he is the model for a Jewish Scholar? Einstein's personal and social life answer this question. (His personal life is depicted in the book *The Private Lives of Albert Einstein* mentioned above). Unfortunately his private life was light-years removed from his mental and intellectual prowess. His private life was extremely deficient in morals and self-discipline, sometimes even to the point of immorality. He had an illegitimate daughter, whose whereabouts he never bothered to trace. He had a number of affairs. His two marriages were rocky. However, on the positive side, his skill as a violinist showed a deep emotional sensitivity, and his accomplishments in physics showed his intellectual creativeness. His pioneering crusades for pacifism and international peace showed his high sense of ethics. In toto, he was not a complete and harmonious Jew in the ideal sense of Jewish values.

In contrast, the *Talmid Chacham* (Torah Scholar) cannot claim any recognition at all if he is not complete in his morals as well as in his intellect. If he does not personally exemplify the highest standards of self-discipline and self-sacrifice, his learning means nothing. Therefore while we all pay homage to Einstein as a genius and great intellectual, we cannot honor him in terms of such Jewish standards.

# Walther Rathenau (1867–1923): Jewish Foreign Minister and Tormented Jew

In the course of our long history Jews have occupied the highest government offices. An outstanding period of such excellence was the "Golden Age" in Spain lasting some 200 years. Shmuel ha-Naggid was the commander in chief of the Sultan's army. Chasdai ibn Shaprut was minister of finance to his king. Besides the period of the Court Jews in Central Europe in the 17th and 18th centuries, it is only in recent times that Jews have reached Cabinet posts.

Luigi Luzzati was foreign minister in Italy before World War I; Leon Blum was prime minister in France before World War II. Denmark had a Jewish minister of finance, Cohn, before World War I. (In fact he was strictly Orthodox and is known as the minister who kept the three Scandinavian kings waiting until Shabbat was over before he would leave for an important royal conference in Malmö in southern Sweden.) Finland's Jewish foreign minister, Jakobson, almost became secretary general of the United Nations. Henry Kissinger's name comes to mind as a recent Jewish secretary of state—equivalent of foreign minister.

In these days the latest Jewish foreign minister has entered the arena of Jewish pride: Malcolm Rifkind of Great Britain. It is to Prime Minister John Major's credit that he appointed Rifkind—a traditional Jew from Scotland—to the post, despite grumbling from Arab tyrants, such as Qadaffi of Libya. A hundred years ago, this could not have happened in the United States. When Henry Morgenthau helped Woodrow Wilson win the election as president, everybody expected that he would be appointed Secretary of State or some other Cabinet post. But Wilson wavered and sent him to Constantinople to be American ambassador.

The case of Walther Rathenau, the German foreign minister after World War I, was, however, quite a different case.

Rathenau came from a highly cultured but assimilated Jewish family in Berlin. His father, Emil Rathenau, had acquired Thomas Edison's European patent rights and had founded the Allgemeine Elektrizitaets Gesellschaft (AEG), the equivalent of General Electric in this country.

His son Walther grew up in a very affluent and highly cultured home. Walther's genius extended beyond science; he was also a deep-thinking philosopher and author. The conflict he felt with his Jewishness arose soon in his youth. On the one hand he admired the Nordic Germans, but on the other—after years of brooding—he realized that the Jews had a great future. He lived through the Dreyfus tragedy, which—as in the case of Theodor Herzl—turned his mind to Zion as a possible solution for the Jewish people.

Yet he was tormented throughout his life with the problem of finding a place for the Jew in German society. Although he reached the highest circles, even under the Kaiser before 1918, he knew that he was the eternal outsider. This torment almost drove him to hostility toward his own people, which however, he ultimately turned into sympathy and admiration. While he once thought the Jew was basically a *zweckmensch*—a man only fit for functional purposes—he later emphasized the Jewish *geist* (spirit) as the predominant Jewish feature.

In my childhood I saw rows of books of Rathenau's writings in our home, which were strictly literary and cultural. Very seldom was anything political found there, although he rose to the rank of minister of reconstruction. My late father was a great admirer of Rathenau and this admiration went beyond the tragic, almost predictable end of that great Jewish statesman.

After World War I the Weimar Republic appointed Rathenau its Minister of Foreign Affairs. Rathenau did everything to alleviate the hardships that German's surrender to the Allies incurred. His Nazi enemies, however, accused him of favoring Russia over Germany, which of course was preposterous. But to the Nazis, no Jew could be accepted as a true patriot.

And so in 1923, a handful of Nazi hoodlums ambushed Rathenau and shot him to death.

Here, however, follows a sequel of which in my childhood we heard more than about his accomplishments as foreign minister: The mother of Rathenau appeared before the judge who was about to convict his murderers. She pleaded for their lives and freedom! Only a Jewish mother could show such an extreme gesture of mercy and compassion. One of his assassins upon being released from jail joined the French Foreign Legion, and in a gesture of atonement, is said to have helped a large number of Jews escape from the Germans in Marseilles in 1940.

The memory of Walther Rathenau, a true Renaissance man who lived centuries beyond his times, should live on as a source of pride to every student of Jewish history.

# On Music Appreciation

Most lovers of classical music will tell you when and where their love was kindled. The inspiration usually comes from a very good music teacher or the exposure to especially good music early in life.

I had the good fortune to have been influenced by exactly these two forces. My parents were deeply interested in good music. My father played the piano, and I remember how from my early childhood on he played piano music by Wagner. My parents, especially my mother, loved the opera. When I was 9 years old my father took our whole family to Salzburg, Austria, to attend the famous Mozart music festival. As young as I was, the impression was very deep. Of course, as most European youngsters, I was given piano lessons, but disliked the ordeal of practicing by playing unending scales in different keys, which then was the popular method of teaching piano.

But my real interest took off before my 15th birthday. Sweden, my native country, was the haven for an unusual number of the most famous conductors and performers who had escaped from Hitler's Germany. The Stockholm Philharmonic Orchestra became one of the world's best under the baton of one outstanding conductor after the other. A friend and I had wisely figured out that it was more educational to attend rehearsals rather than the actual concerts, because during rehearsals the conductor "dissects" the music and trains the musicians in the exact interpretation that he wants to express. By the time a concert takes place, there is, in a sense, really no need for a conductor anymore. The musicians have been trained in rehearsal after rehearsal in exactly the way the conductor wants them to play. During such rehearsals the conductor has the musicians play individual sections of the score, going over it again and again, until the performance is fine-tuned and the sound of the music is according to the conductor's musical insight and taste.

The problem for us boys was figuring out how to attend rehearsals. We had a solution typical for adventure-seeking young boys: we would slip into the concert hall when the rehearsals took place and hide between rows of seats in the concert hall.

This actually worked for some weeks. The trouble was, we were so nervous about being discovered by the guards and then probably evicted, that we did not really appreciate or enjoy the music enough.

And then the inescapable happened: One morning the guard discovered us cowering on the floor between rows of seats, grabbed us by our collars and *schlepped* us to the conductor's dressing room.

The conductor at the time was one of Germany's finest maestros, Fritz Busch, who—while not Jewish—had emigrated from his native Germany out of protest against the undemocratic practices of Hitler. Busch was a tall, rather ferocious Teuton, with the typical straight back of his neck. However, when Busch saw us and heard from me what had driven us to seek attendance at rehearsals, his ferocious look changed into a bright smile. He must have found our behavior charming, and promptly offered to admit us for free to any rehearsal we wanted to attend. Fearing a possible change of heart by the maestro, I quickly asked him—of course in German—if he would confirm this permission in writing. He gladly agreed. I tore out a page from a concert program and penned in German a few lines expressing the conductor's permission for us to attend rehearsals, which he immediately signed. That was some victory!

In the following weeks I heard some of the most beautiful pieces of classical concert music. By loosely following the conductor's instructions, and often criticism, for the musicians, I learned a great deal about how classical music should be played.

Fritz Busch, luckily, preferred to perform such great classical composers as Beethoven, Mozart, Brahms and Bruch, and once in a while he also conducted contemporary music, which the musicians evidently detested. I remember one rehearsal of a violin concerto by Alban Berg, a modern German composer. The musicians broke into laughter at the odd, disharmonious and atonal passages. They simply stopped playing and put down their instruments, laughing. I don't remember if they ever did play the whole piece at the full concert.

Fritz Busch was of course not the only conductor Stockholm had. The most famous maestros of the time gave guest performances. The most memorable appearance was the visit by Arturo Toscanini. It was early 1937 and Toscanini, the world's greatest conductor ever, had arrived from Tel Aviv where he had conducted the Palestine Philharmonic Orchestra founded by Bronislav Huberman. Toscanini, also a non-Jew, had left his native Italy in protest against dictator Mussolini and had gone to Palestine to demonstrate his solidarity with the many Jewish refugee musicians who had been forced to emigrate from Germany and Italy.

I managed to visit Toscanini at his hotel and asked him for his impressions of the Jewish musicians he had just left behind in Tel Aviv. His face, known for its sour and dour expression, turned radiant as he exuded praise and enthusiasm for the struggling but highly gifted musicians. He also gave me his autograph, which is to this day a very rare and coveted collector's item, as Toscanini on principle never gave autographs.

Another guest conductor, Bruno Walter, the Austrian famous for his renditions of Brahms and Mahler, would always be totally exhausted and perspiring after a concert. I remember visiting him in his dressing room after a concert. He sat at the piano and gladly gave me his autograph. I noticed that he wrote his name "Bruno Walter S." Only later did I find out that his original name had been Schlesinger, and the "S" was an abbreviation of his original Jewish name.

The conductor Erich Kleiber made only rare appearances in Stockholm. He, too, gave me his autograph. He later emigrated to Argentina, where today his son is a famous conductor.

Among the many performers whom I learned to admire before World War II were pianists and violinists. Fritz Kreisler, the Jewish virtuoso from Vienna, was a thoroughly charming man. He not only played some of the famous classical violin concertos—especially that of Felix Mendelssohn, the grandson of the famous Jewish philosopher Moses Mendelssohn—but also his own compositions, which have become among the most popular pieces of many violinists' repertoires today. Interestingly, the autograph that he gave me shows that he wrote the "F" in "Fritz" in the form of a G key. This was either done as a deliberate homage to music, or by habit of seeing the G key all his life in his music scores. His rendition of Mendelssohn's E Minor Violin Concerto was a simply unforgettable experience. This concerto has remained my great favorite.

Yehudi Menuhin came to Stockholm in April 1940—just before the Nazi invasion of Denmark and Norway. His concert fell on Pesach, which of course annoyed me. I took courage and wrote him a letter appealing to him to change the date of the concert so that Pesach-observing Jews could attend. He replied in a very courteous postcard in which he assured me that next year he would be careful not to have any conflict with a Jewish holiday. Of course, there was no next year, or the year after or the year after that—the war had taken over Europe and the world.

The great Polish-Jewish pianist, Artur Rubinstein, came to Stockholm shortly before the war. I was overwhelmed with his brilliant piano playing. He gave me an autograph, which I treasure. After the war, he steadfastly refused to step on German soil where so many of his relatives had been killed. He severely criticized Yehudi Menuhin, the Jerusalem-born former child protege, who immediately after the war gave concerts in Germany. I saw Rubinstein again many years later in Paris, but he was then very old and pale, and almost blind.

A pianist whom I only heard a few years ago was Vladimir Horowitz, the Jewish pianist who was Toscanini's son-in-law. He had just come out of retirement when my wife and I heard him in London; he died shortly thereafter.

In 1938 Sergei Rachmaninov, the Russian composer, came to Stockholm and played one of his famous piano concertos. It is of course not often that a composer plays his own composition, but when that happens you can be sure to hear the correct way the composer meant his piece to be played. He had left his native land right after the Russian Revolution in 1917 and had settled in the United States, where he died in 1943.

Sweden is actually a very fertile country for composers. Most of them are unknown outside Sweden, but since they often draw on well-known Swedish folk songs, their compositions are popular at home. I once met Wilhelm Petterson-

Berger, Sweden's leading composer. Beyond his autograph that he gave me, I have no recollection of the encounter.

My dream had always been to be responsible for an important composition and to promote such a musical venture myself. The opportunity arose when my wife and I sought a fitting way to memorialize our late son Jamie, *z"l*, who had been a great lover of music.

His favorite composition was Beethoven's Fantasy in C Major for Piano, Orchestra and Choir.

This piece was a forerunner of Beethoven's Ninth Symphony, in which a choir supplements the musical instruments. The piece begins with a hauntingly beautiful piano recital, which after a while flows into a full orchestra. Finally a choir chimes in repeating a most singable theme.

We therefore chose a similar form to honor Jamie: an oratorium for orchestra, tenor, children's choir and narrator. The oratorium is called *"Tseror Hachayim"* ("The Cycle Of Life") and describes the various phases in a Jew's life, using melodies of Jewish holidays and verses from the Tenach and Midrashim. *"Tseror Hachayim"* is a most unique and moving composition, which has been performed a few times in New York and Israel. In fact, it was chosen by Israeli television as the concert piece on the 1993 Memorial Day program and was watched on television by the whole nation of Israel—a great tribute to Jamie's memory.

Thus music, from my earliest childhood on until this very day, has played an important part in my life, and I am thrilled that my wife, my daughters and their children are unusually musical.

# Mrs. Albright: You Can Be Proud of Your Centuries of Jewish Ancestors

In the current flood of press comments on the revelations that Mrs. Albright—the new Secretary of State—has Jewish ancestors, it has been reported that she seems quite a bit shaken up by the revelations. She is quoted to have said, "It is the duality I will have to live with for the rest of my life." References are made to her "Jewish roots" and her "Jewish ancestry." Such expressions seem to remove her from her true identity. Her mother, grandmother and no doubt all the mothers before them, were good Jewish women. In Jewish law, you are a Jew when your mother is Jewish—in her case, there is no evidence of a single Christian in her family tree. So, she is 100% Jewish.

To be a Prague or Bohemian Jew is the highest badge of honor and pride. No European Jewish community had a more glorious history, albeit sprinkled with much suffering meted out by the Christian church. Jews came to Bohemia almost 800 years ago, and despite occasional expulsions and book burnings, they reached unmatched heights in the religious, cultural, financial and political world.

The pride of Prague Jews in their ancient history was driven home to me during a visit to Prague on Purim. Different from most other communities, where the Megilah is read on the 14th day of Adar, in Prague, as I found out there, they read it on an additional day, Shushan Purim, the 15th of Adar, to prove according to Jewish law that Jews lived there already in a walled city, in the days of Joshua of the Bible.

During these many centuries the Jews of Prague produced the greatest minds in science, astronomy, Talmud, music, literature and statecraft. Tycho de Brahe, the Danish born astronomer, lived in Prague in the 16th century in the company of the brilliant Jewish astronomer David Gans. Jewish soldiers defended Prague against the onslaught of the Protestant Swedish armies in the 30 Year War. (As a reward, the government gave the Jews the so-called "Swedish flag" still displayed in the Altneuschul.)

The brilliance of mind of the great Prague Talmudists are of course legend: The Maharil, the Maharal, the fabled Rabbi Yehuda Loew ben Betzalel (reputed creator of the Golem), Yeheskiel Landau (Noda Biyehuda), David Oppenheimer (statesman, Talmudist, book collector), Rabbi Lippman Heller (Tosfot Yom Tov), Rabbi Zerach Eidlitz (Talmudist, astronomer and mathematician), Rabbi Jonathan Eybenschütz (Talmudist, kabbalist, community leader)—all scions of the academies of Prague. In the field of every science and art, Prague Jews excelled. Franz Kafka, the eminent modern novelist, was a product of Prague, and so was Gustav Mahler, the composer.

Is it surprising that Mrs. Albright mirrors the same qualities of the heritage of this overwhelming cultural inheritance, which is still so strong to this day? The charm, wit, intellect, acumen of Mrs. Albright can therefore be traced to this enormous Jewish patrimony so typical for Jews of Prague and Bohemia. She has every reason to be immensely proud, and the American people should be grateful to benefit from her, as Secretary of State, with such a rich store of the highest degree of culture and diplomatic skill.

It is interesting to note that past generations of leading Prague Jews excelled in statecraft: Rabbi Wolf Wertheimer and Rabbi David Oppenheimer were outstanding court Jews who carried out great political missions. When Empress Maria Teresa (1717-1780) issued an edict for the expulsion of Jews from Prague, the Court Jews of all European countries united—a first in Jewish history—under the leadership of the leading Prague Jews, to oppose the edict and achieve its cancellation despite enormous obstacles. The heritage of such diplomatic acumen is certainly a good antecedent for Mrs. Albright.
I own Hebrew books printed in Prague before America was settled by Europeans. From the beginning of the 16th century, Jewish book printers were actively printing Biblical and Talmudic books in contravening the Papal edict by Pope Clemens VIII to have all Jewish books confiscated and burned!

Among the many fascinating Jewish monuments in Prague which have survived every misfortune in history, the most gripping is without a doubt the Altneuschul built over 800 years ago. This unique structure, following the Gothic style, seems to hold the very spirit of the vanished generations. I would recommend Mrs. Albright to pay a visit to that fabled building and steep in the message of the past centuries. It will be an experience which—next to visiting the Wall in Jerusalem—remains unforgettable for life!
But, I think we who are proud of our Jewish heritage—regardless of the sufferings we have endured—should welcome her back into our fold with joy and love, and assure her that it is not a burden to be Jewish, least of all to be a Czech Jew.

The Jews of Czechoslovakia—mainly Bohemia and Moravia but always centered in Prague—had an outstanding history of religious, intellectual, financial and political and military achievements. The Jewish ties to Prague are simply overwhelming. The Jews lived there for centuries and their fate was always closely tied in with the history of the city as a whole. Of course, tales about the Golem and the Maharal ("Der hohe Rabbi Löw") are part of the Czech patrimony. The nearby Jewish town hall, from the 1700's complete with a clock which runs "backward," reminds the visitor of the "Noda Biyehuda," Rabbi Yehezkel Landau. The nearby cemetery is a unique site in the Jewish world. Hundreds upon hundreds of ancient Jewish tombstones—some stacked one upon the other—bespeak past generations of great Rabbis, community leaders, and scholars. The tomb of the Maharal is at the center of this, one of the most important sites in Jewish Europe. Of course, pilgrims constantly go there to pray at his grave.

The Jewish Museum is a very hallowed structure—it was started at the command of the Nazis, as a "memorial" over the "perished" Jewish people. Hundreds of Jews were ordered to arrange all exhibits describing the Jewish ceremonials during the year. Many of them hoped to be spared death, but in the end, all were gassed. Maybe Mrs. Albright's ancestors were among them. One display is especially significant: the white cloak of Shlomo Molcho, a Portuguese Jew forced into conversion, but who, in the 16th century had re-converted to Judaism, and followed David Reubeni, the pseudo-Moshiach. Molcho was burnt at the stake by the Church when the Christians feared that his conversion to Judaism would lead to a mass movement to Judaism among the Christian population.

The Jews of Prague were known for their advance science of astronomy. The Christian astronomers such as Tycho de Brahe learnt their science from Jews.

Prague had enormous collections of Hebrew books. The famous David Oppenheim, rabbi and book collector, left behind more that 6000 volumes when he died in the 18th century. These books are now in the Bodleian Library in Oxford.

I own many manuscripts written by brilliant Talmudists who lived in Prague. Some I have published, some still await publication. All bespeak an unbelievably high level of intellectual brilliance, and religious piety. Prague sent many of its rabbinic personalities to other countries to lead the Yeshivot there. Thus, Prague could properly be called an "*Ir v'em be Yisrael*," a town and mother in Israel.

The war put an end to this precious community. Yet after the war, it was revived. Czech Jews were extremely important in helping the young State of Israel to defend itself against the murderous onslaughts of Arabs. The famous Czech heavy Skoda industry contributed weapons and planes to the fledgling country. Since the Czechs themselves had successfully achieved independence from the Habsburg empire of Austria–Hungary, under the leadership of the great Czech patriot Thomas Mazaryk, supported by President Woodrow Wilson, they knew how to appreciate the efforts of the Jews to recreate their own independent state. They had full sympathy with the Jews, and felt complete solidarity. I am sure that these memories will find an echo in Mrs. Albright. She will understand the danger of harboring the Nazi Sudeten Germans inside the country, who therefore had to be deported. The parallel with the murderous Arabs with aspirations to undo Israel should thus be clearer to her.

Again, welcome back to your exalted Jewish roots, Mrs. Albright.

# Communities

To be a Jew means being one with Jews everywhere. I have been privileged to visit a mass of Jewish communities in Europe, North and South America, Africa and Asia. My impressions of some of them are contained in this section. The fascinating lives and customs of some of these communities help enrich our own appreciation of our rich history. I hope this section will encourage my readers to continue my own search for our brethren in far-flung corners of the world and thereby strengthen our resolve—"Haverim kol Yisrael."

## Williamsburg, 1940

Many people, when they hear the name "Williamsburg," think of the old colonial town in Virginia. Others may associate the name with the aircraft carrier of the same name. But to the rest of us, Williamsburg is that part of Brooklyn where over 50 years ago Jewish life started sprouting, with an influence of over several generations.

My own exposure to Williamsburg came shortly after I arrived in this country in May 1940. My old friend from our family's days in Hamburg, Rav Walter (Zeev) Gotthold, was in charge of finding a suitable yeshiva for me. He had first taken me to Yeshivat R. Yitzchak Elchanan, but for some reason the right "chemistry" was not there. My only knowledge of a yeshiva was what I had heard from my brothers Bert and Gabriel and from my teacher Rav Shlomo Wolbe, who had spent some years in the Mir Yeshiva in Poland and who gave me a picture—perhaps glorified—of what a yeshiva is like.

So my attention was diverted to the Mesivta Torah Vodaat which at that time was located at 515 Bedford Avenue in the Williamsburg section of Brooklyn. In those days Williamsburg had very few chasidim and few black hats. The Mesivta was under the influence of the Lithuanians. Even its leader, Mr. Feivel Mendlovitz, himself a Hungarian, chose Lithuanian teachers and *roshei yeshiva*.

The process of my acclimatization was not easy. My preparations for Gemara were limited, since in Sweden there was no Jewish education. I was placed in a class headed by Rav Pam, who was then a clean-shaven recent college graduate. My fellow students were all much younger than I. I took on a private tutor who helped me a great deal in advancing. My memories of Williamsburg relate more to Jewish life there as a whole than to my own education. The impact of the community on me was intense. I used every opportunity to visit great men, to participate in gatherings and to absorb the yeshiva spirit.

My activities were influenced by the tragic events in Europe. I tried to be helpful in *hatzalah* (rescue) work. Rav Abraham Kalmanowitz, called by some "The Last *Shtadlan* (intercessor),'' was close to me. He helped set up a network of *hatzalah* linked to my father in Sweden. Rav Kalmanowitz was constantly working in Washington and New York to save as many yeshivot in Lithuania from destruction as possible. Much of the work took place in the offices of the Agudah, at 5 Beekman Street, from where I placed my calls to Sweden to transmit messages and arrange money transfers for food packages and other rescue operations, through my father in Stockholm.

But what impressed me enormously was that with all his weighty contacts in so many parts of the world, he did not stop being a *rosh yeshiva*. I remember well the *shiurim* (classes) he delivered before the whole student body of the Mesivta; he blended his *shiurim* with *mussar* (ethics). In this manner he helped to transmit to the United States the Lithuanian traditions which we all tried to salvage.

Being cut off from my family, I was fortunate that my grandmother, Mrs. Sophie Taub, and my brother, Bert, lived in Manhattan and offered me hospitality most Sabbaths. In the beginning I roomed in Washington Heights in Manhattan and traveled every day by subway (5 cents) and streetcar (2 cents) to Williamsburg.

After a while I took a room on Keap Street in Williamsburg to save traveling time. It allowed me more time to get acquainted with the many personalities at the yeshiva. My routine became standardized. To enter the classroom at the Mesivta, each student had to pass the scrutiny of Mr. Feivel Mendlovitz, who was a very strict taskmaster and did not tolerate lateness. There was also Dr. Lyman, head of the English department, who also checked on each student's studies and conduct.

Although I had sufficient credits from my Swedish school, I had to supplement them with English and civics courses. I had very fine fellow students. Among them were Louis Glick, with whom I have maintained a close friendship during all these years. He is a great supporter of Torah and enormously generous in his philanthropy. Another fellow student was Eliyah Schwei, today one of the great luminaries in the world of Torah. He heads the Philadelphia Yeshiva but exerts deep influence the world over. Some of the greatest Torah sages consult him.

The Mesivta at that time was a relatively small yeshiva. Rav Shlomo Heyman, its head, was a disciple of Reb Chaim Soloveitchik. Although at my level I had little contact with him, it was inspiring to watch him take walks with his "*Beis Hamedrash*" students. His excitement over every bit of Torah was contagious.

The other great men at the Mesivta at that time included R. Gedalia Shor, R. Dovid Bender, and Rav Quinn. As the war proceeded, some of the great men of Torah were able to venture across the ocean to America: Chief Rabbi Yitzchak Isaac Halevy Herzog came all the way from Yerushalyim and delivered a *shiur* in the Mesivta before an enthusiastic audience. Shortly before that, the Mesivta itself moved to a new location, on South Third Street. That move was a memorable manifestation, with Torah Scrolls being carried under canopies, singing and music. In the new building the Mesivta grew rapidly. A few years later it had to move again to Ocean Parkway.

One of the great personalities living in Williamsburg was the aged R. Simche Soloveitchik, the half brother of Reb Chaim. He was over 90 years of age when I attended his Friday night talks. He always wore an impeccable black top hat, and his words of Torah remained in my memory.

One Sunday Mr. Mendlovitz invited me to join him in Spring Valley, N.Y., for a meeting about the establishment of a new organization: Torah Umesorah. Until this day I don't know why he singled me out to join in this meeting, which was to inaugurate the start of this enormously important educational organization. He explained to a few of us that since the European sources of Jewish education were being destroyed, they must be replaced with American resources. He expressed his enthusiasm for American yeshiva students, whom he considered superior even to the European ones.

Toward the end of the year, refugees from Europe began arriving. Of course they were pitifully few and the tragedy of the vanishing European Jews became distressingly clear. One family which arrived from Lithuania was the Leshinsky family. The mother, Mrs. Bas Sheva, was a legendary personality in the Mir. She was a real *mashgiach* (supervisor of students) with all the *mussar* qualifications. Yeshiva students would flock around her to hear her *shmuessen* (talks).

A special treat was in store for me when I changed rooms and moved closer to the apartment of the Moshitzer Rebbe, Rav Taub. This great composer of *niggunim* (chassidic melodies) and master in presenting his music had his apartment right across from my own. During the summer, through my open window, I used to listen to his Friday night gatherings. The rebbe divided his chasidim into sections, and like a conductor, he directed their singing in harmony.

Another interesting personality in Williamsburg was Dr. Fritz Neuberger, the favorite physician of the yeshiva world. A native of Germany, he and his family had settled on Bedford Avenue. Dr. Neuberger was a very erudite and learned person and impressed me a great deal.

After a year I decided to seek another location. Frankly, conditions in Williamsburg were so cramped—there was so little air and nature—that I felt choked. One day, in a small square near Bedford Avenue I spotted a tree that had a plate placed around it, saying simply, "Tree." That did it! Coming from the huge forests and natural resources of Sweden, I felt I had to find some location with more air, trees and flowers. Having partaken of the educational advantages of Williamsburg, I now gave preference to Baltimore after a visit there with Rav Gotthold, my mentor.

And so, in August 1941, I moved to Baltimore and enrolled in the Ner Israel Rabbinical College.

Williamsburg, like so many other sections of New York, has gone through several changes. After World War I it was known as a rather affluent German-Irish area. When Orthodox Jews moved in, there was a transition. Today, the chasidic element predominates. Satmar and other communities set the tone. The original yeshivot have moved out, but I am grateful that I participated in life in Williamsburg at a much earlier and quieter stage. No doubt Williamsburg will always remain an important source for Yiddishkeit in America.

# Baltimore Half a Century Ago

I ended my column last week, titled "Williamsburg, 1940," with my move from Mesivta Torah Vodaat in the Williamsburg section of Brooklyn to Ner Israel Rabbinical College (NIRC) in Baltimore. During the year I spent at Torah Vodaat, I had advanced from Rav Pam's class, the lowest class in the Mesivta, quite a few ranks higher in the Mesivta hierarchy. I would have entered the *beth hamedrash* if I had stayed on.

My initial impression of Balimore was that the NIRC was a much smaller and more compact Yeshiva than the Mesivta was, so the learning would benefit. At that time there were basically only two classes in Baltimore: the *beth hamedrash* under the rosh yeshiva, Rav Jacob Ruderman, and the lower class, under the *mashgiach*, Rav Yitzchok Boruchson. During my first two years in Baltimore I attended Rav Boruchson's *shiur* which pleased me to no end. (Thereafter I was promoted to the *beth hamedrash*.) Only two years previously Rav Boruchson had visited my father in Stockholm on behalf of the Slobodka Yeshiva. I have retained a very vivid memory of his unusually friendly, almost shining face, which radiated all the warm qualities of *mussar*. And now I was a disciple in his *shiur*. I also shared my meals with Rav Boruchson, which placed me very near this great *baal mussar*.

As the years passed, Rav Boruchson, cut off from his family back in Slobodka, asked me often to go to New York for him and try to send food packages to his hometown. There were German organizations that claimed they could make such deliveries through enemy lines and war fronts. Although certificates came back after months of waiting, claiming to be receipts for Rav Boruchson, I could easily see that they were forgeries to entice him to send more packages. I could not bring myself to tell my teacher of this observation, for it was his last hope of being in contact with his wife and children. (After the war, when I met his surviving children, they denied having ever received any packages.)

The Yeshiva was housed in a very primitive wood building on Forest Park Avenue. Yet in later years the students would agree that the learning was more intensive when sitting on a hard wooden bench than it was in more comfortable facilities. In fact, Rav Boruchson admonished his students not to sit on comfortable chairs or sofas during davening but to move to bare wooden benches. He told us that the feeling physically comfortable was an impediment to having true religious feelings.

Baltimore was the scene where important Torah scholars came to visit. Among them was Rav Eliezer Silver of Cincinnati, who would don a black top hat before delivering a *shiur* in our Yeshiva. Others were Rav Rif of Camden, N. J., and Rav Sheftel Kramer, the father of Rebbetzin Ruderman. Rav Ruderman himself was exemplary in his modesty. He was not ashamed to confide to his students that he considered a great Torah sage in Baltimore, Rav Forschlager, his true teacher and mentor. On some occasions Rav Ruderman would walk for more than an hour to visit his great teacher. This happened especially on Sukkot, as Rav Forschlager had the only *esrog* from the Holy Land.

The Beth Hamedrash in Baltimore was made up of outstanding students. Among them was Rav Moshe Sherer, brother-in-law of the legendary Michael Tress. After the latter's death, Rav Sherer has become the shining example of a *shtadlan* (public servant) concerned with the fate of every Jew. The work started by Mike Tress during the war—when rescue work was so essential for the survival of Jewry, especially Torah Jewry—and continued to this day by Rav Moshe Sherer, is of historic proportions.

In those days, rescue work was not institutionalized by professionals as it is today, but was entirely based on individual efforts, in the old *shtadlan* tradition. Yet Rav Ruderman considered it the duty of yeshiva students to apply themselves to learning only rather than going out in the world to do rescue work. He believed that such intensive learning was doing more to save European Jewry. Fortunately for me, I had before me the examples of the giants in rescue work and was personally involved with them, so I could judge how important their work was.

Rav Ruderman, the great *rosh yeshiva* and *talmid chacham*, was a bit of an enigma when it came to secular studies. In my own case, he approved of my attending classes at Johns Hopkins University under the world-famous Bible scholar Professor William Foxwell Albright, even though Bible criticism was part of the curriculum. On the other hand, I remember that he refused to examine the just-published essay by Rav J. B. Soloveitchik, "Ish haHalachah," because he had spotted a footnote quoting Soeren Kierkegaard, the Christian Danish theologian.

Among the personalities I remember from those days in Baltimore was Rav Shimon Schwab, who headed a German congregation and also occasionally gave classes in the Yeshiva. Another was my teacher in Arabic and Jewish philosophy at Johns Hopkins, Rabbi Samuel Rosenblatt, son of the famous Cantor Yossele Rosenblatt. Dr. Bernard Lander, today a tremendous force throughout the world in establishing institutions of Jewish learning, back in 1941 headed a small synagogue in the Park Heights section of Baltimore.

Soon after I came to Baltimore, the Yeshiva made plans to acquire a new building on Garrison Boulevard. There were some seventy students when I arrived. At that time there were no black hats, not even beards, nor any chasidim, among the students. The Lithuanian influence, especially by the *mussar* teachings of the Mir Yeshiva, dictated that any outer demonstrations of *frumkeit* (piety)—like black clothes, *peyes*, etc.—were signs of *gayve* (haughtiness) and had to be shunned. Hence the emphasis on light-colored suits and hats and clean-shaven faces—even among the oldest *talmidim*. All that has changed dramatically.

The power behind the growth of NIRC was Rav Naftoli Neuberger, a dynamic and brilliant executive director. His amazing connections in Washington enabled him to win for the Yeshiva grants and funds otherwise hardly known to Orthodox institutions. Rabbi Neuberger had studied in the Mirrer Yeshiva in Europe at the time my brothers Bert and Gabriel studied there, so I have followed his career for over 60 years. Fortunately, his talents and genuis have spilled over to his sons, who are active in the support of the Yeshiva.

Soon the stone-laying of the new building took place. I remember vividly how Theodore Roosevelt McKeldin—the mayor of Baltimore and later governor of Maryland—made a speech there, in which he used the only "Jewish" passage he could quote, namely Psalm 23: "The Lord is my shepherd I shall not want..." with a thick Irish brogue.

I used Baltimore's proximity to Washington often for visits to the various government war offices, as I tried everything to alleviate the plight of my parents, who were trapped in "neutral" Sweden. Sweden miraculously escaped being touched by Hitler and played an important role in rescuing hundreds of yeshiva students, who were first taken to Japan and later to Australia and the United States. Washington in wartime was certainly a different place than today. Foreign officers—Russian, Chinese, British, French—in their colorful uniforms were seen everywhere. Temporary, prefabricated buildings filled every open space in Washington to house the growing bureaucracy.

Baltimore, more provincial than New York, had only limited cosmopolitan cultural life. Some of the old Jewish families were of German origin, such as the Adler, Ney and Strauss families. They were Othrodox and supported Rav Ruderman. I was intrigued to discover that the Peabody Musical Institute, the oldest academy of its kind in Baltimore, was founded in the 1860s by a fellow Scandinavian, a Danish Jewish composer by the name of Emmerich. I started working on his biography and still hope to complete it one day. Emmerich is the name of a well-known Danish-German-Dutch rabbinical family.

I recently acquired a historical document that shows how Sir Moses Montefiore was part of the growth of the Jewish community in Baltimore. The letter, signed by the great British-Jewish benefactor, is dated 1872 and is a receipt for donations to the collection fund of R. Shmuel Salant, the leading Ashkenazic rabbi in Jerusalem. The donors are the following Baltimore congregations: Shevet Achim; Chevrat Aron Yisrael; Chizzuk Emunah; and Sheerith Yisrael. Of these, two congregations still exist. The money was earmarked for distribution among "the poor who live in our Holy Land." Thus the well-known Baltimore tradition of tzedaka is documented from the earliest times and makes the community exemplary until this day.

The first Baltimore Jews benefited from the liberal rule instituted by Lord Baltimore, the colonial governor in the British colony of Maryland. They were Sefardic and German Jews who brought Reform Judaism with them. As more waves of immigrants arrived, Orthodoxy gained an important foothold. A few of the old synagogues, which were congregated around East Baltimore Street downtown, can still be seen, but most have moved uptown and beyond where beautiful residential areas exist, including some fine parks—which made Baltimore very attractive to me.

Since Baltimore has a very humid climate during the summer, I would take the opportunity to go north, where I visited Boston and took courses at Harvard University. My trips to Boston afforded me the opportunity of spending much time with Rabbi J. B. Soleveitchik, who has remained an inspiration throughout my life. When I first met him he was a 37-year-old scholar who had recently come from Berlin. He loved the German language and preferred to converse with me in German.

Thinking back half-a-century, I am struck at how the Jewish community, and especially the Yeshiva, made newcomers feel at home. I am grateful that I benefited from this warm and friendly atmosphere. It alleviated somewhat the fright and worry that the horrible war years brought with them. And it offered a calm background for intensive studies, whether in the yeshiva or in the university, and I made the best of both worlds.

# Memories of Jewish Life In Boston 50 Years Ago

A very significant book has just been published which can teach us all a telling lesson, entitled *The Death of an American Jewish Community*, by Hillel Levine and Lawrence Harmon (Maxwell Macmillan Co. Inc., New York, 1992). The community the book talks about is that part of Boston—Roxbury, Dorchester, and Mattapan—where most of Boston's Jews lived decades ago. After a combination of organized black rioting, vandalism, violence, anti-Semitic outbursts and blockbusting, an exodus of Jews took place in just over two years, 1968–70. Today the area is totally black. The death of this Jewish area took place some 25 years before the disturbances in Crown Heights and Los Angeles. Jewish leaders should have learned a lesson and been forewarned so that the survival of Jewish sections elsewhere could be assured. Too many parallels to be accidental can be drawn between what happened in Boston with what happened later elsewhere. It is not, however, too late to learn that lesson, especially when one hears so much about new programs which offer black underprivileged groups "home ownership opportunities." The book encapsulates what this meant in Boston in the 60's: "Under the guise of expanding home ownership opportunities for the city's black community, the heads of 22 Boston savings banks were complicit in establishing a limited and carefully well-defined inner-city district within which blacks could obtain the attractive, federally insured housing loans. Falling exclusively within the defined district was almost the entire of Boston's Jewish community, an unproductive neighborhood for the city's bankers because so many of the residents had paid off their mortgages. By forcing blacks with home ownership aspirations to compete in a limited geographic area, the banks created an eruption of panic selling, blockbusting, street violence and rage." You can clearly see why every Jew concerned with recent events should read and study this book.

In short, the death of Jewish neighborhoods was not part of the traditional "recycling" of ethnic groups, as perhaps was the case with Harlem, which 70 years ago was considered an affluent Jewish neighborhood. (I should know, because when my own grandmother moved from East Broadway on the Lower East Side to 118th Street, my family rejoiced at her social advancement.) No, the Boston tragedy was the result of political and social forces which saw in Jewish neighborhoods an easy target and a solution for placating black demands, to which no meaningful Jewish leadership stood up.

Since I am an eyewitness to the Boston Jewish communities of long ago, before the tragedy unfolded, I see it my duty to share some reminiscences of that long-forgotten period.

When I came to this country in 1940 as a youngster, I had heard about the greatness of Rabbi J. B. Soloveitchik and wanted to visit him. My good friend Walter (Zev) Gotthold, whom I had known since childhood and whom I still meet regularly in Jerusalem, was a student of Rabbi Soloveitchik's as part of a small group of yeshiva men, mostly recent arrivals from war-torn Europe, with whom the Rov tried to form a yeshiva. I took the train to Boston just after Succot. At this point I must tell a comical story: My English at the time was less than sufficient, as were also my finances. On the train I boarded the restaurant car and took a look at the menu. The prices were staggering: $1 or $1.50 for most dishes (this was at a time when *The New York Times* cost 3 cents, a bottle of milk cost 8 cents and letter postage was 3 cents). I scanned the menu for something affordable—there it was: "dressing—15 cents." I had never heard the word "dressing" and did not know what it meant, but the price was attractive. I pointed at it on the menu to the waiter, who hesitated to take my order, somewhat inexplicably to me. "I insist!" I said. The waiter returned with a tiny jar of dressing on a giant silver platter which he served me with the grandest of dramatic gestures!

During that visit, and again during 1942 and 1943, I lived in Roxbury. The Rov, who had arrived in Boston in 1932, lived in Roxbury, too. He held no official title in town, and his official duties were limited to exercising "*hashgachah*" on the kashrut of the meat, an assignment he had taken over from Rabbi Eliezer Silver of Cincinnati, Ohio, who had previously included Boston in his supervisory duties. Of course, the Rov was for all practical purposes the Chief Rabbi of Boston. In 1935 he was a candidate for the post of Chief Rabbi of Tel Aviv. I own a remarkable document: a letter of recommendation for the Rov by his own father, Reb Moshe Soloveitchik, to the selection committee in Tel Aviv. The 8-page letter is a testimony to the prophetic powers which Reb Moshe must have had: in it he describes in detail the unparalleled talents, qualifications and genius of his son, and predicts his worldwide role as a leader and molder of generations, with his unmatched excellence in Jewish and secular learning. Fortunately for this country, he lost the election, and Rav Amiel of Antwerp was chosen for the position in Tel Aviv.

Boston, as a city, hardly exists. It is really a cluster of towns which since colonial days grew into one urban fabric: Chelsea, Newton, Cambridge, Malden, Brookline, Charlestown, Sommerville, etc. But to me Roxbury and Dorchester spelled Boston. The only other community of interest to me was Cambridge, where I attended a few summer terms at Harvard University. On my first visit the Rov lived in Roxbury; on later visits I found that he had moved to Dorchester, a somewhat more affluent section then. Today he lives in Brookline.

Roxbury has a main thoroughfare, Blue Hill Avenue, where practically all shops were Jewish-owned, among them the GG Delicatessen, a popular meeting spot for Jews. Many an evening I would meet there with my friends and discuss our respective accomplishments in our studies for the day.

During the three years that I visited Roxbury, I had the privilege to spend much time in the house of the Rov, especially on the Sabbath. There were memorable occasions when a group of us would be taken by him on a walk through Franklin Park. We would then sit down on a bench and listen to his discourses in philosophy, sometimes on Spinoza, sometimes on Greek philosophy, and other subjects as well. I remember one such occasion, when as we sat near the golf course, suddenly a shiny white golf ball landed a few feet away from us. Chaim, the Rov's little son, jumped up, ready to pick up the ball, when the Rov got very agitated and cried out: "You must not touch it; don't take it!" I felt sorry for little Chaim and in the process, forgot to ask the Rov for the exact halachic reasons for his excitement. Thinking that the traumatic incident would leave a mark on the child, I asked Chaim, many years later, if he remembered the incident. To my surprise, he did not.

Once while taking a Shabbat afternoon walk along Blue Hill Avenue with the Rov, he decided to enter a large shul on the spur of the moment. The people in the shul were waiting to daven *minchah*. The startled rabbi invited the Rov, who promptly walked up to the *bimah* and delivered a scathing piece of criticism of the rabbi of the shul. I do not remember the subject of the criticism, but the incident showed that the Rov had informal jurisdiction over any Orthodox synagogue in Boston.

I often sat at the Rov's table for *shalosh seudos*. He would not only talk on Torah learning, but also on philosophy. Soeren Kierkegaard, the 19th century Danish philosopher, was often discussed by him. The Rov had just published his significant essay "*Ish ha-Halacha*," a masterly portrait of his grandfather, Reb Chaim Brisker. There too, he quoted Kierkegaard. (As a result, a certain Rosh Yeshiva told me he would not even read the essay.)

Tonya, the Rebbetzin, a towering lady with a stern face but full of charm and warmth, was the mistress of the household. Being fluent in Russian she explained to me, as I remember, that the name Soloveitchik means "nightingale." It was she who, as soon as Shabbat was over, went down to get the newspaper of the day. And it was she who almost single-handedly built and maintained the Maimonides Day School which till this day is the leading Day School in New England.

An unusual practice had developed during the war years: after Shabbat, rabbinic and lay leaders of Boston would gather in the Rov's house. He would place a globe in the middle of the living room, and would give his analysis of the war campaigns of the week on the various far-flung fronts in the war against Hitler and Japan. I remember particularly how he predicted General MacArthur's forthcoming campaigns in the Pacific.

Recalling his student years in Berlin, the Rov would often converse with me in German. He extolled Reb Chaim Heller, who also lived in Berlin at the same time as the Rov, as his great teacher. The Rov revered Reb Chaim, especially when it came to knowledge of the Tanach. When Reb Chaim would deliver special public lectures at the Pennsylvania Hotel in New York on Biblical themes, the Rov would come and "sit at his feet," like any other student.

In January 1941, Reb Moshe passed away. I was among the hundreds of yeshiva students who came by bus from the few yeshivos in existence then, to attend the *hesped* in the Lampert Auditorium of Yeshiva College (now Yeshiva University). One hesped after the other was delivered, but the Rov's own was, of course, the most significant. Some speakers called on the leadership of the yeshiva to appoint Reb Yoshe Ber on the spot as his father's successor. (The powers in the establishment were unmoved, however, and Rabbi Shmuel Belkin was appointed instead.) From that time on, the Rov travelled each week to New York to deliver the *shiur* to his class. His plans for a yeshiva in Boston evaporated. He was simply not as good an organizer as his wife.

My main memories from Boston of these many years ago concern understandably the contacts I was privileged to have with the Rov. Of course, I understood initially very little of what he said. That understanding grew somewhat with the years. I only regret that I was never equipped to understand him fully. Others were, and his wisdom has been recorded and partially published. He once told me that in his family, the printing of *sefarim* was shunned. All we have from his grandfather is a thin book holding some shiurim noted down by disciples. Likewise, the Rov has been very reluctant to permit the printing of his lectures and shiurim. If we find a book bearing his name, we must be careful to inquire whether it really has his approval and authorization.

But Boston also offered me exposure to other personalities. At Harvard my teacher in philosophy was Professor Uhlich, whose main call to fame was his wife, Elsa Brandstroem, a world-renowned fighter for human rights during World War I, when human rights were not yet heard of. I had heard of her as the "Swedish Angel of Siberia," because of her work among war prisoners during the War of 1914–1918. When I visited Frankfurt in 1938, I stayed with friends on the Elsa Brandstroem Strasse. I was, of course, thrilled to meet her in person and treasured every opportunity when Professor Uhlich invited me to his home where I could chat with his famous wife in Swedish. I had signed up to take courses in Jewish philosophy under Professor Harry Austryn Wolfson, the famous scholar whose books on Spinoza, Crescas and other Jewish philosophers were classics.. However, unbeknownst to me, Professor Wolfson hated teaching and always found excuses for the classes to be cancelled. I remember visiting him in his little office, filled with books, in the basement of the Widener Library. I was flattered when many years later he came to attend a lecture of mine when I addressed the Society of Jewish Bibliophiles in Boston about my own Hebrew manuscript library.

A happy interlude in my life was when I met a young couple, just recently married, who played an important role in my life: Moe and Shirley Feuerstein. Moe had in 1936 attended the same Jewish boarding school in Switzerland which I attended in 1938: Ascher's Institute in Bex-les-Bains, so we shared some common memories. Moe and Shirley not only extended their generous hospitality to me, but also engaged in profound, meaningful discussions. Moe soon became an enduring leader in Orthodox organizations and movements, and was always an inspiration to me, as I am sure also to countless others. I also met Shirley's parents, patrician Orthodox Jews who left a deep mark on American Orthodoxy. The Feuerstein dynasty, starting with its founder, Samuel Feuerstein, is largely responsible for the Torah Umesorah movement without which there would be little Jewish education throughout the 50 states today.

There were very few Jewish students at Harvard in those years. In fact, most of its past presidents had been rabid anti-Semites who kept the quota of Jewish students to a minimum. Orthodox students were practically non-existent. I remember my problem when Professor Demos, my teacher in Greek philosophy, scheduled a written examination on a Sabbath. The Jewish proctor who, under a Harvard system adopted from the universities of England, was part of the teaching staff for the class, refused to listen to my pleas to move the date or to let me take the test on another day. It was only after I presented my case to the Christian Professor Demos that my request was granted. The Jewish proctor simply did not want to call attention to a Jewish concern.

I never returned to Roxbury or Dorchester. When I visited the Rov for a *shiva* visit when his Rebbetzin passed away, his home was in Brookline. A visit to the old Jewish neighborhood would be too upsetting, I suppose. On top of it I had a personal loss there: In 1952 a crime took the life of Rav Jacob Zuber, who had been my rabbi and a teacher in my native Stockholm, Sweden. A Lubavitcher, born in Russia, he had participated in the underground activities of the Lubavitch network in Communist Russia, till he was called to take up a position in Sweden in 1930. During the War he did a lot to ameliorate the fate of the Holocaust survivors, especially many *agunot* for whom he found halachic solutions to their plight. For all those years he had dreamt about migrating to America. After the War, his dream was fulfilled. He moved to Boston with his family. And then tragedy struck: he was killed by an unidentified black hoodlum, the first sacrifice in a series of violent crimes which led to the flight of Boston's Jews. A few years ago I helped publish his writings as a memorial to a great scholar and a saintly Jew.

Although the old-time Jewish neighborhoods of Boston are "gone with the wind," as so many other Jewish settlements in our history, Jewish life is prospering and growing in other parts of Boston. The eternal survival of our people is never in doubt.

# Worms—One of Our "Mother Cities"

In Hebrew we have a wonderful name for cities which are of cardinal importance in our long history. We call such a city an *"ir va'em be'yisrael,"* literally, a city and a mother in Israel. Worms was one such city which richly deserved this honorary title. All of us have, at one time or another, had an encounter with the ancient Jewish community of Worms, in the German Rhineland. At most Jewish weddings, the text of the *"t'naim"* (terms of the financial marriage arrangements) are read wherein we find a reference to *"chachmey Shum."* Who were they? They were the sages of the early Middle Ages in the cities of Speyer, Worms (called Wermayza or Germayza in Hebrew) and Mainz (called Magentza in Hebrew), abbreviated to Sh.W.M., or *Shum*. These three cities were settled by Jews at the dawn of history. When the Roman armies under Caesar marched up along the Rhine River, Jewish merchants accompanied them and established trading posts all along their route. These grew into communities, eventually encompassing some thousands of souls. Thus by the year 300 C.E. Jewish communities already were established in the Rhineland. By the 11th century the network of such Jewish communities—all outstanding for the high concentration of piety and scholarship (the famous *chasiday Ashkenaz*) encompassed not only the above mentioned three cities, but also Cologne, Durren (Dura in Hebrew), Bonn (Buna in Hebrew), Trier, Frankfurt and many more.

The sages of Speyer, Worms and Mainz were unique in that they had a well organized system of mutual cooperation in all communal and legal matters, so that there was great unanimity among them in all decisions concerning the conduct of their congregants.

While Mainz was famous for the great *paytanim*, composers of liturgical poems, who lived there, like R. Shimon Hagadol and the members of the Kalonymos family, Worms was outstanding for its great Talmudic scholars: Rabbenu Gershom Meor Hagolah, R. Jacob ben Yakar and R. Yitzchak ben Eleazar, their great disciple Rashi, and R. Eliezer ben Yehuda (also known as the Baal Harokeach). The unbelievable tragedy of the First Crusade in 1096 put a temporary end to the Golden Age of Worms, when most of its Jewish inhabitants were brutally massacred by the hordes of murderers unleashed by the Church. Rabbenu Gershom had died shortly before that terrible date, and Rashi, our enduring and beloved teacher, was providentially absent from Worms at the time. He was visiting his mother's vineyards in Troyes, the city of his birth in the Champagne area of today's France.

My own encounter with Worms goes back to 1931, when as a very young child, I accompanied my parents and brothers to Worms. My late father wisely realized that such a visit would make a lasting impression on us. We visited the ancient cemetery outside Worms where we saw the huge tomb of the martyred R. Meir of

Rothenburg, called the Maharam. The Maharam was kidnapped by the German ruler around 1235 and held imprisoned, in wait for a heavy ransom from the Jews who considered him the highest leader and authority in all of Germany. The Maharam, however, forbade his followers to ransom him, lest the Christian rulers make it a habit to kidnap for ransom all Jewish leaders! After 14 years in the Sinsheim castle he died, and several more years passed till his body was ransomed by a humble Jew, who was eventually buried right next to the holy martyr as a reward for his great mitzvah.

I still remember clearly the awe we felt when we visited the ancient synagogue of Worms, with "Rashi's seat" where, according to tradition, Rashi had sat while he wrote his monumental commentaries on the whole Tanach and the Talmud. We also saw with our own eyes the vestige of a miracle which took place there: Rashi's mother, shortly before his birth, was walking along the narrow alley behind the synagogue when a farmer with a carriage heavily laden with hay came charging down at top speed. Without doubt she would have been crushed to death by the carriage, but miraculously, the wall gave in and formed a niche, big enough to hold and protect Rashi's mother! The incident has been recorded in many Jewish sources, including an old Yemenite manuscript, written in Judeo-Arabic, which I possess. And there I saw that very niche, the bricks of the synagogue wall having gently bent towards the inside!

Because of this early experience, I have always held the words and works of Rashi to be especially precious; he is somehow a living teacher to me. And recently I became further attached to this "mother city in Israel" by the acquisition of two important manuscripts which I have now published. These manuscripts record the astounding communal and rabbinic structure of the religious life of Worms throughout centuries. Worms was unique in that all customs and rules were carefully recorded from generation to generation. By studying these records we gain a very clear and graphic picture of the life of an unusually pious and peaceful community—disrupted only by the occasional pogroms and expulsions organized by the Church.

Let me share with you some of the insights which my manuscripts allow us to glean. Reb Yehuda Leib Kirchheim, born in the mid-17th century, wrote a voluminous book on the *minhagim* of Worms. He displayed an unusual ability to grasp and encompass events covering several centuries: the earliest entry I found records an event in the year 960 C.E., and the last, in the year 1631 C.E. During the intervening years Worms had the distinction that the Christian authorities, out of respect for the superior Jewish community in their midst, awarded the Jews the right to have an *"Epicopus Judaeorum"* or *"Judenbischof"* (Jew-bishop), who represented the community to the Christian authorities. Amongst themselves, however, the Jews of Worms gave their communal leaders unique titles, such as *"Katzin," "Aluf," "Ha'eshel Hagadol,"* and *"Gaon."* Rabbis had the usual rabbinic titles.

For the customs he recorded, Kirchheim also included the reasons in most cases: e.g. at a circumcision, the *"aleynu"* prayer is only recited after the circumcision is over, because they did not want to insult the baby with the reference to the uncircumcised in that prayer, and therefore only recited it once the baby had entered the fold of the Jewish people. Incidentally, the *sandek* was given higher honors than the *mohel* during the services.

    The Jews of Worms continued for centuries to elaborate their memorial prayers for their martyrs, killed in the massacres of the Crusaders in the beginning of the month of Sivan. Special prayers were recited in which the names of the martyrs were enumerated. In our own service, the "*Av Harachamim*" prayer has remained from that period. Significantly we do not say this prayer on a Sabbath when the new moon is announced, except in the case of the month of Sivan, when that rule is broken and Av Harachamim is said in solidarity with the Jews of Worms and neighboring communities, victims of the First Crusade.

    The Kirchheim Manuscript is also rich in historical accounts. It contains a long poem or lamentation written by R. Eliezer of Worms (1140–1225), in which he describes the slaughter, before his own eyes, of his wife and two daughters. He also describes for us the virtues of each one of them: About his wife he wrote a paraphrase of the "*Eshet Chayil*" by King Solomon, adding that his wife spun wool for the making of tzitzit; she stitched together the parchment sections of the Torah Scrolls, and helped make tefillin; she was a member of the Chevra Kadisha and washed the bodies of the dead; she helped outfit young brides, and sewed suits for yeshiva students; she recited Tehillim and sang Zemirot and prayers, said a daily *vidduy*, and taught women in various towns prayers and songs; she prayed morning and night, and she was first in the synagogue; she stood on her feet all Yom Kippur, and she could decide legal questions of kashrut. All that besides the obvious mitzvot of visiting the sick and feeding the hungry. Then R. Eliezer sang the praises of his daughter Blatt, aged 13. She had learned all prayers and Zemirot from her mother, and attended to all her father's needs. She was chaste, and truthful in all her words. She knitted and cooked and helped her mother in all household chores.

    R. Eliezer's youngest daughter Channah is described as follows: She recited the first portion of the "*Shema*" every day, at the age of 6. She too knitted and sewed and helped in the kitchen. Her songs were a delight for her parents.

    The rest of the poem, full of anguish and sorrow, is truly heartrending and moving. It is a jewel of Jewish poetry, of great historic importance and a surprising find in the midst of a book of minhagim.

    The Kirchheim account describes the ordinances of the various rabbis. At one time, the rabbis tried to forbid playing with cards and dice on Chanukah. On Purim, one girl was crowned Queen Esther; she would march into the men's shul accompanied by another girl carrying a torch, followed by young men wearing masks. On Sukkot, the *shamash* was responsible for having three sets of lulavim and etrogim ready, to be sold daily to members of the community. When a man purchased his set he would also send it to his wife in the women's shul, where she and her lady friends would make the blessing over the Four Species.

Another important manuscript from Worms is that of the fabled *Yushpe Shames*, who was not only the sexton of the community but also a great scholar in his own right. He lived a generation before Kirchheim, and died in 1649. His document is not so much concerned with history as with painstakingly recording each and every prayer and liturgical poem recited on different occasions in Worms, along with all the customs and laws observed.

These two manuscripts have now been published, along with my introduction in Hebrew, at Machon Yerushalayim, in Jerusalem. My wife and I have dedicated these important works, as we have done with all other manuscripts and works published by us, to the memory of our beloved son Jamie z"l, who was so interested in *piyyut*, liturgical poetry, that we recently endowed the Jamie Lehmann Chair in Piyyut at Bar Ilan University.

I am sure my readers will enjoy being transported into the mostly idyllic but often dramatic atmosphere of the outstanding and exemplary community of ancient Worms, by studying these newly published volumes.

# The Jews of Yemen

A startling news item appeared in the press last week to the effect that various Jewish groups in this country and in Europe are trying to "organize a discreet departure from Yemen of some 1,600 to 1,700 Yemenite Jews, the last of an ancient community that once numbered 50,000." It is therefore appropriate to consider the history of this marvelous Jewish community, probably the oldest—with the exception of the Jews on the fabled isle of Djerba off Tunisia—Diaspora community.

Anyone who has been privileged to meet a Yemenite Jew will have been impressed with the refinement, modesty and piety which are the Yemenite hallmarks.

The roots of the Jews in Yemen—*Teman* in Hebrew—start at the dawn of our history. Besides being mentioned in the Tanach (Job's friend Elifaz came from Teman, and many of the Prophets speak of Teman), the Queen of Sheba is said to have heard about King Solomon from Jews in Yemen, located next to the kingdom of Sheba. Even in Islamic tradition it is reported that the contact between King Solomon and the Queen of Sheba was established through the Jews in Yemen, and there are reports of Jews in Yemen during Roman times. In the old Jewish cemetery at Beth Shearim there are tombs of Jews whose remains were brought there from Yemen in the 2nd century C.E. Despite their isolation, the Yemenite Jews maintained contact with important Jewish centers, especially with Egypt and Babylonia. Their scholarship was of the highest standard throughout their history. Some important Midrashim, unknown elsewhere, were composed and preserved in Yemen, including the *Midrash Hagadol*, written in Aden in the 13th century, and *Chemdat Ha-Yamim*.

The Genizah in Cairo yielded many letters dated from the 11th century onward, exchanged between rabbis in Yemen with the heads of the Jewish community in Cairo. The Rambam, Maimonides, became their teacher "par excellence"—he taught them through special Epistles and sent them copies of his Code at an early date. No holy book, besides the Tanach, was copied so meticulously in Yemen as Rambam's *Mishneh Torah*. I own several manuscript volumes besides hundreds of fragments of medieval copies of the Rambam penned in Yemen, mostly written on parchment, going back to the 13th century, less than a century after the Rambam's death.

The Yemenite Jews also maintained contact with Jewish scholarship in Europe. The writings of the great rabbis of Germany and France were known to them, and this is how it happened: In one of my Yemenite manuscripts I found a description of how the Yemenite Jews would line up in their harbor whenever a ship arrived bringing Jewish merchants from Germany on their way to India to buy silk. They would ask the merchants for their sacred books, which they then would hand-copy before the ships continued on their way. Through one of those unusual exercises, the Jews in Yemen acquired a copy of Rashi's commentary on the Torah; I recently published a Yemenite copy of Rashi, handwritten many years before the printing press was invented, which contains several important variants from the known, printed text of Rashi. The Yemenites are till this day exceptionally skilled scribes. There never was a Hebrew printing press in Yemen, with the exception of Aden, and all the thousands of holy books used by the Jews there were handwritten.

The Jews in Yemen clearly had very early contact with the Jews in Moorish Spain, the medieval center of Jewish poetry, for they soon adopted the style of the Spanish-Jewish *paytanim*. This contact led to a flowering of poetic genius which outlived and almost surpassed their Spanish masters. A book containing Yemenite songs and poems is called a *diwan*. My own collection of such diwans is now being catalogued by a great Yemenite scholar, Professor Yehuda Ratzaby, and contains over 5000 poems, many hitherto unknown.

The Yemenite Jews were barely tolerated, treated as *dhimmis* (i.e. pariahs) by their Moslem rulers, as is legislated by Islam for all "infidels" under their rule. Their fortune fluctuated throughout the centuries depending on the benevolence or lack of it of the respective rulers. While the Moslems were mostly farmers, the Jews were in charge of crafts on which the Moslems often depended. This meant that even the most hateful Moslem ruler was loath to expel the Jews, unless they could teach their trades to their Moslem neighbors.

An intense longing for the Moshiach and for a return to Eretz Yisrael and to Jerusalem was kept alive throughout the countless centuries of exile in Yemen. With the end of the First World War, a sudden desire for mass emigration to the Holy Land arose. Some Yemenite Jews had already begun to emigrate to the Land from 1882 on, and they had informed their brethren by a steady flow of letters of the situation there. The opening up of the doors to emigration, even in a very limited sense, brought electrifying results in Yemen. I quote from a very moving and historic letter which I own, written by a Yemenite Jew in Jerusalem on the 17th of Tammuz, 1925, to his relatives back home:

"Oh my beloved relatives, let me tell you about the situation in Eretz Yisrael. The Land is improving and growing from month to month and is becoming doubly beautiful and glorious, much more so than when we came here in 1912. Behold, every year Jews are taking over areas of land, and every area they take over they build up, thank G-d, whether in Judea or in the Galil. And now Jews can even take part in the British Government and can fulfil their every wish. Each year more and more Jews are arriving here from all countries, and soon G-d will grant you, too, the right to come here. This is so, because the Zionist leadership is casting lots, and the lot of the Yemenite Jews has now won. It also happens with the permission of the British Government and with permission of the Jewish ruler, the High Commissioner Herbert Samuel, which is his goyish name, but his Hebrew name is Menachem Ben-Uziel, may his glory be uplifted. And you, my relatives, choose the good that is offered you, and remember, I can only give you hints, but the wise among you will understand what I mean.

"P.S. Please send my regards to Menashe Djabani and tell him on behalf of his brother, Salaam Djabani, that he lives among the Yemenites in Rehovot and has found himself a Yemenite wife from the Shamsaan family."

During this time many Yemenite Jews started to move. They gave up their belongings and moved to Aden, a part of Yemen under British Colonial rule since 1839. There they camped for years—until the fabled "Operation on Wings of Eagles" or "Magic Carpet" fulfilled their dream to come to Eretz Yisrael. The Jews of Aden itself stayed on a little longer. The last ones left in 1967, and so I had the opportunity—perhaps I was one of the last travelers to witness Jewish Yemenite life "intact"—to spend Tisha B'Av in Aden, Southern Yemen, in 1960. Here is the entry from my diary reporting on that memorable visit. As we have just commemorated Tisha B'Av last Sunday, my report is especially timely:

"Aden in Southern Yemen is situated in the southwestern-most corner of the Arabian Peninsula, bordering in Hadramaut—akin to Biblical Chatzar-Mavet. Of course, the heat and the barren landscape of the area are among the most extreme in the world. Aden in itself covers a narrow strip of land, along some of the most rugged and steep mountains I've ever seen. One of the first sights on coming from the airport was a large Jewish cemetery along one of the mountainsides. Row after row of raised stone sarcophagi can be seen, facing north. A narrow gorge has been cut through one of the mountains, making a narrow, zigzagging road leading into neighboring Qrater, the old city. I hired a taxi to take me to the Jewish Quarter. My Arab driver, Ibrahim, said, 'Oh, you want to go to Afd el-Yahud,' saying that this was the Arabic name for the Jewish ghetto. He went on to tell me sadly how that region had been completely inhabited by thousands of Jews until 12 years ago, but since then, most of them had gone to 'Falastin' (Israel). Ibrahim took me to the largest synagogue in Aden, a spaciously built stone structure easily capable of holding hundreds of worshippers. The central section has only a marble tevah in its midst, with no benches or seats around it at all. Two parallel rows of high pillars are on either side of the tevah, and in the eastern and western wings are row upon row of very low wooden benches. In the front of the northern wall a wide aron kodesh houses the Torah scrolls, each encased in round wooden boxes in the Yemenite fashion. As is the custom in Oriental synagogues, scores of elaborate silver lamps, donations of individuals, are suspended from the ceilings, right in front of the Ark. A special room bordering the eastern wing and separated from it by a high iron fence is the room reserved for women. I first met the shamash, an unbelievably thin Yemenite, wearing white clothes and a black skull cap. His black beard and side curls make his white face seem even paler, and his deep-set black eyes even more penetrating. We conversed in Hebrew, the only language spoken by most of the Jews in Aden besides Arabic. Two young boys standing next to him were introduced to me as Shmuel and Hanan, who spoke fair Hebrew. Their younger sister whispered excitedly to them, 'Yehudi?' pointing to me.

"At night, a scene right out of the *Arabian Nights* meets me in the synagogue for the Tisha B'Av services. The men wear red fezzes, are dressed in white, flowing robes, and are followed by their sons and grandsons. Clusters of these families place themselves comfortably in various spots of the synagogue. The grandfather, patriarchally placed in the middle, sits on a carpet, sometimes barefoot, resting against a high cushion or box; next to him his son, also a little on the heavy side, but without the elder's flowing white beard and side curls. Around the group are children, usually barefoot, of all ages, of whom the youngest will soon fall asleep while the older ones compete with the grownups in chanting the *Kinot*. With the synagogue built for a community of thousands, only a few hundred are left; the enormous spaciousness of the basilica-type synagogue leaves room for approximately fifty adults and an equal number of children to disappear into their respective corners.

"For the youngsters, it is like Purim or Simchat Torah. Happy groups of boys in holiday dress, barefoot, with Israeli-made skullcaps on their heads, run back and forth. Then a stern looking young man with a red fez and black beard lets his rod out through the air with a whistling sound, but miraculously misses the children each time he charges into the groups. For a while he gets them to congregate at the foot of the Ark and even gets them to chant a few lines, but soon they are dispersed again in mirth, to the charging of the *melamed*.

"Behind the bars along the east wing, women are following the services in a darkened hall. I noticed that their faces are uncovered, although their heads are covered by kerchiefs. Surrounded by Moslems whose married women are literally mummified from head to toe, it must have required enormous strength of character on the part of the Jews not to force their women into adopting similar garb.

"As the reading of the Lamentations proceeds, I am struck by the peculiar Yemenite pronunciation applied. Each *komatz* is pronounced as an 'o' and each *cholem* is pronounced—similar to the Lithuanian manner—as an 'ay.' (A typical Oriental differentiation between the *aleph* and *ayin*, between *kof* and *qof*, between the 'hard' and 'soft' sounds, is observed. This mixture of Oriental consonants and 'Lithuanian' vowels creates a rather weird-sounding Hebrew.)

"After the services, as a group of worshippers gathers around me for conversation, I query them about this. They reply that their forefathers have lived in Aden for over two thousand years and that they have no other pronunciation. When I asked them why their cemetery as well as their synagogue faces north and not east, they shake their heads in wonderment, since they have never heard of another direction other than north for praying and burying their dead. After all, Aden is practically due south of Israel. I am informed about their institutions, their yeshivot for boys up to the age of fifteen, their shechitah. I meet their rabbi, Rav Zecharyahu, a venerable sage with a long white beard and wise, knowing eyes. I hear complaints about the unhappy lot of the approximately one thousand Jews still living in neighboring Yemen, whose king refuses them the right to emigrate.

"Practically all Jews in Aden are Orthodox and every Jewish shop is closed on Shabbos. The shadow of the tragic events of 1948 still lingers here: Twelve years ago mobs of murderous Arabs swooped down and set fire to Afd el-Yahud while the Colonial British troops looked on idly for a few days. Comparing the Jews I met with the Arabs, whom one can see lounging lazily in the bazaars or working in the harbor, it is obvious that the Jews are cleaner, better educated and better mannered than their Arab neighbors. What untold tension and strife must have charged the two thousand years of history of this proud community.

"A curious experience illustrates the impact of Jewish culture on the Arabs. In the course of my taxi trip, I returned to the car from the synagogue after one of my stops, and found 180 shillings missing from my jacket. Challenged, my Arab driver exclaimed heatedly in English, 'Torah Temimah! Nobody was near the taxi while you were away!' In my surprise over this Hebrew expression I completely forgot my monetary loss. Ibrahim explained to me that this is a common oath used by Arabs, which they had heard from their former Jewish neighbors.

"It was, of course, a rewarding experience to visit the birthplace of so many Aden Jews who are now scattered around the world."

If the present effort to bring out the remaining Jews from Yemen succeeds, a long and glorious chapter in Jewish history will be closed, and a true *kibbutz goliyot* will have been accomplished. We can all benefit from the rich religious and cultural legacy which the Yemenite Jews have brought to us and which is a true blessing for us all.

# The Jews of Gibraltar

If I am asked which, in my opinion, is the most charming Jewish community outside of Israel, I will without hesitation say: Gibraltar! There, at the southernmost tip of Western Europe, and within viewing distance of Africa, is a unique enclave, remote from anything one usually associates with European Jewish communities. It is, in fact, an historic hybrid of Spanish, British and Moroccan communities, which, over the span of centuries, has developed its own gentle and hospitable character. The character of Gibraltar's Jewish community is only matched by the breathtaking scenery provided by its unique geographic location (including the monkeys which have inexplicably settled there for centuries). In olden days called "The Pillars of Hercules," the Rock of Gibraltar is a steep rock bluff, protruding out of the Spanish plains, which is surrounded by a small piece of land, just enough to hold its population of some 29,000.

My first encounter with Gibraltar goes back some 53 years. In May, 1940, I was on my way out of Europe. As a 17-year-old, I had travelled alone from Sweden through Nazi Germany. The Blitz against the West was then at its fiercest. I could not travel at night, so after a train trip from Sweden to Berlin, I was forced to stay overnight in a hotel. The next day I got as far as Munich, and again stayed at a hotel overnight. The Nazis, probably knowing that I was a Jew, still honored my Swedish passport and gave me no trouble. Yet, at every railroad station, I heard the voices of one or two Jews, hidden from view, calling out to me, thinking I might be a Jew fleeing persecution whom they could help and shield.

In this manner I personally experienced the extent of Jewish self-help during the height of the Holocaust. I have often wondered what happened to those self-sacrificing, heroic Jews, whose brotherly love motivated them to take such risks in the face of ferocious Nazi persecution.

From Munich I crossed into Italy, where I spent a few days with relatives in Milan. Finally I reached Genoa, where the *U.S.S. Washington*, on its last sailing, was to take me to New York. Two days into the Mediterranean we were stopped at Gibraltar. British warships ordered the giant American ship to stop, and for a whole day the ship was searched for Nazis or war contraband. America was not yet involved in the war, and as a "neutral" nation, it had relations with both Germany and the Western Allies.

I had time to admire the scenery. South of us were the gentle Moroccan mountain ranges, veiled in an azure hue. North of us stood the imposing Rock of Gibraltar. It was several decades before I visited Gibraltar again. It is a visit worth recommending to any traveller who is looking for natural beauty, historic sites and a warm Jewish community.

The name Gibraltar is a contraction of the Arabic words "*Jibr el-Tariq*," the Mountain of Tariq, named after the Moslem hero who invaded Spain in the 8th century and established Moorish rule over the Iberian Peninsula, which lasted till 1492. Geographically, it is part of Spain, but militarily and politically it is vital for Britain, which has fought many wars over the tiny territory, and has held on to it to this day.

It was in the Treaty of Utrecht of 1713 that Spain ceded Gibraltar to Britain. But since Jews were banned from Spain after the Expulsion of 1492, the Spaniards inserted a clause in the Treaty reading: "Her Britannic Majesty, at the request of the Catholic King, does consent and agree that no leave shall be given, under any pretext whatsoever, either to Jews or Moors to reside or have their dwellings in the said town of Gibraltar." These may be called Spain's "famous last words" because Jews, in fact, did live in the shadow of the Rock, before and after 1713, although Britain did try to live up to the vicious Catholic attempt to extend the Church's deathly campaign against the Jews even beyond Spain's boundaries.

As an isolated outpost of Britain's colonial Empire, Gibraltar was dependent on nearby Morocco for food supplies. Since the Kingdom of Morocco was traditionally friendly toward its Jewish citizens, Morocco helped the local Jews circumvent the restrictions on Jews living in Gibraltar as a condition for supplying the British garrison on the Rock with food.

Only a few years elapsed before a treaty was signed between Britain and Morocco in 1721, which clearly guaranteed the right of Jews to live in Gibraltar. The corresponding clause is couched in flowery language: "The subjects of the Emperor of Fez and Morocco, whether Moors or Jews, residing in the dominion of the King of Great Britain, shall entirely enjoy the same privileges that are granted to the English residing in Barbary." In other words, this was a reciprocal agreement: Englishmen were permitted to live in Morocco (Barbary), and Jews were allowed to live in British Gibraltar.

But the Spaniards did not give up. In 1726 Spain claimed that Britain had violated the Treaty of 1713, because she "had permitted Jews and Moors, enemies of the Catholic religion, to reside in the city." This claim became a pretext for Spain's attack on Gibraltar, a siege that lasted from 1726 to 1727. The Jews of Gibraltar excelled in their heroism and patriotism in the defense of their beloved Gibraltar. The cooperation between the Jews and the British Government led to long-lasting historic ties till this day, as well as close ties between the Spanish-Portuguese Congregation of London with their brethren on the Rock.

In 1749, Gibraltar's first rabbi or *chacham*, Isaac Nieto, came from London to found the first synagogue, Shaar Hashamayim, which is still in use today. Many other *talmidei chachamim* have served the Gibraltar community over the years.

Gibraltar was the home base of Lord Nelson's fleet before its engagement nearby in the Battle of Trafalgar. In fact, Lord Nelson's closest friend there was a wealthy Jewish merchant, Aaron Cardozo. When I visited the cemetery along

Gibraltar's main street, I noticed graves of sailors who had died in the Battle of Trafalgar.

As the Jewish community grew, more synagogues were built: Nefutsot Yehuda (one of the most beautiful and richly decorated of Gibraltar's synagogues) in 1781; Etz Hayim in 1781; and Abudarham in 1820.

During World War II, Gibraltar was an indispensable part of Allied strategy. Since Gibraltar guarded the entrance to the Mediterranean, any convoy of supply ships trying to reach Malta or Egypt had to pass Gibraltar. The danger of Spain under Franco, Hitler's friend seizing Gibraltar, was ever-present, and would have placed a fatal stranglehold on the Allies' War effort. It could also have threatened the survival of Eretz Yisrael during the War, especially with Nazi General Rommel standing near her gates. Providentially, Franco (who was aware of his Marrano roots) desisted from any hostile action. As for the Jews, he even reportedly extended an invitation to any Jew of Sephardic origin to come to Spain for protection.

Most of Gibraltar's Jews were evacuated during the War. On their return, it was noticed that their religious practices, of which Gibraltar had always been so proud, had slackened. Judaism was on the decline. But then a radical change set in, due mostly to one man, Rabbi Josef Pacifici, the son of a prominent Italian thinker and lawyer, a graduate of the famed Gateshead Yeshiva in England. Rabbi Pacifici assumed the rabbinate in Gibraltar in the late 1950's, and totally revolutionized Jewish education and religious observance in the 600-member community. He made sure that the young, future leaders of the community attended yeshivot abroad; once they returned, they gave Gibraltar a practically 100% Orthodox character.

When I first came to Gibraltar I was immensely impressed with the piety and enthusiasm of its Jews. First, Sir Joshua Hassan, the Mayor—and later Chief Minister for more than 30 years—was an honored member of the Jewish community. Also, many of Gibraltar's Jews have served as Cabinet Ministers, and several have been appointed as diplomatic representatives of various foreign rulers as well.

When I first met Sir Joshua, Levi Eshkol was Israel's Prime Minister. I therefore made a pun on the famous words of the immortal Spanish Jewish bard, Yehuda Halevy, who lamented, *"Libbi bemizrach ve'ani b'sof maarav"* (My heart is in the East, but I am at the very edge of the West) by suggesting *"Levi bemizrach ve'ani b'sof maarav"* as there were now two Jewish heads of state, one at each end of the Mediterranean, Levi Eshkol in the east, and Sir Joshua in the west.

Sir Joshua's nephews include Rabbi Abraham Levy, who is now the head of the Spanish-Portuguese Congregation Shaar Hashamayim in London. He is also the author of an excellent book titled *The Sephardim*, which has just been published and which is a "must" for every student of Jewish history.

Another nephew, James (Chaim) Levy, a lawyer, is president of the Jewish community in Gibraltar. Moe Garson, a prominent accountant, is the mainstay of Gibraltar's religious activities. He helped establish a *kollel* there, which naturally had an enormously strong influence on the community. A local school and kosher restaurant are well established.

All Jewish stores, without exception, are closed along the main street on Shabbat—probably a record in our world today. A Shabbat in Gibraltar is therefore a very pleasant experience. After the Jews attend services in any of the four beautiful synagogues, and take their Shabbat meals, they are seen promenading along the narrow streets of Gibraltar, in a serene Shabbat atmosphere.

I had the good fortune of being the guest of the Levy family on my first visit to Gibraltar. One of the members of the family was a high-ranking British officer in the garrison on the Rock. On Friday night I observed the entire family singing the hauntingly beautiful Sephardic song *"Bendigamos,"* sung in Sephardic congregations around the world—except in New York it is only sung once, on Sukkot, in the synagogue. Here are some of the Ladino strophes with their translations:

> *Bendigamos al Altísimo*
> *Al Señor que nos crió*
> *Dèmosle agradecimiento*
> *Pos los bienes que nos dió*
> > *Bendigamos al Altísimo*
> > *Por su ley primeramente*
> > *Que liga a nuestra raza*
> > *Con cielo continuamente*
> > > *Bendita sea la casa esta*
> > > *El hogar de su presencia*
> > > *Donde guardeamos su fiesta*
> > > *Con alegria y permanencia*

> Let us bless Him, the Most High,
> Bless the L-rd, for us He made.
> Thanks to Him, Who did supply
> The rich fare before us laid.
> > To the Most High blessings rise,
> > First, because it is our race
> > He Himself to heaven ties
> > For all time, by His law's grace.
> > > May this house be blessed, 'tis here
> > > At this home, G-d's presence stays,
> > > And His feast we keep brings cheer,
> > > Happiness throughout our days.

It can be noted that no Hebrew word occurs in this song, perhaps because Marranos singing it had to shield their Jewishness. Yet the pride in the glory of Judaism and its laws is evident.

On one of my visits to Gibraltar I made a unique historic observation. I have, for some time, collected "diplomas of introduction" issued in the 19th century for "*shadarim*," i.e., emissaries who left the Holy Land during past centuries for Jewish communities scattered around the world to collect money for needy institutions and communities in Eretz Yisrael. Some of these diplomas are elaborately written on large parchment sheets, full of Biblical verses and rich vocabulary, describing the oppression under which Jews lived in the 19th century Turkish Empire.

One such diploma is addressed to the community in Gibraltar, along with communities in other countries, such as Brazil, Peru, Algeria, etc. The purpose of the emissary's mission was to collect money for "Kotel Hamaaravi," an institution for poor orphans and widows in Jerusalem, as well as for the redemption of prisoners taken by the Moslem government. When I visited the Abudarham synagogue in Gibraltar, I noticed a *pushke* (charity box) which had been permanently attached to the wall, bearing the name Kotel Hamaaravi. When I enquired about the pushke, I was told that some emissary had left it behind, long ago, but had never returned to collect its contents. Well, it was obvious that I knew the background of this pushke and even the name of the emissary, spelled out in his diploma: Avraham Mursiano. It was a rewarding experience to find the solution to a century-old mystery.

Gibraltar is also a role model for tolerance and good neighborliness among communities of different religions. There has always been perfect harmony between the Jews, Christians and Moslems in Gibraltar. One of the factors which binds them together is their common loyalty to the British Crown; none of them would want to come under Spanish rule. Sir Joshua Hassan has therefore earned the abiding love of his constituents for defending Gibraltar's freedom of choice in countless international conferences.

We can all be proud of this small but vibrant Jewish community in a far-off corner of Europe, which offers living proof that a totally observant Jewish community can earn the respect of its non-Jewish surroundings, making constructive and appreciated contributions to the general welfare.

# Aleppo and Its Jews—A Proud History

Over the years I have taken my readers on visits to the most far-flung communities. Together we have travelled in my columns to such scattered cities and communities in the Diaspora as Worms, Germany; Aden, Yemen; London, England; Djerba, Tunisia; Carpentras, France; Karachi, Pakistan; Recife, Brazil; Amsterdam, Holland; Gibraltar; Madrid, Spain; Stockholm, Sweden; Newport, Rhode Island; Kingston, Jamaica; Vancouver, British Columbia; Helsinki, Finland; New Orleans, Louisiana; Vishau, Rumania; St. Petersburg, Russia; Cairo, Egypt; Moncalvo, Italy; Mexico City, Mexico; Jodensavanne, Surinam; Halberstadt, Germany; Izmir, Turkey, and many more. Quite an impressive array of cities and their communities, representing important aspects of Jewish history of which we should be profoundly proud.

But few cities and communities can match the glory of Aleppo, Syria, a city which spans the millennia from the days of David until our own time. Whenever I meet a Jew whose roots are in Aleppo, I know I am facing aristocracy and nobility. Aleppo is certainly the crown jewel of splendor in the Sephardic world. Although I have never physically been there, I feel that I have touched its hallowed ground because of its people and its books which I have encountered.

Sometimes one hears the city referred to in Arabic as Halab, from which the name Aleppo is derived, but Aleppo's original name in Biblical days was Aram-Tzova, which its Jews have preserved throughout all the 3,000 years since King David's great victory there, as reported in the Book of Samuel (II, Chapter 10) and in Psalms (Psalm 60). This name bears witness to the fact that in the days of our Kings the land of Israel extended through what is today Syria and according to my interpretation of the Jonah story, Jeroboam II almost captured Niniveh, the capital of Assyria.

Throughout its long history Aleppo has been characterized by its exemplary communal life. Always headed by great Talmudic sages, whose benevolent authority was always followed with awe and total dedication, Aleppo has the enviable record of unbroken communal peace and spiritual productivity. Early Jewish travellers, such as Benjamin of Tudela, reported Jews living there in 1173. Before him, the great Rav Saadia Gaon visited Aleppo in 921, and found great Talmudic scholars there. The Cairo Genizah fortunately contained surviving remnants of handwritten responsa originating from Aleppo in the 12th century. Rabbi Petachya of Regensburg, Germany, visited Aleppo from 1170–80 and expressed his admiration of its great scholars.

The famous Spanish poet Yehuda Alcharisi, translator of the Rambam's philosophical work *Moreh Nevuchim*, visited Aleppo and reported that it had Talmudic scholars, medical doctors, poets and authors. The Rambam's famous disciple, R. Yosef ibn Aknin, for whom he wrote the *Moreh Nevuchim*, settled in Aleppo after passing through Egypt.

Ancient inscriptions still exist today in Aleppo, dating back over 1000 years. I knew Israeli diplomat Dotan when he was Ambassador to the Dominican Republic, and he told me of timeworn Hebrew inscriptions he had seen inside Aleppo's ancient city-fortress. (Dotan, a fine elderly gentleman, was tragically killed in a traffic accident.)

In the early 1500s the Aleppo Jewish community was providentially changed when the Ottoman Empire opened its gates to the influx of Spanish Jews who were expelled from Spain in 1492. This immigration was led by a true Spanish "grandee," R. Shlomo Kassin, who bore the Spanish noble title "Señor" throughout his life. He arrived in Aleppo in 1504 and was soon appointed head of the ancient community because of his great wealth and administrative genius. Besides his wide business interests he devoted much of his time to Torah study. His contemporary was R. Yosef Caro, author of the *Shulchan Aruch*, who had settled in nearby Safed in the land of Israel. Another great Sephardic personality of the time was Rabbi Shmuel Laniado, who was sent to Aleppo by R. Yosef Caro. (Israel's famous Laniado Hospital bears his family name.)

Señor Shlomo Kassin's sons were Señor Ephraim Kassin and Menashe Kassin, who were the mainstays of Aleppo's many charities and communal administrations. Testimonies to their outstanding communal ventures are found in the biographical notes of their contemporaries.

The first member of the Kassin family to serve as the community's Chief Rabbi was R. Yom Tov Kassin, followed by his son, the great Talmudist and Kabbalist, Rabbi Yehuda Kassin, who was born in Aleppo in 1708. Yehuda was the great-grandson of Señor Shlomo Kassin, and during his life he was beset by much suffering in health, poverty and communal burdens. His main work, *Machaneh Yehuda*, was recently published by his descendants in New York. It contains hundreds of responsa and displays the most profound erudition and mastery of all phases of the vast Talmudic literature.

This *sefer* is a remarkable book, quite unique in our vast literature over the centuries. Over 200 pages of the printed edition deal with a communal problem which had arisen between the original Jews of the ancient community and the so-called "Señores Francos," recent arrivals from such countries as France and Italy. It seems that upon arrival in Aleppo they made an arrangement with the local Jews that they would be exempt from community taxes and would not be subject to the edicts and ordinances of Aleppo's other Jews. Although most of the Francos settled permanently in Aleppo and intermarried with the native Jewish families, they continued to claim total immunity from the traditional laws of the city-folk. Their exemptions covered such indigenous ordinances as the prohibitions against Jewish women taking walks in the public parks and holding public gatherings on Jewish holidays (out of fear of attracting the attention and jealousy of the Moslems). They were also exempted from charity collections for the needy locals or for the poor in nearby land of Israel, and they were allowed to maintain their own channels for sending charitable contributions to Israel.

In the days of Rabbi Yehuda Kassin, Chief Rabbi Rephael Shlomo Laniado, who headed Aleppo's *Beit Din*, tried to put a stop to these exemptions and to force the Francos minority to submit to all the public regulations. R. Yehuda Kassin thereupon composed a very lengthy and erudite defense for maintaining the old order of exemptions, and even brought the supporting approval of several leading Sephardic authorities of the time, including R. Yom Tov Algazi of Jerusalem. An interesting feature in this controversy, from the perspective of our collective history, was that the Francos threatened that they would cease attending services in Aleppo's synagogues and would establish their own places of worship if they could not have their way. Rabbi Laniado held that they could be prevented from forming such separate synagogues, but Rabbi Kassin defended their right to do so. Throughout the controversy Rabbi Kassin's main goal was above all else to maintain peace and harmony in the community.

Rabbi Kassin's humility was legendary, and many stories still circulate about his exemplary character. He lived to the ripe age of 76, and was buried according to the custom which many Sephardic communities reserve for their outstanding scholars and saints, in the courtyard of the ancient Great Synagogue of Aleppo, where the Jews could venerate his grave.

The Kassin dynasty is one of the most fabulous in our history. The name Kassin comes from the Biblical word *katzin*, captain or judge, which occurs many times throughout the books of the *Tanach* (e.g., Judges 11:6 and Proverbs 6:7). While most Spanish Jews had Spanish-sounding names, such as Caro, Amigo and Esperansa, the Kassin family's Hebrew name pre-dates the expulsion from Spain, indicating that they held positions as judges and leaders for hundreds of years before coming to Aleppo.

All of R. Yehuda's descendants were leading rabbis, Talmudists and Kabbalists in Aleppo. One of his descendants is today's Rabbi Saul J. Kassin, rabbi of the Syrian community in Brooklyn, whose book on the 613 mitzvot has been published in both Hebrew and English. His son Jacob is one of the leaders of the Sephardic community at large, and a great supporter of Sephardic institutions in Israel.

Thus the Kassin family spans over 500 years of unbroken piety, scholarship and leadership, and compares favorably with the great Jewish dynasties in Germany, Lithuania and Poland. Only the Jewish people can point to such outstanding families spanning centuries upon centuries, throughout times of oppression, expulsion and suffering.

Aleppo is famous for its greatest treasure: the fabled Aleppo Codex (Keter), one of the world's oldest Hebrew *Tanach* manuscripts. It was written 1000 years ago in Tiberias by a member of the famous Ben-Asher family, and shows the final vocalization and punctuation of the Biblical text. After some vicissitudes it ended up in Aleppo where it was venerated as an object of great sanctity. In 1947 it was burned and partly destroyed by an attacking Arab mob. Miraculously, most of it was saved, and it was smuggled from Syria to Jerusalem, where it is presently housed in the National Library. Some believe it is the Biblical text to which the Rambam refers in his *Hilchot Sefer Torah*. Parts of it are displayed in the Shrine of the Book in Jerusalem's Israel Museum.

Anyone who becomes familiar with Aleppo's marvelous Jewish community will be profoundly impressed with the contributions its Jews have made to our glorious history. They deserve our closest attention, so that all of us—Sephardic or Ashkenazic—can learn from their lofty example, and each in his own way can emulate their record of scholarly and communal achievements.

# The Jewish Community in France

The Jewish community in France today is vibrant and growing, counting some 800,000 souls, *kain yirbu*—but it has no connection with the great French centers of the Middle Ages which existed along the Rhine River and in Provence along the Mediterranean. Those communities vanished when the Church and the king of France ordered their expulsion around 1391.

French kings in the Middle Ages had been very subservient to the Church. For example, in 1243 King Louis IX had 12,000 copies of the Talmud publicly burned in Paris at the urging of the Pope in Rome. For this "good deed" the king was sainted, and therefore he is known in history as St. Louis, the only French king ever to be sainted!

The only Jewish communities permitted to continue to exist were those around Avignon, a territory outside the realm of the Roman Popes. One such location was Carpentras, where the oldest French synagogue stands today.

Only the French Revolution in 1789 brought deliverance to French Jews, leading to their full emancipation in 1791, with Napoleon as their great benefactor. He not only instituted a Sanhedrin in Paris, but also, in 1808, organized the "Consistoire Centrale des Israélites de France," the administrative organ for all French Jews. This Consistoire has been functioning uninterruptedly ever since—except for the Holocaust years, 1940–45—until today.

In 1994, I paid a visit to the Consistoire at the kind invitation of its senior officers. They were especially proud to show me their brand-new building, sparkling, modern and clean, which just opened at 19 Rue St. Georges, near the traditional Jewish section in the 9th Arrondisement. The seven-story building holds not only the office of the President of the Consistoire Central, but also that of Chief Rabbi of France, as well as offices for the administrative heads of all the 17 French regions.

They also have installed a beautiful museum section where right now a very educational and tasteful exhibit of the beautiful synagogues of France is being shown. Partly through expertly executed scale models, partly through large photographs, you get an idea of the architectural beauty of these houses of worship, which in some cases go back hundreds of years. No visitor to France this summer should miss seeing this exhibit.

Traditionally, the Consistoire Central has had as its President a member of the Rothschild family. Its rostrum of past Presidents contains such names as Alphonse de Rothschild, Edmonde de Rothschild, Edouard de Rothschild, Guy de Rothschild and Alain de Rothschild—all French Barons. With the decline and assimilation of the original French Jews, the influx of Algerian, as well as Moroccan and Tunisian Jews, has providentially improved the whole face of French Jewry.

The last French-born Chief Rabbi was Jacob Kaplan, who was a friend of General Charles de Gaulle. I saw him some 20 years ago, and was pleasantly surprised to learn that as a sprightly 97-year-old, he is still very active in Jewish community affairs. But after him, the Chief Rabbis, Rabbis Sirat and Sitruq, have been Algerian-born Jews, as is the present Consistoire President, Jean-Pierre Bansaro.

Under the guidance of the Consistoire, French Jewry has developed one of the most dynamic and vibrant communities in the Diaspora—but other groups, most notably the Lubavitch movement, have also had a lot to do with it. As unbelievable as it sounds, there are 60 (!) kosher restaurants in Paris, all under the supervision of the Beit Din. I remember a time when there were only two or three. In 1988 there were 27 Jewish schools and 111 kindergartens, and more are opening all the time. There are regular Jewish television programs, many organized by Chabad. The danger of assimilation and intermarriage, which worried the first North African arrivals in France (as I can remember from the 1960's), is mercifully gone.

"Jeunesse Lubavitch" in Paris offers 80 *shiurim* a week for adults around the city. They have recruited thousands of *baalei teshuva*.

Maybe the Rebbe's special attention to France stems from the fact that about 60 years ago he studied engineering at Sorbonne University in Paris, and of course, he speaks fluent French and has intimate knowledge of the country. Incidentally, I heard that he was persuaded to move his studies from Berlin to Paris by Rabbi J. B. Soloveitchik, who together with Rabbi Yitzchak Hutner, later of Chaim Berlin fame, was his fellow student in Berlin. Soon after Hitler took power in Germany, the Rebbe abandoned Berlin for Paris.

One can gain good insight into French Jewish life by reading some of their publications. The current issue of *Tribune Juive* carried an interview with Danielle Mitterand, wife of the French President, in which she mentions that her son, Jean-Christophe, lived for some time at Kibbutz Hanassi in Israel. Another publication is *Chroniqueur—Information Juive Internationale*. With so many French Jews nowadays of Sephardic origin, their interest in the fate of Israel's Shas Party is understandable. This magazine devotes much space to the Deri affair, but in a friendly spirit, also airing the suspicion that the attacks on the Minister of Interior are partly based on anti-Sephardic prejudice. The magazine has a revealing story on Jerzy Kluger, an intimate personal friend of Pope John Paul II from the time of their youth in Poland, who defines himself as the Pope's only Jewish friend.

The Consistoire's vast organization is led by a triumvirate consisting of Jean-Pierre Bansard, President; Irène Arditi, Chief of Staff; and Leon Masliah, Director General. Mr. Bansard, a prominent self-made and self-taught businessman, was born in Oran, Algeria, in 1940. He heads business and banking ventures in France and Israel, and has undertaken a great number of communal and charitable enterprises in both countries. He was elected President of the national Consistoire in 1992, and was also elected President of the European Jewish Councils.

Of Sephardic origin, the majority of French Jews know the Arabs very well, and naturally have no illusions about the chances of peace with them. They are extremely militant in matters of Israeli politics, and will go to any extreme to protect the security of Israel and Jerusalem. I hope to have established good cooperation between the Consistoire and equally concerned Jews in America.

To many of us the name Pissarro is identified with the Italian town where one of the earliest Hebrew printing presses existed—I own copies of the Talmud printed in Pissarro in 1507. But to the world at large, Pissarro is the name of one of the greatest 19th century painters; in fact, he can be called the father of French Impressionist painting. Giants in the world of art, such as Cezanne, Monet and Renoir, got their first initiation into the impressionist style from Pissarro. But who was this famous artist?

An exhibition totally dedicated to Pissarro is now taking place at the Royal Academy in London, which I had the occasion to visit last week. It is scheduled to remain open until October 2, and surely will be a major attraction to this summer's tourists traveling to Europe.

Pissarro was born on July 10, 1830, to an observant Sephardic family in Charlotte Amalie, the capital of the Danish Virgin Islands. These islands were sold to the United States in 1917, and today they are known as the U.S. Virgin Islands.

Pissarro's father, Frédéric, was born in Bordeaux in southern France, a center of Spanish-Portuguese Jews, including many Marranos who escaped from Spain or Portugal—I own a beautiful illuminated *ketuba* from Bordeaux from 1832, in which all signatures are Portuguese names. Frédéric, a merchant, moved to Charlotte Amalie in 1824.

In 1826, when he wanted to marry the widow of his mother's brother, the local synagogue objected on *halachic* grounds, because his bride was his aunt by marriage. Frédéric had to invoke the intervention of the King of Denmark in order to go through with the marriage. The local Jewish community still treated the couple with some hostility, which bespeaks a high degree of religious observance in an otherwise almost unknown Caribbean community.

The third son of this marriage, Jacob Abraham, later changed his name to Camille. As a young man he was a fully observant Jew, but when he moved to Paris for his art studies he was again treated as a stranger, all of which caused him to feel hostile toward organized society and religion. In fact, he had anarchist tendencies, although he was totally peaceful in character.

Although his colleagues hailed his genius as a painter, some of them showed anti-Semitic resentment toward him. During the Dreyfus scandal, some of the best known impressionists sided with the anti-Dreyfus party, and therefore hated Jews.

Foreign visitors of the time marvelled at this symptom of reactionary backwardness. One such foreigner was Norway's national composer, Edward Grieg, who was friendly with some of the impressionist painters. When they found out that he sided with Dreyfus and the Jews, he, too, was ostracized by some of his supposed artist friends. Although by then, in the 1890's, Pissarro was indifferent to religion, he was still a staunch defender of Jews, and quite outspoken on the subject of anti-Semitism.

As an artist he particularly loved landscapes and city scenes. In fact, the London exhibition concentrates on his countless paintings of certain streets and boulevards in Paris, although in my opinion his country scenes are even more significant. Pissarro's children were also gifted painters.

He died in 1903, and thus 1993 marks the 90th anniversary of his death. Since he spent much time in England, and painted English countrysides profusely, he is particularly beloved in that country—and hence this summer's exhibition in London.

He takes his place among the great Jewish painters who pioneered in their particular styles: Marc Chagall of Russia, Max Liebermann of Germany, Isaac Gruenewald and Ernst Josephson of Sweden.

Today, Israeli art, too, is immensely popular around the world. There must be something in Jewish genes which produces excellence in painting, as well as in so many other fields of human achievement which demand ingenuity and innovation.

# A Visit to the Synagogue of Piedmonte

Most tourists to Italy visit Rome, Venice, Florence—sometimes also Naples. Few visit the Northwestern Province of Italy called Piedmonte—the Foot of the Mountains. Very few know that Piedmonte is a veritable treasure chest of magnificent, albeit abandoned Jewish synagogues. When I heard about them I decided to take out time from a business trip to Milan for a "cultural safari" to this almost forgotten corner of our Jewish past. I invited my daughter Karie to accompany me on this trip. We met in Milan where we met our Jewish tour guide, Mrs. Annie Sacerdoti, the author of several books on Jewish antiquities in Italy.

We left Milan and after a 45-minute drive west soon reached Casale-Monferrato. There we were in for a wonderful surprise. After we reached the ghetto, the synagogue was opened for us. This synagogue is a sparklingly beautiful Baroque structure, built in 1595.

The ceiling in the synagogue was adorned with a few Hebrew words. All around the walls there are many biblical verses as well as historical texts. We couldn't see or photograph enough of this beautiful edifice.

Afterwards, we inspected the little narrow alleys of the old ghetto, and even saw the hinges of the gate that once had shut off the Jews from the outside world every evening.

In order to find the wife of the president of the community we walked a few blocks to a movie house where the cashier turned out to be the wife of the president. Mrs. Ottolenghi had studied at the Univesity of Wisconsin and spoke very fluent English. She told us that there are only 12 Jews in the city. Her own 24-year-old son had become quite religious and wanted to perpetuate the traditions of the family in Casale-Monferrato.

We continued the ride through the Italian countryside, now reaching hilly sections covered by vineyards and poplar trees beautiful in their different shades of green.

Our target was Moncalvo, a city so dear to my heart because of its Jewish community's important manuscript, a *machzor* (holiday prayer book), handwritten in 1799, which I own, and about which I have corresponded for some time with Dr. Carlo DiBenedetti, head of the Olivetti industrial empire, whose family had created this *machzor*.

We proceeded to a hill outside town where a very stately, aristocratic manor is owned by a Jewish family who are in the wine business. We were immediately received as members of the family as they showed us their wine cellar and wine manufacturing areas.

We returned to town and visited the beautiful, large city square on top of the hill. Interestingly enough, the town synagogue was placed at the center of that square, instead of the usual church. Unfortunately, the synagogue is closed, having been totally stripped of its interior, which had been sent to Israel and partly installed in the Bnei Brak Yeshiva.

Next we drove to Asti. Asti is one of the three Jewish communities covered by the abbreviated expression "*Apam*," standing for Asti, Fasano and Moncalvo. The *machzor* in my possession, covering the rite for all three communities, is called "*Minhag Apam*," or "*Minhag Tzorfat*," since its Jews came across the Alps as refugees from the pogroms in the French provinces in 1391.

We drove into the center of Asti, and parked the car near the central city square. After meeting Mrs. Sacerdoti, we proceeded on foot to the old Jewish ghetto. We were told that the Jews of Asti, as a one-time exception, were allowed to have windows in the outside building of the ghetto, which faced the Christian part of the city, but that as a result of this, the Christians invoked the rule that a Madonna had to be attached to that building, which the Jews were thus forced to look at. This Madonna is still there!

After passing some very old courtyards and the large wooden doors that led into those courtyards, we reached the Via Ottolenghi—a street named after one of the outstanding Jews of the Asti community—where we finally arrived at the magnificent synagogue. This synagogue, which was completed in 1809, reflects a much later period than the one we had seen in Casale-Manferrato. The large building was mainly characterized by tall marble pillars, and the ark was beautifully gilt-laid.

We concentrated on the ark, and I had the non-Jewish guardian of the synagogue help me take out one Torah scroll after the other. To my surprise, almost all of them were written on brownish leather in typical North African script.

We went upstairs to the women's section where we saw on the wall a framed document referring to the "Israelite University," which I understand refers to a Hebrew school.

In this synagogue a small museum had been organized, with very neat and clearly marked objects. These were mostly handwritten short prayers; printed prayer books from Venice and Livorino with handwritten annotations; besides an array of scrolls, Torah mantles, and historic documents. A number of mimeographed publications had been prepared for visitors, as well as an unusually beautiful and colorful printed brochure.

Mrs. Sacerdoti had presented me earlier with a very rich folder of historical facts on the Asti community, including a complete chronology of the historical highlights covering the period 1812 to 1984, approximately 110 years. Sadly, there is a repetitive sequence of expulsions and reinstatements of the Jews in this community.

We now headed for the cemetery. The cemetery itself was rather depressing in that it was filled with rather garish and somewhat gaudy tombstones, often holding a photograph of the deceased, or even sculpted busts. There were mausoleums and monuments very similar to the ones seen at the Mosseri compound at the Basatin cemetery outside Cairo.

The guide proudly pointed to the tombs of outstanding Jewish officials, including an Isaac Artom, who was the principal advisor to Cavour, the hero-prime minister of the first United Italian Government back in 1870.

One man whose tomb we saw was the inventor of the study of fingerprints. Another man, whose very prominent tomb held his bust, was the inventor of a marine communications device for ships.

The name Ottolenghi dominated the cemetery. As expected, with such an assimilated community, Hebrew inscriptions were in the decided minority. I noticed a peculiarity: "The day of his death" was given as *Yom Halfato*, ("the day of his turning over") instead of *"Petirato"* (his passing), as would be expected. When I asked Mrs. Sacerdoti about this later, she said that I was right in my assumption that this could be considered a translation from an Italian expression for death, such as "he changed his life."

It seems that originally cemeteries were inside the city boundaries, but that Napoleon, about 180 years ago, ordained that all cemeteries must be moved far outside the cities for hygienic reasons. As a result, the Jews were forced to "gather the bones" of old graves and move them along to the new cemeteries. In Asti there was one communal grave that held all the bodies collected from the old cemetery, all placed under one large stone.

## Part II
## Travels in Piedmonte, the Northwestern Province of Italy

We arrived in Mondovi as scheduled. This is a beautiful medieval city perched up on a mountaintop, with the "modern" part of the city down in the river valley, where a rapid river flows under the main city bridge.

We looked up Mr. Marco Levi, the only surviving native-born Jew in Mondovi. He is a 74-year-old accountant who is exceptionally nice and of course happy to finally have Jewish visitors.

At first he took us to the cemetery outside the city. None of the tombstones in this cemetery dated further back than the early 1800s. Surprisingly, I found one stone with an English inscription, for an Esther Hardman, who died around 1848. The other stones were completely dominated by two families: Levi and Mongliano.

It was a very moving sight to see Mr. Levi tend his parents' graves, which held large, black marble gravestones in modern style. As slowly as the old man had been walking before, he now quickly ran back and forth between rosebushes and these graves, placing one long-stemmed rose in an urn in front of each of three graves. He is the only surviving Jew, and only surviving child—he is unmarried and leaves no family behind—I was very touched by this gesture of filial love for parents who had died over 40 years ago. Of course my daughter Karie and I wondered who would take care of everything Jewish in this town after Mr. Levi was gone. The community comes under the jurisdiction of the largest Jewish community in Piedmonte, which is in Torino; but will they continue to care?

We returned to town and proceeded up the steep hill going to the old medieval part of town. This was quite an experience.

As we reached the ghetto, we left the car parked and walked up slowly through the winding narrow alleys, until we came to one house that bore a plaque dedicated to one of the Ottolenghis. We entered this house, which houses a beautiful old synagogue on its second floor. It is of course much smaller than any other we had seen on this trip, but it had a certain intimate, warm atmosphere. Only the ark was gilt-laid and was practically a "walk-in closet." In the center of the synagogue we saw something we hadn't seen in any of the others: a *bimah* surrounded by columns and having in its center a beautiful, movable lamp made of mirrors. According to Mr. Levi, this lamp would be detached during Sukkot and placed inside the Sukkah so that the *berachot*, which were painted along the walls of the Sukkah, would be reflected in the mirrors.

We walked into the women's section and then into one small room that held a bench still left over from the days when this was a children's school. We saw various objects such as *tzedakah* boxes; one Queen Esther's crown used for Purim plays; a donor's silver lamp, which was due for repair; a plaque used for noting *nedavot* (pledges) by members who had gotten *aliyot*; and similar objects.

We noted that one window faced outside the ghetto into the wide fields and vineyards surrounding the city. As with the other ghettos we had visited on our trip, the synagogue was placed in such a way that the Jews could reach it by walking through different houses of the ghetto without venturing outside the ghetto.

Mr. Levi took us upstairs where we reached the attic—complete with its original medieval beams. We saw an oven that was used for baking matzot. It was a moving sight to see these crowded quarters in which Jews had been cooped up for so long.

After the visit to the ghetto, Mr. Levi took us to the highest spot in town. It seems that each of these mountain cities has a spot marked *"Belvedere"* (Beautiful View), mostly close to the city tower or fortification from where one has a fabulous view over the enormous expanses of vineyards, hills and fields surrounding the city. It must have been from here that the knights of old controlled the farming areas and villages around them, which they held in servitude.

We traveled next to Cuneo and checked into the hotel, which was comfortable and adequate. Cuneo struck us as a nice, large city, relative to the country area.

One family name that appears in most of the cemeteries of Cuneo is "Foa." However, on one tombstone in Asti, which we had visited earlier, I noted that the Hebrew transcription of that name was spelled "Foar," no doubt meaning "glorious" or something similar. Our guide had said that it was thought that the name came from a French town with a similar name. But that seemed to be wrong. Also the name "Jerach" occurs frequently in Asti. I correctly guessed these people must have been refugees from Lunel in southern France, a city known for its great Talmud academies! (A similar derivation of that city name is "Yarhi," the well-known medieval author.)

When one sees the crowded and oppressive conditions of the ghetto, one must marvel at the great Jews who lived there and who produced such fine works—in rabbinics, science and poetry! In Moncalvo, all the Jews lived—about 300 of them—in one, single street, shorter than an average New York City block. They were herded together here, from where they were allowed to do "banking" business in many of the surrounding villages and towns.

And it was here, in this little street, that the beautiful 1799 *mahzor* (holiday prayer book), which is in my possession, was written, and perhaps partly composed! I'm also thinking back to the small, murky *beth midrash* of the Rambam in Cairo, where I had similar thoughts about the great works of historic and monumental value, which he had written under such oppressive, crowded conditions. All this means that we are wrong if we think that we need rich, affluent and spacious surroundings to give us inspiration to thought.

## Part III
## Travels in Piedmonte, the Northwestern Province of Italy

I started the day by taking a walk across the huge piazza of Cuneo, before we all started out.

Our first stop was at the shop of Mr. Cavaglion. It turned out that he dealt in Persian and Oriental rugs and art objects, and we very quickly bought some amulets and similar ornaments written in Hebrew that had come from Persia.

Mr. Cavaglion turned out to be an extremely friendly and lively person, as was his wife and the other members of his family. He had invited his brother and his brother's wife—who turned out to be a professor of Italian Jewish literature at the Hebrew University, whose maiden name is Ben Zimra of Gibraltar origin—as well as his own wife, who was very quick in telling us that she came from Vincelli, a place known for its huge synagogue, which we unfortunately could not include on our itinerary this time.

A great deal of talk ensued between everyone present. Mr. Cavaglion then produced a number of Hebrew manuscripts coming mainly from Yemen, and I selected a few for purchase. At the same time, he gave my daughter Karie a present—two fragments of a sacred Torah written on red leather!

Finally, we were ready to move in two cars toward the old ghetto in town.

On this trip I have discovered something I never knew about the Italian ghettos. All the ones we visited were extremely small, sometimes covering just one street or just one courtyard into which hundreds of Jews were herded. This is a far cry from the ample ghetto in Venice! Perhaps the situation was different in each place. Here in the Piedmonte area, the Jews—lured by the permission granted them by local rulers to carry on money-lending activities in many of the Piedmonte towns—accepted the closed-in life of the crowded ghetto. On the other hand, in Venice Jews always lived in large numbers and were an important part of the thriving commerce of that republic and therefore could not be restricted, even if the Church wanted them confined.

The ghetto in Cuneo actually consisted of just one courtyard and the small buildings around it. There were four gates leading into this crowded courtyard, one of which is still visible in its original form.

As we entered the courtyard, we stepped into the rooms connected with the synagogue, which was on the second floor. At the street level was a community room in which quotations from Pirkei Avot were still visible. As we walked up the staircase, we came into the large synagogue, which was most unadorned, except for the ark, which was completely gilded. Mr. Cavaglion later pointed out how much of a sacrifice it must have been for the very small community of poor Jews to raise the money to buy the gold for the ark.

We all marveled at one phenomenon: In a corner of the outside wall there was a hole that indicated a spot where a cannonball had hit the synagogue during one of the sieges of town, while children were studying inside. Miraculously, the cannonball never entered the synagogue. This historical event was celebrated every year as a "Cuneo Purim"!

On the floor above was a small room that was once used as a school for children. I also saw piles of Hebrew books that were in a miserable state of decay. They were of no particular interest but showed that some learning had been going on in this community.

Cuneo is very near the French border. During the days of the Avignon popes, the Jews were liberally tolerated there, but in later times the Jews were expelled from the Provence and came across the Alps at the border into Italy. They brought with them their French rites and old melodies. I arranged with Mr. Cavaglion to record some of these melodies in the afternoon!

We now proceeded to the Jewish cemetery, which is located inside a large Catholic cemetery. We walked though large areas of Christian tombs before we came to another enclosure to which Mr. Cavaglion had the keys. As we entered the Jewish cemetery, I noted certain families were predominant there, particularly the Cassin family, whose name in the few Hebrew tombstones was spelled "Qatzin." Of course, this is the family of the famous Cassin who was Gen. de Gaulle's adviser during the war and who received the Nobel Prize for authoring the U.N. Declaration of Human Rights.

The tombstone of one rabbi mentioned in Hebrew the name of his rabbinical teacher. There had near been any *yeshivot* in these small Italian towns, so those young men who wanted to study for the rabbinate had to visit Padua, Venice, Florence or Rome.

Afterward we went back to the hotel to pick up our luggage and proceeded to the home of the Cavaglions for our "recording session." I was very happy and satisfied at taping one or two typically Provencal melodies, which must be strictly "endangered species." There are no Jews left in the Provence in France, and those on the Italian side of the border are clearly dying out. The melodies that he sang were said to be of local character from Cuneo and may constitute an important contribution to Jewish musicology.

Mr. Cavaglion kept saying to me in French that "this is a feast day for me, as I have Jewish guests!" I must say at times I was moved to tears over his exuberant enthusiasm at our presence. His wife joined him and she was even more exuberant than he. She comes from Vincelli and showed me portraits of her rabbinical ancestors. She too contributed some melodies, mainly from the Seder, always telling with great enthusiasm what her father sang and what he didn't sing.

After having a drink in the family living room, we left and Mr. Cavaglion escorted us all the way out a few miles into the countryside to make sure that we were heading the right way.

About an hour later we arrived at Cherasco—a small, provincial town with no Jews left at all. This is where Napoleon had signed the treaty that gave him control of most of Italy and France, where he emancipated the Jews. However, the owners of the house in which the old synagogue is still housed had come specifically from Turin to be on hand and show us around. First we met Mrs. Silvana Segré who turned out to be fluent in Hebrew since she had been trained at a teacher's institute in Jerusalem. She was now teaching in a Jewish school in Turin, which had about 120 students and 14 Italian-born Jewish teachers. She showed us the very small compound that contained the ghetto, including the house at which the synagogue was located. We walked up the narrow steps of the synagogue until we came to a water fountain that had been donated by the members of the community, according to a fine inscription on top of it.

As we entered the small synagogue hall I noted that its *bimah* was similar to the one we had seen in Mondovi the day before. On top of each window a poem had been written composed evidently around the personal names of members of the synagogue. It was the first synagogue we had visited where that the walls were not decorated with quotations from either the Bible or the Talmud.

Of course, we checked the Torah scrolls. One was written on leather and the rest were on parchment with no special peculiarities.

The staircase leading up to the women's gallery was too weak to hold us. On the other hand, we found the room that had been used as a schoolroom.

As in the case of other synagogues we visited in Piedmonte, its entrance was from inside the ghetto so that the Jews did not have to go outside the ghetto to reach the synagogue.

After a while, Mrs. Segré drove us out of town to see the Jewish cemetery. We saw the monuments, which were well kept and preserved. Here the name Segré, which indicates the Spanish origin of the family, predominated the cemetery. However, a beautiful, large, black stone with very clear, golden, engraved letter—the only one with a complete Hebrew text—was the grave of a Mrs. Hendele Rothstin. Mrs. Segré had no idea who she had been. (In the Cuneo cemetery we had seen three graves of Viennese and Hungarian Jews who had been executed by the Nazis only three days before the war was over.)

We said good-bye to Mr. Segré and Mrs. Segré—after they had shown us their apartment in the remodeled ghetto building—and were off for the last leg of our trip leading back to Milan. On the way we stopped over in Fossano; I wanted to be sure that I had visited each of the three cities that made up the famous APAM "tri-state" community!

Fossano, too, is a typical medieval town perched on top of a hill. Unfortunately the synagogue has disappeared. No one could tell us the location of the cemetery, which was still supposed to be in existence. We returned to our hotel in Milan a bit after 10:00 p.m. after an exhausting but totally gratifying and revealing cultural safari into the past of the rich Italian Jewish heritage!

On the way back to Milan, Karie talked about the great importance of having personal experiences such as this one, which make everything Jewish come so much to life, especially past history and our rich Jewish heritage.

In the morning we barely managed, each on his own, to return to the city.

Our trip through Jewish Piedmonte taught a great deal about Jewish history. By the 13th century, the Church realized that it had failed to eradicate Judaism in France, the land of the great *yeshivot* of the Provence and of the descendants of Rashi and his successors. The Church had tried to achieve success by burning precious Hebrew manuscripts, beginning in 1243 in Paris, when tens of thousands of copies of the Talmud were thrown publicly into the flames.

Next, the ferocious onslaught by the Church on Judaism was tried through public disputation and forced conversion. This, too, failed. That is when the Church decided to massacre the French Jews and deport the surviving Jews.

So in 1391 the great bloodbaths perpetrated by the Church took place. France was emptied of its once majestic Jewish centers. Those who could escape crossed the Alps into Italy. They took the rites with them, called "Minhag Tzorfath" to this day.

The communities of Piedmonte are therefore the transplanted French communities that had survived the outrages and pogroms of the Church. The *Machzor Apam* that they left us is a monument to the strength and resilience of the Jewish spirit.

Our visit to Piedmonte was therefore our way of paying homage to the memory of our great Jewish heroes.

# A "Shared" Jerusalem Equals a "Judenrein" Jerusalem

Orchestrated to coincide with the brutal political pressure on Prime Minister Netanyahu amid Arafat's deliberate dragging out of the so-called Hebron Accord, comes a full page advertisement in *The New York Times*, part of an anti-Semitic, anti-Israeli campaign composed of a combination of Arab oil money and extreme leftists who are deceptively trying to lend a religious character to their hate campaign.

The ad is a masterpiece of lies and deception. It is also totally misleading and dishonest. It is signed in the name of "Christians." Which Christians? The extremely fine print allows one only with difficulty to unravel the names that the ad bears. But it is obvious that in the main Marxist leftists in Christendom spearheaded the drafting of the ad. Presbyterians, known for their anti-Semitism, are prominently represented, along with Lutherans—the Protestants with roots in Germany, the original home of anti-Semitism. Prominent through their absence are members of the huge membership of Southern Baptists, the largest segment of American Protestantism.

The dishonesty and falsehood represented by the ad is that it hides the fact that it is based on a similar previous ad published some year ago, also calling for "A Shared Jerusalem," which was the result of a meeting in Jerusalem of Marxist Arabs and Jews. However, that meeting was more honest than the present one: It cleared up the question, which "share" do these leftists have in mind for the Jews, the original owners of Jerusalem? Well, if we are lucky, they will benevolently present us with the King David Hotel, Holiday Inn, the Biblical Zoo and surrounding areas. And the share of the Arabs? All of biblical Jerusalem, i.e., the entire Old City.

Below the surface there always lurks in such circles the demand of the pope for control of Jerusalem. The Vatican reserves no place for Jews in the control of Jerusalem, just as the Catholics reserve no space for Protestants in the Church of Nativity in Bethlehem. Protestants are allowed only once a year to stand outside in the courtyard and sing hymns!

In short, "a shared Jerusalem" is a Judenrein Jerusalem. The obsession with always taking away Jerusalem from the Jews has its roots in the classical Christian anti-Semitism of centuries ago—the Church claims to be "Verus Israel" (the True Israel) and Jerusalem only exists in heaven, not on earth. Because the Jews forfeited their right to their capital, they must eternally wander around landless and homeless.

Although the signatories claim to be churchmen, not one biblical or religious word appears in the ad. This is logical considering that the signatories are inspired by leftists, in contradiction to the claim of *"caritas"* (Christian love). The ad also spells the end of inter-faith fraternization. Two thousand years leave Christians where they always were: out to eradicate Judaism and Jewish existence. The years when there was a pretense of a common agenda for Jews and Christians through inter-faith activity are down the drain, as far as these hate-filled Christians who signed this vicious ad are concerned.

I was heartened by the first reaction to the hate campaign against Jewish Jerusalem which came from the prestigious International Christian Embassy in Jerusalem. Its head, Rev. Willem van der Houven, a wonderful human being and deeply religious Christian, immediately discussed with me plans to counter the leftists with an ad expressing the true Christian feelings about the Jewish claims to Jerusalem. He set himself a very short deadline for inserting a full-page ad in the *Jerusalem Post* in order to make an impact on the final negotiations concerning Hebron. Despite the brief time limit, dozens of Christian groups and churches from all over the world clamored to get aboard and have their signatures on the new ad. Many more could not be accommodated but deserve to be mentioned.

If the spectacle of the anti-Semitic ad would not be so dangerous and tragic, it would be amusing to observe how the episode proves that in Christendom, just as in some segments of modern Judaism, there are totally secular, anti-religious segments who have only a "liberal" agenda, far removed from the original religious mission of their faith. We are learning through this episode that Christians with these leftist, Marxist leanings have no right to invoke arguments on historical rights since they abjure any weight to history. (Similarly, Shimon Peres has often said that Jews should "forget" the past and their own history!)

The fact that this ad is not pioneered by religious Christians but by cold-blooded leftists is shown by the fact that the ad contains a mechanism to influence congressional hearings in the approval of new State Department personalities nominated by President Clinton. Fortunately it is not likely that the broadly religious conservative Christian electorate, which is becoming increasingly powerful, will follow the lead of the secular leftists. It is up to Israel's friends to demonstrate the hypocrisy and deception of the signatories, who claim to be religious Christians while identifying themselves with Moslems and anti-Christian leftists.

The ad mentions not one Jew or Moslem among the signatories. Yet the previous ad listed many Jewish and Moslem founders of the "Jewish Peace Lobby," a leftist PLO front, founded by the likes of Letty Pogrebin and other pro-PLO members of Americans for Peace Now (APN). The current controversy helps finally to ferret out the people who for years pretended to be Zionists and shared the Israeli government's faith in a united Jerusalem under undivided Jewish rule. Having won membership in the Conference of Presidents of Major American Jewish Organizations by a ruse, the APN's true anti-Zionist program is now apparent,. There is still time to disbar them from mainline Jewish organizations so that President Clinton can be shown that the 93 percent of the Jewish electorate which voted for him was convinced that the United States government will support a Jewish Jerusalem.

In confronting the underhanded political propaganda of the anti-Semites who signed *The New York Times* ad, Jews—as individuals or as groups—should write to members of the United States Senate Foreign Relations Committee and impress on them that the newly nominated secretary of state, Madeline Albright, should declare her adherence to the traditional American concept of an undivided, united Jerusalem under Jewish control.

We should at the same time encourage our religious Christian friends and express our appreciation for their solidarity in this critical situation.

Hans Lehmann ז״ל
1885-1949

# Family

I am privileged to be a member of a very old family, rich in tradition. Its roots can be found in many countries: On my parents' side, in Germany and Lithuania, on my wife's side in Rumania, Hungary and Czechoslovakia. In my own life, Sweden, Germany and the USA played the greatest roles in cementing a many-colored spectrum of Jewish experience, for which I am profoundly grateful. My ancestors, and especially my late father, are an ever-present inspiration to me. My son Jamie ז״ל, to whose memory this volume is dedicated, was the embodiment of the excellence in ethical behavior and scholarly accomplishments for which our family has always striven.

## 'D'Yukna Shel Abba': A Profile of My Father, ז״ל

There is an unusual verse in the Book of Tehillim (45:17) that states, "*Tachat avoteycha yihyu banyecha*" (In the place of your fathers will be your sons). The language is hardly the type of "Tehillim language" we are used to. In fact the entire Chapter 45 is different from almost all of Psalms: It is not addressed to either G-d or to the individual worshiper. It is an expression of adoration of a king by a scribe at the court of the king—the "*sofer mahir*" (skilled scribe) mentioned in Verse 2. Therefore, the verse expresses the hope for a continued royal dynasty, where grandfather, fathers and sons harmonize in the same destiny.

I have often thought how this verse applies to my own family. And it brings to my mind many of the things that my own father, *z"l* (1885–1949), used as his motto in life. One of his main themes in life was the verse at the end of the Book of Malaki referring to the prophet Elijah in the end of days: "And he will turn the hearts of the fathers to their sons, and the hearts of the sons to their fathers." He stressed that it is not the fathers, the old generation, which is to discipline the young generation into respect and obedience to their elders. It is the elders who have to turn their hearts and understanding to the young generation, which will in the end bring about the harmony between generations.

I was privileged to have had an unusual father—a Jew who lived an unusual life and who benefited enormously from his experiences. His shining example was enough to place an imprint on his children—no regimenting or nagging, so often found in parents, was ever his conduct, only through personal example. But to understand the unusual aspects of his life, I must outline his biography.

My father came from a very long line of German Jews. Their roots were in

Halberstadt in Central Germany, a city made famous not only through its many outstanding rabbis and scholars and institutions, but also because of the outstanding deeds of our namesake, Behrend Lehmann, who was the finance minister to the King of Saxonia and who lived about 300 years ago. His outstanding example achieved social relief for his fellow Jews and brought Jewish scholarship to its greatest height in Germany by establishing an important Torah academy in Halberstadt shortly after the 30-Year War and the Chmelnetzky pogroms of the 1640s.

My father was born in Leipzig, also in the Kingdom of Saxonia. Leipzig was a unique city in that it was a meeting point of East and West. The annual Leipzig Fair, still maintained today, brought Russian fur and bristle dealers to sell their ware at the fair. Many of them ultimately settled in Leipzig, thereby making the city a thoroughly mixed community of Eastern and German Jews. The German Jews were quite assimilated by the end of the last century, and it was a G-dsend that the Russian Jews—many of them outstanding Talmidei Chachamim—brought strong Orthodoxy and learning to the town.

Although German Jews traditionally looked down on "Eastern" Jews, in Leipzig there was more amalgamation of the different groups than elsewhere in Germany. My father had many good friends among the Russian Jews—for example, the outstanding banker, Hans Kroch, a first generation German Jew, whose grandfather had been a great Russian Talmid Chacham whose works the grandson would publish one volume for each Yahrzeit. My father was also friendly with leading Russian fur dealers, among them the Merkin, Eitingon and Kestenbaum families.

A turning point in my father's life occurred when a young, charismatic rabbi, Ephraim Carlebach, of the famous German rabbinical family, arrived in Leipzig. He organized the youth and brought enthusiasm into their life. He formed a Hebrew school, and my father taught there from time to time. A young lady, Fannie Taub, born in Berlin but of Lithuanian lineage was also one of the Carlebach enthusiasts. She came from a very poor home, but my father paid no attention to her financial standing. Once he had made up his mind to marry her, he followed her through nine years of separation, after she and her family had emigrated to New York. And so in 1912 they got engaged in New York, and a year later were married by Dr. Meyer Hildesheimer of the famous rabbinical family of Berlin, who happened to be in New York on assignment for the Agudah. The result of the influence of Rabbi Carlebach on my father was that throughout his life he made it his goal to be in the company of scholars and teachers. He also decided that he would sacrifice everything for a Jewish education for his children.

My father refused to settle down in America—a country he considered much too materialistic and superficial. Instead they returned to Leipzig, where my father had meanwhile started his own business. But when World War I broke out, in 1914, they moved to Sweden, where my father had an active business. As the family grew, the problem with Jewish education became precarious, as Swedish Jews were almost all assimilated Reform Jews, without a proper Jewish school. At first my father engaged private tutors for my brothers, but in 1928 decided to move the entire family to Hamburg, known for its outstanding day school, the Talmud Torah Realschule.

During our stay there, I remember countless rabbis, roshei yeshivot and other scholars who visited our home. One of them, Professor Isaak Markon, an outstanding Russian scholar, was the librarian of the Jewish library in Hamburg, and he initiated me—at the tender age of 10 years—into the various uses of a library.

One of my father's main logos was *"Torah u-gedulah be-makom echad"*—Torah and worldly greatness in one person. He admired greatly those figures in our history who personified this slogan, although there were admittedly not too many of them. But he impressed on me this ideal, which I have always tried to pursue.

He also used a German saying to the effect: "Each person must contribute something for eternity." With this he meant that it is not enough to follow the average course of life, but one must achieve something that excels and surpasses usual standards in order to leave a mark on history forever. This attitude impressed on me a search for accomplishments which others have not necessarily achieved. It is a principle that does not apply only to learning and religious observance, but also to general academic scholarships and even business. It can best be described as a *"koach hachiddush,"* ability to innovate! My father undertook business transactions that were quite unusual. In my own career my wife and I have pioneered commercial transactions and constellations which broke new ground—in many parts of the world.

Papa—as we called him—was a history buff. Even before my Bar Mitzvah my father would spend long sessions with me during which he related world history, going back to Otto von Bismarck and the First World War, of which he knew every battle, general and campaign.

He was an enthusiastic Zionist and had dreamed of a Jewish State long before it became a reality. He knew all the writings of Moshe Hess, Herzl and other early Zionists. Yet he used to warn me that Zionism is something like a "Para Aduma"—the Red Heifer—which defiles the pure but would purify the impure. This meant that religious Jews sometimes turned irreligious in pursuit of Zionism, while it would attract to Judaism those had been alienated through assimilation.

Papa was fluent in German, Swedish, French, English and Italian. He loved to teach us proverbs in these languages. One which has stayed with me throughout life, in Italian, can often be applied: *"Si non e vero e ben trovato"*—If it is not true, it is nevertheless a good invention. How many times have I thought of this when I hear *"pilpul"* or forced Dvar Torah, which even its author knows is not really true, although it sounds clever.

He was exceptional in that he had no ambition to be ahead in education of his own children, for some parents like their children to advance no further than their own level of education. But Papa wanted me and my brothers to surpass him in Jewish and secular education, and he rejoiced in our academic and cultural accomplishments.

My parents spent the entire War (1939–1945) in Sweden. My father had personally rescued one synagogue from destruction by the Nazis and had brought it to Stockholm where it still is in use today. He was an essential link in all rescue operations, since Sweden was neutral and had links with Germany as well as with the Allies. Entire Lithuanian yeshivot were saved to Japan and the United States through my father's untiring efforts. He also arranged South American passports for Jews whom he never knew—as long as he could save a Jew! Toward the end of the War, he was the first Western Jew allowed into Russia and he used the time to mobilize Russian Jews with hope of emigration and rebuilding of Jewish life.

A few weeks before he passed away in 1949, we had the *zchus* of his coming to New York for my wedding. He returned to Sweden, where he died. We buried him in Israel, the Land he—like Moses—had not been privileged to visit himself. In his memory I established a few buildings in leading Yeshivot in Israel and published Sefarim which are important for Torah study. This life which began in Germany, and brought Papa to various countries, ended in the fulfillment of his most cherished dreams, the redemption of our people, and the re-establishment of Judaism after the Holocaust. As the verse in Tehillim states, a royal dynasty deserved that generation after generation live up to the aims and principles established in the past.

May my father's memory always be blessed.

James H. Lehmann, ז״ל (1950-1982)
The Lehmann family honors his memory with an annual
Memorial Lecture given at New York's Fifth Avenue Synagogue.

# Remembering My Son Jamie Lehmann ז״ל

Every year, a Memorial Lecture is held in memory of my son Jamie, *z"l*, who passed away in June of 1982. The memorial meeting will take place at the Fifth Avenue Synagogue, at 5 East 62nd Street. As in previous years, the Memorial Volume will be published, containing last year's lectures, along with two of Jamie's essays and a number of Hebrew poems which were dear to my son.

The meeting will start with the *Kel Male Rachamim*, sung by the world renowned cantor, Yosef Malovany. Rabbi Sol Roth of the Fifth Avenue Synagogue will speak about Jamie and his writings. Thereafter, I will deliver "A Father's Appreciation." The Memorial Lecture in 1995 was delivered by Professor Sid Z. Leiman, who teaches Jewish history and literature at Brooklyn College and Yeshiva University. Professor Leiman was one of Jamie's teachers. The theme he will speak on is "The Architect of the Jewish Response to Modernity." The reference is to Chacham Bernays of Hamburg, who was born in 1792 and died in 1849 and who was among the very first Orthodox rabbis to have a secular academic education. His influence is felt to this day. It was he who taught R. Samson ben Rafael Hirsch, the initiator of the "Torah Im Derech Eretz" concept.

I publish herewith my "Father's Appreciation" of last year, which has been published for this year's memorial meeting. I have also added an excerpt from Rav Aharon Soloveitchik's Memorial Lecture of last year.

These memorial meetings have become the highest cultural Jewish event of the year and attract growing numbers of participants. I sincerely hope that this year's event will be as well attended as previous years. You are invited to pay respect to my late son. Admission is free. Collation follows the lectures.

### *A Father's Appreciation*

The *yahrzeit* of Jamie always falls shortly after Shavuos and after *Parshas Noso*, and you know that for the past twelve years we have been learning a continuous *Shiur* on the Book of Ruth which we read on Shavuous and which Jamie learnt with his wife Marcia shortly before his death. It seems to me significant that there is a line going from Nachshon ben Aminadav to Dovid HaMelech—three generations from Nachson ben Aminadov to Boaz, and three generations from Ovad [?] to Dovid. I mentioned often that our son Jamie often invoked the *Chut Ha-Meshulosh* in the sense of a family—three generations of a family, grandfather, father and son, or grandparents, parents and children, whether daughter or son—are a cord of strength that cannot be severed. If you take a look at Nachshon he personifies some qualities that were inherent in Jamie. The twelve *korbanot* of the

*Neseim*; Rabeinu Bachai makes a very interesting observation: all other *korbanot* started *korbano* and Nachshon, although he was the first, starts *U-korbano*, as if it were the second in line and not the first. He was the first and gave the first *korban*, but appears in a sequence of various *korbanot*, to show that Nachshon was so humble that he didn't mind appearing as if others came before him. Equally, Rabainu Bachai points out that the word *Nasi* is missing in the *parshah* of Nachshon; all others were called *Nasi* or *Nesei'm*, and he isn't called *Nasi*. This kind of humility was very characteristic of Jamie. Everybody knew that he excelled; everybody knew that he was a leader, that happened without question. But he never had to stress it; I don't think that he was ever president or chairman of any kind of organization, and yet from childhood on he was the head of any group.

The Gemara also points out that Nachshon ben Aminadav was the one who jumped into the Yam Suf before anybody else dared; he took on the *mesirat nefesh* to brave the waves and when he got into the water, the water split. So we have two qualities in Nachshon: his humility and his *mesirat nefesh*.

If we go on three generations further, we come to Boaz and Ruth. We have two persona in Megillat Ruth: Orpa and Ruth. What was the difference between the two? In the case of Orpa, she decided to classify human beings around their ethnicity, so to speak, and therefore she went back to *amah* (her nation) and *elohehah* (her gods). She decided that she was a Moabite, we were all Jews, and she had her god—Kemosh—and she wasn't interested in the Jewish religion. But Ruth was totally different. Ruth had real deep interest in what Naomi stood for. She said to Naomi, "*El asher telchi ailaich*"—in the future, I know that you have a great future in front of you, you are going to amount to a great deal, and I want to emulate you. Then she goes on, "*Ubeasher talini alin*"—even in the dark sides of life, when there is sadness and mourning and death and night, she admired Naomi's conduct and wanted to share in that. As a result of that, she says "*Amchah ami*." That kind of nation that produces a person like Naomi, is the nation that I want to be part of. And "*ve-Elokaich Elokai*"—the kind of G-d who created that kind of nation is the G-d for me. So therefore, she was deep in her appreciation of her fellow men, completely different from Orpa. And I would say again that Jamie was certainly a Ruth person, somebody who had so much compassion, so much interest in people around him, that it is just amazing how many expressions of admiration come pouring in to this day. Just read what Yale University published in a volume where they said that Jamie's character was such that he was kind and always concerned with others, and he would at times drive through the night to comfort somebody in need. Interestingly enough, the *goyim* noticed that in Jamie there was this *Ahava* and this *Chesed*, this *Chut shel Chesed* that Jamie so often talked about which was so apparent in his life.

Now let us look again at what Ruth said. She comes back to say at the end, "*Ba-asher tomiti ehmot*." She thought (she was not Jewish at this point) that death is the end, there is no more; "where you die I die," and that seems to be the end. But her grandson Dovid must have pondered over that. Is it really true that death is the end? And we find in the famous *hesped* that Dovid HaMelech pronounced over his best friend Jonathan, he uses similar words to those that Ruth used. But he says, "*Bemotam lo nifradu*"; where his great-grandmother said "*Hamavet yafrid*" he said "*Bemosom lo nifradu*," which means, according to David's full statement, "*Haneahavim vehaneimim bechaiyaihem ubemotam lo nifradu*." The Jewish ethical concept, the Jewish philosophy of life and death is totally different, in the sense that life goes on and there is no separation through the process of death. This is something I think we are demonstrating here: Jamie passed away twelve years ago and after twelve years the love for him, the desire to emulate him in his excellence in every respect shows that *bemotam lo nifradu*—we were not separated through death.

Now what is it, if you again trace the generations from Nachshon all the way down to Dovid, what do we learn? We learn that the example of a *Godol*, of a great person, is a driving force in Jewish education, in Jewish life. And it has been so in our family. I know that on my wife's side, our children were blessed to have had grandparents like Reb Faish Moskovits and Anyu—he was a *Godol HaDor* in his own right and we and everybody looked up to him. In my own family, my father was exemplary in seeking out *Gedolim*. His first influence was Rabbi Ephraim Carlebach and later Rabbi Yosef Carlebach and many others throughout his life. He taught us to seek out *Gedolim* even if you don't learn with them, but even having seen a *Godol*, a *Godol b'Torah*, a *Godol b'Midot*, makes you a totally different person than somebody who never saw a *Godol*. I remember my teacher, Rav Shlomo Wolbe, who is one of the *Gedolim* to whom I was very much exposed, told the story that the Alter from Kelm had the following encounter: when the Darwinian evolution theories reached the small town of Kelm, where the yeshiva was, a *talmid* came running in to the Rebbe all excited, and said, "Rebbe, Rebbe, there is a *goy* in London who claims that he descends from apes. What do you say to that?" Very calmly the Alter said, "Of course, he has to come to that conclusion because he never saw Rav Yisroel Salanter." It sounds funny, but it is really very very profound: a person who has seen Rav Yisroel Salanter, which means a person who has seen a *Godol*, has seen the fantastic and supreme development of *Midot* and wisdom and depths and profundity of learning and scholarship, can see no link between monkeys and such a person. Those who haven't fall into a different category. Therefore I would like to use this occasion to call on my children and grandchildren especially, to make it a focal point in their education to seek out *Gedolim*. No matter how far you have to go, seek them out so that you will have seen at some time a *Godol* in *Midos* and learning and in conduct to his fellow men and G-d. With that in mind, we are all privileged to see the *Godol HaDor* among us, and I hope that that will be a stimulation for all of us along the lines that I have spoken.

## Rabbi Ahron Soloveitchik's Appreciation of Jamie Lehmann

*B'reshus* Dr. Manfred Lehmann and *b'reshus haKehal*, I am taking the liberty to deliver a memorial lecture in the memory of Jamie Lehmann. In the course of the last fifty years I have delivered numerous memorial lectures as well as eulogies over different people, but in respect to all the people I memorialized or eulogized, I knew them very well as a result of my contact and acquaintance with them for a long time. However, Chaim Menachem, *z"l*, or Jamie, as he was commonly called by everyone, was an exception.

I met Jamie Lehmann only once in 1982, a few months before his passing, at the Fifth Avenue Synagogue. I came there to his lecture, even though I hadn't met him before, because I was eager to hear a lecture by a young scholar of 32. After his lecture I spoke to him for about 15 minutes only, within which I expressed to him a few comments on his lecture. It is needless for me to tell you that I was very impressed with his lecture. However, I was primarily impressed with Jamie's personality. Why? In the course of the years I had heard numerous and multifarious lectures by different people: Rabbis, *Roshei Yeshivot*, scientists, artists, politicians and such; I was not so impressed with their lectures as I was impressed with Jamie's lecture. The main reason was that Jamie *motzaw chain b'einai*—he found grace in my eyes. I don't know why. What is *chain* or grace? *Chain* or grace cannot be defined; it can only be felt. The Torah says in connection with Yosaif—*Vayemotzaw Yosaif chain beainov*. Yosaif found *chain* in the eyes of those he met. The Torah also says in connection with Noach, *VeNoach motzaw chain beainei HaShem*—that Noach found grace in the eyes, so to speak, of the Lord. And the Ramban there asked, what is *chain*? *Chain* the Ramban says means *Ma'asov na'im vene'emim, vecahn vaitain chaino b'einei sar bais hasohar*. What the Ramban means can be expressed succinctly in the following statements: grace consists in the fact that a person's external and internal behavior is beautiful and correct. It means that he is humble and unassuming. There are many speakers and lecturers who are very eloquent, but they try to impress the audience through their eloquence and rhetoric. Such speakers and lecturers are not internally beautiful, even though they appear externally polished and correct. When Jamie spoke, I felt that he was full of grace and devoid of malice, jealousy and even ambition; he was even devoid of constructive and productive ambition. He did not try to impress the audience, nor did he try to impress himself (sometimes you hear an eloquent speaker full of so much *naches* of himself—when Jamie spoke I didn't see that he enjoyed his own lecture).

# How One Jew Saved Yiddishkeit in His Country

Jews have lived in Sweden since about 1755. By the beginning of this century, Sweden was enveloped in Reform Judaism and assimilation. World War I (1914–1918), however, brought a contingent of observant Jews to the country to whom Reform was anathema. The Reform congregation-called "Mosaic Congregation"—was headed by a rabid Reform rabbi, named Ehrenpreis, who originally had been a learned yeshiva *bachur* in Galicia. However, his life was the story of a turncoat.

After taking on a rabbinical position in a Reform community in Bulgaria, he spurned authentic Judaism. He even turned against his erstwhile Zionist colleagues: In 1897 he had been Theodore Herzl's secretary for the First Zionist Congress in Basel, but by 1913 he had accepted the post of Chief Rabbi of Sweden on condition that he forswear Zionism. (In 1933 when Hitler came to power, Ehrenpreis became, again, a Zionist.)

Whatever was left of authentic Judaism in Sweden disintegrated under his leadership. The handful of observant Jews had a giant fight on their hands to save *kashrus*, Jewish education and the mikveh. My late father, Hans Lehmann, was a leading spokesman for Torah-true Judaism and often engaged in sharp debates with the Reform in town. The most erudite and explicit document he left behind is the following statement in defense of the mikveh in Stockholm, written 74 years ago. With or without help by Reform Jews, the mikveh in Stockholm survived.

During World War II, Ehrenpreis was accused by Christian Parliament members of doing less than the Christians themselves did to save German refugees. It goes without saying that his children and grandchildren intermarried and are today Christians.

After World War II a large influx of German, Polish and Hungarian Jews—survivors of the Holocaust—came to Sweden and totally revived Jewish life. The memory of the Reform Rabbi Ehrenpreis, for his disloyalty to Judaism and Zionism, is of course tarnished until this day. My father—product of the enthusiasm for Judaism planted in him by his teacher, Rabbi Ephraim Carlebach of Leipzig—always distrusted the Reform. His distrust for Ehrenpreis was sadly vindicated.

My father's example shows how even one staunch defender of Judaism can win a historic battle for our survival. . . . We can all learn from his example. His life illustrated the prophetic verse, "G-d's paths are straight, the righteous advance on them, while the wicked stumble on them" (Hoshea 14:10).

May his memory be blessed.

Here is my father's statement in defense of the Stockholm mikveh.

"The following statement is submitted on my own behalf and on behalf of my associates, Mr. Heyman Nathan and Jacob Ettlinger, in response to the statement of August 30 issued by Dr. Ehrenpreis:"

As is well known, my associates and I submitted a request on January 6, 1922, for a declaration of support by the Mosaic Community of Stockholm for an annual subsidy of S.Cr. 1500 for the maintenance of the local ritual bath (Mikveh). Dr. Ehrenpreis, the chief rabbi, gave his promise at the time to approve such a subsidy. We are therefore profoundly surprised to learn of the devastating and critical attack by Dr. Ehrenpreis against a Mikveh in general, and in Stockholm in particular.

Before I respond in detail to his statement, I wish to point out that there exists in Stockholm—a fact some of your members may be ignorant of—in the southern part of our capital a traditional congregation based on traditional Jewish values. Its name is "Adass Yisroel." Its constitution stresses prominently the support of a Mikveh. Furthermore, I wish to point out that within the last few years, the maintenance of the Mikveh was entirely supported financially by members of said traditional congregation. This Mikveh has recently been renovated in order to comply totally to the religious requirements involved.

Until now the financial contribution by the gentlemen who sign this petition amounts to about S.Cr. 400-500. However, the Mikveh has now been forced to present to us a new contract, which imposes a substantial financial burden on us in order to comply with the annual expenditures. This obligation we cannot assume by ourselves without the contribution by the Mosaic Congregation. Closing down the Mikveh is unthinkable. On the other hand it is unthinkable for traditional Jews to see the Mikveh cease to exist. I therefore take the liberty to renew my petition to give a favorable response to our new request.

We are forced to express our profound surprise that the leadership of the Mosaic Congregation has simply put aside our petition. Being a minority within the community, it would seem to us that you are guided by the slogan "Might Makes Right." Such a policy corresponds neither to the Jewish concept of Law, nor the maxims of modern Liberalism. Even if our traditional co-religionists cannot insist on a place in the sun, I nevertheless believe they have the right to expect understanding for their religious convictions. And so little is requested by us: an annual contribution of S.Cr. 1500 for a flawless compliance with the Jewish requirements especially for the maintenance of the Mikveh.

The claim of Dr. Ehrenpreis that the need for a ritual bath in Stockholm does not exist is incorrect. I enclose documentary evidence by the bath installation, that during the past five years about 1,880 persons made use of it. Such a number is proof enough that the existence of a Mikveh is a necessity. I am of the opinion that it is part of the duties of a Liberal congregation also to accommodate the convictions of dissidents, if their requirements are justified. In today's political climate, the needs and aspirations of minorities are met to the widest possible degree. Why should such tolerance not also be extended to the requirements within Jewish communities?

Even Christian scholars, without necessarily being philo-Semites, have had to admit during past centuries that the survival of the Jewish people in its excellent form can be traced to the exemplary chastity and family purity. These virtues in our people are entirely based on the institution of the Mikveh and its symbolism. To deny this truism and the value of the Mikveh would be an historical untruth.

As to the claim by Dr. Ehrenpreis that there is no theological foundation for the Mikveh but that the Mikveh in oldest times was merely used for hygienic reasons, I rebuff this claim totally. As our previous statement emphasized, the purifying spiritual and emotional influence of the Mikveh is of paramount importance, and it is regrettable that Dr. Ehrenpreis ignored the cardinal biblical commandment for the Mikveh, as found in Leviticus 11:36: "*Akh mayon u'bor mikveh mayim yihiyeh tahor...*" This reference proves clearly that the institution of the Mikveh is a basic religious command in the Jewish religion, side-by-side with the oral tradition.

I also take the liberty of disagreeing with Dr. E's claim that 45 percent of all Jewish communities have eliminated the Mikveh. Claims based on such statistics are totally unreliable. Even in such communities as Genoa, Copenhagen and Oslo, where Torah-true Jews are in the minority, the communities consider it a call of duty and honor to comply with all Jewish laws.

The Reform rabbis whom you mention as "authorities" are by no means authorities. (e.g., Stein, Geiger), nor are their opinions respected widely. These extreme rabbis occupy, in Germany, a tiny minority within German Jewry and have never been accepted as authoritative by the Jewish masses until this day. I will avoid quoting Reform rabbis and their ideas, in order to avoid disagreement, friction and strife within our community.

Even though the Mosaic Congregation of Stockholm has refrained from supporting the Mikveh in the past, there is no reason to assume that this sad state of affairs will also continue in the future. On the contrary, I consider it honorable and desirable to change and correct the attitude, so that the shortcomings of the past can be corrected. But my main point is that for the sake of unity and harmony in our community, the needs of the minority be recognized and met.

I appeal, that in the interest of peace your Council approve our justified request for a contribution of S.Cr. 1500. Otherwise we will not waive our rights, and will, in the case that our request is turned down, find other ways to defend our legal rights.

# My Wife—Anne

The time is June 1941. The place, the Moscow Central Railway Station. The Trans-Siberian express is stoking its locomotive, sending out clouds of white vapors. At one of the windows a handsome dapper man of about 50 with a Franz Joseph-style mustache and a little vandyke beard is looking out at the platform with his wife, a petite, elegant lady, standing next to him. Her freckled face is furrowed, betraying anxiety. Peering out of the next window stand two good-looking tall young men, their sons, of about 18 and 20, and the youngest boy of fourteen. At the third window, staring anxiously at the platform, is Anne, their beautiful pigtailed daughter of sixteen.

The Moskovits family was on their way from Budapest, Hungary, to America by way of Sophia, Bulgaria, then on to Moscow and Vladivostok on the mysterious Trans-Siberian Express which traverses all of Russia. A trip to last all of ten days and eleven nights—from Vladivostok on to Japan by boat on the Chinese Sea and from there on to the USA. They were to land in Seattle, and after a five-day train trip arrive in New York.

The oldest, their daughter Edith and her husband Joel Rosner, had sailed for the USA in the early part of 1940, a few months after their wedding, the trip lasting over six weeks. The Moskovits' oldest son, Zoltan, followed through the Soviet Union and Japan, arranging for the transit visas for the family along his way.

Not long after arriving in New York, Edith began to bombard her parents with daily telegrams and phone calls, urging them to leave and not to delay their departure. "You are too close to the happenings to see the danger you're in," she repeated incessantly. The final impetus for Mr. and Mrs. Moskovits to take the giant step with the rest of their family was the commencement of repeated raids (razzias) that they were subjected to.

The Jews of Slovakia were already being transported to Poland to concentration camps. Some of the braver and luckier men jumped the trains as they crossed Hungary and tried to hide in Budapest. Every once in a while, some of these men would knock on the Moskovits family's door for help. And then the raids began. Three or four detectives would barge into their apartment and after searching the flat, stationed themselves in the hall inside the entrance door, arresting anyone who entered without a travel permit to be in Budapest or an ID certifying their residence in the city.

Among those arrested in late 1940 by the KEOK, the Hungarian Gestapo, was the husband of an adopted poor girl who had grown up in my in-laws' house. They were visiting my parents-in-law with their two little babies.

Neither my father-in-law or any of my brothers-in-law were in Budapest at the time, having already left for Sophia, Bulgaria, where the family was to congregate to leave for the USA by way of a Black Sea port. Only my mother-in-law and Anne, then a girl of 15, were still at home.

Anne, unafraid, went up to the KEOC and asked to speak to the chief inspector. A beautiful young girl, she was taken to the chief and pleaded for the man's release and for permission to visit him in the detention camp. The man was released.

My mother-in-law meanwhile telephoned a retired Hungarian army general, a man supported by Mr. Moskovits. At that time, it was already difficult for Jews to function in their business as heretofore, and it was a practice to engage some influential gentile to front for the business. Mr. Moskovits was a grain dealer and supplied the governments of Hungary and Bugaria with grain. Mrs. Moskovits told the general that Anne had gone to the KEOK. The general became extremely upset and implored Mrs. Moskovits never to allow Anne to even go near the KEOC again. Nor should she take matters into her own hands. These were dangerous times, he concluded.

They were to leave Budapest in May 1941. Unhappy that she would lose one year of gymnasium (high school) by leaving before the year's end, Anne asked the general to arrange for a special year-end examination by a representative of the Ministry of Education (which she knew was done in exceptional circumstances). She accompanied the general to the Ministry of Education, waiting in the anteroom while the general went in to the office to speak to the person in charge of such matters. The general told Anne that he had not been able to obtain a special examination. The general drove her home and left.

Anne waited for the taxi to pull away from the curb and returned to the Ministry. She sought out the official and convinced him to arrange for a special exam for her and received her certificate for the year.

Anne incessantly pleaded with her parents to heed her sister's urging. She looked forward to going to America with great excitement. After Mrs. Moskovits's beloved father passed away Mrs. Moskovits agreed to leave for America.

The plan had been to ferry the family over one by one to nearby Sophia, from where they were to take a boat on the 26th of June of 1941.

However, a few weeks after Anne landed at the Sophia airport without a visa, and her mother with her youngest son Bubi, also arrived in Sophia without a visa, Mr. Moskovits was called up to the police and was told, with no ifs or buts, that unless they left the country by June 6th, they would be deported back to Hungary. None of his highly-placed connections could help Mr. Moskovits in this case and they were faced with either finding an alternate way of travel prior to the June 26th boat or face deportation back to Hungary.

In order to make the June 6 deadline, Mr. Moskovits chartered a Russian plane to fly the family to Moscow.

As the family deplaned in Moscow, the government-appointed tourist agents, the Intourist, met them and hovered around them. Notwithstanding, the family explored the attractions of Moscow, including the ballet and the opera which Anne attended with her mother, unaware of the danger they were escaping. Their luggage, with the contents of their lavish Budapest home, had bulged to fifty-four suitcases. When, four days after they arrived in Moscow, the time came to board the Trans-Siberian Express, the Intourist representative announced that the luggage would go by a separate van. Mr. Moskovits refused to allow them to take his three suitcases and his *tallis* and *tefillin*. When they boarded the train, they saw their 54 cases, neatly stacked, standing on the platform.

The train gives a shrill whistle. Steam escapes, fogging the window, as the train slowly begins to leave the Moscow station. And there, still on the platform, stand all their trunks. The father rushes to grab the emergency brake to stop the train. Anne jumps her father from the back, pinning down his arms in a stranglehold so that he cannot reach the emergency brake.

"What are you doing?" he cries out in surprise.

"Don't try to stop the train," Anne says, holding on with all her strength. "We'll be arrested and wind up in Siberia. Never mind the trunks."

"At least you have your three suitcases," Mrs. Moskovits says, trying to calm her husband.

"And my *tallis* and *tefillin*," says the father. He turns to his sons, "Never leave your *tallis* and *tefillin* for anyone else to carry."

Not until they reached Seattle did any one of them, except their father, have a change of clothes, except the kimonos they bought in Tokyo.

*Puppchen* (little doll), as Anne was called by her family and friends, hesitated not an instant to push down her father's arm—to avoid the danger she foresaw should her father stop the train.

Her independence showed up at the earliest age, even as a child in Szatmar, Roumania, where she was born. When she did not want to take her French lessons, and was locked into her room to await her tutor, she stood at the window and when she saw the tutor turn in at the gate she climbed out the window and disappeared for the afternoon. She made deals with the bus conductor; in exchange for costly Simon Arzt cigarettes she took from her father's office, she would take over the bus, collect the fares, and guide the bus to its destination. She made deals with the taxi drivers to let her drive, and with the policemen to close his eyes when she drove by sitting next to the driver.

At ten she entered the Catholic girls' gymnasium run by nuns. It was a very strict school, not very much to her liking. When the teacher punished her for carrying a comb and a mirror, which signified vanity, she was given the choice of apologizing or kneeling on corn kernels. Rather than apologize for something she did not feel was wrong, she kneeled for an hour on corn kernels digging deeply into her knees.

When she was eleven they moved to Ungvar (Uzhorod) in Czechoslovakia. Just as the population of Transylvania was a mix of Hungarian and Romanian speaking people, in Ungvar Hungarian, Ruthanian and Czech was spoken. When the Moskovits family moved to Ungvar, Puppchen was enrolled in a Hungarian school for a year, during which time she was privately tutored in the Czech language so that she could enter the Czech gymnasium. After the year, her knowledge of the Czech language was still wanting and instead of the gymnasium she was enrolled in the Czech folkschule. Anne was determined to get into the Czech gymnasium, so that she could go to University when she grew up.

After a year in the Czech folkschule she applied to the Czech gymnasium, even though her mastery of the Czech language still left much to be desired. When the day came to take the entrance examination, she asked her uncle to say *Tehillim* during the hours of the examination.

As she left the house, her uncle waved to her, holding up the book of *Tehillim*. She was one of two out of thirty-two applicants who were accepted into the school. To this day she is a great believer in *Tehillim*.

When, in 1939, Czechoslovakia was dismembered, Ungvar became Hungary. The Czech gymnasium became a Hungarian gymnasium. All of the Hungarian teachers sent down from Budapest were extremely anti-Semitic. Anne was constantly punished. She begged her parents to permit her to go the Hebrew gymnasium, a Zionist school. It was, as she tells to this day, the happiest year she ever spent in school in Europe.

Her father felt they would be safer were they to move to Budapest. In such a metropolis, a Jew with a not very politically correct background (Mr. Moskovits was a known Czech patriot) could more easily "disappear." Anne was enrolled in a girls' gymnasium—which did not abide by the numerus clausus and one-third of her class were Jewish girls. She was happy in Budapest, a beautiful city with theaters, opera, concerts and other cultural activities to be enjoyed. Hungarian was her mother tongue and school was therefore easy.

After two years in Budapest they were now travellng on the Trans-Siberian Express. The train finally puffed its last puffs of vapor and smoke as they arrived in Vladivostok. They passed Birobidjan, the Jewish state—the vast snow-covered, barren lands of Siberia—saw the largest lake, the Bajkal, and met Russian officials who spoke Jewish (an unusual experience for people coming from Hungary).

THE DATE, JUNE 21, 1941. It was Friday and they rushed to board before Shabbat. The Japanese vessel waiting in the harbor. The second day after the Japanese vessel heaved out of Vladivostok harbor, on June 22, 1941, the Germans invaded Russia.

Had the family tarried one more day in Moscow, or had the father pulled the emergency brake, or had they been permitted to stay in Bulgaria until their scheduled departure by boat, they would have suffered the fate of all the other Jews in the Holocaust. The vessel on which they were to depart from the Black Sea Port scheduled to leave on the 26th of June never left.

It seems Providential that while my future wife's escape from Nazi extermination took place through a slow eastbound Trans-Siberian train, the last one for freedom, my own rescue took place through a westbound last sailing of an American ocean liner from Genoa to New York. It would seem that Providence lent its hand to save two people destined to lead a dramatic fruitful life together.

After a stopover in Seattle and Chicago, the family arrived in New York to an apartment on the Upper East Side in Manhattan. Joel Rosner, their son-in-law, a certified textile engineer, organized a factory with his wife, Edith, and my father-in-law to manufacture underwear. They were soon booking defense orders.

The family settled in a beautiful home in Crown Heights. Now Anne was determined to learn English. Within a year-and-a-half, Anne passed her college entrance exam to Brooklyn College, where she majored in psychology and English.

At that time, especially where they lived on tree-lined President Street, there were few religious Jews. In fact, when Mr. Moskovits raised a *succah* in the fall of 1941, the Jewish neighbors called the police. Mr. Moskovits was ordered to remove the *succah* within ten days. Two days after the eight days of the *Succoth* holiday was over, the *succah* was dutifully removed.

The family now lived in the most spacious house in Crown Heights—1400 President Street. Soon the former Lubavitch Rebbe arrived. (The one I had accompanied to his departure from Stockholm, Sweden and he too, sailed on the last boat out of Gothenburg heading for New York.) His arrival not only transformed Crown Heights but also New York and the USA as a whole. There soon developed intermingling of the families support for Lubavitch, unbeknownst to either side, in as much as my father in Sweden funded publications by the Rebbe, and in Crown Heights Mr. Moskovits helped fund the establishment of the Rebbe's headquarters.

Mr. Moskovits, who had been the pillar of strength in communities where he had lived, whether in Szatmar, Ungvar, Budapest, Brooklyn and later Miami, Sao Paulo, Brazil and Jerusalem, had managed to revive the old European spirit of the warm, closely knit society based on Torah and *Gemillut Hassadim*. As one of the few survivors of the European scene, he was always sought out by members of the new generation who wanted to benefit from his unbelievable wit, sharpness of mind, wise counsel and burning religious piety. His wife, the matriarch of the family, reigned with imperial exaltation, not only over her family, but also over the communities where she lived. Her modest and charitable life is a legend. Whenever her husband did a good business, she would immediately exclaim: "Now we can give more for *Tsedoko*!"

She was especially close to her two daughters. But Anne being the younger, had her special love. "Lechtig Leben" she would call her younger daughter: The mother's blessings were heaped on her lavishly.

An unusual incident will illustrate the influence Mr. Moskovits had, on earth as well as in heaven. When he married, his wife who was 18, an enormous mass of people had been invited for the one week celebration. Just before she was heading for the Chuppe, there was a lot of commotion. The beautiful silver, especially bought as a wedding gift, was suddenly missing. A thorough search was conducted but yielding nothing. An old man who had been sitting near the silver, was immediately suspected as being the thief. The young bride, however, conducted her own thorough search and she found the silver hidden under some tablecloths. Exonerated, in his elation, at being freed from suspicion, the old man pronounced a blessing: "May the young bride live to be 88!" The amazing fact is that Mr. Moskovits died on the eve of Pessach at the age of 88.

My first meeting with my wife came about because of the hospitality her mother practiced. In the Yeshiva in Baltimore, where I studied, I had met a young Moskovits. When he invited me to spend the last days of Pessach in his house in 1945, I readily accepted, unsuspecting that he had a sister or that I was being "set up" for a *Shiddach*. I was overwhelmed when Anne came down to the Yonteff table. Her beauty was extraordinary, her face and deep eyes reflected the wisdom for which her family, for generations, was famous. I was "smitten."

It took, however, four years before we both decided to get engaged. The wedding took place in the garden of Mr. and Mrs. Moskovits' seventeen acre country estate in Irvington-On-the-Hudson. It was a wonderful Simche, with only family and friends invited. My own parents, after a separation of the War years, had come over for the occasion. Fortunately, my father and Anne's father got along splendidly, and they had the greatest respect for one another. A few months after our wedding, my father died after he returned to Sweden. Anne and I rushed over to help with the funeral, but also to take over the business. We stayed over half a year, and on our return we lived for a while in the family country estate in Irvington-On-the Hudson.

Among the countless acts of kindness, love and "Chesed" which my wife has performed, her greatest *Z'chus* is the "Kibbud Av" which she has extended to her parents and to my mother. From the time my mother became a widow, Anne cared for her in our home for 23 years, till my mother passed away. Her own parents stayed with us till 1980 when they, too, passed away. Anne always showed them honor and love which knew no bounds, without concern for her own comfort or convenience. May this *Z'chus* always be an example and inspiration for our children and grandchildren.

Anne not only helped and encouraged me in business, but she also was all in favor of my continuing my academic pursuits. Thus, scholarly articles which have appeared in various scholarly journals over the years are the products of her encouragement.

In February 1950, our son Jamie was born. Anne rejoiced in having a son. He was followed by two daughters. When Jamie suddenly passed away in June 1982 at the age of 32, the loss seemed insurmountable. It took all the strength of Anne's character and trust in Divine Providence, that she managed to reestablish a normal fruitful business and family life.

We have over the years lived in various countries and towns. Our business has taken us to Europe, Africa and the Caribbean. Everywhere Anne is respected as an outstanding authority. In Kenya, she is honored by being called "Mother," the highest honor for a woman. (I am called "Mzee"—old man.)

At one time, our firm was able to corner Government contracts from Caribbean states, which previously had been lodged with the British Government for years. The London authorities became curious and sent a commission of inquiry to the area to find out the reason for our success at the expense of the British Empire. The commission came back and reported in London; "Lehmann has a secret weapon, it is Mrs. Lehmann!"

She has, over the years, been able to structure unusual and successful business transactions. It was she who developed, in Washington, the concept of barter deals. Exchanging strategic materials against less needed materials. Other firms, some of the biggest commodities dealers, have simply copied Anne's business strategies and benefited greatly from her schemes.

It was Anne's idea to expand our relations with Ministries of Communications in newly independent countries. This branched out into specialization in modern telecommunications equipment which we introduced to various young nations. This has helped the rural development in those countries and has brought them prosperity and modern advance.

Throughout these busy years, Anne has always practiced what she saw at home: respect for own parents, charity to the needy in any part of the world, especially in Israel, and encouraged the education of her children. She has also supported me in position I have taken in synagogues which I have founded, especially the Young Israel of Lawrence-Cedarhurst and the Young Israel in Woodmere, both of which today prosper beyond every measure of expectation. Anne and I have regularly visited Israel where Anne is acting as a grandmother to her many nieces and nephews. She has supported an institute for post-natal care in Jerusalem, another hospital in Ashkelon, she has helped me support a Yeshiva in Givat Shaul and the famous Jamie Lehmann Mussar Institute, all in memory of out late son. In America she has helped build two Yeshiva buildings in memory of her parents.

Her charitable instincts simply know no barrier. If a needy cousin in London shows that he is destitute, she helps him lavishly without regard to the cost.

It is easy to understand that I admire and love my wife beyond compare. We have been blessed with wonderful children and grandchildren, and only mourn the terrible loss of Jamie who promised to surpass mankind's fondest hopes. I can only wish that my wife will merit to live many more years together with me, with the satisfaction that all her dreams for her children and grandchildren will be fulfilled, and that she can help as many needy people as she wishes. And that her great love for Israel will be rewarded with seeing the full Geulah in our days.

One of the greatest accomplishments in her life, due to her boundless piety and love for her mother, and her boundless energy, was that she attained the permission by the Rumanian Government to transfer her grandfather from Vichau to Tiberias, next to her own mother's grave, as had been her mother's dream.

Anne has actually never sought out an activity just because it pleases her. She always made sure that I, as her husband, and her children are equally interested in what she is doing. As an accomplished painter, she has painted some marvelous canvasses. Her first paintings were of her parents and landscapes in Israel, with special emphasis on Jerusalem, which she has never tried to display in galleries or museums. She painted them for herself and her family. In her upbringing of our children, she has succeeded in opening their minds to every aspect of life, with an open and free mind. Her indebtedness to our Jewish past and tradition is never far from her, and there is no one she despises more than one who denies his Jewishness. To be with her is an unending challenge. I have never in our 48 years of marriage had a dull moment in her company.

The words of King Solomon have never been spoken about a more deserving woman than Anne: (*Rabbot banot assu chayil v'at alit al kullana*) Many women were of valor but you surpassed them all.

May my deep sense of gratitude to my wife, and my gratitude to Hashem for having such a wife, never leave me.

Dr. Lehmann and Mrs. Lehmann with New York Mayor Rudolph Guilliano and
Rabbi Sol Roth. Dr. Lehmann was presented with an award for his defense of Jerusalem.

# A Message To My Grandchildren

As we are nearing the end of the 20th century, we live in a world of much confusion. The Germans speak of *"die Umwerung aller Werte"*—the re-evaluation of all values. In this turmoil we are blessed with the steady beacon of Jewish values, and the inspiration which Jewish history brings us. Having my grandchildren in mind, I feel the obligation to pass on to them the treasure which I was privileged to acquire during the past three quarters of a century. If my late son Jamie, of blessed memory, would still be with us, my task would be easier, for he was ahead not behind the flow of the times. Fortunately my two daughters carry on our family traditions and so I lovingly embrace them in thanksgiving for conveying to their children and grandchildren my message.

I commend anyone who seeks guidance in this world, to refer again and again to that magnificent and supreme book of beauty and perception, the Book of Psalms. Who but a divinely inspired Jewish king could have composed such symphonies of words as are found in Psalms Chapter 29? And he also tells us his source of wisdom—namely, the memory of historic events of the past. "Oh, G-d, we heard it with our own ears, our forefathers told us, the great deeds which You performed, in days of old." (Psalms 44)

The center of our perception of the world, is the centricity of man himself. Man may be lowly in the zoological range of things, but we must remember the majesty of man's soul, and therefore his enormous potential. As King David put it (Chapter 49) *"Adam bi'yekor*—Man's glory." Generation after generation is at work to distill and refine that glory. We are all partners in the monumental effort to reach the heights which man is destined to reach.

And G-d placed us before a multitude of paths to reach our goal. As the prophet Hosea says, "G-d's paths are just, the righteous will advance on them, while the wicked will stumble on them." The question which begs to be asked at the end of the life of each one of us is: Did I choose the path of advancement, or did I stumble? Part of the road to fulfillment is to enrich our lives with all the knowledge that life in this world can yield. We must not pass up the opportunities to learn and do good in this world. A passive person represents a wasted life. I have sought to explore as many aspects of life as possible, and to define and record what I have learned in the process.

The cardinal question to be solved is: Where do we find G-d? In my own case I am convinced that G-d has manifested Himself to us again and again—in history. It is by studying our history that we realize that G-d is timeless, and that He can only be explored and understood if we try to adopt His own timeless sense of history. We Jews have the unmatched privilege to see the world from the vantage point of 4,000 years of history, and the inexhaustible richness of our literary heritage.

If I may digress a moment: the "*Koach ha-Hiddush*" is at our command not only in the process of learning, but also in the material life. My wife and I have created and innovated new constructions in business, with international implications, which we pioneered, and which to this day are being emulated by the greatest business firms in the world. It all started by our realization that we do not have to copy and repeat what has been done for centuries before us, but to create and innovate new paths. *Koach ha-Hiddush*. That is why we feel closer to G-d when we are steeped in learning and suddenly feel the discovery of a "*hiddush!*" We come closer to His "*me-haddesh betuvo bechol yom*"—"He innovates for the good every day." Also, our practice of the Mitzvot of Judaism—we are commanded—should never appear old and thrashed out, but as new as the day we received the Torah at Sinai.

The element, which drags us down and prevents us from lofty understanding of the timelessness is Time. When the centuries vanish in our minds, and we are able to overcome inertia and blindness, we discover the interconnections in our history—and G-d's own manifestations in history: When Christopher Columbus' ships sailed out of the Iberian port, he spied other ships carrying the exiled Spanish Jews into their long Diaspora. It took centuries before it became apparent that the discoveries of Columbus would save the lives of the future descendants of these very exiles. Without a powerful America, Jewry would have been lost in our generation. Now, 500 years later, we discern the divine pattern. Or: When these exiles sailed East, they found that the Ottoman Empire—(because of economic interests and not being laden with the guilt obsession of the Christian Church) opened its doors to the Jews, who soon were able to found thriving communities and academies where the heritage of Sefarad was continued. If the Ottoman Moslems had been as intolerant and intransigent as they were later and before, the Jews would have perished. Or: the Spanish provinces in North Western Europe had just won independence and founded Holland as a new nation, which soon admitted the tired and impoverished exiles, and permitted them to develop international business concerns, whose activities led to the establishment of Jewish communities in Brazil, the Caribbean, Venice, the Balkans, Palestine and the United States. The Jewish heritage which was close to extinction in Spain and Portugal, thus had an unmatched revival from which Jews the world over still benefit. The timing of Holland's independence fight had prepared the ground, almost to the minute, G-d's way to prepare the very ground for the coming of the messianic age, can, in my opinion, be found in the appearance of such "pseudo-Messiahs" as David Reubeni in the 16th century and Shabbatai Zevi in the 17th century. They ignited such fervor and enthusiasm among Jews throughout the Diaspora which led to an organized movement to Eretz Yisrael—which had never happened before in the history of the Diaspora. Although these movements failed, they showed that Jews could merge their efforts jointly in all countries and achieve hope to resettle our Promised Land. Step by step these developments led to religious and political Zionism which, in turn, gave us the State of Israel. This, no doubt, is the beginning of the rule of Moshiach.

These developments were paralleled by the political events, of the Turkish hold on Palestine crumbling under Britain's invasion of Eretz Yisrael. Britain's involvement had been inspired by a movement in Christian Britain throughout the 19th century, towards the realization of messianic missions, by helping the Jews to reach Statehood for the first time in 1900 years.

None of these events and developments could have happened by chance. If closely observed and analyzed we clearly find G-d's fingerprints at every turn.

In the process, we tragically lost millions of our fellow Jews. Maybe by tracing the interconnections we can find answer and solace in our quest for explanations for the tragedies of the Holocaust and other tragedies. Our search for these answers will also help us overcome the apparent threats to the survival of Torah Judaism. While the ancient tree of Jewry is being pruned from time to time, its ultimate survival can not be doubted. As we see, in the unparalleled revival of Torah learning and Torah observance in our own time, all over the world.

These events show the strength of Hashgachah Kelalit—Providence for the nation as a whole. But Papa often spoke of Hashgachah Peratit, the Providence in the lives of individuals. How else can I explain that the Moskovits family was miraculously plucked out of the European Holocaust, and the Lehmann family miraculously surviving the war in Sweden, while I myself sailed across the ocean to the United States in the midst of the burning war—only to lead to the union of my wife and myself? And so I ask myself what was the purpose of our lives—so clearly selected out of the storms of history—if not for a higher purpose? And the fulfillment of that higher purpose is now left in the hands of my grandchildren, with all my love and encouragement.

I can only hope and pray that my grandchildren and their children will be part of this great revival and, with their inheritance in a rich patrimony of our family, will make meaningful contributions to the glorious continuity of our people and religion, on the soil promised to us.